The Atonement
and the
Sacraments

The Atonement and the Sacraments

The relation of the Atonement to the Sacraments of Baptism and the Lord's Supper

ROBERT S. PAUL

Wipf and Stock Publishers
EUGENE, OREGON

Wipf and Stock Publishers
199 West 8th Avenue, Suite 3
Eugene, Oregon 97401

The Atonement and the Sacraments
The Relation of the Atonement to the Sacraments of Baptism and the Lord's Supper
By Paul, Robert S.
©1960 Paul, Robert S.
ISBN: 1-57910-280-8
Publication date: July, 2002
Previously published by Abingdon Press, 1960.

This book is humbly dedicated
to the members of the church and congregation of
Christ Church (Congregational), Leatherhead in
the County of Surrey, England,

*who by their questions raised the central issues
of the faith, and who in their lives have revealed
him on whom all our faith rests*

Preface

THE PREFACE OF A BOOK, I IMAGINE, SHOULD BE LIKE AN HONEST MENU —it should give a fair account of the bill of fare with some indication of what the reader will be expected to pay in terms of interest or tedium.

The contents of this book are concerned with the doctrine of the Atonement and the Gospel Sacraments. At first sight it appears to be far more about the Atonement, although we shall discover that our discussion of that doctrine comes to its natural focus in the Sacraments. However, the reader had better be warned that a great number of books have been written on the Atonement, and the addition of one more would seem to demand a fairly formidable excuse.

My excuse is the doctrine itself. If the heart of the Protestant exposition of the Christian faith is the great act of God in Jesus Christ for our redemption, then we must needs struggle continually with this doctrine in order to express in ever new and living terms what it means to the Church. This is one of our primary aims. The book is written by a minister for those ministers and other Christians who have discovered that they cannot altogether dispense with theology and who are involved in relating the Christian faith they profess to the Church's life of worship and witness.

The theme was conceived in a parish ministry and came to birth in an ecumenical ministry. It originated in questions that were put by church members in a pastorate that lasted nearly ten years in post-war England. I discovered that the post-war minister could not depend upon the theological images and formulations of the past. Nor could he reject them as entirely worthless. Other doctrines might be adequately safeguarded by creeds and confessions, but the doctrine that deals with what God has done for us in Christ has never been so irrevocably defined.

Why is that? Can it be because these facts of the gospel are so fundamental to our salvation and so charged with saving grace that no human theory of their meaning in past, present, or future can claim to be the Holy Spirit's last word on the subject? Yet all the attempts of faith to wrestle with their meaning have some value. This means that we are less concerned with defending Irenaeus against Anselm or Abelard against Bernard than with trying to discover what may be of value to our own day in the historic theories of the Atonement. We shall discover that those fundamental aspects of the doctrine which can be expressed for all time bring us to the very heart of Baptism and the Lord's Supper.

The vital task of relating this to the Church's apologetic still remains, but that is outside the scope of our present study. Our concern is with the prior questions, what the Atonement means to the Church, and its relationship to the Church's own life of worship centered in the preaching of God's Word and the Sacraments given to us by our Lord. For only by constantly reassessing in each generation the meaning of the work of Christ for her own salvation can the Church equip herself for the task of interpreting that same gospel to the world. Until we can say clearly what it means to us, and particularly what it means to us *now*, we shall not be able to prove its relevance to the rest of mankind.

Like the classical sermon and Caesar's Gaul, this book is divided into three parts.

I. *The Legacy from the Ancient World.* We commence with an examination of the doctrine of Atonement from the early Church to the nineteenth century. It is a task which has been done many times, sometimes at inordinate length and sometimes like the Levite in the parable—with a brief glance backward for the sake of decency and a speedy maneuver to pass by on the other side! I have attempted an independent review of the classic theories in what I hope is a reasonable compass. Sometimes I have been led seriously to qualify previous judgments, and it cannot be pretended that the results will be to everyone's liking. Like any substantial *hors d'oeuvre* this section should be treated with discretion, according to appetite and need.

II. *Disputes About the Inheritance.* One recent writer listed over seventy books on the Atonement by British theologians written during the first fifty years of this century. The list was not complete. This illustrates one of the ecumenical aspects of our subject, for national and geographical emphases in theology are just as much a part of the ecumenical encounter as the issues arising from our confessional allegiance. Often in ecumenical discussion American Methodists, Presbyterians, and Episcopalians will find that they have as much or more in common as Americans than they have with their European co-confessionalists. Just as sometimes within the same setting English Anglicans and Free Churchmen—with a shock of surprise—discover themselves saying the same things, although they could never agree on the soil of Albion. Over against the clash between "Anglo-Saxon" and "Continental" theologies (often limited to the issues between American and Swiss-German theology) I suggest that British theology has had its own contribution to make which has centered in the Atonement and its relationship to Church and Sacraments. Of course, one could drive this thesis too far. British theologians are not tied to one doctrine any more than they have a monopoly of interest in it. Until the death of Horace Bushnell in 1876 the interest was certainly shared in America, and there have been great continental theologians like Ritschl who treated the doctrine with characteristic erudition and profundity. Nevertheless, I think we can say that the Atonement has received special attention within Britain during the past hundred years and has become the point of reference from which theological thinking in that country has begun and then spread into other areas of doctrine. In this part of our study we shall therefore concentrate upon this aspect of recent British theology which deserves to be better known on both sides of the Atlantic. It will demand a good deal of concentration from the reader.

III. *Treasure in Earthen Vessels.* At this point we shall apply the results of our previous study to our understanding of Baptism and the Eucharist. We are well aware that the interpretation of the Sacraments is a central ecumenical problem. We live with the results of the historic divisions over Baptism, and we have been all too conscious of the rival interpretations of the Eucharist—Roman, Lutheran, Calvinist, and Zwinglian. But today all the answers of the past seem curiously irrelevant in face of the mute scepticism of an indifferent world. Perhaps ministers who are most alive to the needs of their people and to the silent questions of those who watch the churches without ever entering them are less concerned with denial than with affirmation, less concerned with denying other people's experience of

Christ's presence than with asserting the reality of the Presence they themselves have known in Word and Sacraments.

How is a modern Protestant to understand the Sacraments? He can only understand them *evangelically*, i.e., as related to and included within the great act of God which redeems his people and creates his Church. For him there is no theology of Sacraments to be developed as an interesting sub-theme in liturgics, but he must study the meaning of the Sacraments because they are given by Christ and therefore have their place *within* the gospel. They are central in worship because that which is declared through them is the same gospel of reconciliation that is proclaimed in the preaching of the Word. They are a means whereby the living and victorious deeds of Christ are revealed once again in his Church.

There is, however, a further problem at which we shall glance from time to time—the interplay between doctrine and the historical situation in which it is formulated. At first sight this seems to be a long way from our subject, but we touch it at almost every point. A man standing in Montana and watching a stream tumbling down the Rockies to join the Missouri will not immediately think of it in close relationship to the water which is cascading at that moment down the Allegheny Mountains to the Ohio River. Two thousand miles divide the two, and yet they ultimately flow together in the waters of the great Mississippi. It is something like that within this question of the relationship between history and doctrine. Traces of this will flit and shadow across our page, but they will all come to focus in the one central issue, to show how the Church makes explicit by Word and Sacrament the message that "God was in Christ, reconciling the world unto himself."

In trying to acknowledge all those to whom I ought to express my thanks, I can only echo the writer to the Hebrews, that the "time would fail me" to tell of all who by their prayer, precept, writing, or example have contributed to this book. I am particularly grateful to former students of the Ecumenical Institute's Graduate School of Ecumenical Studies (especially the 5th semester) who gave my interpretation of the Atonement and the Sacraments the kind of testing that only students can give.

PREFACE

I must also express my most sincere thanks to Professors Paul Ross Lynn and Chalmers Coe of the Hartford Seminary Foundation, who diligently went through the manuscript to purge my English of its Oxford accent. Their sympathetic encouragement and that of others among my colleagues has given me so much more than I asked of them. Special thanks are due to Mr. Dikran Y. Hadidian, Librarian of the Case Memorial Library, who undertook the preparation of the index.

One other person deserves the rest of my gratitude, and so much more besides. With two aching fingers my wife typed out the whole manuscript. In addition she has done all those little chores that are unavoidable in writing a book but which add up to something so frightening that they must have been responsible for many a prospective literary genius turning to less exacting forms of creativity. May the good Lord repay her, for I cannot.

ROBERT S. PAUL

Contents

INTRODUCTION. MAINLY ABOUT THE
WORD "ATONEMENT" 17
   1. "Atonement" and the Dictionary Definitions 18
   2. The Birth of the Word "At-one-ment" 20
   3. The Word in the English Versions of the Bible 23
   4. Overtones and Undercurrents 26

PART I
The Legacy from the Ancient World

CHAPTER I. THE ATONEMENT IN THE FATHERS . . . 35
   1. The Early Writings 35
   2. Irenaeus and the "Ransom Theory" 47
   3. The Development of the Theory 53
   4. What Do We Learn from the Fathers? 61

CHAPTER II. ANSELM AND HIS SUCCESSORS 65
   1. *Cur Deus Homo:* "Satisfaction" 66
   2. The Theory Reviewed 73
   3. Peter Abelard and the Great Example 80
   4. Thomas Aquinas Tries to Sum Up 85

CHAPTER III. THE REFORMERS AND THEIR
FOLLOWERS 91
   1. Ransom and Penalty: Martin Luther 92
   2. Sacrifice and Penalty: John Calvin 97
   3. The Atonement in the Catechisms and Confessions . . . 109
   4. Attacks upon Calvinism 114
   5. Seventeenth-Century Puritan Reactions: John Owen and
      Thomas Goodwin 117
   6. Eighteenth-Century Puritan Reaction: Jonathan Edwards . . 127

THE ATONEMENT AND THE SACRAMENTS

PART II

Disputes About the Inheritance

CHAPTER IV. THE ATTACK ON "OBJECTIVITY" . . . 135
1. The Evangelical Revival 135
2. New Thinking for a New World 138
3. The Break with Calvinism in Britain: McLeod Campbell . . . 140
4. The Break with Calvinism in America: Horace Bushnell 149

CHAPTER V. OLD FACTS AND NEW THEORIES 162
1. "Vicarious Penitence": R. C. Moberly 162
2. The Rising Tide of Liberalism 168
3. *Abelardus Redivivus*: Hastings Rashdall 170
4. *Abelardus Recogitans*: Robert Franks 181
5. Critique of the Modern Abelardians 186

CHAPTER VI. REACTION AND RETURN 194
1. Robert Dale Reasserts the Objective Atonement 194
2. James Denney Repeats the Theme 206
3. Incarnation as Atonement: the Thought of Westcott, Caird, and Wilson 216
4. Forsyth Attempts a Synthesis 227

CHAPTER VII. PRESENT TRENDS 241
1. The Post-War Climate in British Theology 242
2. The Atonement and American Theology 246
3. Three Formative Theologians: Gustaf Aulén, Bishop Hicks, and Vincent Taylor 253
4. An International Discussion: Emil Brunner and Donald Baillie . 268
5. Toward an Ecumenical Consensus 274

CHAPTER VIII. FUTURE PROBLEMS 282
1. Incarnation and the Church 282
2. "He hath made him to be sin for us, who knew no sin" . . . 287
3. "Ye shall be as gods" 291

CONTENTS

PART III

Treasure in Earthen Vessels

CHAPTER IX. THE ATONEMENT AND THE SACRAMENTS . . . 297
   1. Where Christian Theology Begins 297
   2. Themes and Theories 301
   3. The Divine Drama 307
   4. The Deeds of the Living Christ 313

CHAPTER X. BAPTISM 319
   1. Ecumenical Problems of Baptism 319
   2. The New Testament Dilemma 322
   3. The Place of Baptism in Christian Worship . . . 325
   4. Jesus and His Baptism 328
   5. The New Testament Testimony 335
   6. Mode and Meaning 341
   7. The Exclusive Modes 348
   8. Toward Sacramental Fullness in Jesus Christ . . . 351

CHAPTER XI. THE LORD'S SUPPER 359
   1. The Bread of Life 359
   2. Prefigured Sacraments in Paul 364
   3. Memorial and Act 368
   4. Incarnation and the Real Presence 371
   5. The Institution of the Last Supper 374
   6. Ethics and the Eucharist: the Challenge of the Cross . . . 378
   7. Ethics and the Eucharist: the Response of Faith . . . 381
   8. Epilogue—or Prologue? 386

INDEX OF SUBJECTS AND PROPER NAMES 389

INTRODUCTION

Mainly About the Word "Atonement"

"You see," said Humpty Dumpty to Alice, "it's like a portmanteau—there are two meanings packed up into one word." Perhaps our ideas would be far richer if we were content to leave it so, but in the laudable desire for precision we tend to identify a word with one particular meaning to such an extent that all its other valuable associations are lost. Often the word itself has to be jettisoned when its use for party purposes or as a means of technical definition has passed. Our loss is not only that a word has become unusable, but also in the fact that during the process of redefinition it will be entirely a matter of chance which of its alternative meanings will finally be the one that gains popularity or notoriety, and it certainly need not be the one which is most fruitful or even that which is closest to the original meaning.

In theology this can be serious. Reflect upon the loss that is suffered by the Church when such words as "catholic," "orthodox," "fundamental," "evangelical," and "mission" have become almost unusable for large sections of the Church owing to their appropriation for ecclesiastical party purposes. There was a time not so long distant (it still persists in Wales) when an English Free-Churchman could not use the word "church" with reference to himself without a sense of betrayal. The "church" was the parish church, the national Anglican church from which he dissented and which was the cause of the civil disabilities—he was a "chapel" man. The question I ask is whether the word "atonement" has now joined the ranks of the words that are in the process of becoming discarded by large sections of the Church because of their misappropriation for party purposes.

THE ATONEMENT AND THE SACRAMENTS
1. "Atonement" and the Dictionary Definitions

One of the dullest ways of entering the subject of any book is by starting with dictionary definitions, but in this instance I do so because the dictionaries may indicate difference between the current American and British usage regarding the word "atonement."

Although the academic purpose of the unabridged *Webster's New International Dictionary* and the complete Oxford *New English Dictionary on Historical Principles* to some extent hides this difference of emphasis, I believe it is implicit in the content of their definitions. Webster's defines the meanings of "atonement" as: "1. (Literally, a setting *at one*). The state of, or act of bringing into, concord; restoration of friendly relations; reconciliation." It says that these are archaic, which leaves us the alternative meanings: "2. Satisfactory reparation for an offense or injury," And thirdly, its meaning in theology, "The saving of redeeming work of Christ wrought through his incarnation, sufferings, and death; also, reconciliation between God and men, especially as effected by Christ." [1]

The Oxford definitions are, first, "The condition of being *at one* with others; unity of feeling, harmony, concord, agreement"; secondly as "The action of setting at one, or condition of being set at one, after discord or strife" (i.e., the restoration of personal good relations either by reconciliation or appeasement), which the dictionary regards as an obsolete usage of the word; thirdly, its special uses in theology, "Reconciliation or restoration of friendly relations between God and sinners"; and fourthly, "Propitiation of an offended or injured person, by reparation of wrong or injury; amends, satisfaction, expiation." It notes that the word is also used theologically in this sense, but it adds this general but significant comment, "As applied to the redemptive work of Christ, atonement is variously used by theologians in the senses of reconciliation, propitiation, expiation, according to the view taken of its nature." [2] We are to assume that in British theological usage all these meanings are equally admissible. On the other hand, there seems to be a hint in the American dictionary, that when it speaks of reconciliation as part of its definition of the theological use of the word "atonement," its content will tend to be

[1] Later references are to the shorter *Webster's New Collegiate Dictionary*.
[2] Later references are to the *Shorter Oxford Dictionary*.

interpreted in terms of the common meaning of the word—"satisfactory reparation for an offense or injury."

This becomes more explicit when we compare *Webster's New Collegiate Dictionary* with the *Shorter Oxford Dictionary*, which are perhaps more significant for our purpose because they are more widely used, and for that reason presumably not only reflect popular usage but also do a good deal to form it. In Webster's work the word is here defined as "1. an atoning (i.e., the making amends or reparation for wrong-doing), 2. as the satisfaction given for wrong-doing or injury; amends, expiation"; and 3, in theological usage, (a) the effect of Jesus' sufferings and death in bringing about "the reconciliation of God to man," and (b) this reconciliation.

The *Shorter Oxford Dictionary* gives priority of meaning to "the condition of being at one with others." It then ranks chronologically the idea of concord and reconciliation, and particularly "the reconciliation or restoration of friendly relations between God and sinners" (1526), and finally the idea of propitiation or reparation for wrong is mentioned with its special theological associations. It shows that this was the last meaning of the word to develop in theology, and it is clearly the meaning which is furthest from the original meaning of the word. When we compare this with its parallel volume in America and bear in mind that theological content will be affected by popular usage, it suggests that virtually the latest development has been the meaning which has survived in American usage, so that the modern understanding of the word will be largely governed by one particular conception of the atonement.

If any help were needed to tie this word to satisfactionary or penal ideas of the doctrine, Webster supplies it by speaking of it as the effect of our Lord's death in bringing about the reconciliation of God to man. For one of the distinctive marks of all the satisfaction theories from the time of Anselm onwards has been the fact that they thought of redemption primarily as effecting a change in the attitude of God toward man.

If this is to some extent true, then it suggests that there is a difference of emphasis in the use of the word on the two sides of the Atlantic, a possible tendency in America—and we cannot demonstrate it to be any more than that—for the word to carry a stronger accent upon the satisfactionary theories than it does in Britain, which may be a result of the struggle between "Fundamentalism" and "Modernism." We have to remember that although the issue in that struggle was centered in the interpretation of the Bible, it was also involved with what many regarded as a defense of the "orthodox" doctrine of Atonement.[3] Although those issues were fought out no less vigorously in Britain than in America, it does appear in the usage of the word that within the former there has been a determination on the part of theologians (and philologists?) to insist upon its basic meaning, and to prevent the word "atonement" from being captured for party purposes.

2. The Birth of the Word: "At-one-ment"

This basic meaning of "atonement" is simply the state of being or becoming "at one," reconciled, with someone else. Most of the theological terms in our language have their origin in Latin, but this word is wholly and indigenously English. We see the word both in its nominative and verbal forms in the course of development within the literature of the great Elizabethan age, and there are several interesting examples to be found in the plays of Shakespeare. In *Richard II* the whole plot revolves around the quarrel between Henry Bolingbroke, Duke of Hereford, and Mowbray, Duke of Norfolk. The play opens with the unsuccessful attempt by King Richard to reconcile the two nobles, at the end of which he declares:

> We were not born to sue, but to command:
> Which since we cannot do to make you friends,
> Be ready, as your lives shall answer it,
> At Coventry, upon Saint Lambert's day;
> There shall your swords and lances arbitrate
> The swelling difference of your settled hate:
> Since we cannot atone you, we shall see
> Justice design the victor's chivalry.[4]

---

[3] E.g., the "orthodox" Presbyterians (1923), against whom the signatories of the Auburn Affirmation protested, took "the Atonement" as one of the "five Essential doctrines" in danger from "modernist" theology—i.e., a particular theory of the Atonement, for they maintained that "Christ offered up Himself a sacrifice to satisfy the Divine justice and to reconcile us to God." Cf. F. E. Mayer, The Religious Bodies of America (St. Louis: Concordia Publishing House, 1954), p. 236.

[4] Act I, Scene 1.

INTRODUCTION

One could hardly imagine that there is any idea here of Richard placating or making "reparation" to his two nobles—the meaning is unambiguously "to reconcile."

Two other passages give us an insight into the idea of "atonement" and the common meaning it had during the last decade of the sixteenth century. In *Henry IV*, Part II, the plot centers in the rebellion raised in 1405 against the King by the Earl of Northumberland and his associates. Having decided that the rebellion could not be sustained by the army under their command, the Archbishop of York and the Lords Mowbray and Hastings decide to parley with their opponent, Prince John, for reasonable conditions of peace. In the discussion of this policy the Archbishop remarks to his friends:

> And therefore be assured, my good lord marshal,
> If we do now make our atonement well,
> Our peace will, like a broken limb united,
> Grow stronger for the breaking.[5]

Similarly in *Richard III* Queen Elizabeth, the wife of Edward IV, asks the Duke of Northumberland about her sick husband and is informed that he is progressing well and that he

> ... desires to make atonement
> Betwixt the Duke of Gloucester and your brothers.[6]

From these examples we see that for Shakespeare and his contemporaries atonement and the act of atoning meant reconciliation and the act of reconciling.

A further point to notice from these examples is that there is a certain equality of status in those between whom atonement is to be made. It is something which takes place between peers, and if the king or a prince of the royal blood enters the quarrel as a participant he does so not as a superior being but as *primus inter pares*. Richard II's high-handed action in the dispute between Bolingbroke and Mowbray was a material factor in his own ruin.

There may not be a precise equality of social or political status among the contestants, although Shakespeare almost invariably made them of similar rank and power, but the equality that is represented

---

[5] Act. IV, Scene 1.
[6] Act. I, Scene 3.

is an equality of responsibility that is shared in their quarrel. Richard II intervened as a third party in the quarrel to "atone" the two dukes, and by the punishment meted out to both of them, we assume that they had been more or less equally culpable. Those who had rebelled against Henry IV likewise speak of making atonement with the king, but with an army standing to arms behind them, it is clear that they regarded themselves as in no way his inferiors suing for forgiveness or making amends for any wrong that they had done but as equals in the quarrel. Similarly in *Richard III* the king, in this case Edward IV, speaks of intervening as a conciliating party in the dispute between two groups that were balanced against each other in political power and prestige—his own brother Richard, Duke of Gloucester, and the powerful relatives of his wife the queen.

This equality between the parties emphasizes the basic idea of reconciliation for it is shown to be an action which involves both sides in the dispute, a movement which must be mutual in order to achieve its desired result. The meaning of atonement as it appears here is personal reconciliation between man and man, or between people who, in so far as they shared responsibility for the estrangement, must also share in responsibility for their *rapprochement*.

Another meaning of the word "atonement," which strengthens this basic idea, appears in Edmund Spenser's *Faerie Queene*. The poem was published in 1590, but we know that Spenser was in the process of writing it ten years earlier. Throughout most of the work the word in its various forms seems to have had the simple meaning of "together," "in unison." Often the reconciling effect of that "togetherness" is enhanced by bringing two opposites or two enemies in relationship to each other. In the following passage the two knights who are mentioned had only a few moments before been tilting at each other in mortal combat but now are united in attacking one of the onlookers:

> The warlike Dame was on her part assaid
> Of Claribell and Blandimour attone.[7]

The same use of opposed contrasts is seen in the following figure which Spenser uses. Having declared that he is going to recount the

[7] IV. IX. xxx.

INTRODUCTION

"whiles of a wanton lady" and "knighthood fowle defaced by a faithlesse knight," he goes on to urge his readers not to let the example of the bad offend the good:

> ... for, Good, by Paragone
> Of Evil may more notably be rad [perceived, read]
> As White seems fairer, macht'd with Black attone:
> Ne, all are shamed by the Fault of one.[8]

The meaning is clear, that just as white shows up in clearer contrast when it is matched together (attone) with black, so goodness shows up to better advantage when it appears in close contrast to evil. But the contrast here is very near harmony, for in the idea of "matching" black and white Spenser's words contain more than a suggestion of a reconciliation of opposites.

We can see how the idea of reconciliation, as an expression of that "togetherness" which being "at one" conveyed to the Elizabethan, began to grow out of the personal relationship of a new found unity that followed discord and strife. So Sir Guyon and the Red Cross Knight, having been about to assault each other and suddenly recognizing their error, ask pardon of each other:

> So been they both attone, and doen uprear
> Their Bevers bright each other for to greet.[9]

Here then is the meaning that grew naturally out of the English idea of "at-one-ment"; the personal reconciliation of responsible people who had been violently and even mortally opposed to one another. This was the conception that was taken up into theology in describing how the work of Christ changed the relationship that sinful man had with his Creator.

3. The Word in the English Versions of the Bible

For the early theological use of the word it is interesting to examine its use in the early English versions of the Bible and particularly to compare its use in the King James Version (the Authorized Version) of 1611 with that in its immediate predecessor, the Genevan Version,

---
[8] Ibid., III. IX. ii.
[9] Ibid., II. I. xxix.

published in 1560. The former version has over seventy examples of the word "atonement" used either as a substantive or in a verbal form ("to make atonement") in the Old Testament. Most of the examples are employed in the description of the sacrificial system in Exodus, Leviticus, and Numbers.[10] A comparison of these instances with the equivalent passages in the Genevan Version shows that King James revisers generally were following the Genevan translators. However, in four places they had used "atonement" where their predecessors employed "sanctify," "purify," or "purge," and in thirteen places they used the word "atonement" where the Genevan Version translated the Hebrew as "to reconcile" or "reconciliation." In two interesting instances where the King James Version used "atonement" twice in the same verse, the Genevan translators had used both "atonement" and "reconciliation" as virtual equivalents.

> And yee shall doe no worke that same day: for it is a day of reconciliation,[11] to make atonement [11] for you before the Lord your God. (Lev. 23:28, G.V.)
>
> And the priest shall make an atonement [11] for the ignorant person, when hee sinneth by ignorance before the Lorde, to make reconciliation[11] for him: and it shall bee forgiven him. (Num. 15:28, G.V.)

It is the same Hebrew root (כפר, Kipper, Karphar, etc.) which is being translated in each case. The upshot of this is that whereas "atonement" and "reconciliation" appear to be interchangeable terms in 1560, by 1611 it seems that there was a tendency to use the former as an expression of the theological relationship between God and sinners, or at any rate to describe the reconciliation between God and the sinner in the Old Testament system of sacrifices.

The interrelationship of the two words is further shown in the New Testament. Both versions employ the word "atonement" only once in the New Testament (Rom. 5:11), and the King James translators followed the example of their predecessors. It is important, however, to see this single example of its use in relationship to the previous verse:

---

[10] The exceptions: II Sam. 21:3; I Chr. 6:49; II Chr. 29:24; Neh. 10:33.
[11] כפרים: לכפר: זכפר: לכפר

INTRODUCTION

For if, when we were enemies, we were reconciled [12] to God by the death of his Son; much more, being reconciled [12] we shall be saved by his life. And not only so, but we also joy in God through our Lord Jesus Christ, by whom we have now received the atonement.[12] (Rom. 5:10-11, K.J.V.)

Here again it is the same Greek root which is being translated ($καταλλάσσω, καταλλαγή$), and the change seems to have been made primarily for the sake of euphony, i.e., to avoid employing the same English word too often. In this sense it may be said that the word atonement was "introduced by a mistake." But perhaps the translators are less to be blamed for the later theological constructions that were built upon this isolated New Testament example than thanked for illustrating in so marked a way the fact that *to them* atonement meant reconciliation.[13]

This is by no means all that the New Testament has to say about the *doctrine* of the Atonement. A thoroughgoing New Testament study of the doctrine would demand the consideration not only of such words as $ἱλασμος$ and $ἱλαστηριον$ (usually rendered "propitiation" in our English versions) but also an examination of such important questions as the relationship between our Lord's messianic vocation and his conception of the Servant of Yahweh in Isaiah; the relation between his sacrificial suffering and the idea of sacrifice in the Hebrew religion; the significance of the eucharist passages of the New Testament. We should have to examine the titles that our Lord took to himself and the titles which the early Church ascribed to him. We should have to review these questions both in the light of Jesus Christ's own expression in the Gospels as he drew nearer to the Cross, and as the Church came to understand his sacrificial life and death on the other side of the Crucifixion, in the light of the Resurrection and all that followed. We should not build too much on the single instance where English translators happened to render the original by the native word "atonement." To be complete in our study we should interpret the content of the doctrine not solely

---

[12] $κατηλλάγημεν, καταλλάγεντες, καταλλαγήν$.
[13] Melville Scott speaks of the "disastrous results" which have come from the King James Version's use of the word "atonement" in Rom. 5:11. *The Atonement* (George Allen & Sons, 1910), p. 20. (Where the place of publication is not cited, it may be presumed to be London.)

through the words of the Evangelists, Paul, the writer to the Hebrews, or the Johannine writers, but through the New Testament as a whole. And even then we could interpret the doctrine only against the background of the story of Salvation as it had unfolded through priest and prophet, through life of sacrifice and ways of worship in the history of God's People from the beginning. Our concern, however, is not primarily with expounding the biblical doctrine of the Atonement but with the more modest tasks of trying to recapture the English word so that this very ordinary vessel may be more worthy to contain the treasure of the gospel. We can then illustrate the fact that if we put later associations of the word in their proper subordinate place, we have a word of our own which can express more adequately than any other the doctrine of our redemption.

To describe that doctrine we need a word which has shown itself capable of growth. For the doctrine itself is infinitely rich, and yet at its heart holds the promise and the purpose that we shall be be "at one" with God—not by our own deserving but by his free choice. The promise that in this work of reconciliation, of bringing God's world back to himself, he calls us (again, not of our desert but of his choice) to be free partners with him. These are ideas which are not only at the heart of the biblical doctrine of the Atonement but also at the center of the English word that we have used to describe it.

No preconceived theological opinions should take the concept of reconciliation from our use of the word "atonement." Although we are grateful for the rich connotations it has beyond this, to atone means basically to reconcile, by whatever means. If the doctrine of the Atonement as it is revealed in the Bible has at its center this same idea, then out of faithfulness to our mission to proclaim that gospel we must use a word which describes the fact—"God was in Christ reconciling the world unto himself."

4. Overtones and Undercurrents

On the other hand we cannot ignore all the overtones that the word atonement has taken and which persist long after the basic meaning has fallen silent. Atonement has "reconciliation" at its center, but it tells us more than that. Reconciliation informs us about the central purpose of redemption, and this must be maintained at the heart of the doctrine if the many inadequate and even barbarous interpretations are to disappear, or if the word "atonement" itself is to be any longer any use to us. We ought, however, to welcome the fact that atonement means more than reconciliation; that in our Anglo-Saxon usage the word carries with it hints of the cost that is involved in our reconciliation with God. For a Frenchman, for example, there is no exact equivalent for the word. To render it exactly one would have to coin a term that would contain the meanings of both *réconciliation* and *rédemption*, with perhaps a suggestion of what the French would understand by *expiation*.[14]

The Latin *expiatus* developed the meaning of legal satisfaction demanded by the Law from the criminal which was "expiated" in his punishment. Atonement also has developed the secondary meaning of "making amends for an offense." Although it has in this way often been used as a synonym for expiation, it can never be only that without doing violence to the conception of personal relationships that is at its heart. The idea of reconciliation, of "togetherness," which is at its root, must surely govern any secondary or derivative meaning that the word may have. The re-establishment of a personal relationship must be the central idea. If it is legitimate to use the word in the sense of reparation for an injury done, then this use of the word should be governed by the fundamental idea that this is done not as the expiation of a crime but in order to restore a personal relationship that has been broken. A criminal may expiate his crime in prison or upon the gallows, but there is no necessary reconciliation either to the law or to society involved. But the Prodigal Son atoned for his sins, not so much by his sufferings in the far country as by returning home to receive forgiveness and reconciliation with his father.

In both "expiation" and "atonement" there is the idea of satisfaction given for an offense that has been committed. However, in the one the satisfaction is legally conceived and legally exacted, whereas in the other no satisfaction can be effected without a voluntary act involving a personal coming together. In the one the word is fulfilled when the law has exacted its just penalty, but in the other the word is only fulfilled when the penalty is accepted voluntarily and undergone in order to make personal reconciliation possible.

[14] The Nordic languages appear to be better equipped. Cf. the German *Versöhnung*.

THE ATONEMENT AND THE SACRAMENTS

We might ask ourselves, however, how it was that the word atonement gathered to itself a secondary meaning so close to the idea of expiation. In asking ourselves how it happened, we are really also asking ourselves how far it is legitimate to take up this meaning into our understanding of the Christian doctrine of Atonement.

I think we gain a good deal of help in this from its use in the King James Version of the Bible. We have already noticed that the word "atonement" is used over seventy times in the Old Testament, and we find that it is used invariably with the idea of sacrifice, i.e., with biblical associations which, if they are not wholly expiatory, are nevertheless closely allied to that idea. The English translators of the Bible reserve the use of the word "atonement" for the Hebrew root כפר, which means "to cover" or "a covering" and hence a covering for sin.

We cannot ignore the "expiatory" element, although equally we cannot ignore the fact that as the Hebrews understood their sacrificial system this "covering" for sin was initiated by God himself as a means of restoring personal relationships between his people and himself. The expiatory or "covering" element in respect of human sin is always held within the context of personal relationships that bound together the individual Israelite and the people of Israel and Yahweh. It would be outside our purpose to enter into a learned disquisition on the relative merits of the "communion" theory of Robertson Smith, or the "gift" theory of G. Buchanan Gray, but it would appear that whether one believes that the purpose of the Hebrew sacrificial system was to enable the individual making the sacrifice to re-enter communion with the Deity, or to offer God a gift, the same accent upon a personal relationship of reconciliation is implied.[15]

At the same time we must recognize that if in the word "atonement" the idea of reconciliation is genetic, the "expiatory" meaning of the word has come from its association with Scripture and in particular from its association with the Old Testament sacrifices. In the Bible itself these sacrifices are always held within the context of the personal relationship between God and his people, and therefore the idea of ritual sacrifice is kept within its proper place. But it had its place, and if the ideas that underlie the conception of sacrifice in the

---

[15] Robertson Smith, *The Religion of the Semites* (1927). G. Buchanan Gray, *Sacrifice in the Old Testament* (1925). The two views are not necessarily mutually exclusive, cf. Vincent Taylor, *Jesus and His Sacrifice* (Macmillan, 1937), p. 49-50.

INTRODUCTION

Old Testament are important for our understanding of the Christian doctrine of the Atonement, then the infusion of those ideas into the word "atonement"—*within the boundaries of its basic meaning*—are not only legitimate but an enrichment. It is an indication that the word has grown to the doctrine. The association of such ideas with the word "atonement" is dangerous only when the secondary forms are allowed to take the place of and virtually to exclude the fundamental idea of being or becoming "at one" with God, which both Hebrew religion and the English word itself had at their center.

We have not very far to look to find a reason for the rapid acceptance of the "expiatory" idea into the meaning of "atonement." We have already seen that the King James Version employed the word in the Old Testament even more often than its predecessor, and we must remember that after 1611 this version rapidly won its place in both Britain and America and held its primacy for nearly three hundred years. Thus, the sacrificial element, and what that implied in terms of cost and purification, became inevitable and valuable adjuncts in the idea of "atonement" among people who largely continued to be "people of the Book."

The fact that the basic conception of reconciliation faded into the background is, I suggest, not primarily due to the translation of the Bible itself but to the theology which prevailed and which interpreted it (for reasons that we shall examine later) almost wholly in terms of its own expiatory view of the Atonement. For our part if we are to re-establish the word and the richness of its biblical associations, we must not lose sight of the fact that the English translators of our older versions interpreted the idea behind the Jewish sacrifices by the word "atonement" at a time when its root meaning of reconciliation was unquestioned. If their translation has given valuable overtones to the English word that were not current in their own day, we must also give full recognition to the fact that the basic idea which they found in the sacrificial practice of ancient Israel was "at-one-ment" as *they* understood it. We must interpret their understanding of sacrifice and its purpose by what "atonement" meant to them and not by what their employment of the word caused it to become.

It has been pointed out that theologians who have written on the doctrine of the Atonement have almost completely disregarded the meaning of the word "atonement" itself.[16] But this is surely not so surprising since such a study would have been largely irrelevant to their purpose. Why bother with the English word "atonement" when it would be far more profitable to examine the biblical terms themselves and to review critically the doctrine as it is revealed in Scripture itself? This obviously is the first task of one who has an exegetical approach to the doctrine, and as we shall see, the biblical scholars have already subjected the doctrine to a most exhaustive critical analysis in Scripture. We cannot afford to disregard the results of such study, for sound exegesis must always provide the basis for any faithful exposition of Christian doctrine.

At the same time the primary concern in our present study is not exegesis but exposition, and in this enterprise words—the words of the vernacular language in which a preacher speaks to his congregation—are of vital importance. Perhaps their proper use and the content given to them is the most important problem which faces the Church in communicating the gospel. To be forced out of using a word because it has been captured for party purposes, or because we have been too bemused or lazy to insist upon an intelligent understanding of its meaning, may be the equivalent of throwing away a living vehicle of grace. Moreover, to express the gospel we need words in the fulness of their meaning. To search for a unitary principle is good, particularly if it lays bare the root meaning of a word, but this too can lead to impoverishment rather than enrichment if in our insistence upon the basic theme we ignore the overtones or undercurrent. Doubtless the Christian gospel can be reduced to a very simple phrase—"God was in Christ reconciling the world unto himself"—and yet all the books of theology that have ever been written cannot exhaust or fathom its meaning. We need such a word which hints at the unfathomable if we are to do anything like justice to our exposition of the purpose and act of God in Christ for our redemption; a word which has the heart of the doctrine at its center but which can grow with our understanding of the doctrine's fulness.

So the purpose of this study is to help in the Church's task of communicating the gospel by reviewing what the Atonement has meant and can mean to the Church *herself*. Many people are cynical

---

[16] Melville Scott, op. cit., p. 17.

about the Church, and they have good reason, for Christians cling closely to their sins. But pastoral experience has shown me that the Church faces its present difficulties often not because it lacks the gospel, but because it finds it almost impossible to communicate it in intelligible terms.

The ultimate problem here is the problem of apologetic, of finding the basis whereby Christian and non-Christian can speak the same language to each other so that the world in which the Church is placed will at least understand what is being said in Christ's name, whatever its final response may be. But before this question can be tackled there is the prior question of how far the Church understands the Gospel that is committed to her charge, how far the Church can put into clear terms to herself the saving act of God by which she lives. And by "the Church" here I mean not an ecclesiastical hierarchy, theologians, or even ministers, but the ordinary members who are the spearpoint of evangelism within the world. This is the area in which this study seeks to make its contribution. It deals with the question that will always be prior to effective apologetic, "What does the gospel mean to the Church?" And because Protestant theology finds its center in the Atonement, this is the doctrine in which this book finds its focus.

Within the context of the Church, however, we find that doctrines cannot be neatly separated and labeled like so many articles at a sale. But there is an interrelationship which affects them all, and in speaking about the Atonement we find ourselves drawn into thinking about other doctrines that appeared to be very distant but which in the light of Scripture suddenly become very close, indeed an integral part of the thing we are discussing. In dealing with the center of Christian doctrine we soon find ourselves involved in all doctrine. For in theology the doctrines of the Church are not to be added or subtracted at will, but they are like limbs in a body whereby when we do violence to one the whole body is affected.

This is obviously true in the relationship which exists between the doctrine of the Atonement and the doctrines of the Trinity and the Person of Christ. It is also true of the Church and Sacraments; doctrines that week by week touch our Christian life in a visible and concrete form. For that reconciliation between God and man which the doctrine of the Atonement declares in the life, death, and resurrection of Jesus Christ should be demonstrated within the fellowship of the Church. And this saving act by which the Church lives is both made objectively real and is subjectively appropriated with gratitude by us in the water of Baptism and the bread and wine of the Eucharist.

PART I

The Legacy from the Ancient World

CHAPTER I

The Atonement in the Fathers

1. The Early Writings

LOOK AT THE MOST MODERN CHURCH BUILDING YOU CAN FIND—AN exterior of concrete slabs and glass blocks and an interior of suspended pillars and subdued lighting—and you are looking at an heirloom that has been handed down to us from the time of the New Testament. Church history does not take place and church doctrine does not come to birth in a vacuum. Not only is every part of the Church as we know it today—its life, its ways of worship, its faith and sacraments—part of a historical web that catches up all worship and witness from the first century until now, but in the same way to examine any doctrine of the Church in its most modern expression is to find that it is inextricably linked to a historical and theological chain that leads directly back to the New Testament and the Apostles. That is true of the doctrine of the Atonement as it is of every Christian doctrine; it is linked to its own history of explanation.

I speak of a "history of explanation" because what we have in the history of the doctrine is not an account of the *doctrine's* development —the Atonement is a fact and one cannot "develop" a fact to make it more so—but it is the history of the way in which the doctrine has been explained by the Church to succeeding generations of its members. What is offered here is a review of that history, necessarily partial and selective, but I hope it will be sufficient to show more clearly what each age has contributed to the Church's understanding of the Atonement's meaning. For sometimes the Church has used elaborate pictures and theories to describe the mystery of redemption, but at other times it has been content to rely on the words of Scripture and the drama of its liturgy.

Possibly it was through these repeated expressions of the Christian faith in worship that "the faithful" were kept faithful to the inner meaning of the work of Christ during the age that immediately followed the passing of the Apostles. Certainly one feels there must have been something which supplemented the dry moralism of the Apostolic Fathers. For one seems to witness in their writings a very remarkable and rapid falling off from the doctrine of grace in the New Testament, brought home to us particularly by their shifting the work of Christ from its central position in the gospel. How else is one to explain the fact that in the *Didache* virtually the only reference to atonement is the suggestion that if your salary is high enough you ought to "pay a ransom for your sins?"[1] This is a doctrine of works, and in a primitive form at that!

On the other hand it may be that the meaning of the work of Christ was not elaborated by the writers because it was generally recognised by all Christians, i.e., that the personal assurance of the Atonement as a fact had been already appropriated by faith, and they did not see the need of "laying again the foundation of repentance from dead works, and of faith toward God" (Heb. 6:1). In support of this we must point out that almost all these writings were addressed to Christians, and the concern of the pastor at that time was that Christians should bear some fruit to the gospel in the quality of their lives. The apologist on his part pointed to this ethical fruit confidently as evidence for his case.

At the same time, in the almost total accent upon ethical aspects of the Atonement, it is hard to avoid the conclusion that we witness here a radical shift from the gospel of grace revealed in the New Testament, a regression from Christ-centered faith to man-centered works. I feel that this case against the Apostolic Fathers is too strong to be altogether explained away. Whatever the depth of their personal faith as they read the Scriputres or partook of the sacraments, they did not reveal an understanding of the gospel in terms of faith. In the writings that have come to us, therefore, in so far as the writers represent a view

---

[1] *Didache* iv. 4, 6. Cf. "The Teaching of the Twelve Apostles" in Vol. I of the *Library of Christian Classics* (Philadelphia: Westminster Press, 1953). Most of the quotations from the Fathers in this chapter are from Vols. I and III of the series. (The writers of the early centuries have been so well translated in this and other series that there is little excuse for any minister not making himself familiar with their thoughts.) From *Early Christian Fathers*, Vol. I, Library of Christian Classics. Published, 1953, The Westminster Press. Used by permission.

which is different from that of the New Testament, we must say that they had misunderstood the gospel.[2]

But if this was a *total* misunderstanding, into what faith, then, were the converts of the Church converted? To put the issue in another way, was that misunderstanding so complete that the gospel which the Church proclaimed ceased to be Christian? That is a judgment that I believe we dare not make, for it would come very near to saying that the Church had ceased to be the Church. We must recognize the limitations of these writings, but also within those limitations we are concerned to try to understand the positive elements of the faith in which the writers lived.

There is a good illustration of the break between the New Testament faith and the Apostolic Fathers' lapse into moralism in the *First Epistle of Clement* (ca. A.D. 95). The Roman bishop called upon his Corinthian readers to fix their eyes upon the blood of Christ, realizing how precious it is to the Father because "it was poured out for our salvation and brought the grace of repentance to the whole world."[3] T. F. Torrance has pointed out that what Christ's death here is said to win for us is not atonement but an opportunity to repent,[4] and we might go even further to suggest that here we have almost the beginnings of a sacrament of penance. On the other hand Clement usually stays very close to Scripture, and in the passage where he speaks of our Lord as the fulfillment of the prophecies, "the high priest of our offerings" and "the protector and helper of our weakness,"[5] we see side-by-side both his concern to keep within these Scriptural terms and his interest in practical ethics. His argument

---

[2] Cf. Thomas F. Torrance, *The Doctrine of Grace in the Apostolic Fathers* (Edinburgh and London: Oliver and Boyd, 1948). To deal with this question adequately would demand a full-length study which would defeat the purpose, even as it would be beyond the scope, of this book. Professor Torrance has made such a study, and he has made a very convincing case to show that the Apostolic Fathers demonstrate a doctrine of grace (or the lack of such a doctrine) radically different from the New Testament. He argues that the coincidence of Judaistic and Hellenistic presuppositions within the Christian context meant that the early Fathers failed to grasp the central significance of the death of Christ in the New Testament (cf. op. cit., pp. 136-39). To me he has made his case almost too well, for at the end I am left asking the question, "In what sense, then, could the Church change this much and still be the Church?" For a less negative interpretation of the Fathers, see H. E. W. Turner, *The Patristic Doctrine of Redemption* (Mowbray, 1952).

[3] *I Clement* 7.
[4] Torrance, op. cit., p. 46.
[5] *I Clement* 36; cf. ibid., 61, 64.

was quite frankly exemplarist—"because Christ did this, therefore you should follow him. . . ." Therefore, although the work of Christ is expressed in the traditional words of devotion, they are almost entirely used to call forth an ethical response in the Church.

This is even more pronounced in the pseudonymous homily from the middle of the second century that has come down to us as the *Second Epistle of Clement*. The work is quite clearly not a letter but the sermon of a presbyter,[6] in which the work of Christ is very clearly related to the ethical response that the preacher expects to win from his hearers. For example, he declared that Christians sinned in not realizing "whence and by whom and into what circumstances we were called, and how much suffering Jesus Christ endured for us," and he immediately pointed the question, "How, then, shall we repay him, or what return is worthy of his gift to us? How many blessings we owe to him! For he has given us light; as a Father he has called us sons; he has rescued us when we were perishing."[7]

Our estimate of a passage like that will depend very much on whether one regards the ethical advice that follows as being suggested by the preacher because such effort is "worthy," or because it is the response to grace. Perhaps in view of the fact that he says it was God the Father's divine initiative which was active in our Lord's saving work, we can afford to take the charitable view: "For he took pity on us and in his tenderness saved us, since he saw our great error and ruin, and that we had no hope of salvation unless it came from him. For he called us when we were nothing, and willed our existence from nothing."[8] It is true that sometimes in the Apostolic Fathers the acts of Creation and Redemption are confused.[9] But if—as appears here—they are brought together in the almighty purpose of God because they subsume the same act of divine grace, then the confusion may have its own insight!

The preacher then went on to make his point of practical ethics, for he said that we can truly acknowledge Jesus Christ only by obedi-

---

[6] Despite the fact that it reproduces the image of the vine from *I Clement* 23 (*II Clement* 9), the form appears clearly to be that of a sermon, and it has been suggested that the source was Alexandria. Cf. C. C. Richardson in *The Early Christian Fathers* p. 186.
[7] *II Clement* 1.
[8] *Ibid.*
[9] Cf. Torrance, *op. cit.*, p. 113.

ence to him and by honoring him not only with our lips, but with heart and mind. "Thus, brothers," he declared, "let us acknowledge him by our actions, by loving one another, by refraining from adultery, backbiting, and jealousy, and by being self-controlled, compassionate, kind." [10] He was addressing the faithful. Is such a passage, I wonder, to be interpreted as his whole doctrine of the Atonement—if so, it is meager enough—or is it a homily intended to stimulate in Christian believers the fruits of the Spirit?

The ethical implications of the gospel are stressed so constantly in the writers of this period that sometimes it seems as if our Lord's work itself was regarded as having primarily a didactic purpose, which may indeed indicate gnostic influence.[11] So although Justin Martyr (ca. 100-165) hinted that the sacrifice of our Lord meant victory over the demons,[12] he also said that Jesus Christ, "taught us these things for the reconciliation and restoration of the human race." [13] The intention of the apologist was, of course, to convince the pagan world of the superiority of the Christian faith over pagan religions and philosophies—a pagan world that understood something of comparative ethics but which thought of superior conduct as coming from superior "knowledge" ($\gnosis$). In commending what they announced as the revelation of a divine "gnosis," the Apologists would inevitably concentrate upon the Incarnation and upon the ethical implications of belief in Christ, for their main argument was in the final analysis either proved or disproved by the change brought about in the Christian converts. It should be remembered in reading a writer like Justin Martyr that his sole intention was apologetic, and it is for this reason that he plays down the scandal and shame of the Cross. On the other hand he makes no attempt to allegorize or explain away the event of the Cross itself—it really happened; "that these things really happened," he declared, "you can learn from the Acts of what was done under Pontius Pilate." [14] It is the way it is presented which gives the impression that Justin is more anxious to represent

---

[10] *II Clement* 4.
[11] Cf. what Torrance says about Clement of Rome (op. cit., pp. 47 ff.). Compare with what is said by H. E. W. Turner about Clement of Alexandria, *The Patristic Doctrine of Redemption*, pp. 40 ff.
[12] *Apology* I. 63; cf. *ibid.*, 28.
[13] *Ibid.*, 23; cf. 13 and 20 where our Lord is called "our Teacher."
[14] *Apology* I. 35.

the work and Passion of Christ as the inevitable sequel to his humility in the Incarnation than as the central act of sacrifice in the gospel by which we are saved.

This accent upon the Incarnation is to be found in the reputed "Letter to Diognetus" (ca. 129?), the message of which can be summed up in its own declaration, "God sent him to men.... He sent him as God; he sent him as man to men." There is also, however, in this letter the emphasis upon the divine initiative of God himself, which is typical of the way in which these writings stress the action of God the Father in the plan of salvation:

> O the overflowing kindness and love of God toward man! God did not hate us, or drive us away, or bear us ill will. Rather, he was long-suffering and forbearing. In his mercy, he took up the burden of our sins. He himself gave up his own Son as a ransom for us—the holy one for the unjust, the innocent for the guilty, the righteous one for the unrighteous, the incorruptible for the corruptible, the immortal for the mortal. For what else could cover our sins except his righteousness? In whom could we, lawless and impious as we were, be made righteous except in the Son of God alone? O sweetest exchange! O unfathomable work of God! O blessings beyond all expectation! The sinfulness of many is hidden in the Righteous One, while the righteousness of the One justifies the many that are sinners.[15]

This is piety not theology, but I personally dare not say that I find no doctrine of grace in it. For all its lack of precision on Atonement, it stresses one vital aspect of it which later theology often forgot—the work of the Father in our redemption. Such a passage should remind us that behind the ethical writings of the Apostolic Fathers and the Apologists there stood the faith of those who knew themselves to have been brought out of darkness into light, of faith that was loyal in the face of martyrdom, and of piety that had been nurtured by Word and Sacrament in the liturgy of the Church. Their doctrine of Atonement might be grievously defective, but while Scripture and Sacrament and the gifts of the Spirit remained in the Church, it could not fail ultimately to get to grips with the theological meaning of the whole work of Jesus Christ.

At the same time, their exposition of the Atonement did not go

---

[15] *Epistle to Diognetus* ix. 2-5.

much beyond the ethical response that the death of Christ is able to inspire in us. The writer of the "Letter to Diognetus" frankly appealed to the gratitude of believers as sufficient incentive for imitating within their own lives what God had done in Christ, for "when you love him, you will be an imitator of his goodness." [16]

This is clearly an exemplarist attitude to the work of Christ but not entirely so, for can you "love him" unless led to do so by the Holy Spirit? Furthermore, the same writer speaks of the work of redemption as God showing us "the Saviour's power to save even the powerless." [17] Somewhere underneath the expression of his *imitatio Christi* there was the more objective faith in a God who had acted in Christ, and who in acting helped us when we could not help ourselves. Perhaps a great part of the stress which the writers of this early period place upon the Christian's ethical response must be seen in the light of their consciousness that the Christian was always in the showroom. As Ignatius, the martyr bishop of Antioch, urged the members of the church at Magnesia, "we have not only to be called Christians, but to be Christians." [18]

It has been said that of all the early Fathers Ignatius is the one who most nearly approaches the apostolic figures of the New Testament, and particularly in his Christ-centered devotion.[19] As we think of him, we are reminded of one special aspect of the Atonement in its relation to Christian ethics among these early Christians, their attitude to the pressure of persecution and the constant threat of martyrdom.

Ignatius wrote his epistles to the churches on his way to martyrdom, and both objective and subjective aspects of the Atonement are to be found in them. On the one hand he spoke of Christians being prepared as stones for God's Temple and said, in a picture which is nothing if not graphic, "you are being hoisted up by Jesus Christ, as with a crane (that's the cross!), while the rope you use is the Holy Spirit." [20] This is the objective act of God on our behalf, so that Jesus is our High Priest with the Father,[21] and our faith is grounded

---

[16] *Ibid.*, x. 4.
[17] *Ibid.*, ix. 6.
[18] Ignatius, *To the Magnesians* iv.
[19] Torrance, op. cit., pp. 56-57.
[20] *To the Ephesians* ix.
[21] *To the Philadelphians* viii. 2.

in the historic facts of our Lord's birth, Passion, and Resurrection.[22] It has been justly pointed out that he seems to think of Christians *being built* into God's Temple, whereas the New Testament speaks of believers *having been built* into it by the work of Christ.[23] At the same time the idea of atonement as future consummation—and as a present process—is not unknown in the New Testament, and Ignatius certainly believed that God had taken the original initiative in man's redemption. For this objective reason he could speak of Christians "being completely at peace by reason of the Passion of Jesus Christ, who is our Hope." [24] On the other hand he drew out the ethical implications of this for himself and other Christians to the point where ethics demands a complete identification of the individual with the Passion and sufferings of Christ.

It is difficult for us to appreciate the narrow but passionate intensity with which Ignatius sought to demonstrate his faith in martyrdom. If it cannot be said that he sought it for its own sake, he undoubtedly believed, like Spintho in G. B. Shaw's *Androcles and the Lion*, that martyrdom would be the immediate passport into heaven. It is perhaps unfair to compare him with the coward Spintho, for Ignatius was fanatically almost too brave, and yet sometimes one feels that he looked to martyrdom itself to purge him and present him pure before his Lord. In somewhat gruesome imagery—the eucharistic significance of which should not be lost on us—he says, "I am God's wheat and I am being ground by the teeth of wild beasts to make a pure loaf for Christ." [25] With all his sterling qualities one wishes that Ignatius in the face of a martyr's death had shown a little less immoderate haste to embrace it.

Yet fundamentally it is not martyrdom for its own sake which he seeks—"that is whom I am looking for—the One who died for us." [26] He seeks Christ: he gives his life for the Cross and sees himself as having the opportunity to share in the Passion of Christ.[27] He describes himself and his fellow Christians as part of the fruit of Christ's

---

[22] *To the Magnesians* xi.
[23] Torrance, *op. cit.*, p. 68.
[24] *To the Trallians* pref.
[25] *To the Romans* iv. 1-2.
[26] *Ibid.* vi. 1.
[27] *To the Ephesians* xviii. 1, and *To the Smyrnæans* iv. 2.

Passion [28] and says of the docetists that if they had really been of God's planting "they would have shown themselves as branches of the cross, and borne immortal fruit." [29]

All these citations illustrate the fact that for Ignatius, on the way to his own death, the death and Passion of our Lord constituted not only the basic act of God on which the certainty of his own salvation rested but also the call to him to become in his own person and martyrdom identified in the sufferings and sacrifice of his Lord. The imitation of Christ meant self-identification to the point of martyrdom. This could be either an act of the deepest futility or one of the highest saintliness according to whether Ignatius regarded it as something he was doing by his own strength, or as a response to grace through the power of the Holy Spirit. It was in this identification that the danger lay for Ignatius, for perhaps the reason we are reminded of Spintho is that Shaw's character believed that martyrdom would *of itself* guarantee his salvation. We sense this danger for Ignatius, although we have no right to assume that he fell into the trap.

In several other ways the epistles of Ignatius are relevant to the later theories of the Atonement. First, in opposition to the docetists there is his insistence upon the Incarnation and the Virgin Birth. It is when this is seen in relationship to his equal insistence upon the authority of the Church's hierarchy that we begin to see its possible implications for the future, in the identification of Church structure with a continuing incarnation of the Body of Christ. For Ignatius himself, we do not feel that the Incarnation was absolutely to be equated with the Atonement. The former doctrine was stressed because of the actual danger of docetic ideas in the Church at that time—the question whether Christ really suffered or only seemed to. Ignatius may not have had a carefully thought-out doctrine of Atonement, but he saw the vital importance of a real incarnation in a truly human Christ if there is to be either any ground for our faith or any genuine ethic. Fundamentally (whatever later emphasis upon the

---

[28] *To the Smyrnæans* i. 2. Was this kind of self-giving the "fruit of the vine" which our Lord declared he would not drink until he drank it now in his Father's Kingdom? (Cf. Mark 14:25; Matt. 26:29.)

[29] *To the Trallians* xi. 2.

THE ATONEMENT AND THE SACRAMENTS

Incarnation may have led to) Ignatius' concentration upon the doctrine was in defense of God's plan of redemption. He said:

> Be deaf, then, to any talk that ignores Jesus Christ, of David's lineage, of Mary; who was really born, ate, and drank; was really persecuted under Pontius Pilate; was really crucified and died, in the sight of heaven and earth and the underworld. He was really raised from the dead, for his Father raised him, just as his Father will raise us, who believe on him, through Christ Jesus, apart from whom we have no genuine life. And if, as some atheists (I mean unbelievers) say, his suffering was a sham (it's really *they* who are a sham!), why, then, am I a prisoner? Why do I want to fight with wild beasts? In that case I shall die to no purpose.[30]

We can see here the inextricable relationship between the doctrines of Incarnation and Atonement. There could be no objective redemption, no redemption achieved *for* us as distinct from redemption achieved *by* us, unless it was won for us by the historic human Christ.

The second point regarding the Atonement may be touched upon very briefly. In his letter to the *Ephesians* he says that "Mary's virginity and her giving birth escaped the notice of the prince of this world, as did the Lord's death—those three secrets crying to be told, but wrought in God's silence." [31] I think it is worth remarking, without indulging in lengthy comment, that here we may have the beginning of the later Ransom theory that interpreted the Atonement as a deception of the Devil.

Finally, we must note what Ignatius says about the Eucharist. In one place he spoke of dissident members of the Church at Smyrna who "hold aloof from the Eucharist and from services of prayer, because they refuse to admit that the Eucharist is the flesh of our Saviour Jesus Christ, which suffered for our sins and which, in his goodness, the Father raised." [32] We cannot tell from the context which Ignatius condemned the more, their skeptical views of the Eucharist, or the fact that they absented themselves from the common worship, although be observed that "they would have done better to love and so share in the resurrection." What we must be careful to see, however, is, his identification of the *blood* of Christ with the *love* of

---
[30] *To the Trallians* ix, x; cf. *To the Smyrnæans* v. 2-3.
[31] *To the Smyrnæans* vii. 1.
[32] *To the Smyrnians* vii. 1.

Christ.[33] For the first thing Ignatius notices about those who neglected the Eucharist is that "they care nothing about love: they have no concern for widows or orphans, for the oppressed, for those in prison or released, for the hungry or the thirsty." [34] Practical Christian ethics —through the offering of the church members?—had something to do not only with the doctrine of redemption but also with the Lord's Table at the center of the Church's life.

We find similar emphases in Polycarp's letter to the Philippians, as we should expect from one who had close connections with Ignatius. On the one hand Jesus Christ "endured for our sins even to face death," [35] but on the other hand Polycarp called on his readers to be imitators of Christ's endurance and said that he set us an example in his own Person.[36] Indeed, "he endured everything that we might live in him." [37] The saints and martyrs of the past shared in the sufferings of Christ, but it was a sharing in the sufferings of One "who died on our behalf and was raised by God for our sakes." [38]

In the account of the *Martyrdom of Polycarp* the writer said that the martyr overcame the powers that were ranged against him and so gained immortality to glorify God and "to bless our Lord Jesus Christ, the Saviour of our souls and Helmsman of our bodies and Shepherd of the Catholic Church throughout the world." [39] Here is a recognition of that which our Lord himself achieved for us by his own Passion, but it is caught up in a present experience in which both his suffering and his glory are shared by those who are faithful to him. This is illustrated by the prayer which Polycarp is reputed to have offered at the point of his death. It has been pointed out that it bears many similarities to the Eucharistic prayers of a later period and may be taken as typical of the prayers of Consecration that were used in the Church at Smyrna about that time. There is certainly nothing improbable in the suggestion that at the moment of martyrdom Polycarp spontaneously broke into the prayer that would be hallowed to

---

[33] Eg., "being rooted in love by the blood of Christ," *To the Smyrnæans* i. 1; cf. *To the Ephesians* i. 1.
[34] *To the Smyrnæans* vi. 2.
[35] Polycarp, *To the Philippians* i. 2.
[36] *Ibid.* viii. 2.
[37] *Ibid.* viii. 1.
[38] *Ibid.* ix. 2.
[39] *To the Philomelium* xix. 2.

him not only by its association with the Sacrament of the Body and Blood of our Lord [40] but also by his own long and deep experience of breaking the bread and raising the cup as the pastor and bishop of the Church in Smyrna. With such associations sacrifice and sacrament could not remain separated and distinct and would inevitably be understood (albeit dimly) as parts of the same act of God whereby in Christ God gives himself to the Church, and in which the members by receiving him, offer themselves in the Spirit of Christ to God the Father, for the reconciliation of the world.

What then are we to say of these earliest church writings? That there was a weakened sense of the central importance of the atonement wrought by Christ, there seems no doubt. T. F. Torrance suggests that the theological failure of the period was due to the fact that Hellenistic and Judaistic ethics came together under the aegis of Christianity, and that there was a consequent failure to understand the unique nature of the gospel in its saving faith.[41] The result was an inevitable lapse into legalism.

This at least in part explains the emphasis upon Christian conduct. It was an emphasis that held grave dangers for new Christians, for it could so easily become a new Law to take the place of the old Law. If we have to smile, it is with a wry smile, when we read in the *Didache* "Your fasts must not be identical with those of the hypocrites. They fast on Mondays and Thursdays; but you should fast on Wednesdays and Fridays"! [42]

But although the point may be well taken, the Church—as Horace Bushnell saw many years later[43]—by holding close to the scriptural images had its own guarantee that the truth would not be lost. It has been well said that if we can be sure that the Christianity of this period meant at least what Hastings Rashdall said it meant, "it is probable that it means a great deal more besides." [44] Even during this

---

[40] M. H. Shepherd in *The Early Christian Fathers* (Library of Christian Classics, I, 143.

[41] Torrance, op. cit., pp. 136-37.

[42] *Didache* viii. 1.

[43] Cf. Bushnell, *The Vicarious Sacrifice* (New York: Charles Scribner's Sons, 1866), p. 474.

[44] H. E. W. Turner, op. cit., p. 12; also pp. 44-45. Cf. Hastings Rashdall, *The Idea of the Atonement in Christian Theology* (2nd ed.; Macmillan, 1920) pp. 189-208. Turner also stresses the devotional aspect of the doctrine in the Apostolic Fathers, op. cit., pp. 43-44.

period there were signs that she was soon to grapple with the meaning of the Atonement along the lines of the ransom theory which was developed by the Greek Fathers. For the rest, while there were men and women who in becoming Christians were prepared to become martyrs for the faith, I believe there were those whose simple faith carried them to the heart of the matter, even though they would have been as unwilling as they were unable to theorize about it.

2. Irenaeus and the "Ransom Theory"

It is not until the time of Irenaeus (140?-202) that an attempt is made to arrive at a theory that would explain the facts of the doctrine of the Atonement. The contrast is made all the more pointed if one compares what Irenaeus says on the subject with the views of his great theological contemporaries, Clement of Alexandria (150-215), or Tertullian (ca. 155-225) who tend to repeat the kind of things we have read in the earlier writers. Of all the earlier theologians of the Church one would have expected to find a clearly formulated doctrine of the Atonement in Tertullian, not only because his method and style were forensic but also because he found the essence of the Christian faith "to lie in a historic revelation, an act of God, which is to be accepted by faith and expounded rather than constructed and proved by human reason." [45] We should also have expected him at this point to have come under the influence of Irenaeus. However, Tertullian appears to have a no more systematically worked out doctrine of the Atonement than his predecessors.[46] He has the same concern as Ignatius and others against the docetists to maintain the historic actuality of our Lord's sufferings and the relation of his passion to a true incarnation—for if Christ was not truly man then the whole purpose of God would be destroyed [47]—and he believed that in suffering, our Lord was fulfilling the Scriptures. In one way—almost incidentally—Tertullian prepared the way for a later theory of the doctrine by appropriating the term "satisfaction" from Roman law and employing it with reference to penance—it was that which the repentant sinner paid back to God by his penitence and good works.

---

[45] S. L. Greenslade, article in Chambers' Encyclopaedia (Newnes, 1950) ad. loc.
[46] J. F. Bethune-Baker, An Introduction to the Early History of Christian Doctrine (7th ed.; Methuen, 1942), p. 333.
[47] Adversus Marcion iii. 8.

He does not apply the idea to the doctrine of the Atonement itself, but it is at least possible that by using the term "satisfaction" he opened the way for Anselm's later use of the word and thereby became the unconscious precursor not only for the Western conception of penance and atonement but also for the Reformation reaction from it.[48]

It should be remembered that all three men were Christian apologists. That is, they were concerned with commending the Christian gospel to the world in which they lived, and that when, for example, Clement of Alexandria asserted the superiority of the Christian's "true knowledge," he was taking up the categories of the society of that time. Irenaeus, on the other hand, took his starting point not so much from the place that contemporary thought had reached but from the world's actual need. He understood, as Paul had done before him, men's need for the assurance of victory over the ancient enemies —sin, death and the devil—and again following the Apostle of the Gentiles he understood the collective nature of Man.[49] Therefore, in presenting his view of the Atonement Irenaeus showed that by his sacrifice and death our Lord has done something for humanity as a whole. He tried to make explicit the "objectivity" that underlies the religious experience of the earlier writers: it was a reaffirmation of the Pauline conception of the solidarity of the human race—indeed, of the whole creation—and of our Lord's action on its behalf.

This representative character of Christ's work is central in Irenaeus' doctrine of the Atonement and in particular in his use of the Pauline doctrine of the "Second Adam."[50] Just as David and Goliath faced each other as the chosen representatives of their respective nations, and the hopes and fears, victory, or defeat of the nation were concentrated in the person and deeds of its own appointed champion, so

---

[48] S. Cave, *The Doctrine of the Work of Christ* (Nashville: Cokesbury Press and University of London Press Ltd. 1937), pp. 90-91. But cf. what Dr. John McIntyre says of Tertullian's use of "satisfaction" and his reply to the suggestion that it had influenced Anselm in *St. Anselm and his critics* (Edinburgh: Oliver & Boyd, 1954) pp. 84 ff.

[49] Cf. "S. Irenaeus concerns himself primarily with religion; the Apologists rather with philosophy. For them cosmology takes pride of place over soteriology, ... S. Irenaeus stresses the uniqueness of the act of God in Christ; the Apologists prefer to dwell upon the Incarnation as a continuation of the work of the Logos before the coming of Christ." H. E. W. Turner, op. cit., p. 39.

[50] Rom. 5:14-17; I Cor. 15:20-22, 45-49.

the destiny of the total race of mankind had been centered in its own protagonists—first Adam and then Jesus Christ. Christ "recapitulated in himself the ancient making of Adam." [51] Through apostasy man was held in bondage, and because he could not release himself, God's Word entered into the situation and "gave himself a ransom for those who had been led into captivity." But although "the apostasy" had tyrannized over us unjustly, God had to act in accordance with his just nature, "not redeeming his own from it by force, although it at the beginning had merely tyrannized over us, greedily seizing the things that were not its own, but by persuasion, as it is fitting for God to receive what he wishes by gentleness and not by force." [52]

Here we have what is perhaps the governing idea in Irenaeus' doctrine of Atonement—what is "fitting" to God—for even the distinctive concept of recapitulation (*recapitulatio*) is really governed by this basic idea. He works it out by an appeal to the types and parallels in the Old and New Testaments: our bondage to sin had been caused by the fruit of a tree, so we are redeemed by the fruit of the Cross; Adam had been tempted and by the disobedience of a virgin, Eve, and therefore it was fitting that our salvation should also come through the obedience of the Virgin, Mary; the wisdom of the serpent had been responsible for our Fall, but the simplicity of the dove (the Holy Spirit) conquers our sin. This parallelism comes to its climax in the Fall of Adam, and in the redemptive work of Christ, the Second Adam, our Lord "recapitulates" the scene of the Fall on behalf of the whole hman race and turns the abject defeat of Adam into his own complete victory. Irenaeus also demonstrates the indispensable relationship between the Incarnation and the Atonement, for Christ would not "have truly redeemed us by his blood if he had not been truly made man, restoring again to his own creation what was said in the beginning, that man was made according to the image and likeness of God.[53]

This use of analogy and typology may be very far from us. Dean Rashdall said that Irenaeus "was in the state of mind—frequently repeated in the history of religious ideas—in which analogies to duty

---

[51] *Adversus Haereses* V. i. 2.
[52] *Ibid.* V. i. 1.
[53] *Ibid.* V. ii. 1.

for reasons, for arguments, for thought." [54] But despite the qualms of a liberal theologian and leaving aside the question whether we can accept as arguments the examples Irenaeus used, we may ask whether we can dismiss so easily the fundamental theological idea on which the use of this typology rests. Is there not a "fitness" in the way in which God acts, was not Irenaeus defending a vital principle by insisting that God acts only in conformity to his own nature? It is this central idea which leads Irenaeus to insist that even in his dealings with the Apostasy (the Devil) which had us in bondage God was bound to act justly and not arbitrarily.[55] We see that not only does his conception of Christ's representative work rest finally upon his justification of God's ethical nature, but also that in taking up the conception of Christ's "solidarity" with us, Irenaeus asserted the only kind of objective Atonement that does justice to the Fatherhood of God revealed in Jesus Christ—it is redemption which is cosmic in its proportions and all-inclusive in its intention. To put the issue another way, he shows that when Christ acted he redeemed not only men but Mankind, not simply creatures but Creation.

A theological liberal living in an age of individualism might very well reject this as an impossible conception of redemption, but most people today have been born into a world that has become thoroughly disillusioned with individualism, and in which the old false securities, upon which the nineteenth century's supreme confidence in individual man were based, have been swept away. The world of concentration camps and atomic power, of technology and totalitarianism, not only brings home to us our solidarity in sin and guilt but also demonstrates that on the level of human society we live or die as a race. Redemption on that level, at any rate, must involve both me and my neighbor, and involves us in reconciliation. It is useless to speak to the member of some small central European or Asiatic country about his democratic freedom of choice and his individual responsibility when he knows that his own country is too poor to afford atomic weapons, and that because of this simple economic fact its fate, along with his and that of his children, is entirely in the hands of the juggernauts of world power. He knows that he is involved, whether he likes it or not, in cosmic ruin or cosmic salvation. In the face of the world in which

---

[54] Hastings Rashdall, *The Idea of the Atonement in Christian Theology*, p. 237.
[55] Cf. *Adversus Haereses* V. i. 1. and ii. 1.

we live, in the face of atomic bombs, hydrogen bombs, and all subsequent horrors, it is surely of some significance to know that right at the heart of the Christian gospel is the announcement that God in Christ has linked his "destiny" with man for his redemption.

Two other aspects of the thought of Irenaeus are important. First, there is a direct line in his thinking between his view of the Atonement and his view of the Eucharist, but again it is the link of analogy. When he wrote against those who denied the salvation of the flesh and the possibility of the incorruption of the body, he declared:

> For if this is not saved, then neither did the Lord redeem us by his blood, nor is the cup of the Eucharist the communion of his blood, and the bread which we break the communion of his body. For blood is only to be found in veins and flesh, and the rest of [physical] human nature, which the Word of God was indeed made [partaker of and so] he redeemed us by his blood. So also his apostle says, "In whom we have redemption by his blood and the remission of sins." For since we are his members, and are nourished by [his] creation—and he himself gives us this creation, making the sun to rise, and sending the rain as he wills—he declared that the cup, [taken] from the creation, is his own blood, by which he strengthens our blood, and he has firmly assured us that the bread, [taken] from the creation, is his own body, by which our bodies grow. For when the mixed cup and the bread that has been prepared receive the Word of God, and become the Eucharist, the body and blood of Christ, and by these our flesh grows and is confirmed, how can they say that flesh cannot receive the free gift of God, which is eternal life, since it is nourished by the body and blood of the Lord, and made a member of him? [56]

Irenaeus argues that the salvation of both soul and body is a fact, and the proof that Christ's redemption extends to the body is to be found in the Eucharist where God shows that he redeems the material creation by taking the bread and wine and making them his own body and blood. If God redeems and consecrates created matter in this way, how can anyone doubt that he will also redeem and consecrate by incorruption and life eternal the material bodies of men? Irenaeus urged the analogy between material and spiritual things so strongly that he felt it was quite sufficient to argue from one to the other, it was part of the "fitness" of God's action. But it was Christ's

[56] *Ibid.* V. ii. 2-3.

action that redeems, "for we gave nothing to him first, nor does he desire anything from us, as if needing it; but we are in need of communion with him. Therefore he graciously poured himself out that he might gather us together in the bosom of the Father."[57] If this is what the doctrine of the Atonement declares, it is also dramatically revealed to us in the action of the sacrament.

Secondly we must notice what Irenaeus said about "ransom," for although there is little to suggest that he intended the word to be any more than a descriptive picture of what the victory of Christ in our redemption meant to us, it provided the framework in which the later ransom theories would be cast. Adam was conquered and driven out of paradise,[58] and Eve was seduced by the word of an angel,[59] as a result of which we were in bondage to an "apostasy" which "tyrannized over us unjustly"[60] until the Eternal Word entered our nature and "gave himself a ransom for those who had been led into captivity."[61] He expressed the same idea in the image of a fight or battle against the Devil:

> He therefore completely renewed all things, both taking up the battle against our enemy, and crushing him who at the beginning had led us captive in Adam, trampling on his head, as you find in Genesis that God said to the serpent, "And I will put enmity between you and the woman, and between your seed and her seed; he will be on the watch for your head, and you will be on the watch for his heel." . . . The enemy would not have been justly conquered unless it had been a man [made] of woman who conquered him. For it was by a woman that he had power over man from the beginning, setting himself up in opposition to man. Because of this the Lord also declares himself to be the Son of Man, so renewing in himself that primal man from whom the formation [of man] by woman began, that as our race went down to death by a man who was conquered we might ascend again to life by a man who overcame; and as death won the palm of victory over us by a man, so we might by a man receive the palm of victory over death.[62]

[57] *Ibid.* V. ii. 1.
[58] *Ibid.* V. i. 3.
[59] *Ibid.* V. xix. 1.
[60] *Ibid.* V. i. 1.
[61] *Ibid.*
[62] *Ibid.* V. xxi.

It is difficult for the modern reader to decide how far the ancient author intended his description of the Atonement to be understood as fact or parable, but it is to be doubted whether Irenaeus would have recognized any important distinction between the two. In the final analysis it would not greatly concern him whether his pictorial account of Man's redemption was "true" in its factual details or not—it was the reality behind the description which mattered. Man was in bondage to sin and death, but God in Christ had intervened, and by a supreme act of grace, had redeemed him.

3. The Development of the Theory

Nevertheless, whatever limitations Irenaeus himself may have set to the interpretation of his own metaphors, we can see how a simple parable might very easily be extended into a detailed allegory, or how in the hands of literal-minded traditionalists the picture might become distorted into a blueprint of salvation. It has been said that in his conception of the solidarity of the human race Irenaeus was following the thought of Paul in Rom. 5:19, and that the point of departure for the later writers was the place at which he began to follow the writer to the Hebrews, where the epistle speaks of our Lord as destroying "him that had the power of death, that is, the devil" (Heb. 2:14).[63] That may be true, although Irenaeus would certainly have denied any inconsistency in putting the thought of the two writers together. The fact remains that although the later writers also took up the idea of human solidarity, it was the idea of ransom and of God's dealings through Christ with Satan which stirred their imaginations and which they proceeded to elaborate.

This aspect of Irenaeus' "theory" of the Atonement contains three related ideas. First, that Man is in bondage through sin to the Devil as a real and authoritative power; secondly, that in order to effect his release man must be bought back by a ransom to which the Devil would consent; and thirdly, that this redemption depends entirely upon the nature of God, upon a justice that would give even the Devil his due, and upon the merciful love that showed itself in readiness to intervene on Man's behalf. The later writers developed the first two lines of Irenaeus' idea of the Atonement, without giving sufficient recognition to the fundamental conception upon which Irenaeus had

[63] Bethune-Baker, *An Introduction to Christian Doctrine*, p. 335.

built his doctrine, that the Atonement depends upon God's own nature. So in explanation why such action on God's part was necessary and how it was effected, they begin to represent the Devil's claim upon man, not as an unjust usurpation but as a just claim because of man's voluntary sin, and they push the ransom theory further in the attempt to explain how the Devil was induced to give up his claims.

Origen (186-253) took the next step in the development of the theory by the suggestion that the Devil deceived himself. Satan thought that by engineering the death of Christ he would prevent the influence of his teaching, but the possession of the sinless soul of Christ caused him intolerable torture—an issue which had been forseen by God. Origen does not attempt to explain how the deception is to be reconciled with Satan's supposed rights,[64] nor does he develop the theory beyond this. It should be pointed out that while it was this aspect of the Atonement which found its echo in the later Fathers of the Church, Origen also speaks of Christ's sacrifice both as a "propitiation" and as a moral incentive to produce sacrifices of like kind within Christian people. Hastings Rashdall admitted that "there are no doubt abundant passages in which Origen speaks of Christ's death in the conventional language as a sacrifice, or a propitiation for sin," [65] but he found such a distinct emphasis on the moral influence of our Lord's death in the writings of Origen that he regarded him as "the greatest mind among the Christian Fathers." [66]

Nevertheless, it was the aspect of "ransom" that the later theologians took up, and Gregory of Nyssa (ca. 335-395) made explicit the suggestion that was implicit in Origen. The Devil was jealous of Man's happiness and had succeeded in seducing him, and this power which he exercised over mankind fed his pride. When he saw the goodness of Jesus—the glory of the Eternal Word hidden within human flesh—he wanted to destroy him: "Hence it was that God, in order to make himself easily accessible to him who sought the ransom for us, veiled himself in our nature. In that way, as it is with

[64] Cf. Rashdall, op. cit., p. 337 and note.
[65] Ibid., p. 263.
[66] Ibid., p. 256.

greedy fish, he might swallow the Godhead like a fishhook along with the flesh, which was the bait." [67]

It is a grotesque image (perhaps, as Luther saw, based on the picture of Leviathan in Job 41), and yet we should remember that even for Gregory of Nyssa himself it was only an image. Gregory is not unaware of the moral problem how to reconcile the absolute justice of God with perpetrating a deception in order to achieve his ends. He discusses this question at some length and concludes that the deceit was in reality "a crowning example of justice and wisdom," for what God did was a supreme example of paying the Devil with his own coin: "Justice is evident in the rendering of due recompense, by which the deceiver was in turn deceived." [68] To modern ears this is reminiscent of the justice of Gilbert and Sullivan's Mikado, whose object all sublime was "to let the punishment fit the crime," but it would hardly appear to be a sufficient apologia for the righteousness of God.

It should perhaps be said in Gregory's defense that he does not present his picture as a statement of what happened but as an analogy of what happened. The same kind of theory and imagery is given to us by Rufinus[69] (345-410), and however bizarre the image appears to us, we must remember that it could hardly have won such general acceptance that it almost became the official doctrine of the Church if it had not demonstrated real spiritual truths about the redemption of man. Sir George Adam Smith, writing about the book of Jonah, pointed out that our modern sense of humor is bound to make the picture of the prophet being swallowed by a whale seem ludicrous and

---

[67] *Oratio Catechetica*, xxiv. The doctrine is expounded in chs. xxii-xxvi. An Eng. tr. by C. C. Richardson is to be found in *The Christology of the Later Fathers* (Library of Christian Classics, Vol. III) as "An Address on Religious Instruction." From *Christology of the Later Fathers*, Vol. III, Library of Christian Classics. Published, 1954, The Westminster Press. Used by permission. I am grateful to one of my students, the Rev. J. W. McCann, for pointing out that the image of the bait and the fish-hook had already been used some years before this by a former student of Origen, Gregory Thaumaturgos (ca. 210-70). In a sermon "On all the Saints" he described the Devil "casting his hook at the Godhead and seizing the wonted enjoyment while he deems himself the captor and discovers that in place of the man he has touched the God." The Ante-Nicene Fathers (1956 reprint of the Edinburgh edition, Grand Rapids: Eerdmans) VI, 72.

[68] *Ibid.* xxvi.

[69] Rufinus *Commentarius in Symbolum Apostolorum*, 16.

grotesque,[70] but the same factor also prevents us from understanding the imagery of the Greek Fathers in respect of the Atonement. It is essential to realize that at a time when sailors would not venture far from sight of land the idea of the "big fish" was not a matter for humor. The sea had a sense of mystery and power that filled men with terror of the unknown. The sea serpent or dragon appears as a constant motif in ancient maps and reminds us that the dread of being swallowed by a great beast from the sea, the place of evil spirits, was near and real to the people of that time. When Sir George Adam Smith comments with regard to Jonah, "How many have missed the spirit of the book in amusement or offence at its curious details,"[71] we can say the same of those who dismiss too easily the pictures of the Atonement given to us by Gregory of Nyssa or Rufinus, and miss their insistence that Christ has redeemed us from an Evil that threatened to engulf us completely. We also have to recognize that to the writers themselves this was a picture rather than a theory.

Furthermore, it has been pointed out that the crudity of the image is considerably modified by Gregory himself when he goes on to liken God's "deception" of the Devil with a beneficent deception that may be practiced by a physician to ensure the cure of his patient. For Gregory believed that even the Devil himself would ultimately benefit from the saving action that God had taken: "by so doing he benefited, not only the one who had perished, but also the very one who had brought us to ruin. For when death came into contact with life, darkness with light, corruption with incorruption, the worse of these things disappeared into a state of nonexistence, to the profit of him who was freed from these evils."[72] This is an aspect of the doctrine of the Atonement put forward by Gregory of Nyssa which has not been sufficiently recognized and which must be set over against his bizarre picture of the Devil being trapped by God. Indeed, it shows that it was only a picture and that like all pictures its uses were limited, for a theory of the fish hook, even one of cosmic proportions, can hardly be reconciled literally with the idea that the hook was ultimately baited for the benefit of the fish!

Strangely enough it was within his own lifetime and from the pen

[70] *The Book of the Twelve Prophets* (Hodder & Stoughton, 1928) II, 485.
[71] *Ibid.*
[72] *Oratio Catechetica* xxvi.

of his own intimate friend, Gregory of Nazianzus, that Gregory of Nyssa's ransom theory was attacked. Gregory of Nazianzus (329-389) agreed that we were in bondage to the Devil, and that ransom is usually paid to the one who is in possession. But he asked, "Was the ransom then paid to the evil one? It is a monstrous thought. If to the evil one—what an outrage! Then the robber receives a ransom, not only from God, but one which consists of God Himself." [73] The writer finds that impossible to believe, and he proceeds to demolish for equally good reasons, even before it has appeared, any suggestion that the ransom was paid to God the Father, for how could the Father delight in the blood of his Son?

It will be seen that Gregory of Nazianzus, in standing against this theory, had an independent and powerfully critical mind, but he found it more difficult to put any satisfactory theory in the place of the views he tried to pull down. He took up the representative character of Christ's work and the idea of the Second Adam from Paul and at the same time stressed the obedience of Christ:

"As for my sake he was called a curse who destroyed my curse, and sin who takes away the sin of the world, and became a new Adam to take the place of the old, just so he makes my disobedience his own as head of the whole body. As long, then, as I am disobedient and rebellious, both by denial of God and by my passions, so long Christ also is called disobedient on my account... But as the Son subjects all to the Father, so does the Father to the Son... Thus he honors obedience by his action, and proves it experimentally by his Passion." [74]

We are left with Athanasius (296-373) and Augustine (354-430), one the representative of Greek and the other of Latin thought. It is perhaps not without significance that neither of these great Fathers of the Church writes specifically about the doctrine of the Atonement but deals with the problem incidentally in the course of his treatment of other doctrinal subjects. Athanasius set out to deal with the question of the Incarnation (the *De Incarnatione*) and Augustine with

---

[73] From *Oration* xlv. 22 quoted in Bethune-Baker's *Introduction*, pp. 343-44. We are reminded that another opponent of the theory was the anonymous author of *De Recta Fide*; cf. H. E. W. Turner, *The Patristic Doctrine of Redemption*, pp. 58-59.

[74] *Oration* xxx. 5, 6. ("The Theological Orations" iv. 5, 6 in *The Library of Christian Classics*, III).

the doctrine of the Trinity (the *De Trinitate*). The fact that they found themselves forced to tackle the problem of our redemption, why it was necessary and how it was achieved, is an illustration of that sense of unity between all Christian doctrine that is so pronounced in the Fathers. As the same time it is evidence of the directions from which Athanasius and Augustine approached the problem of Atonement and indicates the doctrines which they placed at the center of the gospel.

It is precisely this fact which gives to Athanasius his special significance regarding the doctrine of the Atonement, for in a real sense he sees the Atonement as a development of that which our Lord took upon himself at the Incarnation. It is the Eternal Word who created us, who saw that man was under the penalty of death, and who entered our situation in order to turn his creation from their fate and

> quicken them from death by the appropriation of his body and by the grace of the resurrection. . . . For the Word, perceiving that not otherwise could the corruption of men be undone save by death as a necessary condition, while it was impossible for the Word to suffer death, being immortal, and Son of the Father; to this end he takes to himself a body capable of death, that it, by partaking of the Word who is above all, might be worthy to die in the stead of all.[75]

Athanasius said that by offering his own body for the life of all, the Word of God "satisfied the debt by his death," but he did not venture any clear-cut opinion on the questions to whom the debt was due, or in what way the satisfaction was made. He incorporated the idea of Christ as our Representative [76] and also the idea that Christ came to restore the *imago dei* that is to be found appearing earlier in Irenaeus[77] But one has the impression that for Athanasius the real act of Atonement and Reconciliation was in the fact that "the Word became flesh and dwelt among us."

This set him a problem regarding the death of Christ, for if the Atonement centers in the Incarnation, why was the death of Christ necessary, and why should it be the death of the Cross? In respect of the first he argued that it was necessary for the Word to take a body

---
[75] *De Incarnatione* viii, ix.
[76] *Ibid.* x.
[77] *Ibid.* xiii.

which was capable of death and which would become subject to death, "that he might offer it as his own in the stead of all, and as suffering, through his union with it, on behalf of all, 'bring to nought him that had the power of death, that is, the devil; and might deliver them who through fear of death were all their lifetime subject to bondage.' "[78]

The death on the Cross presented him with more difficulty, but he argued that it was the only death which was fitting to Christ—he must receive "at others' hands, the occasion of perfecting his sacrifice."[79] If he had devised for himself a more glorious or respectable death, he would have given grounds for the suspicion that he could not prove himself victorious over every form of death: a good wrestler does not pick his own opponents but stands against all comers.[80] Furthermore, by suffering the death of the Cross, he became curse for us for he took upon himself the curse of the Cross.[81] And for these reasons, Athanasius argued, "in no other way than by the cross was it right for the salvation of all to take place."[82]

Because Christ died in this way, death is destroyed and the cross is the victory over it and its power, and Athanasius demonstrated this by pointing to the behavior of Christians in the face of martyrdom. Just as when a tyrant is bound by a great king, the subjects of the king can ignore the tyrant. So it is with Christians. It does not mean that the tyrant, Death, is weak, but it demonstrates the strength and the victory of their King,[83] and Athanasius could point for proof to the multitudes who were coming over at that time to the Christian faith. Moreover, not only was this proof of the fact that death had been slain, but the deeds of Christians in their change from sin to goodness were also proof of the Resurrection and of the fact that Christ was alive and triumphant in the world.

Such is the thought of Athanasius in the *De Incarnatione*. All the scriptural elements are present and most of the emphasis that followed from them in the thought of the early Church—the total work of Christ, his life, his passion and death, the Resurrection, and the con-

---

[78] *Ibid.* xx based upon Heb. 2:14-15.
[79] *Ibid.* xxi.
[80] *Ibid.* xxiv.
[81] *Ibid.* xxv; cf. Deut. 21:23; Gal. 3:13.
[82] *Ibid.* xxvi.
[83] *Ibid.* xxviii.

ception of a victory which brings victory to his people in the struggle with sin and death. But the starting point, the real point of contact between God and man, is the fact that the Word took flesh, and the rest followed as a natural sequence from that. Nevertheless, at the deepest level the Atonement is central to Athanasius, in that within his thought the purpose for the Incarnation was entirely redemptive. Christ came in order that man might be redeemed. When Athanasius speaks about the Word becoming flesh, this is not a theological speculation nor simply the revelation of divine nature but divine action— God's initiative for the salvation of the world.

Augustine's doctrine of the Atonement is to be found principally in chapters 10-16 of Book XIII of the *De Trinitate*, and it appears to be rather more incidental to the theme of the whole work than is the case with the *De Incarnatione*. However, he posed the fundamental question, why it was necessary for God's own Son to die for us. For Augustine it is not sufficient to show that the method used to redeem us was good and fitting to the dignity and honor of God, but we must ask ourselves whether there could have been any other way for dealing with our situation. He said it was necessary to give us hope in the face of our despair, and that there was no better way of doing this than by demonstrating the infinite cost that God was prepared to pay in order to save us: the gift of his Son revealed the extent of his grace. How are we justified by the blood of Christ, and how are we reconciled by his death? Augustine rejected any idea of the death of Christ appeasing the wrath of God, but he said that the human race had been delivered into the power of the Devil by the justice of God when Adam sinned. This did not, however, remove men from God's grace and power, and as man's sin delivered him to the Devil, so the remission of sins in Christ frees him from the Devil's power.

Augustine also contended that the Devil must be conquered through the exercise of God's justice rather than by an act of almighty power. He explained the justice of God's acting in this by pointing out that when the Devil slew Christ, he took something that did not belong to him, thereby shedding innocent blood. For this act in which he exceeded his "rights," it was no more than justice that he should deliver up those that were in bondage to him. Augustine recognized that even when sins are forgiven the trials of mortality remain, but he saw these as opportunities for ethical endeavour. For besides the objective atonement that Christ achieved for us, he gives us the supreme example of obedience in the manner in which he won redemption for us, which should bear fruit in our own lives. So to Augustine the "objective" and "subjective" aspects of the Atonement are not to be set against each other but to be seen rather as the two sides of God's initiative on our behalf and our response in the power of his Spirit, whereby we are given the victory and saved not only from the guilt of past sin but also from its power here and its judgment hereafter.

4. What Do We Learn from the Fathers?

A single chapter that attempts to cover the doctrine of the Atonement throughout the patristic period probably deserves all the criticism it is likely to get, for the omissions will be obvious and no mere catalogue of theologians and their views can represent what the doctrine meant in the life of the Church as the redeemed community. But cursory and selective as the study has necessarily been, a review of the main positions taken within the first few centuries of the Church's history does tell us something about the way in which the Church developed its thinking about this doctrine, and we are provided with some facts with which to assist our approach to the total history of the doctrine of our Redemption.

The first thing we notice is that it was a comparatively long time before the Church began to formulate a theory of the Atonement. For 150 or 200 years (as far as we can tell from the available literature of the period), little attempt was made to produce a "theory." The language of Scripture, the close relation between the work of Christ and the Old Testament prophecies, the sacrificial images, and the writings of the Apostles and others that were developing into the New Testament canon were sufficient to express the Church's faith in what Christ had won for man by taking flesh and by enduring the death of the Cross.

If anyone should wonder that the Church remained so long without attempting to elaborate a theory of Atonement, we have to remember that these same biblical images were also to be found in the continuing life of worship and liturgy with the sacraments at its center. Moreover, with the constant threat and challenge of suffering and martyrdom before them, the early Christians were not likely to forget

THE ATONEMENT AND THE SACRAMENTS

either the cost of their own reconciliation with God or what participation in that act implied for them. The strong ethical imperative in their conception of the Atonement must be seen in the light of that ever-present possibility. There was no danger of imagining that one could follow Christ, the Great Example, simply in one's own strength when that path might lead to the arena or to the flames. Only the strength of the Holy Spirit could make possible the suffering endured by a servant girl like Blandina, or a boy like Ponticus in the name of Christ.[84] Pelagius was not likely to arise in the Church until the fires of persecution had begun to die down.

A further point to notice is that when eventually the theologians came to grips with the problem of explaining how Jesus Christ had won salvation for mankind, the demand for a theory seems to have come from the necessities of apologetic. To explain what God in Christ has done to win the redemption of man is simply another way of challenging the individual with the historic facts of the gospel and of putting into the most graphic and revelant terms the reason why you, I, and our neighbor *ought* to believe in Jesus Christ and be followers of him. By no means all the apologists who were trying to present the issues of the Christian faith to a pagan world moved toward developing a systematic theory of Atonement, but the problems of apologetic pushed them in that direction. Later on we are conscious that the form in which the doctrine was cast was developed by theologians as much for the Church itself as for the world around it. This is perhaps an indication of the problem of catechetical instruction and even of the inevitable change in the quality of membership that arose as soon as the threat of persecution began to lessen and the great mass of the populace pressed for entry into the Church. But perhaps the first steps toward a theology of Atonement came from the challenge of evangelism and the needs of effective Christian apologetic.

We must also notice the images that were used. We owe Gustaf Aulén a debt of gratitude for reminding us that the great "classic" or "patristic" theory of the doctrine of the Atonement, which theologians dismissed too contemptuously, was cast within the dramatic picture forms of redemption from the devil and victory over the

---

[84] Martyred at Lyons during the persecution A.D. 161-80. Cf. Eusebius *Ecclesiastical History* V. 1.

powers of darkness.[85] We need to be reminded that in its essence and origin this theory was not a "theory" and still less an attempted factual account of the truth of Atonement, but it was a dramatic representation of that truth in pictorial figures, and that if these images used by the early Church are understood and used as *images*, they contain truths about the doctrine which should never be lost. At the same time we have to recognize that if this form of the doctrine did not quite become the official dogma of the Church, it became the accepted form of the doctrine for nearly nine hundred years. By its very popularity it became more than a rich and suggestive representation of the truth about the Atonement until it was in danger of being accepted as the truth itself. We have to be clear about the distinction, for whereas we can accept it as the classic or patristic *theme* about the Atonement, containing invaluable aspects of the truth, modern Christians cannot accept it as a ransom *theory*.

Finally, the period of the early Church emphasizes the unity of all Christian doctrine. Properly speaking there is no heretical doctrine of the Atonement (apart from the simple apostasy which denies the efficacy of Christ's redeeming work), because although there have been periods in Church history when one or another theory has held popular allegiance, the Church has never defined the doctrine in a creedal form. On the other hand, to study the early history of the Church is to face the fact that in the development of Christian doctrine all the doctrines are interrelated.[86] There were direct implica-

---

[85] *Den kristna försoningstanken* (1930). Eng. tr. by Fr. A. G. Hebert, *Christus Victor* (S. P. C. K., 1931).

[86] H. E. W. Turner emphasizes that there was no unified doctrine of Atonement in the Fathers and suggests that this was because the Church was preoccupied with defining doctrines that were more immediately pressing from the point of view of Christian Apologetic. But no doctrine affects Apologetic more vitally than the Atonement, and we may regard it as providential that the Church was prevented (in the Latin sense!) from trying to define it until the time when she had "lost the habit of Catholic and ecumenical thinking" (*The Patristic Doctrine of Redemption*, p. 114). Canon Turner shows us that there were four themes on the Redemption that become very difficult to unravel—the stress on moral influence, the theme of Recapitulation and *Christus Victor*, the mystical theme from the East that interpreted Redemption as incorporation into Christ, and the Sacrificial and Satisfactionary themes which led directly to Anselm. Of these we have neglected the mystical theme which found its culmination in the idea of man being transfigured into the divine nature through Christ. Admittedly it is for the Westerner "the hardest to appreciate and to grasp," (*ibid*, p. 121), but the only reason for not concentrating upon it is that it cannot be shown to have had any real effect upon the later writers who constitute our main study. Nevertheless, it is interesting to notice that ideas which are characteristic of this theme seem

tions for the doctrine of the Atonement in those things for which the Church was contending in its struggle with the ancient heresies, in the denial of which one is more often than not involved in a denial of the real efficacy of the work of Christ for salvation.

Perhaps one of the omissions which the limitations of this chapter have imposed upon us is the failure to consider the Atonement in relationship to the "heretical" writings. But a moment's reflection will show the implications, for example, of docetism or gnosticism—which denied the real humanity of our Lord—for the doctrine. Any deviations affecting the doctrines of the Person of Christ or the Trinity were bound to have serious effects upon the doctrine of the work of Christ itself. Therefore, although the doctrine of the Atonement appears to stand free from the Christological disputes of these early centuries, in fact it was inextricably involved, and in contending for a full doctrine of the Person of Christ, the Church was also contending for the possibility of a full doctrine of the work of Christ. There can be no salvation as the Bible announces it and as the early Church lived it, unless Jesus of Nazareth lived as a man and is also the Christ of God.

---

to have been revived independently by later Western writers, who had little or no knowledge of Eastern thought.

CHAPTER II

Anselm and His Successors

ONE COULD MAKE OUT A FAIRLY GOOD CASE FOR SUGGESTING THAT most of the really explosive writings in the history of human thought have been short ones. Into this category we should certainly have to place Anselm's *Cur Deus Homo*, for with this brief treatise Anselm completely destroyed the predominance held by the theory of a ransom paid to the devil and substituted a completely new series of categories in which the doctrine of the Atonement was very largely to be cast for the next eight hundred years.

Anselm was archbishop of Canterbury, from 1093 to his death in 1109, during the troublous reigns of William II (William Rufus) and his brother Henry I. Although Anselm is the see of Canterbury's brightest ornament in theology, it must be remembered that he was a native-born Italian who had voluntarily gone into exile in order to enter the cloister. His thought was Latin and Western, and his natural allegiance was to Italy and to the Roman pontiff. He had been born in 1033 into a noble Italian family and had left home in order to enter the monastery, joining the community at Bec where he eventually became abbot. It was while he was at Bec that he came under the influence of his learned and able countryman, Lanfranc (a close adviser of William, Duke of Normandy), who in 1070, after the Norman Conquest, became Archbishop of Canterbury following the deposition of his English predecessor, Stigand. When Lanfranc died in 1089 soon after his friend and patron, William I, William Rufus delayed nominating a successor for about three years while the rents and perquisites of the see of Canterbury went into his own treasury. In March, 1093, however, the king became ill, and fearing death, he sought to square his accounts with the Church by sending to Bec for Anselm, who was then more or less forced to accept the archbishopric against his will.

As archbishop Anselm tried to correct the more obvious abuses within the Church in England and to strengthen the bond between that Church and the see of Rome. But he did not possess Lanfranc's good political sense and nearly half the time he was Primate of All England he spent in exile, mainly over the bitterly contested question of "lay investiture" with William Rufus' successor, Henry I. Although Anselm could not escape the tensions of ecclesiastical diplomacy, for which he had not much taste, his real interests were theological and philosophical, and from the theological point of view the years that he spent in exile were a blessing in disguise, for they enabled him to develop these interests. The *Cur Deus Homo* was begun in England in the midst of his struggle with William II and completed in 1098 in Italy, when his dispute with the English king had forced him to appeal to Rome.

1. Cur Deus Homo: "Satisfaction"

In the preface Anselm sets out the plan and intention of the book. It is divided into two parts, the first containing the objections raised by unbelievers against the Christian faith, and the answers to those objections with a view to showing (by means of reason alone) that it is impossible for anyone to be saved without Christ. The second part of the book continues the same method and tries to show ("as if nothing were known of Christ") that human nature was made for immortality, but that this cannot be obtained without the work of Christ, the "God-Man." Anselm is seeking a common ground for debate between the believer and the unbeliever, and he finds this in human reason.

How far this is a valid ground for apologetic modern theologians would find arguable, and how far Anselm actually conducts his argument without recourse to the Christian revelation is questionable, but we must not misunderstand the motive and purpose behind this method. He is not trying to demonstrate the reasonableness of religion, and still less that the Christian faith is a religion of reason. His arguments are conducted not to show the reasonableness of belief but to demonstrate the sinfulness of unbelief. An unbeliever who is convinced by his reasoning has not the satisfaction at the end of having discovered reasonable grounds for belief in Jesus Christ, but he discovers that his reason faces him with the indictment and judgment of Almighty God, against whom he stands as a sinner. Anselm's book is Christian apologetic in the best sense of the term, not as simply offering a reasoned or reasonable defense of the Christian faith, but in presenting a challenge to unbelief and in trying to discover ground on which the revelation of God in Christ may be presented to unbelieving man with some hope of being recognized for what it is. Anselm recognized that this kind of apologetic could also be a means of strengthening those simple believers who are unable to give a reason for their faith. For on the questions why God became man, and why he chose to save man by his own death, Anselm declares that the unlearned ask for help.

The Cur Deus Homo* was therefore written with a double purpose —first that of evangelism or apologetic, to convince men through their reason about their need of God's help in Jesus Christ, and secondly, to support the faith not only of the theologically literate but also of the simple believer who wanted to be able to give a reason for the faith that was in him.[1] This attempt to present theology in a form which could be understood by the simple is perhaps not the least important lesson that theologians have to learn from Anselm. It is ostensibly the reason why the book is in the form of a dialogue between Anselm (giving the Christian answer) and the mythical "Boso," who voices the doubts of the unbeliever and the difficulties of the unlearned Christian. But it should be noticed that there was a very practical advantage in this method, for it often enabled Anselm to attack through "Boso" a traditionally held position without necessarily implying that it was his own view! Through "Boso" he takes up the point that Augustine had made previously; namely, that it was not sufficient simply to show that it was good or "fitting" for God to

---

* NOTE: For the sake of consistency the quotations in English from Anselm and Abelard are from the translation in *A Scholastic Miscellany*, Vol. X., Library of Christian Classics. Published, 1956, The Westminster Press. Used by permission. A detailed study of the *Cur Deus Homo* is to be found in Dr. John McIntyre's *St. Anselm and his Critics* (Edinburgh: Oliver and Boyd, 1954). Another important recent study of Anselm is that of G. H. Williams of Harvard, "The Sacramental Presuppositions of Anselm's Cur Deus Homo," in *Church History*, September, 1957 (American Society of Church History), pp. 245-74. Other studies will be found in the histories of doctrine, such as *Le Dogme de la Rédemption* by l'Abbé Rivière.

[1] *Op. cit.* I. i. The point is made even more explicitly later on in the book, when Boso reminds Anselm that he was being asked to do something for Boso and for those who had enquired through him, "and not for the learned." II. xvi. Cf. McIntyre, *op. cit.*, p. 49.

save man through the sacrifice of Christ, but it must be clearly shown that there was no other way. Here it is the Eastern theologians who are under fire, but at the same time it can be shown that Anselm does not so much criticize the idea of what is "fitting" to God as push it to its absolute conclusion. His whole argument is based upon the idea that God's plan of redemption comes from God *a se*, from God's own nature. If in one sense, therefore, Anselm demonstrates the inadequacy of the Greek theories, in another sense he develops what had been the fundamental concept in Irenaeus.[2]

On the other hand there can be little doubt that his main intention is to destroy those elements in the ransom theory which appeared to him to be contrary to this fundamental principle, and he uses Boso to criticize particularly the idea that the devil has "rights" over man. The devil's seduction was much more like the action of a mutinous slave who has persuaded a fellow slave to join his treacherous rebellion against their common Master. Man deserved to be punished, "But the devil had earned no right to punish him; on the contrary, this was the height of injustice, since the devil was not moved to do it by love of justice, but was driven by malicious impulse." We must not forget that Anselm was attacking a theory that was still generally accepted in the Church and which had the majority of Church Fathers on its side, and he goes on (we assume through Boso) to attack the idea that man was in debt to the devil by way of debt or usury. Commenting upon the passage (Col. 2:14) where Paul speaks of the bond that stood against us being blotted out and nailed to the cross, he declares that since the bond was the "bond of the decree" it did not belong to the devil but to God, "for by God's just judgment it had been decreed and, as it were, confirmed by handwriting that, since man had freely sinned, he should not be able by himself to avoid sin or the penalty of sin."[3] Boso seems to be given the words but Anselm is really speaking, for all that then follows in the book is to justify this position and to demonstrate the necessity for Christ as God's own

---

[2] Dr. J. McIntyre finds the center of Anselm's soteriology in this concept. "To put the case briefly," he says, "St. Anselm's purpose is to show how the Atonement follows from the nature and Will of God Himself" (*St. Anselm and his Critics*, p. 203). Elsewhere he speaks of it as the *aseitas* within God—the necessity which constrains him to act as he does and which "springs from Himself (*a se*) and from no other person or thing" (*ibid.*, p. 193; cf. pp. 57, 120). We are surprised that seeing this so clearly, Dr. McIntyre does not show its connection with "fittingness" in Irenaeus.

[3] St. Anselm, *Cur Deus Homo* I. vii.

Son making satisfaction *to God* by his suffering and death for the sins of the world. This is his decisive step which undercut the former ransom theory of the Atonement, for although there had been those like Gregory of Nazianzus who had been unwilling to describe our redemption in terms of payment made to the devil, they had all been equally unwilling to think of the sacrifice of Christ as something demanded by and paid to God the Father. What others drew back from, Anselm boldly accepted and sought to justify.

Anselm maintains that the will of God itself "should be a good enough reason for us when he does anything, even though we cannot see why he does it," for the will of God is never without reason. However, he soon has to face the real difficulty with which his theory presents him, to reconcile our Lord's freedom of will with his obedience to the Father, and this he never satisfactorily resolves. He sees the difficulty and rightly holds that if certain passages of Scripture seem to imply that God the Father requires the death of his Son, it must be due to our misunderstanding of the Scripture, since our Lord bore his death by his own free will to save mankind.[4] Boso is not convinced: he can see that Christ bore his death because he was obedient, but he cannot see how that obedience *itself* did not require the death. In reply Anselm says that because Jesus was sinless, God the Father could not require his death, but he claims that God commanded our Lord to fulfill all righteousness, and because Jesus voluntarily chose the way of death in obedience to this command, we cannot say that the Father compelled the Son to die.[5] The question is whether this adequately recognizes the all-important *voluntary* action of our Lord on our behalf in going to the Cross. It is an aspect of Anselm's argument where he is weakest.

There is a sense in which the core of Anselm's thought is his conception of the greatness and majesty of Almighty God,[6] but it is also largely true that he interprets this majesty and greatness in the categories of regal sovereignty and honor that were accepted by the feudal society to which he belonged. Sin is essentially to Anselm a refusal on the part of God's vassals to render to God his due, an affront and out-

---

[4] Ibid. I. viii.
[5] Ibid. I. ix.
[6] Cf. A. R. Wateley's article in *The Atonement in History and in Life* ed. L. W. Grensted (S. P. C. K., 1929), p. 198-99.

rage to the Divine Majesty for which full satisfaction must be made. Just as when one person robs another one of his health, he should not only see that the victim is given back the good health that he has lost but also make recompense for the injury that has been caused. So by our sin we owe to God not only the absolute obedience that is his just due but also recompense for the honor and duty of which we have robbed him by our sin in the past. He argues that God cannot simply forgive sin without punishing it, since the right treatment for any sin that is committed without satisfaction is to punish it.[7] Nothing is less tolerable than that the creature should rob its Creator of the honor that is due to him, and therefore, we have merited the just punishment of God unless we can give full satisfaction for our sin. Men are in the dilemma, however, that nothing we can do can give satisfaction to God for the sins of the past: our penance, obedience, and good works of the present and the future are no more than what is due to God from us, and therefore it is impossible for the individual to pay back to God the satisfaction due to him from the sins of the past and to remove this entail of past guilt.

This is the point where the evangelical and apologetic purpose behind Anselm's use of reason can be seen. The premise from which he argues may be of little value to us, since Anselm presumes that the idea of God is within the consciousness of every human being, and this is itself a matter of doubt for the majority of modern unbelievers. But there is a good deal to be learned from the purpose to which he puts the use of reason—not to reason men into the kingdom of God but to demonstrate the nemesis of reason in man's utter inability to save himself or to justify himself before the claims of his Creator. More than this he argues that man is not only unable to pay to God the satisfaction that is due, but that his inability and failure to do so is not an excuse but an additional condemnation. If a servant has been commanded to perform a certain task and warned in doing it to be careful not to fall into a pit from which there is no escape, he surely is to be blamed if he straightway disregards the warning and falls into the very danger about which he has been warned.[8] The illustration is, of course, only valid if one accepts a corporate view of man in which the sin of Adam is regarded as the sin of the race, and the fact that Anselm

[7] St. Anselm, *Op. cit.* I. xii.
[8] *Ibid.* I. xxiv.

uses it seems to contradict the claim of the late O. C. Quick that the note of cosmic redemption is "no longer heard" in Anselm.[9] It may be played with muted strings in Anselm rather than with the brazen trumpets of the earlier Fathers, but it has not disappeared altogether, for if mankind is *solidaire* in sin only a cosmic Christ could win redemption. The main point of Anselm's argument, however, is the challenge that his use of reason offers to natural man—to demonstrate the impossibility of man, individual or corporate, being able to settle his account with God by his own effort and the necessity for the divine intervention of One who was both God and man.

In his preface Anselm had declared that it was his intention in the second part of his book also to work by reason "as if nothing were known of Christ," but he was unaware to what extent his premises were wholly based upon Christian presuppositions. He commences by stating that man was created to enjoy the blessedness of God and that death would not have entered if man had not sinned. Therefore, he argues that if man is restored, resurrection will follow, but it will follow not of logical necessity but of God's grace; it follows not because God must but because his own nature demands it and of his own grace he wills it: "we should ascribe the whole to grace" (*totum gratiae debemus imputare*).[10] He then directs his attention to the Person of Christ, and underlying the whole of his argument there is the idea of the "rightness" or "fittingness" of God's actions, i.e., that what God does for the redemption of man must be conformable to God's own nature. It was right that as sin had come through man the redemption of man from sin should also come through a member of the human race, and as the cause of man's condemnation was through the temptation of a virgin, "much more is it right that it should be a virgin who would be the occasion of all the good."[11] It is a reappearance of the idea of recapitulation that is to be found in Paul and Irenaeus.

Up to this point Anselm has reasoned that the redemption of man could not be achieved by man himself, and that it must therefore be brought about by God's own initiative in such a way that it is won by a Saviour who is both God and a representative of the human race

---

[9] O. C. Quick, *The Gospel of the New World* (Nisbet, 1944), p. 75.
[10] St. Anselm, op. cit. II. v. Cf. McIntyre, op. cit., p. 199.
[11] St. Anselm, op. cit. viii.

—the God-Man. The question which then presses is how God could possibly take human flesh and become man, and the crucial bases for Anselm's doctrine of the Atonement are therefore the Incarnation and the Virgin Birth. We see something of the medieval monk's distrust of sex in his easy assumption that he need not spend too much time in proving that the Saviour would be more purely and honorably made (*mundius et honestius procreabitur*) from the flesh of either a man or a woman than from the union of the sexes in a normal act of procreation.[12] It reveals one aspect of the difficulties that forced themselves upon Anselm from his attempt to reconcile pure reason with what were, after all, the revealed facts of Christianity and the presuppositions of his own faith. Namely, how was he to reconcile reason to the Church's interpretation of the facts recorded in the New Testament without appealing to faith? How, on the basis of pure reason, could he prove both the necessary and actual sinlessness of Christ which the gospel declared and the possession of a *real* humanity in Christ? Holding as he did a conception of original sin from the sin of Adam, how could that sinless One be taken from the human lump that was permeated and infected with sin throughout?

This, Anselm admits, is one of the ultimate mysteries and as such he might have left it there, but he believed the key to the mystery was in the Virgin Birth, maintaining that through her faith Mary was one of those who was cleansed from sin by the work of Christ even before the Saviour's birth and that our Lord was born within the purity that she had from him.[13] Of our Lord himself Anselm says that he could not sin because he could not will to sin, but he could die because he declared that he had the power either to take his life or lay it down. Therefore, his voluntary death was the one thing that he could give to God in expiation of man's sin, because this was a death which had not been incurred as a punishment but was voluntarily given to God by our Lord on man's behalf.

Before leaving the view of the Atonement set out in *Cur Deus Homo*, however, it should be recognized that Anselm found a place for that aspect of the atoning work of Christ which works upon us by

---

[12] *Ibid.* In fairness, however, it should be said that, although Anselm seems to have regarded celibacy as more honorable than marriage, he does admit that neither can be required of man as a duty (II. xviii).

[13] *Ibid.* II. xvi; cf. xviii and note 29 *infra*.

our Lord's example. He calls to mind the ethical response which our Lord's sacrifice should produce in the believer when he reflects that the life of Christ "is more lovable than sins are hateful." [14] In another passage in defending the actual sufferings of our Lord within his human life he asks, "how could he give himself as an example to the weak and mortal, to teach them not to draw back from justice on account of injuries or insults or sufferings or death, if they did not recognize that he himself felt all these things?" [15] The example of our Lord is not missing in Anselm though it lies hidden, but it is set within the greater context of that which Jesus Christ had done to fulfill the Father's will concerning us, to render his Father due honor in all obedience, and to redeem mankind from the curse of sin and the condemnation of death.

2. The Theory Reviewed

We are now in the position where we can attempt some assessment of the view of the Atonement presented in *Cur Deus Homo*. Anselm seems to represent an almost precisely opposite emphasis to that of Athanasius. For the former the point of contact between God and man is not so much in the fact that God became Man in Christ but in the redemptive purpose that was the reason for his becoming man and in the way in which that purpose was achieved. Whereas in Athanasius the Atonement was the fulfillment of the Incarnation, in Anselm the Incarnation is the means by which God's purpose of Atonement is made possible, and so from the title of his book we are led to expect a treatise on the Incarnation which proves to be a treatise on the Atonement. Of course, one must not drive the distinction too far. To say that the center of Anselm's theology is to be found in Atonement is not to argue that the Incarnation was anything less than indispensable and even central to his theory—a considerable part of his book is spent in proving the Incarnation to have been necessary and a large part of the remainder was devoted to demonstrating how it was effected—but it is simply to say that the Incarnation was not itself the act that brought man's redemption. It was indispensable since it was necessary to show that by man's disobedience death had come to the human race, so by man's obedience life would be given

---

[14] *Ibid* II. xiv.
[15] *Ibid*. II. xi.

back,[16] but Incarnation was simply the means whereby that obedience could be revealed—an obedience that was revealed supremely upon the Cross.

The result and perhaps the intention of the *Cur Deus Homo* was to destroy the theory which interpreted the Atonement as a payment made to the devil, but if one understands Anselm's intention rightly it was not simply to destroy the ancient theory as such, but to re-establish the doctrine of the Atonement upon a firmer basis. In the old "classic" theory the devil's position, if not honorable, is at least legal in the exercise of his "rights" over man, and this, in the light of feudal law, created a double allegiance. Pressed to its logical conclusion and interpreted according to what the law in the Middle Ages recognized about the rights of a *de facto* monarch and the duties of a subject under him, men had a legitimate excuse under the old theory for serving the devil until God could reassert his own claims upon them.[17] It was this aspect of double allegiance which Anselm wished to destroy, and he could destroy it only by shifting entirely the whole basis upon which the idea of a ransom had been developed. He asserts that God alone is sovereign and that the rights of the devil are not the rights of a usurper to the throne but those of a rebel slave; man has one single allegiance to God his Creator. If he declares that the "bond" of Col. 2:14 belongs to God and that the ransom must be won from him, it is because it is fundamental to insist that God alone is King and no one else has any rights over man. Even more to the point, he insists that by his sin man has forfeited any rights he had over himself—he is a rebel outlaw under condemnation to the kind of punishment which the Middle Ages reserved for rebel outlaws. Not only has he broken the personal relationship between himself and God (which kind of personal relationship existed between a vassal and his liege lord), but he has broken his fealty and gone over to the rebel enemy. He has no rights, for absolute obedience is no more than the duty that he owes and nothing he can do can offer satisfaction for

---

[16] *Ibid.* I. iii.

[17] There is an interesting illustration from later history about the place which a *de facto* king held in Common Law. When Oliver Cromwell was offered the crown in 1657, one of the strongest reasons urged was that, by accepting, he would safeguard the actions of his subjects in the event of any future restoration of the Stuarts, since the law covered actions performed in obedience to a *de facto* king, but did not recognize a *de facto* "Lord Protector."

his rebellion of the past, and God, to maintain his kingly honor and justice, cannot allow the rebellion to be unpunished. Of himself, man is hopeless before God. So the whole basis of the doctrine of the Atonement was shifted to meet the questions raised by medieval man, not in the form of an apologetic that tried to reconcile the Christian faith to his way of living by blurring the issues but in a way which, by expressing the truth within his own terms, threw into greater relief the desperateness of his condition before God and the sharpness of the challenge that was presented to him by the gospel.

Anselm asserted the single allegiance that is due to God alone, and that is his great positive contribution, but there is a great deal in the working out of his theory which can be criticized.

1. Although his desire is to enhance the majesty and honor of God, by asserting God's primacy over all things he is sometimes led into representing God's actions in a way which, to the modern reader, is just contrary to his desired effect. We can hardly blame him for failing to meet the questionings of the twentieth century, but his explanations why God has to punish sin (through the terms in which the medieval Church conceived the punishment of sin) simply do not convince anyone today. He rightly insists that man's final and only obedience is to God alone—"against thee, thee only, have I sinned, and done this evil in thy sight." (Ps. 51:4.)—and that the bond of man's indictment belongs to his Creator and not to the devil or any other being. But if these legal terms are to be used we may ask how far the God and Father of our Lord Jesus Christ would insist upon the full satisfaction being paid simply in order to satisfy his honor: if his demand to us is that we should be prepared to forgive unto "seventy times seven," can we set limits to his own mercy?

One of Anselm's most difficult problems is to reconcile his theory with the mercy and forgiveness of God as they are revealed by our Lord in the gospels. He presents us with too great a contrast between the sovereign majesty of God the Father, which must on no account be lessened or impugned, and the merciful humility of God the Son—for our own religious instinct tells us which of these qualities must really be supreme in the God whom Christians worship. The tension is perhaps seen most pointedly when he declares that it is impossible for God to do anything irregularly (*in ordinatum*), such as freely to forgive sin for which no satisfaction has been made.[18] The question which the modern mind asks is, "Which presents a picture more in keeping with the honor and majesty of God—a God who forgives without regard to his own honor, or One who in default of satisfaction condemns men to hell?"

Anselm maintains that for God to forgive a man the satisfaction that is due to him simply because the man cannot pay the debt is to say that God merely remits what he has no chance of receiving, and this makes a mockery of the forgiveness of God.[19] So it does, if that is the only motive for the remission of sins. But supposing the motive is the majesty and honor of God's unconquerable love for man? Did the king in our Lord's parable forgive nothing because his servant could not pay him the ten thousand talents that he owed, and did this make a mockery of mercy? We might argue on the other side that if in the remittance of an unrepayable debt the former relationship of love and trust between creditor and debtor is restored, then that forgiveness has infinite value. Real forgiveness is not in foregoing the satisfaction due by law (although it may include it) but in the restoration of a relationship of trust between two persons, and this brings us near to the heart of the real meaning of atonement.

2. A second criticism of Anselm is in the relationship he presents between the Father and the Son and in what this implied for his doctrine of the Person of Christ. T. F. Torrance, commenting upon Gustaf Aulén's *Christus Victor*, has said that Aulén fails where Anselm succeeded in understanding "the full place occupied by the Humanity of our Lord in the divine act of reconciliation."[20] Whether the judgment is true of Aulén it is not our purpose at this juncture to discuss, but what is here said about Anselm needs to be very carefully qualified. In a certain sense it is true that Anselm bases his whole conception of the Atonement upon the humanity of our Lord, or rather upon the fact that the Saviour was both God and Man. On the other hand, although he holds to the necessity for our Lord having both a divine and human nature, he is far less satisfactory and even far less orthodox when one inquires what kind of humanity he en-

---

[18] St. Anselm, op. cit. I. xii. McIntyre has a very good critique of Anselm and forgiveness, op. cit., pp. 100-109.
[19] Ibid. I. xxiv.
[20] Review of the *Opera Omnia* (Thos. Nelson) of Anselm in *The Scottish Journal of Theology* (Vol. 9, No. 1, March, 1956), p. 89.

visages in our Lord. Certainly, according to Anselm, our Lord is human in the formal, technical sense of having been born of woman and having taken human flesh, and Anselm goes to considerable lengths to demonstrate how Jesus could actually be born of the human stock without actually inheriting human sin. But there are serious limitations in the content he gives to the humanity taken by our Lord. He maintains that it was fitting that our Lord should be like men and dwell among them without sin,[21] but he also stresses the fact that our Lord *could not* sin,[22] could not be miserable in his temporal misfortunes,[23] and could not share the experience of human ignorance.[24]

Furthermore, as we have seen, there is the relation between our Lord's freedom of will and his obedience to the Father. Anselm tried to reconcile those passages in the Bible that seem to imply that our Lord, of necessity, endured the Cross by the will of the Father; first, by emphasizing that Christ voluntarily accepted the Father's command, and secondly, by interpreting the Father's "will" in the general terms of his desire that the Son should fulfill perfect righteousness and obedience. In this sense, he said, "it can even be said that the Father commanded him to die, when he gave him the commandment through which he met death." [25] But did Anselm really get rid of the idea that an *unavoidable obligation* was put upon Christ which prevented him from doing anything other than he did? If—on Anselm's own premise—our Lord *could not* sin, did he have any free will in the choice of the Cross? This is important not only for what it implies about the Person of Christ and the real content in such verses as "tempted like as we are, yet without sin" (Heb. 4:15), but because if it is forced, it destroys one of the essential elements in the sacrifice of Christ which has been most fruitful in winning back men to God—the sense we have that Jesus gave to the Father far more than could be expected of him in the fulfillment of his Sonship. It is the element of the "so much more," the principle of the "extra mile"—that which cannot be commanded or expected—which makes the sacrifice what it is to us, and which illustrates the bond of love between the Father and the Son.

[21] St. Anselm, *op. cit.* I. xi.; cf. Heb. 4-15.
[22] *Ibid.* II. x.
[23] *Ibid.* II. xii.
[24] *Ibid.* II. xiii.
[25] *Ibid.* I. ix.

3. The difficulty is with Anselm's contrast between the honor and majesty of the Father and the sacrifice and humility of the Son, which if driven much further implies either an Arian position regarding the Person of Christ or tritheism regarding the doctrine of the Trinity. Anselm himself never wholly falls into those errors, but in the hands of less skilful writers the danger was present. On the other hand Anselm seems to sense that ultimately a doctrine of the Atonement that asserts the objective action of God in Christ can only rest upon a sound doctrine of the Trinity, i.e., on a doctrine of the Godhead in which all the Persons are so united in purpose that the decision of One is the decision of All, the suffering of One is the suffering of All, and the glory of One is to the honor of All. If such a conception of the Godhead is held in relation to Atonement, there cannot ultimately be any opposition between the justice and love of God, or any false distinction between the satisfaction due to the Father and the sacrifice endured by the Son, for that which the Father receives and that which the Son does are one with that which the Holy Spirit confirms in us.

It is in connection with the same doctrine that the idea of "necessity" in God, upon which Anselm puts so much stress, has to be seen, for that which God does arises from what he is in his wholeness. Anselm insists upon this kind of unity in his doctrine of the Trinity, for he asserts that "the Son, with the Father and the Holy Spirit, had determined to show the loftiness of his omnipotence by no other means than death." [26] The real basis, then, on which Anselm asserts an objective act by God in the Atonement is in his understanding of corporate solidarity and responsibility within the Trinity, so that to God the sacrifice of Jesus Christ was not simply "my Son's sacrifice" but "our sacrifice."

4. There remains the question of the forensic and legal images in which Anselm's theory is cast. Aulén dismisses Anselm in terms of the Medieval *lex et ratio* and the categories of the feudal society in which he lived, and he has been properly criticized for doing so.[27] Perhaps Aulén did not pay sufficient attention to the living personal faith that Anselm reveals in his prayers and personal correspondence,

---

[26] *Ibid.* I. ix; cf. II. xviii.

[27] T. F. Torrance, *The Scottish Journal of Theology* (Vol. 9, No. 1, March, 1956) p. 89.

the starting point and ultimate inspiration of his theology.[28] Nevertheless, Anselm did use the rational form and legal metaphors of his own day, and the fact that he did so has both a negative and a positive aspect.

In the negative aspect Anselm sometimes pushed his metaphors beyond their proper use, which would not in itself have been serious if the metaphors had died with his generation. We have to remember, however, that these were the metaphors and this was the imagery that were taken up by the Western Church and which provided the dominant ideas in the exposition of the Atonement until almost the middle of the nineteenth century. Indeed, they became far more than metaphors and images; they became a theory, a doctrine, and almost a dogma. It is in the light of the later history that we would say that the images used by Anselm—which were still perhaps only images and picture forms for Anselm himself—were dangerous. It was undoubtedly in view of what happened to those images in the hardening process of the doctrine, which produced the modern epitaph to all ransom theories of the Atonement whether paid to the devil or to God—"the one makes the devil into a god, and the other turns God into a devil." At the same time one should in fairness add that Anselm can hardly be entirely blamed for the misrepresentations of his later exponents and critics who read into his legal images the blueprint and architecture of a theological system.

On the positive side, however, we need to recognize the fact that Anselm did not hesitate to use the images of law, feudalism, and chivalry that were distinctive features in the society of his own day, and that he did so in a book which purported to deal with the doubts of ordinary people. It gives a hint which we ought not to ignore, for if the Atonement is the point in the Christian revelation where God's action meets man's need, then we can hardly regard as irrelevant the choice of the analogies and thought forms in which that divine action is presented to each generation. Just as the later history of Anselm's theory warns us that no human attempt to describe and explain this doctrine can be of more than very limited value in time, so no series of categories however blessed by success in the past or honored by

---

[28] E.g., Anselm's "Meditations on the Redemption of Mankind," quoted by N. Micklem, *The Doctrine of Our Redemption* (Eyre and Spottiswoode, 1943), p. 76. Cf. also McIntyre, *op. cit.*, p. 51.

long usage can take the place of the constant theological discipline of retranslating this doctrine into the terms that are relevant to our own day. Anselm's bold use of the legal and feudal ideas of eleventh-century Europe in eleventh-century Europe forces home to us the fact that theology is useless if it fails at this point.[29]

3. Peter Abelard and the Great Example

The need for a revision of the doctrine of the Atonement by the time of the eleventh and twelfth centuries is illustrated by the fact that two distinct interpretations that were destined profoundly to influence later Christian thought made their appearance within a comparatively few years of each other. Over against the "satisfaction" theory of Anselm we have to set the interpretation of Peter Abelard, which through the Liberal theologians of the nineteenth and early twentieth centuries extends its influence into our own time.

Abelard's concentration upon the "moral influence" of Christ's death is perhaps thrown into greater relief by the events of his own tragic but intensely human life. He was born in 1079 of a good Breton family, and very soon he won brilliant success as a scholastic theologian. His tragic love for Heloïse, their secret marriage and separation, his multilation by her exasperated uncle, the condemnation of his teaching by the synod at Soissons in 1121, the opposition of the monks of St. Gildas-de-Rhuys to his being their abbot, the bitter theological antagonism of Bernard of Clairvaux leading to Abelard's condemnation by the pope, and finally his death and reconciliation

---

[29] That Anselm used categories acceptable to his day seems to be incontestable, although J. McIntyre emphasizes that he gave to the idea of "satisfaction" his own distinctive meaning (op. cit., pp. 87 ff.). A further point should be noted with regard to his doctrine of Atonement. Dr. McIntyre has shown us that Anselm's basic position is thoroughly evangelical and "protestant" both in the primacy of faith that he asserts over reason and in a theology that is centered in *sola gratia* (op. cit., pp. 38-54, 77-78, 199). At the same time in the accent upon the sinlessness of Mary, Anselm was preparing the way for later Mariology and possibly for a doctrine whereby the Mother of our Lord would be regarded as co-Redemptrix with our Lord himself (op. cit., p. 161). This has also been noted by G. H. Williams (op. cit., p. 258), who also suggests that the result of Anselm's doctrine of the Atonement was to emphasize the primacy of the Eucharist as the central Sacrament of the Medieval Church rather than Baptism which held the primacy within the Church of the Fathers. We note with interest the sacramental implications of the doctrine, but we can also see how the way in which these were worked out was particularly bound up with the sacrificial theories of Roman Catholic piety regarding the Mass itself. The point to notice is that Anselm's theology of Atonement was seminal both for later Catholic and later Protestant thought.

at Cluny in 1142 while on his way to Rome—all these events build up into a medieval romance in which Abelard is the persecuted "hero." "Love" is the theme, even though a closer reading of the facts reveals that the hero was no saint and that the love had more to do with eros than with agape! It was for these reasons, perhaps, coupled with the fact that he was officially silenced by the Church within his own lifetime, that Abelard had so little influence upon the thought of his contemporaries.

His importance in the history of the doctrine of the Atonement is not for the originality of having evolved a new series of categories in which to expound the doctrine, as is the case with Anselm. The example of the sacrifice and death of Christ as that which calls forth in us a like response of love is not only to be found in the New Testament but, as we have seen, also throughout the patristic period and is even to be found in the *Cur Deus Homo* itself. Abelard's importance is in the fact that he took this aspect of the Atonement as the fundamental meaning of the doctrine and not simply as one aspect of it. In one stroke he attacked the basis of both the earlier Fathers' ransom theories and of Anselm's theory of "satisfaction." If it needed the death of Christ in order to expiate the sin of Adam, he asks what possible expiation will meet the act of murder committed against Christ. Wouldn't it have been much much easier for God to pardon the former sin?

> Indeed, how cruel and wicked it seems that anyone should demand the blood of an innocent person as the price for anything, or that it should in any way please him that an innocent man should be slain—still less that God should consider the death of his Son so agreeable that by it he should be reconciled to the whole world! [30]

Here Boso speaks again! For in the *Cur Deus Homo* Boso had made the pertinent comment, "what justice is there in giving up the most just man of all to death on behalf of the sinner? What man would not be judged worthy of condemnation if he condemned the innocent in order to free the guilty?" [31] Anselm had countered on

---

[30] From Abelard's commentary on the "Exposition of the Epistle to the Romans" II, translated in A Scholastic Miscellany (Lib. of Christian Classics Vol. X), p. 283. (Cf. Migne *P. L.* tom. clxxviii, col. 835).

[31] *Cur Deus Homo* I. viii.

that occasion—not very satisfactorily—by insisting that what Christ had done was not done under compulsion but of his own free will to save man, although as we have seen the real basis of his answer to this kind of criticism rested upon the free decision and corporate action of the whole Trinity. Nevertheless, it is clear from the fact that Anselm puts this criticism into the mouth of Boso that it was a real issue in the minds of men at that time, and Abelard takes up the objection and puts it very much to the fore in his own interpretation of the Atonement.

The positive view with which he seeks to supplant the theories he attacked is expressed in the following passage:

> Now it seems to us that we have been justified by the blood of Christ and reconciled to God in this way: through this unique act of grace manifested to us—in that his Son has taken upon himself our nature and persevered therein in teaching us by word and example even unto death—he has more fully bound us to himself by love; with the result that our hearts should be enkindled by such a gift of divine grace, and true charity should not now shrink from enduring anything for him. . . Wherefore, our redemption through Christ's suffering is that deeper affection in us which not only frees us from slavery to sin, but also wins for us the true liberty of sons of God, so that we do all things out of love rather than fear—love to him who has shown us such grace than no greater can be found, as he himself asserts, saying, "Greater love than this no man hath, that a man lay down his life for his friends." Of this love the Lord says elsewhere, "I am come to cast fire on the earth, and what will I, but that it blaze forth?" So does he bear witness that he came for the express purpose of spreading this true liberty of love amongst men.[32]

Abelard has stated the theory here in all its simplicity and attractiveness. It has been called the "Exemplarist" or "Moral Influence" theory, although one of its most able recent exponents, R. S. Franks, maintained that it is more a religious than a "moral" theory since it has to do primarily with Divine grace demonstrated to us by God's love in Jesus Christ and in our response to that grace.[33] Its attractiveness for the preachers and scholars of theological liberalism can be

---

[32] Abelard's commentary on the Epistle to the Romans, *A Scholastic Miscellany*, p. 283 (cf. Migne, P. L. tom. clxxviii, col. 836).
[33] R. S. Franks, *The Atonement* (Oxford University Press, 1934), p. 38.

understood at once, for at a time when the old categories of religious thought were breaking down, the rediscovery of Abelard seemed a God-given interpretation of the work of Christ which could be set against the outmoded theories of the past and which expressed perfectly the controlling idea of God's Fatherly love that was at the heart of the "New Theology." [34] Nor must we forget that in the eyes of men who were themselves fighting against what they regarded as the false and timid conservatism of theological vested interest, Abelard appeared in the midst of the dark ages as a kindred spirit who had been persecuted and victimized by similar forces of theological cowardice and ecclesiastical obscurantism, but who also illustrated the fact that truth will ultimately prevail. If we cannot dismiss the history of Abelard's own life, and particularly his love for Heloïse, as a formative influence in the development of his own view of the Atonement, neither must we forget that in the later age which was revolting against most of the accepted theological and ecclesiastical traditions, the picture of the silenced and ignored "radical" of the Medieval Church, persecuted and suppressed by "bigots" of doctrinal orthodoxy and ecclesiastical power, was enough to stir the sympathy and assure the loyalty of those who were already predisposed by their own questionings to accept his answers.

We shall have more to say in critique of Abelard's doctrine when we examine the thought of the later theologians who embraced his view in one form or another, but the great characteristic of the Abelardian theory is that it is extremely simple to state but extremely difficult to live. It has little to say to the sinner who is oppressed with the sense of his own guilt for the sins of the past and conscious of his own inability to save himself from the sins of the present. A wise minister once said that to point such a man to the perfect life and sacrifice of Jesus and tell him that all he has to do is to follow our Lord's example is cruel! [35] It is precisely that which the sinner, who is most conscious of his own sin, knows he cannot perform without the

---

[34] R. J. Campbell, one of the acknowledged leaders of liberal theology in England during the first half of this century, took it as the title of his book, although he claimed that it was neither of his own invention nor his choice. Cf. J. W. Grant, *Free Churchmanship in England 1870-1940* (Independent Press, n.d.) p. 132 note. Campbell was at that time (1907) in the midst of his controversy with P. T. Forsyth.

[35] Cyril Follett, "The Church Does Not Stand for This," *The Christian World*, June 11, 1953.

assistance of a power that is greater than his own. In that sense it *is* a moral theory, for the aspiration to follow the example of Jesus is purely moral unless man can be given the assurance that God makes available to him a spiritual power to follow that example which is greater in degree and kind from the inspiration of any human hero or saint. He needs to know that the past has been cancelled by the act of God himself, and that the power of His Holy Spirit in Jesus Christ is dependent upon his gift and not man's effort.

The demand for an "objective" Atonement does not spring in the last resort from the conservatism of the Church or the whimsy of theologians but from the need to know that the forgiveness of sins does not depend upon our own inadequate moral strivings. The forgiveness of sin depends upon an action on our behalf initiated and carried through by God himself. Considering the way he hunted Abelard and secured his condemnation, Bernard does not show up very well, nor is the particular form in which he held the ransom theory one which appears very attractive, but he saw this need of taking Christ's action to oneself in faith and in the life of the Church and the sacraments. In his *Letter to the Pope* denouncing Abelard he said:

> I see three chief virtues in this work of salvation: the form of humility in which God emptied Himself; the measure of charity which He stretched out even to death, and that the death of the Cross; the Sacrament of redemption by which He bore that death which He underwent. The former two of these without the last are as if you were to paint on air. A very great and most necessary example of humility; a great example of charity; and one worthy of all acceptation hath He set us; but they have no foundation, and, therefore, no stability, if redemption be wanting. I wish to follow with my strength the lowly Jesus; I wish Him, who loved me and gave himself for me, to embrace me with the arms of His love, which suffered in my stead; but I must also feed on the Paschal Lamb, for unless I eat His Flesh and drink His blood I have no life in me. It is one thing to follow Jesus, another to hold Him, another to feed on Him.[36]

However one may regret the personal results of this letter for Abelard, the support for Bernard in the history of the Church is not to be found primarily in the learned treatises of theologians but in the lives

---

[36] Quoted in S. Cave, *op. cit.*, p. 163.

of many simple Christians who knew themselves formerly to be sinners without hope of raising themselves an inch nearer our Lord's example, but who have been raised into Eternal Life by faith in what he has done for them.

4. Thomas Aquinas Tries to Sum Up

It has been not unfairly stated that the alliterative list, Anselm, Abelard, Aquinas, comprises the whole of medieval theology for the majority of readers, and that by abstracting them in this way from the total context of medieval thought in which they had their place, we "both pay them a false compliment and do an unpardonable injustice to their contemporaries." [37] The criticism is just, but when we set ourselves an examination of the doctrine of the Atonement in the Middle Ages, so distinctive is the contribution of these three men that we are forced to concentrate upon them. If we pass over the rest of the medieval thinkers, it is not because their contribution to the total theological picture of the period is valueless, but because they do not warrant detailed treatment in respect of this particular doctrine. Their influence upon the later history of the doctrine in Protestantism has been minimal.[38]

We cannot say very much more for the influence of Thomas Aquinas (1226-1274) outside Roman Catholic circles, but the comprehension of his thought and the distinctive emphases that can be traced to him suggest that Protestants ought to know the writings of the Angelic Doctor better than they do. It has been said of Aquinas that the time in which he lived was one which demanded "an architectural genius who could co-ordinate the multitudinous ideas, ancient and new, which were stirring men's minds." [39] It is in the sweep of his thought and the breadth of his theological synthesis that we find both the clue to his method and his significance for our study.

Look carefully at the ways in which Aquinas speaks about our Lord's redeeming work. The Passion and sacrifice of our Lord is "exemplarist," since it inspires us to a similar love. Through it we

---

[37] E. R. Fairweather, *A Scholastic Miscellany*, p. 219.
[38] It has been suggested that it is possible to trace a connection between William of Ockham and John Calvin, but it appears to me the line is extremely tenuous. Cf. R. S. Franks, op. cit., p. 19.
[39] M. C. D'Arcy, *Thomas Aquinas: Selected Writings*, p. vii. Used by permission of the publishers Burns, Oates & Washbourne Ltd. and Benziger Brothers, Inc.

THE ATONEMENT AND THE SACRAMENTS

are made to realize how much God loves us, and also we are given an example of all the qualities that are necessary for salvation—obedience, humility, constancy. All these, together with other virtues are demonstrated in Christ's Passion.[40] This work of Christ is, however, also seen in terms of the victory over sin, death, and the devil that was the great "classic" theme of the Fathers, "for," says our writer, "as man was overcome and deceived by the devil so also it should be a man that should overthrow the devil; and as man deserved death so a man by dying should vanquish death.[41]

Aquinas also takes up the idea of a "satisfaction" given to God, for satisfaction is given to a person when that which is offered is of much more value than the offense for which it is offered; so "Christ gave more to God than was required to compensate for the offense of the whole human race." [42] Furthermore, he speaks of our Lord's work as a "sacrifice" offered to God, for a sacrifice is something which is done to appease God and to render him the honor that is his due, and that which was most acceptable to God in the Passion of our Lord was the fact that he suffered voluntarily out of the fulness of his love. Therefore, adds Thomas, "it is manifest that Christ's Passion was a true sacrifice." [43] He cites approvingly Augustine when he described our Lord as the one true Mediator "reconciling us with God," [44] and Aquinas himself speaks of our Lord's work in bringing the human race in agreement (i.e., reconciliation) with God through his death.[45]

He is not attracted to the idea of a ransom paid to the devil,[46] but he does not reject the metaphor of "ransom," for since Satan had defeated man, he was able to hold mankind in bondage until such time as the debt of punishment which was due had been paid. Because our Lord's Passion was a more than sufficient satisfaction for this debt it was "a kind of price" which met the cost of freeing us from guilt and the debt of punishment. In this way Thomas Aquinas brings together the "ransom" and "satisfaction" concepts in the doctrine of the

[40] *Summa Theologica* III(a). xlix. 1, 3.
[41] *Ibid.* III(a). xlix. 3. The brief excerpts from the *Summa* in this section are from the translation by the Fathers of the English Dominican Province (Burns, Oates and Washbourne, 1911.)
[42] *Ibid.* III(a). xlviii. 2, c. et ad. 1.
[43] *Ibid.* III(a). xlviii. 3.
[44] *Ibid.* cf. *De Civitate Dei* x. 20.
[45] *Ibid.* III(a). xlvi. 1, c. et ad. 2.
[46] *Ibid.* III(a). xlviii. 4.

Atonement: for "the Atonement by which one satisfied for self or another is called the price by which he ransomed himself or someone else from sin and its penalty," and as Christ gave satisfaction not by the payment of money but by giving up on our behalf that which was the highest in cost and value—himself—so "Christ's Passion is called our redemption." [47]

All the metaphors are here, and they are all related to appropriate biblical passages: But whereas we should have expected Thomas Aquinas then to attempt a tremendous synthesis, he simply sets the theories and metaphors side-by-side, and because of this it has been said that his treatment "contains all the materials for a theory of the atonement, but no theory at all." [48] In a sense Aquinas is open to the criticism, but I wonder if the significance of the fact that he did not develop an independent theory of his own, or a great synthesis has been fully grasped. The one thing that comes home to us in his treatment of the subject is that these images are biblical, and that they must all find their place within the Christian faith in such a way that no one of them can be said exclusively to rule out the rest. In the same way it is clear from the manner in which Thomas deals with the different ideas, weaving them into his theological system, that he regards them less as "theories" than as pictures and analogies. They were to him true pictures and analogies because they were biblical, and as such they have vital content, but they could do no more than approximate in terms of human language to the supreme truth that they are trying to convey. In sum Thomas Aquinas is telling us that there can be no one "theory" of the Atonement that can claim to be *the* orthodox and catholic doctrine, and that in any truly catholic doctrine of our Redemption all these channels are complementary ways to the Truth.

The great scholastic theologian has, however, some distinctive emphases which should not be passed over. In the first place he stresses the Resurrection of our Lord as the completion of his work in the Passion and as the means whereby the way to a new life is opened to us.[49] Secondly, he emphasizes Christ's spiritual Headship

[47] Ibid.
[48] O. C. Quick, op. cit., p. 78.
[49] *Compendium Theologiae* 239. Cf. the extract in Fr. Thomas Gilby's *St. Thomas Aquinas: Theological Texts* (Oxford, 1955) No. 239.

of the Church, and the fact that we are incorporated as members in the redeeming work of his Body by membership of the Church. Aquinas believes that as the results of original sin come to us through our natural birth, so the benefits of the redemptive work of Christ come to us through our spiritual rebirth into the Church "thereby men are incorporated in Christ." [50] It is true that he conceives this in terms of the transference of our Lord's "merit" to us, an idea that is foreign to Protestants. But this forms a link between what Aquinas says about the Atonement itself and his third distinctive emphasis, what he says about the Sacraments in relation to this doctrine; for since he regarded the Passion as a sacramental act, we shall expect him to insist that its meaning is carried into the sacraments of the Church.

We must remember that for Thomas Aquinas this meant the seven sacraments of the Medieval Church, but we are concerned particularly with what he has to say about the two Dominical Sacraments, Baptism and the Eucharist. Of the former Aquinas taught that it is the Passion of Christ which works regeneration in the believer, and that as the one who is baptized dies to his old life and rises to the new life in Jesus Christ, the guilt of the past is washed away. This is made effective through the benefits of the Passion and the gift of the Holy Spirit.[51] The meaning of the sacrament is Pauline, whatever might be said of the mode.

It is, however, within the Sacrament of the Bread and Wine that he placed the strongest emphasis upon the benefits of Christ's Passion. A good deal of what he said about the sacrament revolved around proving the real presence of our Lord in the substance of the consecrated bread and wine—the Roman theory of transubstantiation. However, that should not obscure from us the fact that for Thomas Aquinas the Eucharist is, as it were, drenched in the meaning and effects of our Lord's Passion and redemptive work, "for in this Sacrament our sins are purged away, strength renewed, and the mind fortified with generous spiritual gifts." [52] He has no doubt of its primacy within the life of the Church, for the Eucharist is the

---

[50] *Summa Theologica* III(a). lxxviii. 7 ad. 1, xlix. 2; *Contra Gentes* 55.
[51] *Ibid.* III(a). lxvi. 11 c. et al. 2.
[52] Breviary Lessons, Corpus Christi; Gilby, *St. Thomas Aquinas: Theological Texts*, No. 613.

"perfect sacrament of Our Lord's Passion," [53] and "this sacrament which contains Christ Himself, is perfective of all the other sacraments, in which Christ's virtue is participated." [54]

What this meant to him in terms of redemption we discover in the words of his commentary on the Last Supper. The Eucharist, said Thomas Aquinas, "is the everlasting showing forth of his death [i.e., our Lord's death] until he come again; the embodied fulfillment of all the ancient types and figures; the mighty joy of them that sorrow until he shall come again." [55] Notice the words—"the everlasting showing forth of his death ... the embodied fulfillment of all the ancient types and figures." Here is a conception of the Lord's Supper which gets closer to an evangelical understanding of Real Presence in the sacrament than we normally expect from those who hold the theory of transubstantiation; and here incidentally is a conception of the work of Christ in the sacrament which many "evangelical" Christians might do well to ponder.

Or we might approach Thomas Aquinas' view of the Eucharist through a free translation of one of his eucharistic hymns that so nearly reflects the thought expressed above:

> Low in adoration bending,
> Now our hearts our God revere;
> Faith her aid to sight is lending:
> Though unseen the Lord is near;
> Ancient types and shadows ending,
> Christ our Paschal Lamb is here.[56]

His contribution to the doctrine of the Atonement comes to a focus at this point, for just as he showed that all the ancient types and figures have their place in the gospel, so he declares that they all point to the one atoning Saviour who is set forth to us again in the sacrament of the Lord's Supper. Leaving aside the particular doctrine of the Eucharist associated with the Roman Catholic Church, Thomas

---

[53] *Summa Theologica* III(a). lxxiii. 5 ad. 2.
[54] *Ibid.* III(a). lxxv. 1. Questions lxxiii-lxxxiii are devoted to the Eucharist.
[55] Breviary Lessons, *Corpus Christi*; Gilby, op. cit., No. 613.
[56] Translated anonymously, it appeared in the *New Congregational Hymnal* (1859). It is a free translation of Part II of "Pange lingua gloriosi corporis mysterium," written for the office of Corpus Christi. Cf. the note by K. L. Parry in *Companion to Congregational Praise* (London, Independent Press, 1953), p. 161.

Aquinas expresses in these words the universal experience of all the many believers who have received at the Lord's Table the assurance of his redeeming work for them in broken bread and outpoured wine. For at this point all the ancient types and figures have their ending: Christ our Paschal Lamb is here.

CHAPTER III

The Reformers and Their Followers

THE ESSAYIST, AUGUSTINE BIRRELL, ONCE ENTITLED AN ESSAY, "WHAT Then Did Happen at the Reformation?" and a considerable amount of church history has been devoted to the task of trying to answer that question. Although soteriology is only one aspect of the Reformation, both Protestant and Catholic theologians agreed that at the Reformation something happened with regard to the doctrine of Atonement, and until recently there seemed to be a reasonable consensus of opinion on the subject. It was generally accepted that the Reformers were responsible for turning the "satisfaction theory" of Anselm into a theory of "penal substitution, i.e., they had changed the idea of satisfaction paid to God's honor for a theory of satisfaction paid to God's wrath with its penal sentence against sin. In support of this it must be admitted that the penal theory certainly made its appearance at the Reformation and held sway within the churches of the Reformation for about three hundred years, so that in 1905 the president of Princeton Theological Seminary could write, "Lutherans and Reformed are entirely at one in their conception of the nature of our Lord's saving work as a substitutive sin-bearer and an atoning sacrifice." [1] Undoubtedly, this is the concept of Atonement which most Protestant churches adopted, but whether it is entirely to be laid at the door of the Reformers themselves is a matter about which we shall have to do some serious questioning.

At the outset, however, we must remember that medieval scholasticism did not stand still after Thomas Aquinas. A comprehensive history of the Atonement would demand some account of the thought of the Oxford scholar Duns Scotus and of the revival of Nominalist philosophy and theology under the leadership of William of Occam. For the details of their ideas we must be content to direct the reader

---

[1] Benjamin B. Warfield in the Introduction to Junius Remensnyder's *The Atonement and Modern Thought* (Philadelphia: Lutheran Publication Soc., 1905) p. ix.

to the recognized histories of the doctrine. However, the main effects of medieval scholasticism were perhaps to center soteriology in the authority and ordinances of the Church and to emphasize more completely than before both the arbitrariness of the Divine Will and the impossibility that it should ever be comprehended by mere mortals. It was under the direct influence of these later scholastics that Martin Luther received his early training, and it has been pointed out that in their thought the way was being prepared for the ultimate break between reason and revelation.[2]

Although the historian knows that the Reformation was the result of a long historical process, yet the occasion was unpremeditated, almost accidental. When Luther (1483-1546) in 1517 posted his ninety-five theses to the door of All Saints Church, he was concerned far more with checking certain abuses within the practice of the Roman Catholic Church than with presenting a systematic alternative to its doctrine. The question of indulgences appeared to be primarily a matter of practical ecclesiastical reform, and it was only later as the official opposition stiffened that the theological implications underlying the practice were revealed. It was to the practical abuses of the system that Luther's protest was directed at first, and if in the final issue a particular doctrine of Redemption was formulated, it was the outcome and not the cause.

1. Ransom and Penalty: Martin Luther

With this preamble, what was the doctrine of Atonement taught by Luther? Upon that question there is now far less agreement. It has been said that Luther formulated the penal theory and set it against the system he was attacking, because if a man was prepared to accept in simple faith the fact that Christ had taken his sins upon himself, it freed him from all the mediatory paraphernalia with which the fact of redemption by faith in Christ had been smothered within the medieval Church.[3]

Let there be no mistake, the penal theory is certainly to be found in Luther and particularly in his *Commentary on St. Paul's Epistle to the Galatians*. He said that "whatsoever sins I, thou, and we all have

---

[2] S. Cave, op. cit., p. 149; cf. p. 151.
[3] V. J. K. Brook, "The Atonement in Reformation Theology" in *The Atonement in History and Life*, p. 214.

done, or shall do hereafter, they are Christ's own sins as verily as if he himself had done them." He maintained that the prophets had foreseen that "Christ should become the greatest transgressor, murderer, adulterer, thief, rebel, blasphemer, &c. that ever was or could be in all the world"—not that our Lord had committed these deeds, but he had taken the guilt of them upon his own body, so "that he might make satisfaction for them with his own blood"; [4] therefore "sin, death, and hell will belong to Christ, and grace, life and salvation to the soul." [5]

In a sermon he declared:

Because an eternal, unchangeable sentence of condemnation had been passed upon sin—for God cannot and will not regard sin with favor, but his wrath abides upon it eternally and irrevocably—redemption was not possible without a ransom of such precious worth as to atone for sin, to assume the guilt, pay the price of wrath and thus abolish sin.

This no creature was able to do. There was no remedy except for God's only Son to step into our distress and himself become man, to take upon himself the load of awful and eternal wrath and make his own body and blood a sacrifice for the sin. And so he did, out of the immeasurably great mercy and love towards us, giving himself up and bearing the sentence of unending wrath and death.

So infinitely precious to God is this sacrifice and atonement of his only begotten Son who is one with him in divinity and majesty, that God is reconciled thereby and receives into grace and forgiveness of sins all who believe in this Son. Only by believing may we enjoy the precious atonement of Christ, the forgiveness obtained for us and given out of profound, inexpressible love.[6]

Luther used the words "ransom" and "sacrifice" here, but there can hardly be any doubt that in this passage it is the thought and categories of the penal theory of the Atonement which predominate. In the same line of thought he spoke of the flesh of Christ upon the Cross as "sin" to set against his own sin, and declared that upon the

---

[4] A Commentary on St. Paul's Epistle to the Galatians, based on the E. T. by Erasmus Middleton and first published in 1575 (republished and revised by Fleming H. Revell Company). The quotation is from the commentary on Gal. 3:13.
[5] On Christian Liberty. E. T. of the Philadelphia Edition II. 320.
[6] Epistle Sermon, Twenty-fourth Sunday after Trinity. E. T. of the J. N. Lenker Edition (Minneapolis: Augsburg Publishing House) IX. 43-45.

shoulders of Christ "lie all the evils and miseries of mankind, the law, sin, death, the devil and hell." [7] Despite Gustaf Aulén's vigorous disclaimer in *Christus Victor*, one cannot escape or explain away the penal theory in Luther's exposition of the Atonement, and at times the Reformer seems to drive the metaphors of penalty to such an extreme that he speaks as if our Lord not only took the punishment of our sins upon himself but "almost *deserved* eternal punishment in Hell for them." [8] On the other hand when Luther speaks of our faith paying God "the great honor which is due to him," [9] he is using Anselm's own terms, and it is to be doubted whether he realized just how far beyond Anselm he sometimes drives the theory of satisfaction.

However, if the penal theory is strikingly present in Luther's theology, it most decidedly does not stand alone nor is it even the most important *motif*, and here the credit must go to Bishop Aulén for bringing to light what is undoubtedly the predominant theme in Luther's doctrine of Redemption. We have already referred to Aulén's insistence that the "ransom" theory of the Greek Fathers is not to be regarded simply as a primitive form of Anselm's "Satisfaction" theory but as the "classic" attempt by the early Church to describe what it felt about the work of Christ in the dramatic figures of Christ's overwhelming victory over the devil, sin, and death in his life and death and Resurrection. Aulén goes on to maintain that this view of the Atonement and its imagery was recaptured and "with greater power than ever before, in Martin Luther." [10] We may question the details of Aulén's thesis—whether he does justice to Anselm, whether he paid sufficient regard to the "penal" aspects in Luther's teaching, whether, in fact, the "classic theory" remains altogether unchanged, or is concentrated more particularly on the death of Christ in Luther than in the Fathers—but there can be no doubt that in broad outline his case stands. That what he had to say is a very important corrective to the view that the Reformer thought only in terms of "penal substitution."

Certainly the theme of Christ's victory over the powers of darkness

---

[7] Middleton, op. cit. On Gal. 2:19.
[8] V. J. K. Brook, op. cit., p. 216.
[9] *On Christian Liberty* (Philadelphia Edition) II. 320.
[10] *Christus Victor*, p. 100.

comes into its own again in the thought of Luther and often in the very terms used by Irenaeus and the Fathers. So in his *Brief Explanation* of the Apostles' Creed, he wrote:

> I believe that He bore His cross and passion for my sin and the sin of all believers, and thereby has consecrated all sufferings and every cross, and made them not only harmless, but salutary and highly meritorious.
>
> I believe that He died and was buried to slay entirely and to bury my sin and the sin of all who believe in Him, and that He has destroyed bodily death and made it altogether harmless, nay profitable and salutary.
>
> I believe that He descended into hell to overthrow and take captive the devil and all his power, guile and wickedness, for me and for all who believe in Him, so that henceforth the devil cannot harm me; and that He has redeemed me from the pains of hell, and made them harmless and meritorious.
>
> I believe that He rose on the third day from the dead, to give to me and to all who believe in Him a new life.[11]

Side-by-side with phrases in his *Commentary on Galatians* which suggest a rigorous theory of penal substitution, he could speak of Christ as "the conqueror of the law and sin" and use the imagery of the ransom theory. In one place, having more than suggested penal substitution by saying that Christ upon the Cross bore in his body "my sin, the law, death, the devil and hell," he immediately goes on to use the figures of the "classic" theory: "These invincible enemies and tyrants do oppress, vex and trouble me, and therefore I am careful how I may be delivered out of their hands, justified and saved. Here I find neither law, work, nor charity, which is able to deliver me from their tyranny. There is none but Christ only and alone, which taketh away the law, killeth my sin, destroyeth my death in his body, and by this means spoileth hell, judgeth and crucifieth the devil, and throweth him down into hell."[12] Penal and ransom metaphors rub shoulders and jostle each other without regard to any formulated "theory." If in one place he could go so far with the penal idea to declare that God showed himself "more kind to Caiaphas, Herod, and Pilate, than towards his only beloved Son,"[13] he could take over

---

[11] *A Brief Explanation of the Ten Commandments, the Creed, and the Lord's Prayer;* Philadelphia Edition (Philadelphia: Muhlenberg Press), II. 371.
[12] *Commentary on Galatians,* Gal. 2:19.
[13] *The Table Talk of Martin Luther,* E. T. of William Hazlitt, ccxviii.

also the imagery of the "classic" theory entire, including the bizarre figure of the devil as a great fish being caught on the hook of Christ's divinity. He said:

> I often delight myself with that similitude in Job, of an angle-hook that fishermen cast into the water, putting on the hook a little worm; then comes the fish and snatches at the worm, and gets therewith the hook in his jaws, and the fisher pulls him out of the water. Even so has our Lord God dealt with the devil; God has cast into the world his only Son, as the angle, and upon the hook has put Christ's humanity, as the worm; then comes the devil and snaps at the (man) Christ, and devours him, and therewith he bites the iron hook, that is, the godhead of Christ, which chokes him, and all his power thereby is thrown to the ground. This is called *sapientia divina*, divine wisdom.[14]

The story of David and Goliath often reappears as the underlying idea of the ransom theory as it appears in Luther. Christ is represented as a champion who entered the struggle and exposed himself on behalf of the human race, and who at the end finally defeated the giant and killed him with the giant's own sword.[15] This is not only the imagery behind his theology of the work of Christ, but in a more pronounced way it provides the language of his personal devotion and hymns. Read through the great hymn *Ein feste Burg ist unser Gott* ("A mighty fortress is our God"), and it will be found to be full of the imagery of Christ's victory over the Powers of Darkness. Another example might be taken from one of his Easter hymns:

> It was a strange and dreadful strife
> When life and death contended;
> The victory remained with life,
> The reign of death was ended:
> Stripped of power no more he reigns,
> An empty form alone remains;
> His sting is lost for ever.[16]

These images taken from the old ransom theory provide the dominant theme in Luther's exposition of the work of Christ. But they

---

[14] *Ibid.* cxcvii.
[15] *The Fourteen of Consolation* (Philadelphia Edition) I. 150-51.
[16] *Christ lag in Todesbanden*, E. T. by Richard Massie (1800-1887).

are not the only pictures that he uses, and we must agree, in spite of Aulén's denials, that "Luther taught also, if not the Penal theory, yet interpretations of Christ's work of which the Penal theory is a rationalization." [17] Perhaps what becomes clear in Luther is that he is not thinking of a clearly formulated "theory" but his thinking about the Atonement is frankly cast in pictures and images. For if the ransom and penal images come to the fore in his thought, they are by no means exclusive of other ideas in which he represents our Lord's work as our sacrifice or sacrament,[18] and as our example: "with such burning zeal was Christ's heart kindled, when He died for us and descended into hell, leaving us an example that we should be so regardful of the evils of others, and forgetful of our own, nay, rather covetous of evils of our own." [19]

This emphasized the fact that we cannot put Martin Luther's theology of the Atonement into any one category of systematic thought. Perhaps once his appetite for theology was whetted, he simply took the different theories into his own thinking without troubling to systematize them. On the other hand we have the far deeper impression that what Thomas Aquinas attempted by a deliberate theological eclecticism, Martin Luther unconsciously discovered through his own evangelical experience. That sense of personal encounter with sin, death, the law, and the devil which he had experienced, and the sense of complete release which he had gained through simple faith in Christ's atoning work were too great to be confined to one image or to be bound within the forms of a single theory. To quote the late Sidney Cave, "the 'either—or' (*entweder-oder*), beloved of Continental theologians, seems singularly inapplicable to one like Luther, who was not only a master of paradoxes, but a victim of them, and whose Christianity had its unity in his experience, not in his thought."[20]

2. *Sacrifice and Penalty: John Calvin*

If we pass directly from Luther to Calvin, it is not because the theology of Zwingli (1509-1564) is of no interest in itself, but because by reason of his premature death he did not have time to develop a

---

[17] S. Cave, op. cit., p. 183.
[18] *The Babylonian Captivity of the Church* (Philadelphia Edition) II. 258-59.
[19] *The Fourteen of Consolation* (Philadelphia Edition) I. 132.
[20] Cave, op. cit., p. 183.

distinctive doctrine of Atonement, and because his views on the doctrine have had no immediate bearing or influence upon the Anglo-Saxon theologians whose ideas we shall be examining in later chapters.[21] Fundamentally, the intense debate upon the Atonement in Britain and America during the nineteenth century has to be seen in relation to Calvin and Calvinism. This was the theology that provided the battleground, and although theologians from other schools gladly entered the struggle to break a lance or cross swords on the issue, it has been largely those whose militant theology originated in Geneva who have been in the thick of it, and who have both taken and given the stoutest blows.

John Calvin was a more systematic theologian than Luther in the sense that within a single book, *The Institutes of the Christian Religion*, we have his concise but comprehensive exposition of the Christian faith. Undoubtedly a full treatment of his soteriology would ask for a much wider assessment of his writings than the consideration of a single work, but because the *Institutes* became the norm for Calvinistic doctrine, we should be able to find sufficient in it to judge Calvin's central ideas regarding the Atonement.

Calvin has been represented as holding the theory of penal substitution "in its harshest form," [22] and as we found in the theology of Luther, so with Calvin—the idea and images of the penal theory are undeniably there. Writing of the reasons why the Incarnation was necessary he says that "the only end which the Scripture uniformly assigns for the Son of God voluntarily assuming our nature, and even receiving it as a command from the Father, is, that he might propitiate the Father to us by becoming a victim." [23] Anyone who would wish to question too minutely why this was necessary shows, in Calvin's view, that he is dissatisfied with the ordinance of God and even discontented "with that Christ, who has been given us as the price of our redemption." [24] The images that Calvin used here were sacrificial images—propitiation, victim—but it is clear that they are often

---

[21] Some account of Zwingli's emphases is to be found in the chapter by V. J. K. Brook, op. cit., p. 231.
[22] Ibid. p. 234.
[23] Institutes II. xii. 4. John Calvin, *The Institutes of the Christian Religion* (1845), E. T. of Henry Beveridge.
[24] Ibid. II. xii. 5.

being used with a meaning that is close to penal substitution. In another place within the same chapter he says:

> Another principal part of our reconciliation with God was, that man, who had lost himself by his disobedience, should, by way of remedy, oppose to it obedience, satisfy the justice of God, and pay the penalty of sin. Therefore, our Lord came forth very man, adopted the person of Adam, and assumed his name, that he might in his stead obey the Father; that he might present our flesh as the price of satisfaction to the just judgment of God, and in the same flesh pay the penalty which we had incurred. Finally, since as God only he could not suffer, and as man only could not overcome death, he united the human nature with the divine, that he might subject the weakness of the one to death as an expiation of sin, and by the power of the other, maintaining a struggle with death, might gain us the victory.[25]

These and similar passages could be abstracted from Calvin and woven into a very strict penal theory of the Atonement in which our Lord voluntarily (or at the command of the Father?) became the victim of God's wrath against sin, so that the atonement he offered is seen wholly in terms of the satisfaction rendered to Divine Justice by his substitutionary Passion and Death.

Yet even in the passage we have just quoted, these are by no means the only concepts that are represented. The penal element is there—very much to the fore—and Calvin puts an accent upon our Lord's human flesh as "the price of satisfaction to the just judgment of God" and tells us that in this same flesh Christ paid "the penalty which we had incurred." But how did our Lord pay the debt within his flesh? If Calvin suggests to some extent that the debt was paid in suffering, it is surely seen at a far deeper level that if the logic of his view is followed, it must have been paid by our Lord's *obedience*. Since Calvin finds the cause of our sinful state in the disobedience of Adam and since he takes up the idea of Christ's "recapitulation" of Adam, it is essential to his thought to set over against each other not Christ's sufferings and Adam's felicity, but the obedience of Christ and Adam's disobedience.

With this in mind let us see how Calvin approaches the subject. What he says about the work of Christ comes in Book II of the *In-*

[25] *Ibid.* II. xii. 3.

stitutes—at the very center of his exposition of the Christian faith. The theme of Book I is our knowledge of God as Creator and more particularly the source of that knowledge through the revelation of God in Holy Scripture. In the first part of Book II he describes our disobedience and sin in the face of the knowledge of God that is given to us and our need of redemption in view of the fact that we are totally unable to redeem ourselves. Calvin, as Anselm before him, builds up his case to show the absolute necessity of divine intervention if mankind is to be saved, and he shows that the purpose of the Old Testament is *Heilsgeschichte*—the story or panorama of salvation, which in its turn points forward to the divine intervention in the Mediator, Christ. "God," he says, "never showed himself propitious to his ancient people, nor gave them any hope of grace without a Mediator." [26]

We ought to notice from a brief passage quoted previously that Calvin is in line with Anselm in making the Atonement the purpose of the Incarnation and not simply its fulfillment. Because of this one would insist upon the centrality of the work of God in Christ in the thought of Calvin and therefore the centrality of the Atonement in his theology. Although one can find passages which seem to suggest a separation between the Father and the Son, in its totality Christ's work is represented as the intervention of God himself in history. He cites Irenaeus as saying "that the Father, who is boundless in himself, is bounded in the Son, because he has accommodated himself to our capacity." [27] Having demonstrated on the one hand our complete inability to satisfy the God of righteousness who appears "as the stern avenger of wickedness," Calvin goes on to affirm, "but in Christ his countenance beams forth full of grace and gentleness towards poor unworthy sinners." [28] It is God who acted in Jesus Christ, and although in Calvin's view the fulfillment of his purpose involved the satisfaction of a divine justice that he could not repudiate without repudiating himself, the purpose was the salvation of man. The Atonement is central. It was for this reason that he attacked Osiander, who had suggested (because there is no scriptural warrant for showing the contrary) that Christ would probably have become Man even if there

[26] *Ibid.* II. vi. 2, cf. II. x. 4.
[27] *Ibid.* II. vi. 4.
[28] *Ibid.* II. vii. 8.

had been no fall from grace. In reply Calvin quoted from Paul's first epistle to Timothy, "this is a faithful saying, and worthy of all acceptation, that Christ Jesus came into the world to save sinners," [29] and he declared that he was determined to adhere to this to the end: in Calvin the purpose of the Incarnation is the Atonement, that and nothing else.

To prove it he shows that the whole Bible points to Christ, and this is the context in which we have to see what Calvin says about the work of Christ. The Law was introduced to keep the Israelites "in suspense until his advent; to inflame their desire, and confirm their expectations," and he adds that by the Law he understands "not only the Ten Commandments, which contain a complete rule of life, but the whole system of religion delivered by the hand of Moses." [30] In the forefront of this there was the sacrificial system. I suggest that not sufficient attention has been given to the things Calvin said about the Old Testament sacrifices and the significant light they throw upon his idea of the Atonement. Why, asks the Reformer, was the sacrificial system instituted? To a sixteenth-century Protestant it did not naturally commend itself as being of the spiritual and ethical quality that they discovered in the words of the prophets or the witness of Jesus, "for what could be more vain or frivolous than for men to reconcile themselves to God, by offering him the foul odour produced by burning the fat of beasts? or to wipe away their own impurities by besprinkling themselves with water or blood? In short, the whole legal worship (if considered by itself apart from the types and shadows or corresponding truth) is a mere mockery." The Jews would have been as deluded as their pagan neighbors if there had not been a spiritual purpose in this sacrificial worship. To Calvin the meaning was quite clear—it pointed to Jesus Christ, for the Israelites could not attain their true vocation "without a greater and more excellent atonement than the blood of beasts." [31]

Christ and his atoning work are so central to Calvin's exposition of the faith that he holds that "from the beginning of the world Christ was held forth to all the elect as the object of their faith and confi-

---

[29] *Ibid.* II. xii. 5; cf. II Tim. 1:15.
[30] *Ibid.* II. vii. 1.
[31] *Ibid.* II. vii. 1. cf. Ex. 19:6.

dence."[32] As he is the fulfillment of Israel's history and prophecy in his office of Prophet and of her Messianic hope in his office as King, so in his office as Priest he is the fulfillment of her sacrificial worship. The whole passage on the threefold office of our Lord, and particularly that part of it which speaks of his Priesthood, puts the work of Christ within its proper setting if we are to understand the central ideas about the Atonement in Calvin. Plenty of passages can be taken from the *Institutes* where the theory of penal substitution provides all the metaphors, but that emphasis and its imagery have to be put within the context of what Calvin says about the Bible's plan for salvation, which is the sacrificial context. Look at the following passage:

Because a deserved curse obstructs the entrance, and God in his character of Judge is hostile to us, expiation must necessarily intervene, that as a priest employed to appease the wrath of God, he may reinstate us in his favour. Wherefore, in order that Christ might fulfil this office, it behoved him to appear with a sacrifice. For even under the law of the priesthood it was forbidden to enter the sanctuary without blood, to teach the worshipper that however the priest might interpose to deprecate, God could not be propitiated without the expiation of sin... The sum comes to this, that the honour of the priesthood was competent to none but Christ, because, by the sacrifice of his death, he wiped away our guilt, and made satisfaction for sin. Of the great importance of this matter, we are reminded by that solemn oath which God uttered, and of which he declared he would not repent, "Thou art a priest for ever, after the order of Melchisedek," (Ps. cx. 4.) For, doubtless, his purpose was to ratify that point on which he knew that our salvation chiefly hinged... Thus we see, that if the benefit and efficacy of Christ's priesthood is to reach us, the commencement must be with his death. Whence it follows, that he by whose aid we obtain favour, must be a perpetual intercessor... But since God under the Law ordered sacrifices of beasts to be offered to him, there was a different and new arrangement in regard to Christ, viz., that he should be at once victim and priest, because no other fit satisfaction for sin could be found, nor was any one worthy of the honour of offering an only begotten son to God. Christ now bears the office of priest, not only that by the eternal law of reconciliation he may render the Father favourable and propitious to us, but also admit us into this most honourable alliance. For we though in ourselves polluted, in him being priests,

[32] *Ibid.* II. vi. 4.

(Rev. i. 6,) offer ourselves and our all to God, and freely enter the heavenly sanctuary, so that the sacrifices of prayer and praise which we present are grateful and of sweet odour before him.[33]

Here two ways of thinking about the Atonement are to be found side-by-side. The first is judicial—"God in his character as Judge is hostile to us"—and it developed into the theory of penal substitution, but the second is the sacrificial concept whereby Christ is thought of as giving something which is infinitely well-pleasing to God. There can be little doubt that Calvin reconciled the two ideas often by interpreting the sacrificial element in a punitive and expiatory way rather than as the offering of a pure gift in love. Nevertheless, it is the sacrificial aspect of the Atonement which provides the context in which the penal ideas are set, and not the other way around. Calvin was enough a spiritual son of Anselm to speak of satisfaction and enough of a lawyer to speak of satisfaction to the divine Justice. But even when he appears to be setting forth the penal theory at its hardest, it is within the setting of sacrifice because this is the setting which is biblical. So although he speaks of Christ appeasing the Father on our account, it is as a sacrifice that he does it, and in describing the priestly function of our Lord as Mediator he declares that "the honor of the priesthood was competent to none but Christ, because by the sacrifice of his death, he wiped away our guilt, and made satisfaction for sin." [34]

On the other hand the legal categories in which Calvin expressed his conception of the work of Christ led directly to the theory of penal substitution. Before we leave him we must consider some of the force of the theory, and then see the other ways—apart from the sacrificial concept—in which the penal theory was modified in the *Institutes*.

Calvin argues, in language reminiscent of Luther, that Christ was numbered with the transgressors so that he might "bear the character of a sinner." [35] He declares that the very form of his death brought him not under the curse of men but under the curse of the divine Law, so that the whole curse that was due to us might be "transferred to him," and that the sacrifice and expiation that he offered were purifications "bearing, by substitution, the curse due to sin." [36] He lays great

---
[33] *Ibid.* II. xv. 6.
[34] *Ibid.* II. xv. 6.
[35] *Ibid.* II. xvi. 5.
[36] *Ibid.* II. xvi. 6.

stress on Scriptural passages such as Isa. 53; II Cor. 5:21; I Pet. 2:24, which upon any literal interpretation do more than suggest that our sins were laid on Christ in his death by God, and he particularly stresses the descent into hell as our Lord's tasting the meaning of full estrangement from God and the penalty of the spiritual death due to sinners. He maintains that this was introduced into the Creed "to teach us that not only was the body of Christ given up as the price of redemption, but that there was a greater and more excellent price— that he bore in his soul the tortures of condemned and ruined man." [37] This is penal substitution.

At the same time just as we have seen that these ideas occurred with the context of sacrifice, so we discover within Calvin some of the elements of the "classic" theory. The images are not as pronounced as they are in Luther, but they are by no means ignored. There is also a possible difference of emphasis between the two reformers in that whereas Luther thinks of the work of Christ as a victory over sin, death, hell, the law, and the devil and singles out the law as the main cause of our bondage and the special object of Christ's enmity, Calvin often speaks of our Lord's victory as primarily over death. In his descent into the grave our Lord differed from us, for "in permitting himself to be overcome of death, it was not so as to be ingulfed in its abyss, but rather to annihilate it, as it must otherwise have annihilated us; he did not allow himself to be so subdued by it as to be crushed by its power; he rather laid it prostrate, when it was impending over us, and exulting over us as already overcome." [38] Christ's victory over the power of death was consummated by and demonstrated in the Resurrection, for "how could he have obtained the victory for us, if he had fallen in the contest?" [39] Earlier in the *Institutes*, when writing of the necessity for our Saviour to be both God and Man, he declares:

> It was his to swallow up death: who but Life could do so? It was his to conquer sin: who could do so save Righteousness itself? It was his to put to flight the powers of the air and the world: who could do so but the mighty power superior to both? But who possesses life and right-

[37] II. xvi. 10.
[38] II. xvi. 7.
[39] II. xvi. 13.

eousness, and the dominion and government of heaven, but God alone? Therefore God, in his infinite mercy, having determined to redeem us, became himself our Redeemer in the person of his only begotten Son.[40]

These are the terms and images of the "classic" theory, and although they do not appear in Calvin's thought as regularly or as insistently as in the thought of the great German Reformer, they are present to enrich and to qualify the more usual ideas in which he expounds the work of Christ.

There are, however, other aspects of Calvin's teaching about the work of Christ which modify his presentation of the Atonement and which go far beyond the mere use of one image or another in describing the doctrine. These aspects of his teaching are concerned not so much with the picture forms in which Calvin describes the Atonement as in the underlying spirit in which the divine initiative was undertaken—the way in which the redemption of man was conceived by God, the principle by which it was made effective in the work of Christ, and the manner by which it brings forth fruit in us by the Holy Spirit.

1. The first is what Calvin says about the love of God. Often in the grip of his forensic logic Calvin seems to let this slip into the background, but a closer reading of the Reformer reveals that it is the very basis of the view of God's initiative in Christ which he presents. He can speak on one page of Christ expiating with his own blood the sins that make us hateful to God. Yet the whole point of his argument rests upon the fact that it was God the Father's mercy which alone made Christ's action possible, for "had God at the time you were a sinner hated you, and cast you off as you deserved, horrible destruction must have been your doom; but spontaneously and of free indulgence he retained you in his favour, not suffering you to be estranged from him, and in this way rescued you from danger."[41] God does not want to destroy what is his own but tries to find something in us that he can love, "for though it is by our own fault that we are sinners, we are still his creatures. . . . Accordingly, God the Father, by his love, prevents [i.e., "goes before"] and anticipates our reconciliation in Christ. Nay, it is because he first loves us, that he

[40] II. xii. 2.
[41] II. xvi. 2.

afterwards reconciles us to himself." [42] In a particularly striking passage he reveals his own conception of God's love by paraphrasing the words of Augustine:

> Incomprehensible and immutable is the love of God. For it was not after we were reconciled to him by the blood of his Son that he began to love us, but he loved us before the foundation of the world, that with his only begotten Son we too might be sons of God before we were anything at all. Our being reconciled by the death of Christ must not be understood as if the Son reconciled us, in order that the Father, then hating, might begin to love us, but that we were reconciled to him already, loving, though at enmity with us because of sin. To the truth of both propositions we have the attestation of the Apostle, "God commendeth his love toward us, in that while we were yet sinners, Christ died for us," (Rom. v. 8.) Therefore he had this love towards us even when, exercising enmity towards him, we were workers of iniquity. Accordingly, in a manner wondrous and divine, he loved even when he hated us. For he hated us when we were such as he had not made us, and yet because our iniquity had not destroyed his work in every respect, he knew in regard to each one of us, both to hate what we had made, and love what he had made.[43]

"Such," adds Calvin approvingly, "are the words of Augustine," and he then goes on to describe the Atonement in terms of our Lord's perfect obedience to the Father throughout life and in the death of the Cross. This "incomprehensible and immutable" love of God towards us—which we often wish Calvin had brought more into the foreground of his theology—when it is linked with the very strong sense of unity within the Trinity that he had, with the fact that it was God himself whose countenance in Christ "beams forth full of grace and gentleness towards unworthy sinners," presents us with a view of the work of Christ in which even the harshest features of the penal theory are to some extent transmuted.

If it is possible to reconcile in this way the apparent incompatibilities and contradictions of the theory of penal substitution, then the strength and attraction of its objectivity become evident. Perhaps it was not primarily the fear of God's wrath, and still less the thought that God is satisfied with the sufferings of his Son, that brought

[42] II. xvi. 3.
[43] II. xvi. 4.

the theory of penal substitution to the center of evangelical religion and kept it there for three hundred years, but rather the belief that God in his fullness in the Person of Christ took the punishment on "my" behalf that he himself had decreed against "my" sin.

2. A second feature of Calvin's thought which modifies the penal terms in which he often speaks is the principle of obedience in relation to the sacrifice of our Lord to which we have alluded earlier. It was an insight which if it had been developed might have led to a much stronger emphasis in his theology upon the sacrificial aspect of Christ's atoning work. Calvin says that there is nothing more acceptable to God than obedience.[44] He declares that when it is asked "how Christ, by abolishing sin, removed the enmity between God and us, and purchased a righteousness which made him favourable and kind to us, it may be answered generally, that he accomplished by the whole course of his obedience." [45] Quoting Paul's statement in Rom. 5:19—"as by one man's disobedience many were made sinners, so by the obedience of one shall be made righteous"—he declares that our Lord even at his baptism fulfilled a part of the righteousness that was required to redeem us by his voluntary obedience to the will of the Father; "in short, from the moment when he assumed the form of a servant, he began, in order to redeem us, to pay the price of deliverance." Calvin firmly maintains that the Bible places the greatest emphasis upon the death of Christ in the work of salvation and points out that in the Apostles' Creed the transition is directly from the birth of Christ to his death upon the Cross. But he adds that "there is no exclusion of the other part of obedience which he performed in life," citing Phil. 2:7 in proof of his point.[46]

As we have seen previously, this accent upon the obedience of Christ as the central atoning principle actually followed from what Calvin taught about the corporate nature of our disobedience in Adam, for the real "recapitulation" of Adam's defeat and the real "satisfaction" to be given to God must be an ethical and religious victory *in like kind* to the ethical and religious failure in Adam. On Calvin's own estimate of God's nature the Almighty could not be paid simply in terms of physical or spiritual anguish but only in terms

[44] II. viii. 5.
[45] II. xvi. 5.
[46] Ibid.

of that of which by the disobedience of Adam he had been robbed. Had he held closely to this insight and seen it as the center of what he was trying to say about Christ's work for us, he would not only have avoided overconcentration upon punitive ideas which did not honor the God he wanted to honor, but he would have shown that sacrifice is at the heart of the biblical idea of the atonement, and that the sacrifice offered by Christ was a total sacrifice of the whole life which culminates in his death and is vindicated in his Resurrection.

3. The third way in which the penal aspects of Calvin's thought are modified is to be found in his teaching that the love of God calls us to be not merely partakers in the benefits of our Lord's atoning work but sharers in its sacrifice. It is to be found in the passage on the Priesthood of Christ that we have quoted previously, where Calvin declares that although we are still sinners, we can be priests in Christ and through him "offer ourselves and our all to God, and freely enter the heavenly sanctuary." [47] In other words that which our Lord won for us was gained in order that we might be participants not only in his victory but in his sacrifice, not only in his sacrifice but in his glory. He gives us the possibility of becoming sons of God,[48] and relying upon this action of our Lord we have faith that we are the sons of God, "because the natural Son of God assumed to himself a body of our body, flesh of our flesh, bones of our bones, that he might be one with us." Calvin speaks of our "holy brotherhood" with Christ and says that because of this adoption by Christ of us as his brethren, we have a certain inheritance in the heavenly kingdom that he inherits as of right, for if we are brethren, then we are "partners with him in the inheritance." [49] The Atonement issues an ethical call to us by which we enter into our Lord's work of salvation: the blood of Christ is indispensable to the work of redemption, but it is available and effective not only as a means of propitiation but also "as a laver to purge our defilements." [50]

Although the same cannot always be said for his followers, there was no false opposition in Calvin himself between the love of the Father and the love of the Son toward us. His thought was fully in

---
[47] II. xv. 6.
[48] II. xii. 2.
[49] Ibid.
[50] II. xvi. 6.

line with that of the apostle Paul when he said of our Lord that "in him dwelleth all the fulness of the Godhead bodily," [51] and for Calvin the brotherly concern which Jesus Christ exhibited toward us in the sacrificial giving of himself was one aspect of the same prevenient grace which made the Atonement the very center of God the Father's eternal purpose. To inherit the sacrifice and the victory of our Lord was to achieve what God had intended from the beginning. In the words of a later document the *Shorter Catechism* of the Westminster Confession, which perfectly reflects Calvin's own thought at this point, "Man's chief end is to glorify God, and to enjoy him for ever." The fact that this was made possible for us was due not only to the suffering and sacrifice of the Son but equally to the continuing work of the Holy Spirit and to the prevenient grace and invincible love of God the Father.

3. The Atonement in the Catechisms and Confessions

Mention of the Westminster Confession's *Shorter Catechism* introduces a consideration of the way in which the doctrine of the Atonement developed after the time of the Reformers, first in the doctrinal statements of the Reformation and then in its later representative theologians. In the first place, however, let us understand the historical problems with which we are involved.

Two facts stand out regarding the doctrine in its relationship to the history of the churches of the Reformation. First, the "penal" explanation and it descriptive imagery seem to make their appearance at the time of the Reformers, and secondly, although the ideas of sacrifice and ransom, victory, and example occur in the Reformers themselves and continue to crop up from time to time in later Protestants, it was the theory of penal substitution which from the middle of the sixteenth century to the middle years of the nineteenth century became the quasi-orthodox doctrine for the greater part of Protestantism. This poses two historical questions—why did that particular theory of redemption make its appearance at the time of the Reformation? and, since it appears only as one theory among others in the Reformers themselves (in view of the features that it soon began to assume), why did it become so universally adhered to by Protestants?

[51] Col. 2:9.

THE ATONEMENT AND THE SACRAMENTS

It is not my intention to dwell too long upon the first question, although in itself it would provide a fascinating subject for research. To some extent the particular accent may have been brought into being, or at least helped forward, by the Reformation's emphasis upon the individual's responsibility before God, although I am sure that this is an argument which can be pushed too far.[52] Perhaps there are more solid grounds for tracing the theory to the Bible itself and to the literal interpretation that Protestantism adopted in its claim to biblical authority. No less a modern biblical scholar than Vincent Taylor has pointed out how near the New Testament teaching concerning the representative work of Christ comes to a substitutionary doctrine of the Atonement. "In fact," he observes, "a theologian who retires to a doctrinal fortress guarded by such ordinance as Mark x.45, Romans vi.10f, 2 Corinthians v. 14, 21, Galatians iii.13, and I Timothy ii.5f, is more difficult to dislodge than many New Testament students imagine." [53]

Even so, it is doubtful whether the legal and penal categories would have been taken up if they had not been living categories in the thought of that time. We have to remember that the Reformation took place when feudal society was breaking down. The concepts of "law," as something defined by the State, and of the individual's responsibility before the law were ideas which belonged to the new order. Crime was conceived not so much as the breaking of a personal relationship, an affront to the suzerain's honor as it was under feudalism, but it was a sin against the law, and the state was beginning to be regarded as the upholder of the law and its avenger. But even if these factors in the new society were present to stimulate a particular interpretation of the Atonement once it had made its appearance, why did the penal theory become paramount in Protestant theology? This is the question to which attention must be addressed in the remainder of this chapter.

No clear answer to the question is given in the Confessions. For Lutheranism the *Augsburg Confession* of 1530 simply affirms that men are justified freely "for Christ's sake through faith, when they believe that they are received into favor, and their sins forgiven

---

[52] Cf. supra p. 92 and note 3.
[53] Vincent Taylor, *The Atonement in New Testament Teaching* (2nd ed.; Epworth Press, 1945), p. 197.

for Christ's sake, who by his death hath satisfied for our sins." [54] It needs to be read alongside Luther's *Shorter Catechism* where, in expounding the christological articles of the Creed, the catechism speaks of Christ "who has redeemed me, a lost and condemned man, secured and delivered me [even] from all sins, from death, and from the power of the devil, not with gold or silver, but with his holy, precious blood, and with his innocent sufferings and death." [55] No attempt is made to present a theory of atonement—if anything the terms used are more in line with the "classic" view than with the penal theory—but the catechism simply states what Christ has achieved for us. It has been pointed out that Philip Melanchthon in the later editions of his *Loci Communes* appears to have passed over the ransom images that are to be found in Luther and to have concentrated upon the penal theory which rapidly became normative for Protestant theology.[56] But whatever the prestige of Melanchthon as the systematizer of Lutheranism, the doctrinal statements of the Confession as such are not bound to one theory.

It is, however, to Calvinist theology that we must look to trace the development of ideas about the Atonement in the Anglo-Saxon world, but here again we find that the doctrinal statements of early Calvinism are far less bound to a particular theory of the Atonement than we might suppose. The *Heidelberg Catechism* of the Palatinate Churches (1563) declares that Christ is ordained of God "to be our chief Prophet and Teacher, who fully reveals to us the secret counsel and will of God concerning our redemption; and our only High Priest, who by the one sacrifice of his body has redeemed us." [57] The identification of the believer with Christ is made explicit, for by faith the member confessed himself to be "a partaker of his anointing; in order that I also may confess his name, may present myself a living sacrifice of thankfulness to him, and may with a free conscience fight against sin and the devil in this life, and hereafter in eternity, reign with him over all creatures." Christ is "Lord" because, not with silver or gold, "but with his precious blood he has redeemed and purchased us, body and soul, from the power of the devil, to be his own." In all this we

---

[54] *The Creeds of Christendom*, ed. Philip Schaff (New York: Harper and Bros., 1877), III, art. iv, p. 10.
[55] Ibid., III, art. ii, answer p. 79.
[56] Cave, *The Doctrine of the Work of Christ*, pp. 158-61.
[57] Schaff, op. cit., III, answer 31, p. 317.

can notice a strong ethical element with very little that could be regarded as exclusively distinctive of the penal theory, but this emphasis does appear in the catechism's answer to the question what is meant by the word "suffered" in respect of Christ. It says that "all the time he lived on earth, but especially at the end of his life, he bore, in body and soul, the wrath of God against the sin of the whole human race, in order that by his passion, as the only atoning sacrifice, he might redeem our body and soul from everlasting damnation, and obtain for us the grace of God, righteousness, and eternal life." Similarly in explanation of the clauses in the Creed it declares that he suffered under Pilate in order to "deliver us from the severe judgment of God to which we were exposed." He was crucified in order to take on himself "the curse which lay upon me, because the death of the cross was accursed of God." He descended into hell so that "in my greatest temptations I may be assured that Christ, my Lord, by his inexpressible anguish, pains, and terrors which he suffered in his soul on the cross and before, has redeemed me from the anguish and torment of hell." Among the benefits that come to us from his sacrifice, "our old man is with him crucified, slain, and buried; so that the evil lusts of the flesh may no more reign in us, but that we may offer ourselves unto him a sacrifice of thanksgiving."

The penal idea is here, particularly in its concentration upon the sufferings of Christ and in the idea that our Lord's passion is an atoning sacrifice to the wrath of God, but it is certainly no more pronounced than other biblical images which we discover in Calvin. There is the same emphasis upon ethical identity with Christ and upon the sacrificial aspect of Christ's death. Indeed, one of the striking things about the Calvinist Confessions and Catechisms is the fact that although the penal theory of the Atonement appears in them, it is not elaborated and certainly does not assume the importance that it does in later theology. The *Scottish Confession* of 1560 states that "our Lord Jesus offered himself a voluntary Sacrifice unto his Father for us," [58] and that in his descent into hell and resurrection from the dead, he rose again for our justification and destroyed him who was "the Author of death"—statements which would be as conformable to a sacrificial or "classic" theory of atonement as they would be to one of penal substitution.

[58] Ibid., III, art. ix, 446 (cf. art. viii).

Perhaps the penal emphasis falls as strongly in the *Westminster Confession* of 1647 as anywhere—later in point of time, and therefore presumably much more under the influence of "protestant scholasticism." In this Confession it is said that our Lord willingly undertook the Father's appointment to be the Mediator, that he "endured most grievous torments immediately in his soul, and most painful sufferings in his body," and that "by his perfect obedience and sacrifice of himself, which he through the eternal Spirit once offered up unto God, hath fully satisfied the justice of his Father, and purchased not only reconciliation, but an everlasting inheritance in the kingdom of heaven, for all those whom the Father hath given unto him." Even here, however, the theory of penal substitution does not appear in "splendid isolation" and is mixed with the ideas of obedience and sacrifice that we found in the *Institutes*:

> Christ, by his obedience and death, did fully discharge the debt of all those that are thus justified, and did make a proper, real, and full satisfaction to his Father's justice in their behalf. Yet inasmuch as he was given by the Father for them, and his obedience and satisfaction accepted in their stead, and both freely, not for any thing in them, their justification is only of free grace; that both the exact justice and rich grace of God might be glorified in the justification of sinners.[59]

This statement is supported by the *Shorter Catechism* of the *Westminster Confession* where it is said that our Lord fulfills the office of Priest to us "in his once offering up of himself a sacrifice to satisfy divine justice, and reconcile us to God, and in making continual intercession for us." Although the catechism speaks of him suffering "the wrath of God, and the cursed death of the cross," [60] it stresses equally the free grace of God in Christ and the assurance of his love.[61]

In comparison with this we must mention the extreme reticence of the Anglican *Thirty-Nine Articles* on the subject of the Atonement. They simply state that our Lord was "crucified, dead, and buried, to reconcile his Father to us, and to be a sacrifice, not only for original guilt, but also for actual sins of men." [62] True, reconciliation and sacri-

---

[59] *Ibid.*, III, 626-27 (XI, iii).
[60] *Ibid.*, III, 681 (ques. 25, 27).
[61] *Ibid.*, III, 683 (ques. 33-36).
[62] *Ibid.*, III, 488; art. ii.

fice are the terms used, but an unwillingness to be committed theologically does not always pay good dividends, for it is hard to avoid the impression that in the phrase "to reconcile his Father *to* us" the Anglican Church aligned itself with one of the least attractive and least biblical aspects of the penal theory.

The fact which is made clear, however, from an examination of the confessional statements is that there was no one generally accepted doctrine of the Atonement contained in them, and all the biblical images find expression. On the other hand we do notice a tendency to use the legal and penal ideas which would certainly help to swing Protestant theology into that line of thinking. Nevertheless, it is evident that if a strict doctrine of election, an increasingly rigid Biblicism, and the categories of thought in society were to bring the penal theory more and more into the center of Protestant theology, there were elements within the Confessions themselves which might have redressed the balance if events had not accelerated the need to formulate Calvinist doctrine more precisely.

4. *Attacks upon Calvinism*

The events that caused this doctrinal retraction centered in the doctrinal struggle that was going on within Protestantism itself. Just as the radical criticism offered to the Reformers by the Anabaptists led to a stiffening in the doctrines of Church and Sacraments, so the challenge offered by the Arminians to the Calvinist doctrine of Election, and the still more radical criticism levelled by the Socinians, led to retrenchment along the whole front of Christian doctrine by those who had inherited the work of the Reformers and regarded themselves as the guardians of the Reformed teaching.

We should not underestimate the force of the attack launched by the Socinians or the fear and abhorrence with which all aspects of Socinian doctrine were regarded by orthodox Calvinists. The Socinian criticism of orthodox belief was directed on a far broader front than the doctrine of the Trinity alone and significantly came to a focus in the doctrine of the Atonement. In 1594 Faustus Socinus (1539-1604) published his *De Jesu Christo Servatore*, a thoroughgoing criticism of the penal elements in Calvinist doctrine, and he showed that although Christ's death was an affliction it could be regarded in no sense as a punishment because it would be against the nature of God to punish anyone who was innocent. He denounced the idea of imputed righteousness and maintained that we are justified not so much by faith that our sins are blotted out but by our willingness to obey Christ and to believe in his teaching—virtually a re-statement of the position that Abelard had taken against Anselm. Naturally, from the standpoint of the doctrine of God that he accepted, he was not able or willing to concede the force of Calvin's insistence that God was in Christ. Even so his main contentions were never properly met, for he had attacked Calvinism at its weakest point. Therefore, instead of recognizing that the penal theory was comparatively recent and by no means vital to the evangelical faith, the theologians rapidly began to retract into their shell of orthodoxy: the attack had been made by one who denied the doctrine of the Trinity, and inevitably the penal theory against which he had tilted became a bastion of Trinitarian orthodoxy.

We can trace a similar reaction in respect of the doctrine of Election. Although there had been a considerable number of Protestants who had not accepted the view that the efficacy of the cross of Christ was limited to those who were "elect," the Great Remonstrance published by the Arminians in Holland in 1610 brought matters to a head. The second article declared that "Jesus Christ, the Saviour of the world, died for all men and for every man, so that he has obtained for them all, by his death on the cross, redemption and the forgiveness of sins." [63] In itself it was a moderate document that fell far short of universalism, for the Arminians went on to make it quite clear that God's forgiveness was strictly limited to believers, but there can be no doubt that they had attacked the teaching of Calvin at another point where his followers were most sensitive.

When the great exponent of international law, Hugo Grotius (1585-1645), entered the theological arena to expound the doctrine of the Atonement, he did so in the belief that he was defending the Reformers' doctrine against the errors of Socinianism. He called his book a *Defense of the Catholic Faith on the Satisfaction of Christ against Faustus Socinus* [64] (1617) and stated his case thus in the preface:

[63] *Ibid.*, III, art. ii, 546.
[64] *Defensio Fidei Catholicae de Satisfactione Christi.*

THE ATONEMENT AND THE SACRAMENTS

God moved by His goodness wonderfully to do us good, in view of the hindrance of our sins which merited punishment, determined that Christ, voluntarily of His love toward men, by bearing the severest torments and a bloody and shameful death, should pay the penalties for our sins so that, without injury to the manifestation of divine justice (*ut salva Divinae iustitiae demonstratione*), we, through the mediation of true faith, might be freed from the penalty of eternal death.[65]

At first sight this does not appear to be very different from penal satisfaction, until it is seen that what Grotius is saying is that the Passion of Christ is not to be considered as an expiation of Divine Justice but as the demonstration of it. This became known as the "Rectoral" theory, and its significance for the historical situation was that it was generally adopted by the followers of Arminius, which was sufficient to damn it in the eyes of most Calvinist theologians. The penal theory, which was undeniably to be found in the works of the Reformers themselves and which seemed to have the support of Scripture, had been attacked by Socinians who denied the Trinity and by Arminians who wanted to destroy the doctrine of Election. This proved its orthodoxy!

The reaction came at the Synod of Dort (1619) where the delegates of the Reformed Churches expressly attacked the Arminian attitude to Election and the Socinian view of the death of Christ,[66] and in the doctrinal statement regarding the Death of Christ there was a sharp emphasis upon the penal view of our Lord's passion.[67] To some extent the die was cast, the party line for the future had been defined, and it only remained for the theologians to work out the implications.

The significance of this for Anglo-Saxon theology may be indicated by those who took part in the Synod of Dort. Present as an "expert adviser" was the exiled Congregationalist, William Ames ("learned Amesius"), who was later to become the Rector of the University of Franeker, and whose works for many years during the seventeenth and eighteenth centuries were standard theology in the schools of New England.[68] Britain was represented by five official delegates (three from England and one each from Wales and Scotland), and they

---

[65] S. Cave, op. cit., p. 205.
[66] Schaff, op. cit., III, 550-97; particularly "Rejectio Errorum IV," 563.
[67] Ibid., ch. ii., arts. ii and iv; 561.
[68] Cf. Perry Miller's *Orthodoxy in Massachusetts*.

were, of course, representatives of the established Anglican Church, which had by the accession of James I (James VI of Scotland) re-established its position in England and Wales and "invaded" Scotland. It shows the extent to which the Anglican Church at this time considered itself to be allied to the Continental Reformation, but it should be said that there was a growing interest in Arminian doctrine within the Church of England which was supported in "high places."

A few years later the theological temperature was heightened by the publication of a book, *Appello Caesarem*, by a rector from Essex, Richard Montagu, who was associated with the powerful family of that name. The book openly professed Arminian views, but instead of accepting the displeasure of the Calvinist Primate Archbishop Abbott, Dr. Montagu appealed to Charles I who quite clearly supported him. A straw in the wind of English affairs was to be seen in the fact that Dr. Montagu was defended by William Laud, and that Laud was promoted successively to the bishoprics of Bath and Wells and London, and finally became Archbishop of Canterbury. Montagu, after a few years "disgrace," owing to the interference of the House of Commons, ultimately received his reward in appointment to the see of Chichester. Small but significant events like these lead the way to the civil war which broke out in 1642, and which was to find King Charles and his Arminian bishops on one side and Parliament with its Puritan supporters on the other. Admittedly this is a flagrant oversimplification of the issues in that struggle, but these factors were present and played their part. It is in the face of this and all it implied that we must see the doctrine of the Atonement as it was elaborated in the massive systems of Calvinist theology written by the Puritan divines in the seventeenth century: they were written in defense of the Faith and against "spiritual wickedness" in high places.

5. Seventeenth-Century Puritan Reactions: John Owen and Thomas Goodwin

We shall take our main example of seventeenth-century Puritanism from the works of John Owen, the systematizer of English Congregationalism and one of the leading Calvinist theologians in the middle of the seventeenth century. Owen was a member of the Westminster Assembly and belonged to the small but influential group who in ecclesiology refused to be considered either as Presbyterians or as Brownist Independents, but who in the rest of their doctrine were loyal followers of John Calvin. During the period of the Civil Wars Owen rapidly attracted attention as a theologian of some stature, and very soon he rose to be one of Cromwell's leading chaplains and ecclesiastical advisers. He became dean of Christ Church and vice-chancellor of Oxford University and is regarded as the main architect of the ecclesiastical settlement that was adopted during the brief years of Cromwell's Protectorate. These facts indicate that John Owen was no academic recluse, and that he wrote his massive system within the existential situation of a country torn by civil war and in response to the urgent ecclesiastical and theological needs of the time.

During the course of a very busy life Owen managed to produce enough written material to fill twenty-four sizable volumes of the closely printed nineteenth century reprint of his works which now usually grace the shelves of libraries. But the fact that his complete works were reprinted in the middle of the nineteenth century by a Scottish Presbyterian enterprise is sufficient indication not only of the theological battle that was raging around Calvinist doctrine at that time but also of the central place that the work of Owen had in the exposition of Calvinism.[69] Two of these volumes are more or less devoted to the exposition of the Atonement. I do not propose to give a summary of their 1,263 pages but to select some passages which illustrate the way in which he developed the theory of Calvin.

In his *Vindiciae Evangelicae*,[70] having shown that the death of Christ is a price and a sacrifice, he concentrates upon proving that it is a penalty and a punishment, and that the One who inflicted the punishment was God. Basing his argument upon Isa. 53:6, "the Lord laid on him the iniquity of us all," he asks what do the words "laid on him" mean and what is meant by "iniquity." By examining the Hebrew text, he suggests that the use of the *hiphil* tense implies an enforcement; "God made our sins, as it were, to set upon or fall upon Jesus Christ,"[71] and what was done to our Lord was prefigured in the Old Testament example of the scapegoat. He goes on to say that in

---

[69] *The Works of John Owen*, ed. W. H. Goold (Edinburgh, 1850-53). As a matter of interest it may be noted that Owen's contemporary, Richard Baxter, who was not as actively engaged in public affairs, managed to write twice as much as Owen. Cf. Editorial note, *Works*, X, 429.

[70] *Ibid.*, *Works*, XII, pp. 3-581.

[71] *Ibid.*, p. 445.

laying our sins upon Christ there was a twofold action of God as governor and judge:

> The first is "innovatio obligationis," the "innovation of the obligation," wherein we were detained and bound over to punishment. . . . God now puts in the name of the surety, of Jesus Christ, that he might become responsible for our sins, and undergo the punishment that we were obliged to. Christ was ὑπὸ νόμον γενόμενον, he was made under the law; that is, he was put into subjection to the obligation of it unto punishment. God put his name into the obligation, and so the law came to have its advantage against him, who otherwise was most free from the charge of it. Then was Christ "made sin," when, by being put into the obligation of the law, he became liable to the punishment of it. . . . The second act of God, as a judge, is "inflictio poenae." Christ being now made obnoxious, and that by his own consent, the justice of God finding him in the law, layeth the weight of all on him.[72]

Perhaps Owen did not realize how much he was reading the practice of the legal system into his interpretation of the Atonement at this point. The most damning criticism of the penal theory has always been that it is fundamentally unjust to transfer punishment from those who are guilty to One who is innocent. The surprising thing for a modern reader to notice is that Owen seems to have had no difficulty with this idea and does not seem to have expected his readers to have had any such difficulty. The reason seems to have been that he interpreted the penal aspect of the Atonement in terms of the legal practice whereby a guilty person can be "bound over" to appear for trial in his own or another person's recognizances. The right to be granted bail in which a friend might stand as surety is one of the foundation rights of the individual in Common Law, but it should be remembered that these were rights which were being expounded, defined, and defended in the constitutional struggle of the seventeenth century in Britain.[73] Therefore, in suggesting that our Lord had become our "surety," far from introducing an idea that was obnoxious to his contemporaries, Owen was using a legal figure that was a living issue in their minds. He finds his support for the penal theory mainly

---

[72] Ibid., pp. 448-49.
[73] It was not until 1689 in the "Bill of Rights" that the principle was established that bail (i.e., the extent of the surety) should not be unreasonable or excessive.

in Isa. 53, which he examines in detail and deals particularly with "the perverse interpretation of Hugo Grotius."[74] He then proceeds to examine in still greater detail what kind of punishment Christ underwent—what did his "death" mean?

Here Owen illustrates the main difference between the penal theory in the Reformers and in their followers, for whereas in the former it appears as one aspect among several, in Owen the penal aspect becomes the basis of the system, and the sufferings of Christ become the all-important center of the Atonement. For this reason the Crucifixion was painted in the darkest colors and with the fullest wealth of detail, so that the magnitude of what Christ suffered would be brought home to men. In this Owen excels. At inordinate length and with what we should regard as morbid skill, he shows how the death of Christ was the very sum of all that we could suffer: it was first violent and bloody; secondly, ignominious and shameful; thirdly, lingering; fourthly, since it came under the law, an accursed death. Moreover, he shows how there was a consensus of all created things to wound and inflict pain upon our Lord—only the good angels abstained, and even they were restrained from intervening to help him. Both devils and men joined to attack him; and of men, both Jews and Gentiles, rulers and ruled, ecclesiastical and civil governors, friends and enemies—in fact the whole of humanity and even Nature itself joined to bring the greatest possible amount of suffering upon him. This is, however, only the beginning, and Owen proceeds to dwell upon the universality of the way in which Christ suffered. He suffered first in his body—all his senses, feeling, sight, taste, hearing, and smelling ("they crucified him in a noisome place, a place of stink and loathsomeness") were subjected to torture; all parts of his body were afflicted—his head was crowned with thorns, his face was spat upon, his back was scourged, his hands, his feet and his side were pierced, and his mind was invaded with darkness.

After this descriptive *tour de force* about physical suffering, Owen develops his ideas about the sufferings that Christ underwent within his soul. He finally comes to the conclusion toward which he has been working, that

[74] Goold, op. cit., ch, xxv; Works, XII, 455 ff.

on these considerations, it is evident that the sufferings of Christ in relation to the law were the very same that were threatened to sinners, and which we should have undergone had not our Surety undertaken the work for us. Neither was there any difference in reference to God the judge and the sentence of the law, but only this, that the same persons who offended did not suffer, and that those consequences of the punishment inflicted which attend the offenders' own suffering could have no place in him.

Such then are the characteristics of the penal theory developed by Owen and expounded by him in a series of weighty treatises, *The Death of Death in the Death of Christ* (1647), *Of the Death of Christ* (1650), *A Dissertation on Divine Justice* (1653), and also in the 1650's another reply to the criticisms of Richard Baxter, *Of the Death of Christ and of Justification*, and a further *Review of the Annotations of Hugo Grotius*. Nor was he alone in his exposition, for one can find precisely the same kind of approach in the writings of his distinguished colleague, the president of Magdalen College, Oxford, Thomas Goodwin—the same concentration upon the penal aspects of the Atonement, the same insistence upon the satisfaction due to the justice of God, and the same method of dwelling particularly upon the sufferings of our Lord upon the Cross.[75]

But before we hasten to condemn the seventeenth-century Puritans and their treatment of the Atonement, two observations need to be made in their favor. First, their intention was wholly evangelical—they were concerned with bringing the individual to the point of making a decision for Jesus Christ; secondly, the most important reasons for their concentration upon the penal aspects of Christ's death were to be found within the peculiar difficulties and theological dangers of their own day.

1. With regard to the first we might take an example from Goodwin, who having described the pains of Christ, goes on to exhort his readers, "To this end lay all your sins to your own charge; they were laid to his charge to satisfy God's justice, and thou must lay them to thine own charge, to humble thy soul and make thee the more thankful."[76] John Owen too, in his *Dissertation on Divine Justice*, having dwelt upon the necessity for the atoning death of Christ, warns his

---

[75] *Of Christ the Mediator* and other dissertations on the Atonement in Vol. V of *The Works of Thomas Goodwin*, ed. J. C. Miller (Edinburgh, 1863).
[76] *Ibid.*, p. 290.

readers, "If, then, you have the least concern or anxiety for your eternal state, hasten, 'while it is called To-day,' to 'lay hold on the hope that is set before you.' Give yourselves up entirely to him; receive him 'whom God hath set forth to be a propitiation through faith in his blood, that he might declare his righteousness.' " [77]

Nor must it too readily be inferred that fear of hell was the only motive for conversion which they set before their contemporaries, for in dwelling upon the sufferings which our Lord has undergone for us, their intention was as much to inspire love toward him as to inspire fear of God's justice and wrath. Owen tells the story of the wife of Tigranes of Armenia, whose husband saved her from slavery by offering his own life to King Cyrus in exchange—self-sacrifice which led Cyrus to grant the Armenian queen her freedom. When asked if she were thinking about the generosity of Cyrus who had granted her liberty, the queen replied that she was not, but that she was rather thinking of the one who had offered to buy her freedom at the expense of himself. John Owen asks:

> Is not He, then to be caressed and dearly beloved, to be contemplated with faith, love, and joy, who answered for our lives with his own,—devoted himself to punishment, and at the price of his blood, "while we were yet enemies," purchased us, and rendered us "a peculiar people to himself"? We, now secure, may contemplate in his agony, sweat, tremor, horror, exclamations, prayers, cross, and blood, that is God's severity against sin, what the punishment of the broken law and curse are.

Then, breaking into the erotic language of the *Song of Songs*, he exclaims, "May we always, then, be 'sick of love' towards our deliverer!" [78] For all its unwholesome excesses the penal theory, as it was developed in the seventeenth century, was evangelical in its purpose. It placed our Lord at the center of the Christian faith, and as his saving work was shown to be at the heart of evangelical theology, so devotion to him for what he had done became the heart of evangelical piety.

What John Owen did not see was that his own story about the wife of King Tigranes contained a perfect illustration of one of the most dangerous features of the theory of the Atonement that he is

[77] Goold, *op. cit.*, X, 621.
[78] *Ibid.*, pp. 622-23.

at such pains to defend. He had described how a woman lavished her love and respect not upon the king who had granted her freedom but upon the husband who had been willing to win that freedom for her at the expense of his own life. This illustrates exactly, in the response of the Christian believer, the kind of false distinction between the work of God the Father and God the Son which such a penal theory must produce. A theory of penal substitution would be Christo-centric, and because of its insistence upon the actual pains that Christ suffered for us, it would be strong in its evangelical appeal, but it had no way of bringing home to men the love of the Father for them or of inducing them to love him. Theologians might declare that the whole plan of salvation depended upon God's prevenient grace, and that he had taken the divine initiative in prevailing upon his Son to be our Saviour and our Mediator. However, there were always the stumbling blocks and the question marks—why was a Mediator necessary, and why did his justice need to be satisfied with such suffering when Jesus himself had shown us that even human forgiveness ought to be infinite?

Furthermore, apart from any reference to the legal practice of any country, the fundamental question of Socinus, of "Boso" and of Abelard would have to be answered—how could a just God punish One who was innocent? The only way in which this could be met was the way in which it appears to have been met by Anselm and Calvin, by a bold insistence upon such a unity within the Trinity that all Three Persons are seen as equal and full participators not only in initiating the plan of salvation, but in the cost of man's redemption. But this step was either not seen, or else it was too dangerous for the Puritans to take, for reasons that we must now consider.

2. We have already suggested that the work of the Puritans must be considered in relationship to the unsettled and disquieting state of ecclesiastical affairs in which they were fully involved. To see the relation between what happened to the doctrine of the Atonement and the concerns of the immediate situation is of more than general interest. It provides an important illustration of the interplay between the formulation of doctrine and the actual living historical situation in which the doctrine was formulated. It is an indication that a critical study of symbolics involves also a critical understanding of the histori-

cal moment in which a confession, creed, or doctrine becomes alive in the history of the Church.

In the case of the Puritans we are dealing not simply with theologians but with men who were taking an active part in the practical responsibilities of ecclesiastical statesmanship. They were trying desperately to establish a system of church government and form of Christian confession that would do justice at once to their avowed principle of religious toleration, without handing over their country either to the chaos of warring sects or to the uniformity of a persecuting national church. In the case of Owen and Goodwin their situation was particularly complicated in that they were "Independents" (Congregationalists). As theologians they had a special responsibility for defining and maintaining the faith of the Church, since their churchmanship forbade them to regard written creeds as per se authoritative or sufficient safeguards for the faith. These considerations, coupled with their influence upon Oliver Cromwell and their association with him in the experiment of toleration, made them extremely sensitive to attacks from the Presbyterian wing of Calvinism regarding their theological orthodoxy. We can therefore understand their desire to establish the theological repute of themselves and the churchmanship they represented.

It was in this situation, for which they had considerable civic responsibility, that Socinians began to appear, and, claiming the liberty of conscience that the Protectorate proclaimed, began to attack the doctrine of the Trinity. Oliver Cromwell became Lord Protector of the three nations in Britain under two separate written constitutions, for which he was twice inducted into the office of Lord Protector, in 1653 and 1657. A comparison of the ecclesiastical clauses of these two documents is very revealing. In the *Instrument of Government* of 1653 "the Christian religion as contained in the Scriptures" was to be "held forth and recommended as the public profession of these nations," [79] while freedom of conscience was to be given to all "such as profess faith in God by Jesus Christ"—"provided this liberty be not extended to Popery or Prelacy, nor to such as, under the profession of Christ, hold forth and practise licentiousness." [80] In the *Humble*

[79] Art. xxxv, S. R. Gardiner, *Constitutional Documents of the Puritan Revolution* (Oxford: O. U. P., 1906), p. 416.
[80] *Ibid.*, art. xxvii.

Petition and Advice of 1657, however, under which Cromwell had been invited to become King but had declined, there were some significant shifts of emphasis. In the first place "the true Protestant Christian religion, as it is contained in the Holy Scriptures of the Old and New Testament, and no other" was to be "held forth and asserted for the public profession of these nations." [81] Then a confession of faith was to be prepared by Protector and Parliament, and it was to be defended by the law. But the most significant change, which reflected the Socinian threat, was in the basis upon which those who dissented could claim toleration. It was limited to "such who profess faith in God the Father, and in Jesus Christ His eternal Son, the true God, and in the Holy Spirit, God co-equal with the Father and the Son, one God blessed for ever, and do acknowledge the Holy Scriptures of the Old and New Testament to be the revealed Will and Word of God." [82]

This shift of emphasis indicates the concern which the ecclesiastical leaders of the Protectorate had in maintaining the doctrine of the Trinity. In their belief, if this doctrine were destroyed, the basis of the Christian faith they wished to establish in the country would have been smashed. The panic was caused by John Biddle, a Unitarian who openly published the Socinian *Racovian Catechism* and books defending that position. He was eventually imprisoned in 1654 but caused the Protector and his government quite a lot of trouble before his case was finished. In a more settled situation he would not have been in himself of any great significance. But in view of the state of flux in which the church affairs of the country were at that time and in view of the eagerness with which the political opposition was ready to seize upon any possibility of tarring Independency and the government with Biddle's brush, everything was at stake—the purity of the faith, the possibility of a settlement with the Presbyterians, and even the stability of the Protectorate government itself. Historians may differ according to their prejudices as to which of these motives weighed the most heavily upon Owen and his colleagues, but they were all very real incentives in driving the theologians to redefine the doctrinal standards of their own faith and to shy away from any opinions which might seem to jeopardize the "orthodox" faith.

[81] Ibid., p. 454, sec. 11.
[82] Ibid.

Linked to their hatred and fear of Socinianism was a detestation hardly less strong for Arminianism, for they regarded its doctrine of Election as Pelagian and thought that Grotius' theory of the Atonement would lead directly to Socinianism. In John Owens' *Display of Arminianism* (1642), which first brought him to public notice, and in his *Death of Death and the Death of Christ*, he made it his first task to refute the doctrines of the Arminians. Then in the *Dissertation on Divine Justice* he dealt with the views of Socinius and the Racovian Catechism. But most significantly he reserved the full weight of his onslaught for a joint attack upon John Biddle and Hugo Grotius in the massive *Vindiciae Evangelicae*, treating the views of Biddle, the Racovian Catechism, and the atonement theory of Grotius in the same volume, and attempting to trace the correspondence of ideas between Grotius, representing the Arminians, and Biddle as a representative Unitarian. Later on he made this correspondence of ideas quite explicit by publishing letters that had passed between Grotius and a certain Pastor Crellio of the Racovian churches.[83] The point that comes out of this is that Owen interpreted any attack upon the penal substitutionary theory of the Atonement as ultimately an attack upon the real doctrine that he and his colleagues felt to be at stake—the doctrine of the Trinity. I suggest that if this does not wholly explain why the Puritans developed the penal theory it goes a long way in explanation.

It is not suggested that Owen and Goodwin were the only Puritan theologians to be affected in this way. I believe that if a comprehensive study were made of other representative Calvinist theologians in the seventeenth century there would be found a similar tendency in many of them to render more precise, and therefore more rigid, the penal interpretation of the Atonement, not for its own sake, but because—recognizing a unity between all Christian doctrine—they felt that any attack upon it was an indirect attack upon the doctrine of the Trinity. It is significant that in 1682 François Turrettini published his *Institutio Theologiae Elencticae* against the followers of Socinius, and it should be remembered that Turrettini was one of the leading exponents of the penal theory among the Calvinists of Europe.

---

[83] *Review of the Annotations of Hugo Grotius; Works*, XII.

THE REFORMERS AND THEIR FOLLOWERS
6. *Eighteenth-Century Puritan Reaction: Jonathan Edwards*

At this point it is instructive to refer to Jonathan Edwards, for he became to eighteenth-century New England Calvinism what Owen had been to the Calvinism of England a century before. His system of theology, no less than Owen's, was hammered out in the face of new views, which he feared might destroy the Trinitarian faith. We have to remember that when the break with the older Calvinistic forms came, it came at the point of its doctrine of Atonement, and that what McLeod Campbell found it necessary to attack in Britain, Horace Bushnell at almost the same time was attacking in America. Essentially it was the same system of thought which had to be undermined and destroyed, because it had been formulated by men who accepted the same theological presuppositions and faced the same threats to their faith. Even the most casual reading of the list of contents of Edwards' major work on The Freedom of the Will is sufficient to show his concern at the growth of Arminianism, and if eighteenth-century American Puritans tended to confuse Arminianism and Unitarianism, the history of liberal thought during that century in New England seems to justify their attitude.[84]

Although Jonathan Edwards' doctrine of Atonement will be found implicit in his sermons, it is to the *Work of Redemption* that we must go for a systematic exposition. In the preface to this, published in 1773, the great American theologian reveals that the book was the outline of a systematic theology which he had hoped to write, and which he now offered to the public in the form of sermons that he had delivered over thirty years previously (1739) during his ministry at Northampton.

Perhaps we ought to be grateful to him for giving us the outline rather than the comprehensive system, for what stands clear is the centrality of the doctrine of Atonement to his whole thought—"the Work of Redemption." In the comparatively short compass of the *Work of Redemption* we see that it would have been his intention to show "how the most remarkable events, in all ages from the fall to the present times, recorded in sacred and profane history, were

---

[84] See Jonathan Edwards' *The Freedom of the Will* in *The Works of President Edwards* (New York: Leavitt & Allen, 1857; reprint of the Worcester ed.) Vol. II. Cf. also Perry Miller, *Jonathan Edwards* (New York: Sloane, 1949) pp. 22, 107-8, 317.

THE ATONEMENT AND THE SACRAMENTS

adapted to promote the work of redemption; and then . . . how the same work should be yet further carried on even to the end of the world." [85] There can be no doubt on which doctrine Jonathan Edwards places the all-important emphasis.

However, it is significant that when McLeod Campbell launched his attack on the old Calvinism, he coupled the names of Owen and Edwards as the exponents of that system in its classic form.[86] The insight is just, for if Jonathan Edwards succeeds in stripping some of the seventeenth-century verbosity from the doctrine as Owen had expounded it, the doctrine he expresses is very much the same. He speaks of the Saviour "suffering all the waves and billows of God's wrath for men's sins, insomuch that they overwhelmed his soul": [87] Christ did "all that was required in order to satisfy the threatenings of the law, and all that was necessary in order to satisfy divine justice; then the utmost that vindictive justice demanded, even the whole debt was paid." [88] McLeod Campbell recognized that Edwards found the basic quality of our Lord's righteousness in his obedience—an obedience, which he points out, Edwards believed must center in the death of Christ [89] and particularly in the pains of his suffering.

It is the concentration upon the extent of our Lord's sufferings which indicates Edwards' essential agreement with Owen in a most striking way. The American theologian mercifully spares his readers from the excessive length and detail with which Dr. Owen entered into the subject, but he is thorough enough. The aim is to show the superlative extent to which our Lord suffered. Christ had been subject "to uncommon humiliation and suffering in his infancy," for not only were there the humble and painful circumstances of his birth, but he had been persecuted even in his infancy. He suffered not only in the poverty of the home he entered and the manual labor he endured but also in privations and rejection during his public ministry. It is only when he has dealt with these special sufferings of Jesus that Jonathan Edwards proceeds to discuss the sufferings of the death and passion.

---

[85] Jonathan Edwards, *A History of the Work of Redemption*, Works, I, 296.
[86] McLeod Campbell, *The Nature of the Atonement*, ch. iii.
[87] Edwards, op. cit., Works, I, 422.
[88] Ibid., p. 416.
[89] McLeod Campbell, op. cit., pp. 59-60.

He does not treat the cruelties of the Cross as fully as Owen, but there is no doubt of his intention to press home to his audience the fullness of Christ's sufferings on their behalf. "And," he adds, "besides what our Lord endured in this excruciating death in his body, he endured vastly more in his soul." [90] For the reader (and presumably even more so for the hearer!) it all adds up to the fact that Christ endured an infinite amount of suffering on our behalf, and our response should be the response of gratitude in accepting his salvation.

In certain aspects of his treatment, however, Jonathan Edwards is nearer to Calvin (and at the same time nearer to our own day) than was John Owen. Although the penal theory is very near the center of his theology, it is not there alone. He does not ignore the idea of ransom; atonement was to be described in terms of "redemption," just as can speak of Christ's work as a debt being paid or as a "purchase." [91] Even more in line with John Calvin's thought is the fact that although Edwards does not express the idea clearly until the end of his treatment, he places the saving work of Christ at the center of the total biblical account of Redemption, and the penal aspects of the theory are enclosed, as it were, within the sacrificial concepts that permeate the Bible's exposition of salvation. "Now," he declares, "was accomplished the main thing that had been pointed at by the various institutions of the ceremonial law, ... and by all the sacrifices from the beginning of the world." [92]

But if there is this shift of emphasis from Owen, it is still as an example of Puritanism that we look to Jonathan Edwards. Just as he is an example of those things that we criticize, so he is an example of those things that we most commend in the Puritan. Whatever we may say about the less attractive elements of the penal theory, Edwards shows us that the concentration upon the sufferings of Christ had one great evangelical purpose, to stir up the response of gratitude: "O! that you who live negligent of this salvation, would consider what you do!" [93]

For the rest Edwards' theology must be seen as arising out of the

[90] Edwards, op. cit., Works, I, 415.
[91] E.g., ibid., p. 423.
[92] Ibid., p. 416.
[93] Ibid., p. 422.

THE ATONEMENT AND THE SACRAMENTS

same need to defend the Faith as Owen experienced in the previous century, and perhaps our fundamental criticism of these Puritans follows directly from the merits of their loyalty to the doctrine of the Trinity. We criticize them because they were responsible for turning the substitutionary idea from a picture of limited use into a doctrine and test of orthodoxy. We criticize them also because in their emphasis upon penal substitution they presented to the Church a picture that was bound to become irrelevant and obnoxious as soon as criminal law became more humane: as an exclusive theory of atonement it was never adequate to express the honor of the God they wanted to honor. Perhaps most fundamentally, however, we criticize them because in defending the doctrine of the Trinity, they became almost tritheists. The insistence upon absolute distinctions between the suffering of the Son of God and the impassibility of the Father led them to a position where the unity of purpose within the Trinity became merely the acquiescence of the Son and the Spirit in the eternal decree of the Father. On the basis of such doctrine there must inevitably arise in the mind of the believer an opposition of loyalty between the Father, the Son, and Holy Spirit. Even more ironically, by its emphasis upon the subjection of the Son to the will of the Father, it opened the way to Arianism and the very heresies that they were so anxious to avoid. The history of the succeeding decades furnishes dramatic examples of the *volte face* from orthodoxy to Unitarianism, in which, on both sides of the Atlantic, the churches of Calvinism were the chief sufferers.[94]

Fortunately the Christocentric religion that resulted from their teaching was often better than the tritheistic theology which produced

[94] At the end of the seventeenth century a "Happy Union" was projected between the two main churches of Calvinism in England, the Presbyterians and the Congregationalists, both of which were by that time plunged into nonconformity by reason of the unexpected course of events after the Restoration of the royal house in 1660. The union broke down partly because the Congregationalists suspected the Presbyterians of being Arians, if not Unitarians. The fear seems to have been justified during the eighteenth century, for the large Presbyterian Church in England (the Church which formulated the *Westminster Confession*) became almost entirely Unitarian in doctrine, to such an extent that its ancient Trusts are now in the hands of the Unitarian Church of England. Several of the congregations that wished to maintain their Trinitarian position joined the Congregationalists during the course of the eighteenth century in order to do so. It is one of the curious quirks of history that in America, after the defection of the episcopal King's Chapel in Boston, it was among the established Congregational churches of New England that Unitarianism had its greatest effect.

it. If they concentrated too much upon the wounds of Christ and the details of his dying, Medieval Catholic devotion in the west had made precisely the same mistake. Perhaps it was the very devotion to Christ himself which redeemed both Roman Catholic monks and Puritan Protestants. For as it is the eternal function of the Holy Spirit to be anonymous and to point to Christ, so the preaching of our Lord himself must reveal the features of the Father. Despite the barbarities of our theologies and the morbid preoccupations of our inadequate devotions, to become a disciple of Jesus Christ and to meditate upon his passion is to catch something of the vision which sees "the light of the knowledge of the glory of God in the face of Jesus Christ" (II Cor. 4:6).

PART II

Disputes About the Inheritance

CHAPTER IV

The Attack on "Objectivity"

1. The Evangelical Revival

> Was it for sins that I have done,
>   He suffered on the tree?
> Amazing pity! grace unknown!
>   And love beyond degree! [1]

> Father, hear the blood of Jesus
>   Speaking in Thine ears above;
> From the wrath and curse release us,
>   Manifest Thy pardoning love.[2]

THE REVIVAL WHICH SWEPT ENGLAND DURING THE EIGHTEENTH CENtury and which brought the Methodist Church into being underlined the differences between Calvinism and Arminianism regarding the doctrine of Election. George Whitefield, who had started the field preaching, was a firm Calvinist, while the brothers John and Charles Wesley were just as firmly attached to the Arminian views that had predominated in the Anglican Church since the time of William Laud. But when the Evangelicals sang or preached about the Passion of our Lord, they did so in identical terms: it would be virtually impossible to decide from theological considerations alone which of the verses quoted above was written by the Calvinist Isaac Watts, and which by the Arminian Charles Wesley.

The penal theory of the Atonement governed Protestant thinking until the middle of the nineteenth century, but in the perspective of the years the Arminian ideas that appeared to seventeenth-century Puritans to be Satan's trumpet of defiance to the faith seem now to

---
[1] Isaac Watts (1674-1748), "Alas! and did my Saviour bleed?"
[2] Charles Wesley (1707-1788). Cf. *The Eucharistic Hymns of John and Charles Wesley* by J. Ernest Rattenbury (Epworth Press, 1948), p. 199.

be little more than interesting variations on the same theme. John Wesley might break off his association with George Whitefield because the latter would insist that God had eternally limited salvation to the fixed number of his Elect, but there was nothing to choose between them in evangelical fervor. They both described the Cross as a penalty for our sins and concentrated upon our Lord's sufferings on our behalf:

> Hearts of stone, relent, relent,
>   Break, by Jesu's cross subdued;
> See His body mangled, rent,
>   Cover'd with a gore of blood!
> Sinful soul, what hast thou done?
>   Murder'd God's eternal Son! [3]

So sang Charles Wesley. If Calvinists thought our Lord's penal suffering was to be seen in terms of satisfaction to God's justice and Arminians in terms of a manifestation of his justice, the issue would not appear to us to be a very grave one. If Whitefield preached hellfire, so did Wesley—the only difference being that as a good Calvinist Whitefield tended to hold his hearers a little longer and a little lower over the flames before drawing them back and offering them the free salvation which, in the view of his theology, the great majority of them were divinely prevented from accepting! Augustus Toplady's "Rock of Ages, cleft for me" might be a Calvinist counterblast to Charles Wesley's hymn:

> Rock of Israel, cleft for me,
> For us, for all mankind.

But both hymns reveal the same religious experience centered in the atoning work of Christ upon the Cross and the same devotion to his wounds and blood as the seals of our salvation. Indeed, it is one of the minor ironies of church history that these two writers, exemplars in their day of the rival positions, often stand together in the hymnbooks of all denominations and to the devout appear today to be based upon practically identical theologies—because the issue turned

[3] *Ibid.*, p. 202.

wholly upon the point of Election and not on the accepted pattern of the Atonement itself. When they wrote the hymns of the revival, they were, for the most part, more concerned with singing the praise of "the eternal Victim, slain" [4] than with launching theological polemics.

Even the issue regarding Election, however, has to be seen within the context of the need for evangelism that the Evangelicals faced and the response to that need in the revival itself. It is for this reason that Charles Wesley calls upon God to increase, if that be possible, the "perfect hatred" he feels toward "Satan's horrible decree":

> Which feigns Thee to pass by
> The most of Adam's race,
> And leave them in their blood to die
> Shut out from saving grace.[5]

Theoretically the "horrible decree" of Calvinism held that God had already predestined those who were to be saved and that the rest of mankind was irrevocably predestined to damnation. This should have had a stultifying effect on evangelical endeavor, but the logic was not followed. Puritanism was not disinterested in evangelism. The religious ferment of the Commonwealth period arose from a great concern for the salvation of souls, although it must be admitted that it was limited to the geographical confines of the country or "Christendom." The isolated example of John Eliot preaching to the New England Indians throws into relief the fact that the great majority of his contemporaries, like the members and elders of Stephen Leacock's mythical church of St. Osoph, contemplated the world of pagan, Jew, Turk, and Infidel as "a world of sin whose approaching fate it neither denied nor deplored." [6] On the other hand when revival came in 1736, it was started by a Calvinist, Whitefield, and when it overflowed into the great missionary movement at the end of the century, it was largely

---

[4] *Ibid.*, p. 196. "O Thou eternal Victim, slain
　　　　A sacrifice for guilty man,
　　　　By the eternal Spirit made
　　　　An offering in the sinner's stead,
　　　　Our everlasting Priest art Thou,
　　　　And plead'st Thy death for sinners now."
[5] Charles Wesley quoted in Cave, *op. cit.*, p. 211.
[6] *Arcadian Adventures with the Idle Rich* (Bodley Head, 6th reprint, 1952), p. 125.

due to the initiative of Calvinists like William Carey, Joshua Marshman, and David Bogue. They did not accept the strict logic of their theology: even though the doctrine of Election was at first used by those who tried to stifle the missionary enthusiasm of the youthful Carey, it became a great evangelical incentive, for to the Elect of God was given the responsibility of seeking those whom the Lord had predestined to salvation, wherever they were to be found. Furthermore, to kneel at the Cross oneself and enter there the agony undergone by the Son of God for the world was to experience a gratitude which flowed out in a like compassion for the world he came to save.

For these reasons, as we are reminded by P. T. Forsyth, although the eighteenth century was dominated by humanitarian philosophers and scientists, those who showed real compassion in Christian missions, and we might add, concern for the slaves, for the illiterate and for the prisoner, were not the broad-minded thinkers but men whose deepest convictions were governed by what we should regard as a very narrow religious creed: "a gospel deep enough has all the breadth of the world in its heart." [7] This depth they had in the doctrine of the Atonement that stood at the center of their faith and experience. For if this which I witness on the Cross is the love which Christ in his compassion showed toward me, and if this is the kind of self-giving righteousness which is imputed to me and which through the Holy Spirit is to be formed in me, then I can do no other than give myself for his work in his world.

2. New Thinking for a New World

Although the evangelical endeavor can be seen as a fulfillment of that which was best in Calvinism, it could not but bring about the drastic revision and even collapse of many of the old categories of Puritan theology, and in particular the penal theory of the Atonement. As the world was opened up and the teeming races of men were revealed, the very compassion that was born of salvation in the Cross of Christ began to question whether God in his mercy could have consigned so many souls to perdition. Moreover, the revelation of the extent of humanity also revealed the extent of human suffering. This came at a time when more than ever before people were beginning to

---

[7] P. T. Forsyth, *The Work of Christ* (Independent Press, 5th impression, 1952), p. 62.

be sensitive to the sufferings of others in a way which was soon to abolish slavery, reform prisons, start educational ventures, and improve social legislation. People were becoming conscious of how the other half of the world lived, and that threw up in a dark and tragic paradox the extreme misery and cruel pain in which a good many of them died. It showed that although

> We may not know, we cannot tell,
> What pains He had to bear,[8]

many millions of his human brethren had to suffer, at least physically, deaths approaching his own in horror and torment. It meant that it was extremely difficult to speak in quantitative terms about the sufferings of Christ and impossible to concentrate upon them as the unique satisfaction given for the sins of men.

It is difficult to prove how far general cultural factors affected the eventual criticism of the penal theory. Undoubtedly the spread of Deism, Arianism, and Unitarianism during the eighteenth century played its part in undermining the whole Calvinist system of thought, but perhaps these deviations from orthodox faith were less the causes than the symptoms of the reasons for criticism that were more serious because they were less self-concious. The rising demand to humanize criminal law and reform the prisons, associated first with the name of John Howard and later with that of Elizabeth Fry, was the outcome of a change in popular sentiment regarding criminal punishment, which could not but ultimately hold implications for a theology centered in a "penal" theory of Atonement. By the end of the eighteenth century a new wind of criticism was blowing against all the venerable and accepted institutions and beliefs—political, social, and religious—and if in the political arena this showed itself in the American War of Independence, the French Revolution, and in movements that led up to the events of 1848 and the *Communist Manifesto*, we must not forget that the spirit of criticism was bred and fostered in the writings of such men as Jean-Jacques Rousseau, Edward Gibbon, Thomas Paine, and the Romanticists. This spirit of criticism was not limited to the historical movements and events that it helped to produce.

[8] "There is a green hill far away," Cecil Frances Alexander (1818-1895).

Partly as evidence of this general spirit of criticism and partly in its own right might be mentioned the increasing interest in the biological and physical sciences, which discounted the validity of "faith" and tended to reduce the authority of revealed religion. Darwin's *Origin of Species* was not published until 1859, but it was only the culminating event in a process which had been going on for many years. In the same way, although we can say that the whole field of biblical criticism was opened out by the appointment of Ferdinand Christian Baur to the chair of theology at Tübingen in 1826, his appointment was simply evidence of a new openness to critical thought that had already become fashionable. His views had to some extent already been anticipated by the Deists of the previous century.

These are indications of the intellectual climate in which theology had to justify itself during the middle decades of the nineteenth century. They are also ways of showing that the penal theory of the Atonement, as it had been commonly expressed for 150 years, had outlived its usefulness and outstayed its welcome: the attack on it was inevitable.

3. The Break with Calvinism in Britain: McLeod Campbell

By the middle of the nineteenth century the time was ripe for a complete revision of the doctrine, and with the publication in 1856 of John McLeod Campbell's book, *The Nature of the Atonement*,[*] we enter the modern period in our subject. We also enter into what is perhaps the period when there was the most concentrated attempt to rethink the doctrine in the history of the Christian Church. Because Anglo-Saxon theology has made one of its most important contributions to the theology of the Church in this, we shall examine the most significant works in some detail.

To break with the past often demands great courage and personal sacrifice. McLeod Campbell (1800-1872) was a Presbyterian minister in Calvinistic Scotland and had been ordained minister of the parish of Row in Argyllshire in 1825, but because of his views on the Atonement he was twice brought before the General Assembly of the Church of Scotland and eventually condemned as heretical and deprived of his living. His followers built him a church in Glasgow, but although

---

[*] The quotations are from the 6th ed. (Macmillan, 1906).

Campbell continued writing and preaching until his death in 1872, he consistently refused to become the center of a new sect or to join himself to any other branch of the Church.

Immediately on picking up Campbell's book we are aware that we are in the "modern" period of church history. In the Introduction to the second edition he distinguished two tendencies in the thought of his time which made belief in the Atonement difficult. The first was in the current ideas of human progress, and the second was in the fact that the idea of a personal God was being lost in scientific conceptions of universal causes and natural laws. We are at once in a climate near to that of our own day. But although Campbell recognized the difficulties for personal faith raised by the new scientific attitudes, he did not withdraw the absolute claims of the gospel, for he regarded it as "altogether reasonable to ask from scientific men that they should first deal with the claim which the kingdom of God makes on their faith, as what is addressed to them in common with all other men." [10]

In his view the way to reconcile the idea of atonement with the contemporary trends was to concentrate upon the Incarnation—not on the Incarnation alone was being in itself the Atonement, but in the Incarnation as inevitably developing into the Atonement.[11] He found the center of this in our Lord's exposition of the Fatherhood of God and in our personal participation in his divine Sonship: "What God is in that He is love is what God wills us to be." [12] All our Lord's life was a witness to the Fatherhood of God and his Sonship in the Father, and Campbell asked if these were ideas that could command our faith. If they were, then they involved not a blind credulity but "the welcome to a Father's voice, which is the germ of the life of sonship." [13] So he defended our Lord's miracles as "acts of faith and of the divine acknowledgement of faith" [14] based upon the mutual relationship of trust between the Father and the Son.

The relationship of this to our study is shown when he declared that "it is to our personal relation to God as the Father of our spirits that the atonement belongs." [15] This illustrates not only the spirit and

---

[10] Campbell, op. cit., p. xxxiii.
[11] Ibid., p. xviii-xx.
[12] Ibid., p. xxvii.
[13] Ibid., p. xxxii.
[14] Ibid., p. xxxvii.
[15] Ibid., p. xxxix.

temper of Campbell's work but also some of the basic presuppositions upon which it rests; it also makes clear that he was trying to replace at the heart of the doctrine of the Atonement the idea of personal reconciliation between God and man which is the root meaning of the word.

The Nature of the Atonement is not written in an easy style, although the late R. S. Franks described it as the most systematic and masterly volume produced by a British theologian on the work of Christ during the nineteenth century. Its real significance, however, is not in its method but in the way Campbell liberated theology from the old categories in which it conventionally thought of the atoning work of Christ.

He began by defining three questions that concern the doctrine. The question of scope: for whom was it accomplished? The question of purpose: what was it intended to accomplish? The question of its nature: what was it that was accomplished? At the time of the Reformation the issue between the Reformers and the Church of Rome had concentrated upon the second question. In the subsequent disputes within Protestantism itself it was the first question that came to the fore. Campbell proposed to deal with the last of the questions.

The Atonement is the way which God prepared to bridge the gap between our present sinful state and "the good of which God saw the capacity still to remain with us." [16] Campbell emphasized the reasonableness of the demand that we should be able to understand what it is, for the internal evidence of atonement within us "ought to be the securest stronghold of Christianity" and not an unknowable mystery.[17] Conscience, the biblical attitude to sin, the hope of eternal life, and belief in divine forgiveness (which is itself the first demand of the gospel) are all testimonies to our need of atonement, but it is a true instinct in us which recognizes that atonement must mean cost. Against the too easy idea of atonement often put forward by Socinian writers, Campbell insisted that love which is worth anything must necessarily cost a great deal, and infinite love can only be expressed at infinite cost. At the same time he maintained that we may have hope for reconciliation with God not only in the fact of God's love but also

[16] *Ibid.*, p. 4.
[17] *Ibid.*, p. 5.

in his righteousness—he is our Savior *because* he is a just God.[18]

Campbell analyzed the teaching of Luther in the *Commentary on Galatians* and then Calvinism, first in the works of John Owen and Jonathan Edwards, and secondly in the writings of contemporary theologians. He anticipated Aulén by showing that Luther had stressed the "classic" note of victory over the law, sin, death, and the devil [19] and it is perhaps significant that in seeking to illustrate the quintessence of the "Calvinism" to which he was opposed, he turned to the works of Owen and Edwards rather than to Calvin himself. He thought that the basic conception of the Calvinist writers was that of law, and it is interesting to notice that in this respect he regarded "rectoral justice" as simply a variation of the fundamental Calvinist position.

What is the atoning element in the work of Christ? The Puritans and their followers had seen it in the actual pain of Christ's sufferings on the Cross. Campbell confessed that he was not surprised at that, "being indeed that for which alone, on this view, a necessity existed; but my surprise is," he continued, "that these sufferings being contemplated as an atonement for sin, the holiness and love seen taking the form of suffering should not be recognized as the atoning elements—the very essence and adequacy of the sacrifice for sin presented to our faith." [20] He insisted that the Atonement must be seen in its own light and pointed to the zeal [i.e., obedience] of Phineas as an illustration of the quality that could turn away the wrath of God:[21] "The will of God which the Son of God came to do and did, this was the essence and substance of the atonement." [22] This is a focal point in the book because Campbell then turned to his own systematic exposition.

Chapter VI contains what is the core of his view:

That oneness of mind with the Father, which towards man took the form of condemnation of sin, would in the Son's dealing with the Father in relation to our sins, take the form of a perfect confession of our sins. This confession, as to its own nature, must have been a *perfect Amen* in

---

[18] *Ibid.*, p. 26.
[19] *Ibid.*, pp. 31, 42.
[20] *Ibid.*, pp. 99-100.
[21] Num. 25:10-13.
[22] Campbell, *op. cit.*, pp. 106-7.

humanity to the judgment of God on the sin of man. Such an Amen was due in the truth of things.... He [i.e., Christ] responds to it [the divine wrath against sin] with a perfect response,—a response from the depths of that divine humanity—and in that perfect response He absorbs it. For that response has all the elements of a perfect repentance in humanity for all the sin of man,—a perfect sorrow—a perfect contrition—all the elements of such repentance, and that in absolute perfection, all—excepting the personal consciousness of sin;—and by that perfect response in Amen to the mind of God in relation to sin is the wrath of God rightly met, and that is accorded to the divine justice which is its due, and could alone satisfy it.[23]

Taking the view that the Atonement was simply the fulfillment of the Incarnation, he argued that the Incarnation did not merely make atonement possible but inevitable. But the suffering that our Lord endured was no more penal than the suffering and tears of a parent over a wayward child can be considered as penal. Our Lord's vicarious "confession" for us was followed by his intercession—Christ as our Mediator—but this intercession was not an intercession "which contemplated effecting a change in the heart of the Father, but a confession which combined with acknowledgement of the righteousness of the divine wrath against sin, hope for man from that love in God which is deeper than wrath." [24]

So much for the "retrospective" aspect of the work of Christ, but the ultimate aim of the Atonement was prospective—it is "the desire of the divine love that we should become." [25] Christ in his obedience and suffering revealed both the Fatherhood of God and the hidden capacities in humanity, the possibility of sonship, which is eternal life. Our access to God must therefore be in the spirit of Jesus Christ his Son, and this reveals something of the relationship between the "blood" of Christ and our worship—God the Father seeks "the worship which is sonship." "But it further appears to me," he went on to say, "that this conception of the worship for which the blood of Christ is to qualify, sheds back a light on the atonement," for God did demand an atoning sacrifice and "the Father's heart did demand the shedding of blood in order to the remission of sins, because it de-

[23] *Ibid.*, pp. 116-18.
[24] *Ibid.*, p. 127.
[25] *Ibid.*, p. 130.

manded blood in which justice would be rendered to the fatherliness which had been sinned against, and which, therefore, would have virtue in it to purge our spirits from their unfilial state, and to purify us in respect of the pollution that attaches to us as rebellious children." [26] Campbell's contradiction or apparent lack of clarity at this point is due to the fact that he is using the term "blood" in quite a different way from that in which it was used by the theology that he is attacking. It meant to him not so much the *actual* blood shed by Christ in suffering as what we shall see it meant to Bishop Hicks, the response to the Father which our Lord made throughout his life and which poured itself out in blood on the Cross.

To some extent he anticipated the views put forward by Bishop Hicks[27] when he argued that in the Mosaic institution the blood of the victim was intended to purify and prepare the person for whom it was offered for participation in worship. He emphasized the sacrificial idea of our Lord's work by showing that Christ came not to win propitiation, reconciliation, and peace for us, but that he was *in himself* our propitiation, reconciliation, and peace. The verse "the blood of Jesus Christ cleanseth us from all sin" was to be explained not as taking from us our liability to punishment for sin but as a cleansing "having reference to the pollution of sin itself." [28] This ethical concept is taken up later when he declared that "in no view of the atonement can the crucifixion be separated from the previous life of which it was the close." [29]

It is this ethical element in the Atonement—or as Campbell would say, the "prospective" aspect—that illustrates most pointedly the shift of emphasis from the reigning theory and the new basis for most of the theories that were to follow after Campbell. All the theories based upon a conception of "satisfaction" or "ransom" had concentrated upon describing the objective fact of what God in Christ *had done* for our salvation, but most of the views that have followed since McLeod Campbell have put their primary emphasis upon what God in Christ *is* doing and *will* do to save us from sin and have interpreted the facts of the Gospel as the supreme example of general moral and

[26] *Ibid.*, p. 159.
[27] Cf. infra ch. vii, sec. 3, ad. loc.
[28] Campbell, *op. cit.*, p. 169.
[29] *Ibid.*, p. 176.

THE ATONEMENT AND THE SACRAMENTS

spiritual principles. They are variations on Abelard, and they raise the question whether, in the final issue, the believer places his ultimate reliance in what Christ has done for him, or in a general spiritual principle that Christ's Passion illustrates and which we are invited to follow.

This is a generalization, and like all generalizations it may be false. The issue is not as clear-cut as I have suggested, for even as good a Calvinist as Augustus Toplady could see the need of holding the objective and subjective aspects of the Atonement together—

> Be of sin the double cure,
> Cleanse me from its guilt and power.

Furthermore, Campbell would have insisted that his view was based upon an objective conception of the Atonement, for Christ had made a vicarious "confession" for us which because of our own sin we could not make for ourselves. This objective element is revealed as he traced the significance of such terms as "the hour," [30] "the cup," "the baptism" [31] to Jesus himself in the light of his imminent Passion. He even quoted the words of George Whitefield approvingly, that because of our corruption in sin even "our repentance needeth to be repented of, and our very tears to be washed in the blood of Christ." [32]

Nevertheless, when we have properly qualified our generalization, it is still true to say that for Campbell this "objective" action of Christ was centered more in a moral and spiritual attitude than in the historic act itself. Regarding the Cross, he insists, "In respect even of all that was most physical and external, the real value and virtue was strictly moral and spiritual: for the tasting of death for us was not as a substitute,—otherwise He alone would have died: nor as a punishment,—for, tasted in the strength of righteousness and of the Father's favour, death had to Him no sting; but as a moral and spiritual sacrifice for sin." [33] Our Lord's sufferings upon the Cross "are *not* the *measure* of what God can inflict, but the revelation of what God *feels*." This means that the *real* Atonement is seen in the recapitulation of the same attitude and response in us—the *real* salvation is in being saved

[30] John 12:27; cf. Luke 22:53.
[31] Luke 12:50. Cf. 12:53; Mark 14:36.
[32] Campbell, op. cit., p. 124.
[33] Ibid., p. 261.

from the power of sin here and now, and upon this the eschatalogical hope for the believer ultimately depends.

As with all varieties of the Moral Theory, McLeod Campbell's view of the Atonement gains an easily explained theory of the doctrine at the expense of having to hold out to men simply the moral and spiritual conditions for a salvation which they must themselves win. Think what he is implying when he writes, "His death as a propitiation for sin, tasted in the spirit of sonship, and in unity with the Father in His condemnation of sin, that is to say, death, *as tasted by Christ*,—must be not only apprehended by our faith, but also spiritually shared in by us." [34] He maintained that this was not the same as simply inviting men to follow our Lord's example because through the objective and vicarious "confession" that our Lord has made for us, we have an organic relationship with him as branches to the vine "which is quite different from a purely voluntary association."

But is this organic relationship something we have with Christ by virtue of being men, or by virtue of being believers and having entered into the death of Christ? Campbell thinks of the organic relationship with our Lord in terms of the second alternative rather than the first. For him the verse from the parable of the Prodigal Son, "this, my son, was dead, and is alive again," illustrates the spiritual change from death to life to which we are called. It must be understood evangelically and therefore in terms of atonement—in this way the Christian becomes "a living Epistle to the grace of God," [35] and in this way he is called to take up the Cross of Christ himself.[36]

What are we to say as critique of McLeod Campbell's position? It is quite clear that with the appearance of his book we have broken entirely with the old forms in which the doctrine of the work of Christ was normally cast, and we are conscious that we are not only in an atmosphere that is nearer to our own ways of thought, but we also sense that we are nearer to the spirit of the New Testament..

On the other hand we cannot ignore the fact that McLeod Campbell presents us not with a picture but a theory. In their most enlightened moments the older theologians gave us a series of images which represented the work of Christ to us pictorially. They expounded the

[34] *Ibid.*, p. 264.
[35] *Ibid.*, p. 310.
[36] *Ibid.*, p. 319.

Atonement, but they expounded it in terms which demanded understanding not so much by the intellect but by the imagination and the heart. McLeod Campbell, despite his deep insights and reverent treatment, has presented us with a theory which demands first of all to be either accepted or rejected by the intellect, and it is as a theory which tries to *explain* the Atonement that it must therefore be judged.

1. The first criticism that can be offered against it is in Campbell's use of the phrase "Christ's confession of our sins" and still more with the underlying conception contained in it which is basic to Campbell's view. As Scott Lidgett pointed out a good many years ago,[37] it was impossible for our Lord to confess our sins, for not only is it impossible for anyone to "confess" the sins of another but it is even more impossible for our Lord who knew no sin to confess the sins that we have committed—perhaps the one thing that he could not do for us. Canon Moberly regarded McLeod Campbell's phrase as "almost a disastrous one," but he suggested that it does not do justice to Campbell's real thought and that what he meant was that our Lord confessed the sin of humanity "by *being* the very manifestation of humanity, in its ideal reality of penitential holiness, before the Father." [38] Undoubtedly this is what McLeod Campbell meant, but how far it affects the fundamental criticism, we shall have more reason to discuss when we examine Moberly's own contribution to the subject.

2. Campbell does not tell us how the work of Christ is to bear its fruit in men: he failed to link the Atonement with Pentecost and with the work of the Holy Spirit. In R. C. Moberly's phrase, he "discerned with more complete success the nature of the relation of Christ to God, than that of the relation of men to Christ," [39] and Moberly went on to point out that the book does not mention the Eucharist. *The Nature of the Atonement* is weak at those points where those who hold to an objective Atonement are usually strong, for however distant this atoning act of Christ might appear to be, the Reformers and their followers had insisted on its real and effective

---

[37] Scott Lidgett, *The Spiritual Principle of the Atonement* (Charles H. Kelly, 1898), pp. 177-78. Cf. also Horace Bushnell, *Forgiveness and Law* (1874), pp. 28-32.
[38] R. C. Moberly, *Atonement and Personality* (John Murray, 1901), 7th reprint (1911), p. 405.
[39] *Ibid.*, p. 402.

relation to contemporary men through the Holy Spirit's work in the individual, in the Church, and in the Sacraments.

3. This omission in Campbell means that for all the apparent objectivity of Christ's vicarious work, the effective appropriation of grace depends upon our own effort. His theory is easy to explain, but the Atonement he described is hard to win.

Nevertheless, when we have said this, we must agree with R. C. Moberly that it is hardly possible to over-emphasize "the debt which Christian thought owes to that reverent spirit," [40] McLeod Campbell. His book at once cut theology loose from sterile and outmoded categories and placed the discussion on a new basis. He showed that if the doctrine was to be taken seriously, it must not merely be consistent with the letter of Scripture but with the spirit of the gospel. Those who wrote on the subject thereafter would have to be more concerned with seeing that their theories were in sympathy with the spirit of the New Testament than with using the Scriptures as a source book of proof texts. McLeod Campbell reminded the theological world that God is a moral God—a Christian God, who could not act in a way that was morally inferior to that revelation of his nature which had been manifested in the life and death and resurrection of Jesus Christ his Son.

4. The Break with Calvinism in America: Horace Bushnell

There is a very close parallel between the career of McLeod Campbell and that of his American counterpart, Horace Bushnell. Most of the factors in the British scene that made for the radical criticism and re-assessment of Calvinist doctrine were also operative in America. Horace Bushnell (1802-1881) was born in Litchfield, Connecticut, and after graduating from Yale returned as a tutor, where after a considerable religious struggle he made a great impression upon the students by deciding to enter the ministry. It should be remembered that the churches of New England had been split by Unitarianism, and that whereas in England the main sufferers had been the Presbyterian churches south of the Scottish border, in America the impact had been felt most strongly within the recently disestablished Congregational Churches in Massachusetts and Connecticut. Bushnell's de-

---

[40] *Ibid.*

cision to become a minister should be seen within this situation which had to some extent brought theology and the ministerial vocation into disrepute. His work on the Atonement was, at least in part, an attempt to put the Trinitarian faith on a firmer theological foundation by removing the obsolete forms of doctrine with which it had become associated. He was ordained minister of the North Church in Hartford in 1833 and remained there until he retired to devote himself to writing and preaching in 1859. He traveled widely in Europe, and something of his influence may be judged from the remark of the redoubtable Scottish scholar, Sir George Adam Smith, that Bushnell's sermons were to be found on the shelves of every manse in Scotland.

Nevertheless, Bushnell had to face a similar kind of opposition and personal frustration to McLeod Campbell's. On the publication of his first book, *God in Christ* (1849), ministerial colleagues attacked him for heterodoxy in the Consociation of churches, and after a long and bitter struggle his congregation withdrew from the Consociation. But the fact that the congregations of both Campbell and Bushnell supported them so loyally in their troubles, although small enough fact in itself, does have a certain modest significance that might be overlooked. It reminds us that these men approached the problem of reinterpreting their theology from the imperative claims of the pastoral ministry, and it suggests that the new evaluation of the gospel that they put forward had at least met the spiritual needs of the people to whom they ministered.

Horace Bushnell's first book on the Atonement, *The Vicarious Sacrifice*, was published in 1866. In his Introduction he reminds us that no theory of the doctrine has won universal acceptance within the Church, although he believed that there had been a certain historical recurrence of interest in the Moral Theory. He shows a very great and somewhat surprising admiration for Anselm and thought that no writer was ever more unfortunate "in the feeble, undiscerning constructions put upon his argument, by the immense following that has accepted his mastership." [41] Anselm did not think of *justitia* as "retributive justice under the offended wrath-principle of God's nature," but simply as "righteousness." Bushnell maintained that not only was the atoning principle of perfect obedience to be found in Anselm's

---

[41] Horace Bushnell, *The Vicarious Sacrifice* (Sampson Low, 1866), p. xv.

work, but also that the view which the archbishop put forward was very far from any conception of satisfaction by suffering or substitutionary punishment.[42] He said of the theory to be found in the *Cur Deus Homo*, "It is the seed view, in a sense, of the almost annual harvest that has followed; and as all choice seedlings are apt to degenerate in their successive propagations, we are obliged to admit that this original, first form of the doctrine was incomparably better than almost any of the revisions, or enlarged expositions of it since given." [43]

On the other hand Bushnell had not a great deal of use for the so-called "classic" or "patristic" theory that Anselm displaced and regarded it as "very coarse" and "wild looking," although he admitted that there had been considerable degeneration from the original ideas that had brought it into being. Nevertheless, when he himself was moved to describe the meaning of our Lord's death upon the Cross, we find him, in at least one passage, doing so in language which for all its nineteenth-century idiom reproduced the thought and symbols of Martin Luther and the Fathers:

> He came out from the righteousness of God, verily He lived in the world, and now He has gone up clad in its honours to reign. And the justice of God—what is now so visible, as that the Cross itself is God's mightiest deed of judgment? for here goes down, as by a thunderstroke, the prince of this world—all the organically dominating powers of evil; its fashions, its pride, its pomp of condition, its tremendous codes of false opinions, all its lies, all its usurpations. These overgrown tyrannies upon souls are hurled, like Dagon to the ground; and Pilate and the priests, and the senators, and the mob, and the soldiers, are all seen choking in dumb silence, before the Cross and the judgment-day quaking and blackness of the scene. Poor sinning mortals! How weak do they look! How like to culprits judged.[44]

Had Luther belonged to the nineteenth century, he could hardly have done any better.

Like Campbell, of course, Bushnell directed his main attack against the penal theory of the Atonement. If penal substitution is all there is to the doctrine, then he forthrightly declared that there was a good

---

[42] *Ibid.*, p. xxiv.
[43] *Ibid.*, p. xv-xvi.
[44] *Ibid.*, p. 338.

deal to disgust us in God's method of squaring accounts, and he was bitterly scathing against those who thought of the Atonement in terms of a compensation paid to God's justice. He declared:

> On the whole this matter of a contrived compensation to justice which so many take for a gospel, appears to contain about the worst reflexion upon God's justice that could be stated.... The justice satisfied is satisfied with injustice! The forgiveness prepared is forgiveness on the score of pay! the judgment-day award disclaims the fact of forgiveness after payment made, and even refuses to be satisfied, taking payment again! What meantime has become of the penalties threatened, and where is the truth of the law? The penalties threatened, as against wrong-doers, are not to be executed on them, because they have been executed on a right-doer! viz., Christ.[45]

That seems to dispose of the matter, for any theory of penal substitution which, after this, claims to be the statement of fact rather than the description of grace, cannot avoid the indictment Bushnell makes against it here.

He concentrated even more than Campbell on the Incarnation. To him the Incarnation—admittedly a *redemptive* Incarnation—is the center of the gospel. He declared "the real gospel is the Incarnate Biography itself, making its impression and working its effect as a biography—a total life with all its acts, and facts, and words, and feelings, and principles of good, grouped in the light and shade of their own supernatural unfolding." [46] But perhaps we may be forgiven a smile when, in disclaiming any intention of developing a new theory of the Atonement, Bushnell modestly defined his purpose as "only to exhibit, if possible, the Christ whom so many centuries of discipleship have so visibly been longing and groping after"! [47]

The central idea in Bushnell's conception of the Atonement—that which corresponds to McLeod Campbell's conception of "vicarious confession"—is indicated clearly enough by the title of his book, *The Vicarious Sacrifice*. In the first part he seeks to show us that there is no more in this idea than we are to expect from the nature of God and his Son Jesus Christ.

---

[45] *Ibid.*, p. 241.
[46] *Ibid.*, introduction, p. xxxiv.
[47] *Ibid.*, p. xxxv.

THE ATTACK ON "OBJECTIVITY"

1. In the first chapter he very carefully defines the term "vicarious sacrifice" and shows that although the word "vicarious" carries with it a certain idea of substitution, the word neither means that Christ simply "puts himself into the case of man as a helper," nor does it mean a literal substitution by which he becomes "penally subject to our deserved penalties.... He cannot become guilty for us." [48] According to Bushnell, "vicarious sacrifice" as applied to atonement means that our Lord "simply engages at the expense of great suffering and even of death itself, to bring us out of our sins themselves and so out of their penalties; being Himself profoundly identified with us in our fallen state, and burdened in feeling with our evils." [49] Love is essentially vicarious in its own nature, and Christ took our sins upon himself as he took our sickness and our sorrows, by bearing them in his heart "in the tenderness of his more than human sensibility." [50]

The Incarnation is the great act of identity with the human race. It is in terms of the Incarnation and not in terms of the Atonement that Bushnell admitted that there was a certain penal element in the work of Christ. Near the end of his book, in a chapter on God's "Rectoral Honor," he said that it was integral to the view of vicarious sacrifice that Christ should have shared the condition of evil which is the human lot. In this sense there is a kind of penal condition—an entry into "the curse"—for us that is implicit in his taking human flesh, and because this involved a real incarnation in the fullest sense of the word, he believed that our Lord was born of maculate and not immaculate motherhood.[51]

He wrote about those who are associated with our Lord in his vicarious sacrifice—the Father, the Holy Spirit, the good angels (and they are real angels to Bushnell), and the souls of the redeemed. He was not an iconoclast, and he showed here that his intention was to relate his theory of the Atonement to the Trinitarian faith he accepted. But something of the theological audacity and originality of his mind comes out when he made the somewhat startling statement that "God Himself is not any better than he ought to be, and the

---

[48] *Ibid.*, p. 6.
[49] *Ibid.*, p. 7.
[50] *Ibid.*, p. 9.
[51] *Ibid.*, p. 325.

very essence and glory of His perfection is, that He is just as good as He ought to be." [52] Bushnell argued that there cannot be any goodness over and above goodness itself.

It is for this reason, and because he saw the whole Trinity at work in the redemptive process, that he rejected the philosophical objections to the idea of a passible God. Christ was "God fulfilling the obligations of God," and he suffered throughout his life even as God the Father suffered before him. In this work of atonement, said Bushnell, "the whole Deity is in it, in it from eternity, and will to eternity be. . . . Nay, there is a cross in God before the wood is seen upon Calvary; hid in God's own virtue itself, struggling on heavily in burdened feeling through all the previous ages, and struggling as heavily now even in the throne of the worlds. This too, exactly, is the cross that Christ crucified reveals and sets before us." [53] The whole Trinity is involved absolutely in the Atonement, and in the same way that he asserted the suffering work of God the Father, he described in a magnificent passage the vicarious suffering in the Holy Spirit's work for us (ch. 3).

Bushnell's conception of the "vicarious sacrifice" is, of course, another form of the Moral Theory, and he emphasized this when he described how all the redeemed are involved in the work of Christ. Our Lord sets before us the Cross, and for his followers "obedience unto death is to be a law for them as truly as it was for Him." [54] We may question his assertion that there is no reason to believe that in his ministry and death our Lord made a greater sacrifice than did the apostle Paul in his laborious and dangerous missionary life and martyr's death—I imagine Paul would have been the first to disagree with him. But Bushnell and Campbell were certainly right to insist that the ethical aspect of salvation and its fruits in the outpouring of Christian service for the world are aspects of Atonement which had been all too easily ignored. Declared Bushnell:

The supreme art of the devil never invented a greater mischief to be done, or a theft more nearly amounting to the stealing of the cross itself, than filching away thus, from the followers of Christ, the conviction that

[52] *Ibid.*, p. 21.
[53] *Ibid.*, pp. 35-36.
[54] *Ibid.*, p. 74.

they are thoroughly to partake the sacrifice of their Master.... Christ in His suffering love gets never the just degree of power in our feeling, till we are able to love His love and suffer with Him in His suffering. Here only it is that He touches us at the quick, and becomes the soul-renewing power of God. Vicarious love in Him answered by vicarious love in us, tiny and weak though it be, as an insect life fluttering responsively to the sun—this is the only footing of grace in which Christ is truly received, and according to His glorious power.[55]

2. In the second part of his book Bushnell was concerned to show the life and sacrifice of Christ as that which makes him a renovating and saving power. The centrality of the Incarnation to his thought is seen in the affirmation that Christ did not come to earth in order to die, but that he died because he was here. He discovered a special significance in the healing ministry of our Lord but declared that our Lord's prime concern was to heal the souls of men—to reconcile them with God. It is in this section of his book that Bushnell reveals traits that were later to find their full expression in liberal theology. He firmly believed in progressive revelation and maintained that the power of Christ's name was increasing in the world and that it would continue to do so by penetrating all the social and political forms of life until it finally achieved "a complete domination over the race. So the power is working and so it will till it reigns."

If from the twentieth century's position of chastened realism we are tempted to look down upon Bushnell's exuberant optimism, let us do him the justice of remembering that his words were published in 1866. The positive element was his belief that the Atonement of Jesus Christ had something to say to the social and political institutions of his day, and that is a faith which the Christians of the twentieth century might well try to recapture.

A sentimental element, however, entered his theology when he affirmed that the foremost thing that we see in our Lord is not his infinite holiness or sovereign purity but his human qualities—"we like the Friend before we love the Saviour." [56] That may be in a sense true, but we feel that here he is speaking as a preacher rather than as a theologian, and what he said left the way open for others to assume that liking the Friend was the equivalent of loving the Savior.

[55] *Ibid.*, p. 81-4.
[56] *Ibid.*, p. 111.

On the other hand in fairness it should be admitted that Bushnell, no less than Campbell before him, in putting forward his moral view of the work of Christ denied that our Lord is simply our Example. We need far more than "a model to be copied," for we need something that is able to "copy God" into the soul.

3. Horace Bushnell wrote *Forgiveness and Law* (1874) to take the place of Parts III and IV of *The Vicarious Sacrifice*, but there are still passages in the sections he wished to discard which are worth our consideration. Nevertheless, it is undoubtedly here that he laid himself open to some grave objections, for he maintained that there was a law of "Right" before God's will was instituted and that that law is primary. If, in accordance with Bushnell's own view, God simply acts in conformity with his own nature, then he and he alone is primary, but Bushnell sometimes speaks almost as if the Law of Right were itself the First Cause.

On the other hand his reason for taking this position is perfectly clear, since he wishes to undercut the argument of those theologians who held that "God creates all law by His will, and can make anything right, or obligatory, by His enactment"—a view which had been used to support arbitrary and amoral elements in the theory of penal substitution. We must remember that Bushnell was not writing his book as an exercise in abstract thinking but that he was doing his best to destroy a theory that he regarded as thoroughly pernicious. Despite the impression that he sometimes gives us in this section that he regards Law as the First Cause, Bushnell's fundamental contention is that God does not act contrary to his own nature and that the Atonement rests upon the nature of God himself.

It is to this fundamental point that he returned in *Forgiveness and Law*—the redemption of Man depends on the very nature of God, which finds its essential expression in the character of righteousness. God in Christ undertakes atonement for men *because* he is righteous and must therefore go beyond the boundaries of strict justice. In reply to those who thought that God's holiness prevented him from being able to forgive sin, Bushnell exclaimed, "God too holy to forgive an enemy! Rather judge that forgiveness is itself the supreme joy of holiness, whether in God or man." [57]

---

[57] Bushnell, *op. cit.* (New York: Scribner, Armstrong & Co., 1874), p. 56.

THE ATTACK ON "OBJECTIVITY"

However, his main intention in *Forgiveness and Law* was to show that there is no fundamental antagonism between the demands of the Law and the promises of the gospel. In his earlier book he had said that God "should seem, in his justice, to say that he will suffer no jot or tittle of the law to fail; and then to make the saying still more certainly good, He should, for the law's sake, add such an argument of love and mercy, as will restore both jot and tittle and, if possible, the whole broken body of the law." [58] *Forgiveness and Law* is a commentary on this theme by which the writer showed that in the Christian Gospel God does this, for the aim of Atonement is to bring about redemption from sin by implanting within the hearts of men the character and commandments of Jesus Christ.

Arguing that human experience provides us with the best parallels —the "analogical sub-gospels"—he showed, in such normal relationships as that of the mother and her child, the teacher and his pupil, and the general and his troops, that there is an essential relationship between law and grace. But it is of the essence of these relationships that although "grace" more than fulfills the conditions of the law, the law is not thereby destroyed: the two things are autonomous within distinct spheres, and both serve the end, which is to build up character. The boy who has been under the necessary rules of his mother's household as a child will at the end joyfully be obedient to his mother's will simply because he loves his mother, but the principle of law is not thereby destroyed or made unnecessary. "Plainly enough," Bushnell declared, "the law of God never can be taken away from any world or creature. . . . A thousand crosses, ransoms, atonements, would leave it exactly where it was. The taking away of sin was possible, but no taking away of the law. The sacrifice of Calvary itself, set against the law, would have had as little effect on it as upon the principles of Euclid." [59] The purpose of this argument is, of course, to press home the point that the Atonement means an ethical regeneration that will write Christ's nature into the life of man. The period between the writing of this later book and that of *The Vicarious Sacrifice* deepened Horace Bushnell's understanding of the cost that is involved in real forgiveness—he might have gained the point from McLeod Campbell—for even when he argued that we might expect

---
[58] Bushnell, *The Vicarious Sacrifice*, p. 230.
[59] Bushnell, *Forgiveness and Law*, p. 119.

forgiveness from the very nature of God, he did not assume, as some later liberals assumed, that forgiveness is easy for God and therefore almost automatic. There is a paradox here in the gospel. The most holy men "forgive the most easily," but they also are those who are the "most deeply wounded by wrong," and therefore, for God himself the cost of forgiving is the most costly of all.

If God forgives in this way, this is the experience of atonement into which we are called (by the example of Christ) to share, "but whosoever longs to live in the bright cordiality of brotherhood, and have the true enjoyment of his kind, must atone himself into the gentleness and patience of love all the way." [60] For us this is the call of the cross, and whether or not we regard the results as worth what they cost us will depend on the kind of world we want God to give us—a world that consists only of pleasure and rewards, or a world of moral adventure where tragedy and the joy of a costly forgiveness are possible. We need to read Bushnell's words here alongside what Dietrich Bonhoeffer said about "cheap grace." [61]

Horace Bushnell stands out as one of the most provocative, and at the same time one of the most essentially Christian writers of the nineteenth century. In spite of his reassertion of the moral theory of Atonement—"I recant no one of my denials" [62] —there was nothing weak about the figure of Jesus or the gospel that he presented. In almost Forsythian language he declared, "He, the terrible Christ, is the Christ we want. The other I strongly suspect is a conceit of human opinion, representing only a phase or fashion of the time, that will be very soon gone by; while the real Immanuel, coming in much mystery, and raising many hard questions, and fitly called Wonderful, will be proving in all time, His great power and beneficence, only more sublimely." [63]

Like others who have written with understanding on this doctrine, he was essentially an evangelist and a pastor. He said that one of the

---

[60] Ibid., p. 49; but cf. the whole chapter.
[61] "Cheap grace is the preaching of forgiveness without requiring repentance, baptism without Church discipline, Communion without confession, absolution without contrition. Cheap grace is grace without discipleship, grace without the Cross, grace without Jesus Christ, living and incarnate." *The Cost of Discipleship* by Dietrich Bonhoeffer, E. T. by R. H. Fuller (London: S.C.M., 1948), p. 38; The German *Nachfolge* was first published in Munich in 1937.
[62] Bushnell, *Forgiveness and Law*, p. 12.
[63] Bushnell, *The Vicarious Sacrifice*, p. 304.

reasons that stimulated him to review the Atonement was the conviction that the Church must clarify its doctrine at this point as she took more and more responsibility for foreign missions.[64] All through his work he balanced the need for doctrinal restatement against his pastoral concern to find the best pictures in which to present truth to the ordinary person. It is for this reason that he pleaded that the biblical language of sacrifice should not be discarded but given new content, for he maintained that as long as the biblical terms are used to describe the Atonement, the content of the gospel will be eternally safe. He added, "Let anyone contrive to make it safe, by any other guard of orthodoxy, ... and he will not be long in making the discovery that it is gone already." [65]

At the theological level it is worth noting that he is one with McLeod Campbell in anticipating Bishop Hicks's assertion that in the Old Testament sacrifices "the blood is the life." At the more fundamental level he understood and revealed the false position into which a rigid application of the theory of penal substition had forced his Puritan forebears, for he roundly declared that if Christ were wholly other from God, "that would be tritheism and not trinity." Or as he had raised the question previously, "does then God's right hand offer pains to His left, and so make expiation to the sins of the world? How many Gods have we? Not any more truly three, nor less simply one, because we hold the faith of a trinity." [66]

Horace Bushnell's works on the Atonement were just as significant theologically for the American scene as McLeod Campbell's book had been for Britain, but they both represent far more than simply the radical views of two independent but individual thinkers—the ethical figures were to provide the new pattern which the doctrine would take in the attempt to meet the needs of a new age. It is therefore as moral theories, purporting to give an explanation of the Atonement that is all-sufficient, that we must judge them, and it is on that ground that they are open to criticism.

1. In putting forward his view of the Incarnation—which for him was almost identical with the Atonement—Horace Bushnell reveals the great weakness of all theories that explain our redemption exclu-

---

[64] Bushnell, *Forgiveness and Law*, pp. 22-23.
[65] Bushnell, *The Vicarious Sacrifice*, p. 474.
[66] *Ibid.*, p. 425 cf. *Forgiveness and Law*, p. 57.

sively in terms of an ethical response. He says that Christ "had never undertaken to bear God's punishment for us, but had come down simply as in love, to the great river of retributive causes where we were drowning, to pluck us out; and instead of asking the river to stop for Him, He bids it still flow on, descending directly into the elemental rage and tumult, to bring us away." [67]

It is an excellent illustration worthy of the preacher that Bushnell was, but our criticism is that the Christ of the moral theories does not "pluck us out" but having sublimely gone through the flood himself, simply turns and calls us to step out as he does. The command "Follow me!" to the disciples ended in the self-revelation that they could not follow him, for Peter denied him, Thomas doubted him, Judas betrayed him, and the rest fled. Only after the objective events of Good Friday, Easter Sunday, Ascension, and Pentecost—events which dragged them from the flood despite themselves—were they able to obey his original command.

2. The moral theories can so often descend to sentiment. In the first chapter of *The Vicarious Sacrifice* Bushnell says:

Here then, as I conceive, is the true seed principle of the Christian salvation. What we call the vicarious sacrifice of Christ is nothing strange as regards the principle of it, no superlative, unexampled, and therefore unintelligible grace. It only does and suffers, and comes into substitution for, just what any and all love will, according to its degree. . . . Given the universality of love, the universality of vicarious sacrifice is given also. Here is the centre and deepest spot of good, or goodness, conceivable. At this point we look into heaven's eye itself, and read the meaning of all heavenly grace.[68]

The passage illustrates both the strength and weakness of Bushnell's theory. It could easily degenerate into mere sentimental grandmotherliness in respect of God's love, although Bushnell himself is not often guilty of this. On the other hand give full weight to the fact that it is God who suffers in this manner, and we see something of the strength of his theory. Indeed, when we give full weight to that and see that it was God who suffered in Christ, must we not part company with

[67] *The Vicarious Sacrifice*, p. 327.
[68] *Ibid.*, p. 12 f.

Bushnell when he speaks of a difference only in "degree"? Is not the very difference of degree so great that it actually constitutes something "wholly other"?

3. This points to another weakness. Bushnell speaks as if Paul, once the truth of the gospel captured his heart, spent his life in the service of others. Paul did not—he spent his life centered *in Christ*, and because of *that* it was given to others. Once he had faced the immeasurable grace of God in Christ, he accepted a life of sacrifice for himself, but he did this not in his own strength but in the strength he had from Christ through the Holy Spirit.

It is significant that both Campbell and Bushnell wrote from the standpoint of the orthodox Trinitarian faith and declared the need for an objective view of the work of Christ. Yet both were responsible for undercutting the traditional forms in which objectivity had been stated and thus opened the door to the kind of subjective thinking that they denied and deplored.

We cannot help noticing that although they had very different methods of dealing with their subject, they arrived at remarkably similar answers, and in comparison with their more "orthodox" contemporaries, we are struck with the modernity of their writing. What they said about the Atonement was fundamentally the same—the Redemption that God offers us must be seen in terms that are consistent with God's own nature, in terms of God's love revealed in the life and death of Jesus Christ. Whether you describe it as "vicarious confession" or as "vicarious sacrifice," it implies the same, an obedience to death in which we are called to participate.

Undoubtedly we can indulge ourselves in the popular theological pastime of being wise after the event and of criticizing the "blind spots" in the theology of Campbell and Bushnell, but we must be forever grateful to these men for being prepared to help the Church meet a world that was becoming indifferent to its theology and nauseated by its dogmatic analogies. They freed the Church from the dead hand of the past in the form of a penal theory that had become calcined into dogma and from metaphors in its use that in becoming old had become morally disgusting. For that we stand in their debt.

CHAPTER V

Old Facts and New Theories

IT IS VERY DIFFICULT AND DANGEROUS TO TRY TO PUT THEOLOGIANS INTO pigeon holes. Seen from the point of strict chronology, the writers with whom we are dealing in this chapter made their contributions to the subject some years after some of those whose work will be considered later. R. C. Moberly was, for example, to some extent influenced by the thought of Bishop Westcott, and both Hastings Rashdall and R. S. Franks wrote some years after the books of Robert Dale and James Denney. Rashdall at least wrote in reaction to them. We need to remind ourselves that that which the chronicler tends to see in terms of lineal continuity actually took place within a dialectical situation where the time factor, although important, was not all-important. A historical perspective should show us that the progress of the ongoing theological discussion is more like a spirited argument interspersed with exclamations and irrelevancies than a series of progressively reasoned monologues.

The theologians who are considered in this chapter are dealt with here not because they follow next in time to McLeod Campbell and Horace Bushnell but because they represent lines of development from the work of the two previous thinkers, and in particular because they took up in one form or another the search that had been initiated by Campbell and Bushnell to find a meaning for the Atonement that was "grounded in principles of universal obligation."

1. "Vicarious Penitence": R. C. Moberly

In some ways R. C. Moberly's *Atonement and Personality* [1] is not the obvious choice with which to begin. But he had been very deeply influenced by McLeod Campbell's book, although by the time his own book was published in 1901, he could hardly help revealing that he

[1] R. C. Moberly, op. cit. Quotations are from the 7th reprint of 1911.

had also come under the influence of other theologians. By that date also there was not quite the same need to attack the Atonement theories as they had been handed down from the Puritans, for Robert Dale's book in defense of the theory of penal substitution had lifted the discussion to a different plane. Therefore Moberly's book adopts a positive rather than a negative attitude to the subject—he is not so much concerned with attacking and destroying the older theories of the Atonement as with presenting a cogent and reasonable alternative to them. Indeed, he is far more conscious of the need for presenting "the objective fact" of what our Lord accomplished than many other exponents of moral influence theories, particularly in his insistence upon the place of the Church and Sacraments in his view of the Atonement. On the other hand he did put forward a "theory" to explain the work of Christ, and his theory is more fully in line with the basic idea of McLeod Campbell than that of any other representative theologian.

Moberly's method is quite different from the majority of other writers on the subject. He begins with a systematic examination of what we mean by "punishment," "penitence," and "forgiveness." His central problem was to relate the work of Christ to the problem of human "personality," for he maintained that we can have no real understanding of atonement without understanding what we mean by personality, nor could "personality" be explained without atonement. Punishment can only apply to beings that have personality, and the lower down the evolutionary scale one travels, the less the idea of "punishment" has any meaning. In the same way "penitence" also has meaning only for beings with personality, but there is also this corollary that the more a human personality is corrupted by sin, the less real penitence becomes possible, for the legacy of past sin prevents true repentance. "The reality of sin in the self blunts the self's power of utter antithesis against sin. Just because it now is part of what I am, I cannot, even though I would, wholly detest it," [2] and therefore, Moberly argued, "The consummation of penitential holiness,—itself, by inherent character, the one conceivable atonement for sin,—would be possible only to the absolutely sinless." [3]

A similar argument can also be conducted with regard to forgive-

[2] *Ibid.*, p. 42.
[3] *Ibid.*, p. 43.

ness, for this quality also is personal; it concerns the relations of persons to persons. If it is not simply to be the remission of punishment, however, if it is to be real forgiveness, it must involve reconciliation and the reinstatement of the erring person to the position he would have had if he had not sinned. If we expect to receive complete forgiveness, then we ought to forgive others completely—"forgive us our trespasses, as we forgive those that trespass against us." Our dilemma is that we cannot. But God's "dilemma" is that he cannot forgive humanity until it can do this. For divine forgiveness is divine love, and as the love of parents for their children "dare not, cannot—being love—forgive, in the height of the [child's] passion," so "love dare not, cannot—being love—fail to forgive, from the moment when forgiveness is possible." [4]

On these grounds Moberly argued the need for the intervention of a mediator between man and God, so that the divine love might be shown as divine forgiveness toward us. Christ fulfilled his atoning work in his obedience, in his unceasing dependence upon God, and this obedience produced in our Lord the only kind of personality that could make the perfect act of penitence toward God. Human nature was guilty of sin, but in taking human nature upon himself without personal sin, our Lord made the act of penitence on behalf of all human nature, for the vengeance of God is reserved only for sin unrepentant.[5]

At the beginning of a chapter on the objective and subjective aspects in atonement Moberly posed the kind of question that is put by the ordinary man who demands "what, after all, putting all make-believe aside, is the real relation of Calvary to me?" The frequency and nature of this question shows that both an objective and a subjective aspect of the Atonement was necessary if the Christian gospel was to meet men's spiritual need. The older theories had contended for a presentation of the doctrine that would show that the Atonement or reconciliation with God had already been accomplished—it was already won—and in so far as they had done that, what they had said was necessary and true. But this could make no difference to the individual unless he was able to apprehend it. "If it is to be—as in

[4] Ibid., p. 64.
[5] Ibid., p. 132.

purpose and capacity it assuredly is—my righteousness, crushing sin for and in me . . . [it] is of necessity that I should be in a certain relation with it: and upon my relation to it its relation to me will ultimately depend." [6]

Moberly's view of the Atonement in the final issue was a variant of the Moral Theory, but it is considerably more, for he made the supremely important point that the Atonement must be seen in terms of Pentecost. "An exposition of atonement," he says, "which leaves out Pentecost, leaves the atonement unintelligible—in relation to us. For what is the real consummation of the atonement to be? It is to be—the very Spirit of the Crucified become our spirit—ourselves translated into the Spirit of the Crucified." [7] In other words he is saying is that the atoning work of Christ brings about the realization of human personality as it was intended to be, and that we must understand human personality in terms of the doctrine of the Holy Spirit, for the Holy Spirit became in our Lord the "Spirit of Human Holiness victorious over sin." [8]

This might be interpreted in an almost entirely humanistic way, and Moberly does not make a very clear distinction between the Spirit that was in Christ which is given to the believer, and a spirit of goodness and love that might be manifest in any good pagan, although he implies there is a difference. He would probably explain the difference in relationship to the absolute holiness which was in our Lord and into which the Christian believer becomes incorporated. But the Sacraments have to be seen in relation to this work of the Holy Spirit —Baptism because it means not merely enrollment into the society of the Church but incorporation into the very life, death, and resurrection of Christ, and the Eucharist because this incorporation is ratified by Christ and accepted by the believer in Christ's gift of his own flesh and blood.

Therefore, we have these special points of emphasis and progression of ideas in Moberly.

1. The Atonement (i.e., reconciliation) that Jesus Christ achieved for us was his whole life of obedience, and this led to the act of per-

[6] Ibid., p. 140.
[7] Ibid., p. 151; cf. pp. 151-53.
[8] Ibid., p. 204.

fect penitence on our behalf which was able to turn the penalty due to us into penance. Like Campbell and Bushnell before him, he stresses the importance of the Incarnation as itself an atoning act, and possibly under the influence of Westcott's writing, he places great stress on Athanasius. He also shows himself to have been influenced by the ideas of Abelard and of the more recent writers, McLeod Campbell and Bishop Westcott.

2. On the other hand he went far beyond Abelard in recognizing the objective side of the Atonement and our need for this assurance and far beyond Campbell in stressing the work of the Holy Spirit in our redemption. He does this, emphasizing at the same time very strongly the unity of the Trinity against those who in seeking to be super-orthodox Trinitarians virtually end by becoming virtual ditheists or tritheists.[9]

3. The aim and result of the atoning work of Christ is to bring into being the Christian personality, but Moberly went beyond the majority of exponents of moral influence theories by insisting that this Christian personality was not to be attained simply by our own moral effort. "There is indeed Christian effort," he says, "and there is the imitation of Christ. But these are rather the necessary outcome, than the producing cause, of the Spirit of Christ. It is by His initiation rather than ours, and by the acts of His power rather than ours, that we were first brought into relation with Him, and that His Spirit is progressively imparted to us."[10] Moberly had what so many of those who held similar theories lacked, a doctrine of Grace.

Atonement and Personality was an important attempt to reconcile the new theological thinking with the high Anglican views of its author, but Moberly laid himself open to one great and obvious criticism which later reviewers have sometimes unfortunately used as an excuse to foreclose on any further consideration of his views. He had criticized McLeod Campbell for employing the idea of "vicarious confession," but if it is impossible for one person to make confession on behalf of other people, the same must surely be true of "vicarious penitence" which Moberly seems to have put in its place. Indeed, when he discusses the idea of vicarious sacrifice in the work of Christ, he points

[9] *Ibid.*, pp. 84, 156-57.
[10] *Ibid.*, p. 320.

out that the weakness of all ideas based upon vicarious action is that "no one can quite be another." We can see that on the ground of the "objective" theories one man *could* perform a work or an action on behalf of someone else, but it is quite different when the basis for the atoning work of Christ is shifted to that of a sentiment rather than a deed—one cannot have an *effective* vicarious feeling or attitude of contrition or penitence. This objection certainly undercuts the idea which features so prominently in R. C. Moberly's exposition of the Atonement.

On the other hand it can be questioned whether the idea of vicarious penitence was at the heart of Moberly's argument. Undoubtedly it was a conception which he, under the influence of Campbell's book, regarded very highly, and it seems to take its place at the climax of his study of "personality" and of the personal concepts involved in atonement. A second look, however, will show us that the real heart of his moral theory is our Lord's *obedience*, and a closer look at the work of Campbell and Bushnell will reveal that the same idea underlies the "vicarious confession" advanced by the former and the conception of "sonship through sacrifice" put forward by the latter. "Obedience is atoning," says Moberly, "and the atonement itself can be exhibited as one great consummation of obedience." His suggestion that our Lord was the only man who could have given perfect penitence to God (if he had had need to do so) is valuable, since it emphasizes our own incapacity and need—the truth contained in Whitefield's statment that even our tears of repentance need to be washed in Christ's blood—but a vicarious "penitence" by a perfect Man who knew no sin could at best be only analogous to that which we ought to feel.

Moberly's most important contribution to the subject was in showing the relationship between the redemptive work of our Lord and the doctrine of the Holy Spirit and the extension of the Holy Spirit's work in Church and Sacraments. If he had concentrated on showing that although a man cannot be perfectly penitent before God, yet through his incorporation into Christ by the Holy Spirit the believer is enabled to share in the perfect *obedience* of our Lord, Moberly would have presented a more unified theory of the Atonement and one that was less open to objection.

THE ATONEMENT AND THE SACRAMENTS

2. *The Rising Tide of Liberalism*

Although R. C. Moberly appears to have taken up more completely than any other theologian McLeod Campbell's theory of the Atonement, it is in the writings of those who returned to Abelard and found the meaning of the work of Christ entirely in terms of his Example that the ethical emphasis started by Campbell and Bushnell reached a fulfillment that they could hardly have envisaged and of which they would probably have disapproved. Before we examine the neo-Abelardian view, however, we must set the historical stage in which it made its appearance.

Hastings Rashdall's Bampton Lectures, *The Idea of Atonement in Christian Theology*, were delivered in 1915 and published four years later; R. S. Franks published his *History of the Doctrine of the Work of Christ* in 1918, and reaffirmed his position in the Dale Lectures delivered in 1933 and published one year later. Therefore, sixty years separate their work from that of McLeod Campbell, and during those six decades a great deal had happened to change the theological climate. Campbell in Scotland and Bushnell in America had been conscious in their writing that they were attacking the entrenched positions of orthodox theology, which was upheld not only by the confessional standards of the churches within these countries, but also buttressed by a doctrine of the verbal inspiration and inerrancy of Scripture. Rashdall and Franks on the other hand published their historical studies of the doctrine of the work of Christ when the theological systems of old orthodoxies seemed to be entirely swept away under the impact of radical biblical criticism. They wrote in the heyday of theological liberalism. German methods of biblical criticism may have been late in crossing the English Channel, but when they came, they were widespread in their influence and devastating in their effect. In the minds of most Christians—liberal as well as traditionalist—orthodoxy regarding the verbal inspiration of the Bible was held to be indissolubly linked with orthodoxy of theological belief. It was believed that if the foundation of verbal inspiration was successfully attacked, then the whole superstructure of doctrine—Trinity, Incarnation, Person of Christ, Atonement, Church, and Sacraments—would be called in question.

The more perceptive minds saw the fallacy of the common view, but this belief produced unworthy fear in some and an insolent confidence in others. It led to the extreme bitterness of the struggle and to such incidents as Benjamin Jowett's trial for heresy in the vice-chancellor's court at Oxford (after the publication of *Essays and Reviews* in 1860) and the "down grade" controversy of 1887 which divided the Baptist Union of Great Britain and caused the defection of Charles Haddon Spurgeon, the greatest preacher of the century. Spurgeon stood for the old theology in its entirety, and he brilliantly expounded it from his London pulpit. However, his charges against the "down grade" in evangelical orthodoxy show that in maintaining a unity between the verbal inspiration of Scripture and the historic Faith of the Church the churchmen of that time often tenaciously held on to positions that were irrelevant to the main issue.

On the other hand very few people were able to go through the fires of radical biblical criticism and emerge with an evangelical faith that was strengthened and confirmed. Too many of the liberals appeared to be more concerned with tearing down the doctrines of the Faith than with establishing them on a surer foundation—or when they did try to construct something from the ruins, were content to rebuild upon general "Christian principles" rather than upon the historic facts that Christianity proclaimed. This is the background against which the books of Rashdall and Franks must be set, for when, in the years immediately following the First World War, they published their thorough historical studies of the development of the doctrine of the Atonement, the battle appeared to have been overwhelmingly won for theological liberalism and for a liberalism which seemed as if it would get more and more liberal in the post-war years.

It was a significant fact that both books were the results of *historical* studies and largely inspired by the idea of progressive revelation and by the contemporary historical exegesis. It was the time which was inspired by the "quest for the historical Jesus," when scholars thought that by objective critical methods they would eventually be able to sift the simple message of Jesus from the accretions added by later churchmen and reveal Jesus and his teaching in all their simplicity. Although we now are able to see how little "objective" their criticism often was and how subjective were the criteria of "objectivity" that they assumed, we must recognize that this was the prevailing temper of advanced theological scholarship during the first three decades of the twentieth century. Not only were the written documents of Christianity under critical review but even the facts of the gospel seemed to be discarded. If these *had* been revealed ultimately by historical and literary criticism to be different from the facts which the Church had traditionally asserted, then a radical revision of the Church's doctrinal position would have been inevitable. But often it was assumed too readily that because critical scholarship had disproved the Mosaic authorship of the Pentateuch or thrown doubts upon the traditional dating and authorship of the Fourth Gospel, that in some way the Incarnation was thereby proved to be a myth and the Resurrection irrelevant.

It was, of course, overconfidence in what historical and literary criticism had proved or could prove, and modern theology may be in danger of moving too far in an opposite direction, but in those pre-Bultmann days it was assumed that one's views upon Scripture were bound to govern one's doctrinal position. In this way the historical approach to Christian doctrine was in line with the historical approach to Scripture. Just as New Testament scholars thought they had discovered by these methods the "simple gospel" of Jesus beneath the later theologizing of Paul and the early Church, so those scholars who devoted themselves to the history of doctrine "rediscovered" the ethical emphasis in the Apostolic Fathers and the Exemplarist view of Atonement put forward by Abelard. It was a new line of attack upon the presuppositions of the older theology aided by the trend in biblical studies, but it developed the line of criticism which had been started when Campbell and Bushnell demanded that Christian doctrine must be consistent with the spirit of the Christ revealed in the New Testament. The difference between the new followers of Abelard and their predecessors was that they sometimes wrote and spoke as if the discovery of a "historical Jesus" made belief in a living Christ unnecessary. Example took the place of grace, and the result was that historical objectivity became the means whereby the Christian Faith was placed on a basis of pure subjectivism.

3. Abelardus Redivivus: Hastings Rashdall

Dean Hastings Rashdall was an Anglican moral philosopher and theologian who spent the greater part of his life teaching in Oxford until he was appointed Dean of Carlisle in 1917. He was born in 1858

—two years after McLeod Campbell's book on the Atonement had first seen the light of day—and died in 1924. So his life covered the period that witnessed the great critical onslaught in biblical studies, and his contribution came at a time when with the rise of the "New Theology" [11] some attempt was being made to put something in the place of the theological systems that had been pulled down.

The main part of his book, *The Idea of Atonement in Christian Theology* is an examination of the way in which the doctrine developed in the New Testament and in church history. We shall devote most time to the earlier part of the book because the way in which he approached the problem in relation to the New Testament illustrates the typical approach of that time, and also because we must recognize that what Rashdall believed about the New Testament governed both his interpretation of history and his own systematic exposition of the doctrine. He was in line with the demand that had been raised by Campbell and Bushnell that the Atonement must be interpreted not by what later theology had made of it, but by what Jesus Christ had revealed of God's Spirit in the New Testament. But he had his own view of what constituted the New Testament.

Rashdall first dealt with the teaching of Jesus concerning forgiveness, denying that our Lord had ever taught that sin could be forgiven only through the atoning efficacy of his death or any similar doctrine. Jesus became convinced that he was the promised Messiah, but it was clear that he did not regard the kingdom he was to inaugurate either as a political institution or as crowning a cosmic catastrophe that would destroy the existing order. "It was essentially," said Rashdall, "a state of society in which God's will should be perfectly done— done as it is in heaven." [12] Jesus may have thought of the punishment of the wicked, but there is no proof that he thought of it as eternal punishment, and the one distinction between those who were to suffer judgment and those who were to enter the Kingdom of God "was to be determined by their conduct and character." [13] Here is the ethical center where Rashdall places his greatest emphasis: "Goodness thus understood was the one condition of entrance into the king-

---

[11] Hastings Rashdall, *The Idea of Atonement in Christian Theology* (London: Macmillan & Co., 1920). Cf. *Supra*, p. 83, note 34.
[12] *Ibid.*, p. 7.
[13] *Ibid.*, p. 13.

dom—that and not descent from Abraham, not the performance of any outward rite, not the state of a man's intellectual belief, except of course in so far as morality itself implies some measure of belief." [14]

Rashdall showed that throughout our Lord's ministry the idea of forgiveness was associated with his fundamental doctrine of God's paternal love toward all his children, pointing to the Lord's Prayer—"Our Father . . . forgive us our trespasses." He insisted that God's forgiveness is immediately granted where there is true repentance. "There is not the slightest suggestion," he affirmed, "that anything else but repentance is necessary—the actual death of a Saviour, belief in the atoning efficacy of that death or in any other article of faith, baptism, confession to any but God, absolution, reception of the holy eucharist, Church membership—not a hint of any of these. The truly penitent man who confesses his sins to God," he concluded, "receives instant forgiveness." [15] This is the heart of Hastings Rashdall's view of the Atonement. The fundamental contention of Campbell and Bushnell that the Church's doctrine must be consistent with the spirit of the New Testament is endorsed and carried a stage further by defining that spirit as the revelation of a Fatherhood in God that is ready to grant instant forgiveness to true penitence. There are categorical implications that if the later theologies of the Atonement were right, then that which "was taught by Christ Himself was not Christianity at all." [16]

But this position which appears in some ways so close to the gospel had really been answered many years before by Rashdall's Oxford colleague, R. C. Moberly. The views put forward by both men on the doctrine of the work of Christ were based upon the "moral influence" of our Lord, but Moberly had recognized that sinful man can never be "truly penitent"—*that* was possible only to One who was sinless. Rashdall declares that all that is necessary is that a man should truly repent, but Moberly says, in effect, "that is just the trouble. God is ready to forgive us if we are truly penitent, but a sinner, by the very nature of what sin is, cannot give to God a repentance that is true." If this is a right understanding of human nature, then it is difficult to see how Rashdall's position can be tenable. If sin so corrupts that

[14] *Ibid.*, p. 20.
[15] *Ibid.*, p. 26.
[16] *Ibid.*, p. 27.

it make true penitence impossible, then the doctrine of Atonement (if it is to be of any use to sinners) must convince them that Christ, by his own act, on their behalf has done something whereby our faltering and insincere repentance is received as perfect in the sight of the Father. And from the other side, Bishop B. F. Westcott had pointed out that although from a superficial point of view nothing seems simpler or easier than forgiveness, if we look at it more deeply, nothing is more mysterious or more difficult. For true forgiveness demands both a perfect knowledge of the offense and a perfect restoration of love.[17]

There is a passage in Dorothy Sayers' broadcast sequences on the life of Christ, *The Man Born to Be King*, where after realizing what he has done, Judas stands before the High Priest, and throwing down the thirty pieces of silver, declares, "You that are steeped to the lips in the same crime with me, can you stand there red-handed and offer up for us both a spotless and acceptable sacrifice? There is no priest, no victim in all the world that is clean enough to purge this guilt ... Is God merciful? Can He forgive? ... What help is that?—Jesus would forgive. ... and my soul would writhe for ever under the torment of that forgiveness. ... Can anything clear me in my own eyes? Or release me from this horror of myself?"[18] Remorse with its self-pride is clearly not to be confused with repentance, and true penitence is much more difficult than we realize; if everything depends upon this, I am lost.

Rashdall, however, admitted that there are several passages in the Synoptic Gospels that are open to a different interpretation of Atonement—the "ransom" passage (Mark 10:43-45, Matt. 20:26-28) and the accounts of the Last Supper. But he threw considerable doubt upon the authenticity of the first passage and thought it was much more likely to have come from the pen of the Evangelist than from Jesus himself. It was possible that Jesus had presentiments about the way he would die, and if this was the case, then he must have thought of it as a kind of service given to others. "Just as His life had been a

---

[17] *The Historic Faith* (Macmillan, 1883), pp. 130-31.
[18] *The Man Born to Be King* (New York: Harper & Bros., 1943), p. 267. Cf. James Denney, "A man can no more repent than he can do anything else without a motive, and the motive which makes evangelical repentance possible does not enter into his world till he sees God as God makes Himself known in the death of Christ" (*The Atonement and the Modern Mind* [Hodder and Stoughton, 1903], pp. 89-90).

THE ATONEMENT AND THE SACRAMENTS

life of service for others," said Rashdall, "so would His death be. And in this His disciples were to imitate Him. To offer a unique expiatory sacrifice for the sins of the whole world was clearly a kind of service which was wholly beyond their power. To work, to suffer, and, if need be, to die in the service of others was quite within their reach." [19]

In the same way, in dealing with the accounts of the Last Supper Rashdall reviewed the critical difficulties against accepting the passages as they stood and regarded the shorter Lucan version as by far the best account of the incident. He found "no necessary reference to the death" in the account of the Supper but regarded it as possible that Jesus would have been thinking of his possible death very much as any great leader of men might regard his own death as an act of martyrdom for the cause or of self-sacrifice for his followers. "Doubtless He may have felt that the death of the Messiah had a significance which the death of no other man could have, but He claims for it no unique expiatory value." [20] The giving of the bread and the cup suggests, he says, "the idea that our Lord looked upon his approaching death as an act of self-sacrifice for His disciples," and the words "for you" in the Institution were probably a later addition. Rashdall concluded, "We have found, then, nothing in either of the two places which we have examined which can compel us to abandon the conclusion that our Lord never taught that His death was necessary for the forgiveness of sins, or that any condition was required for forgiveness but the supreme one of repentance and that amendment which is implied in all sincere repentance." [21]

At the same time Hastings Rashdall rightly believed that a doctrine of the Cross was implicit within our Lord's life and teaching, but he believed that the doctrine of free forgiveness was simply a consequence of the principle that "love is the highest thing in human life and the highest revelation of the divine nature." "And that being so," he continued, "we are already able to find a meaning in the later doctrine

---

[19] Rashdall, op. cit., p. 32. One would think, on Rashdall's own premises, that if the life and teaching of our Lord were the greatest gift he had to offer to mankind, then to allow himself to be executed at the age of thirty-three after a brief three years' ministry was a great disservice to humanity. If the death of Jesus was a service to us, then Rashdall should have shown how this was of more benefit to men than his continuing to live and teach.
[20] Ibid., p. 43.
[21] Ibid., p. 45.

which sees in the death of the supreme Revealer a pledge or symbol of the forgiveness which He had preached and promised. In so far as "the doctrine of the cross" means the supreme beauty of loving service, and in particular its efficacy in touching the heart and regenerating the lives of others, the doctrine of the cross may be traced back to the teaching of our Lord, and forms the very centre of it." [22]

Dean Rashdall's treatment of the teaching of Jesus illustrates his method, and this is where the heart of his conception of the Atonement is to be found, but he could not neglect the development of the doctrine in the rest of the New Testament. When and where did the pre-Pauline and Pauline doctrine originate? Certainly we cannot regard Paul as its originator, for in I Cor. 15:3 the apostle very deliberately states, "I delivered unto you first of all that *which I also received*, how that Christ died for our sins according to the scriptures" (R.S.V.). On the other hand there is no idea of linking salvation specifically with the death of Christ in Stephen's speech or in the early Petrine speeches in the *Acts*, which concentrated upon the Resurrection. Yet "by the date of St. Paul's conversion, which may have occurred at any time between a year and six or seven years after the crucifixion, the Church or certain circles in it had come to believe that Christ died for our sins." [23]

Rashdall deals with this as a historian. We know that very soon after our Lord's death the disciples concentrated upon "searching the scriptures" for proofs of his Messiahship, and that in this search Is. 53 became the central passage of proof. Rashdall suggests that the adoption of Jewish prophecy was therefore responsible for linking the death of Christ with an expiatory idea of our salvation, even as I Cor. 15:3 suggests.

One feels that there is a good deal of truth in the suggestion that a specific doctrine of salvation connected with the death of Christ developed through the early Church's study of the Scriptures, although we may still question Dean Rashdall's implication that this was a gigantic and regrettable accident. It is at this point that we fail to sense in Rashdall any adequate understanding of the specific work of the Holy Spirit in the infant Christian community. Can we explain away Pentecost so completely as to say that comments made

---

[22] *Ibid.*, pp. 46-47.
[23] *Ibid.*, p. 78; cf. pp. 75-83.

THE ATONEMENT AND THE SACRAMENTS

by the Fourth Evangelist upon the life and teaching of Jesus were misguided, or to suggest that the apostles were left to follow as best they could the Great Example? If that had been the entire gospel, we doubt whether the blood of the martyrs would have been the seed of the Church.

Rashdall continued by examining Paul's idea of Atonement, particularly in Romans where the apostle faced the fundamental question how Gentiles could become Christians without undergoing the observances of the Jewish Law. He said that Paul found his answer, first by denying that any man could be justified by the works of the Law, and secondly by asserting that justification before God was to be obtained only in the new righteousness that the Messiah, Jesus Christ, had made available to all men. Neither Jew nor Gentile could be justified without Christ, for all had sinned and come short of the glory of God (Rom. 3:23). Caught up in this, however, was the idea of the flesh as the source of moral evil and at least the embryonic appearance of a doctrine of predestination. With regard to Rom. 9:18, Rashdall observed, "It is impossible to deny that on the whole the Augustinian and Calvinistic interpretation of St. Paul as regards these questions is justified, with the momentous exception that St. Paul knows nothing of everlasting punishment." [24] So he went on to summarize the doctrine of Atonement in St. Paul: "The objective source or ground of justification is the death of Christ. The righteousness by which the Christian attains justification is a righteousness of God: a righteousness which is not due to the sinner's works at all—not even to his repentance. It is something brought into existence by God as a free act of favour or mercy." [25]

It would nevertheless be wrong, in Rashdall's view, to attribute to Paul a theory of atonement as clear-cut and detailed as in the later systems. Paul does not quite explain why God could not forgive our sins without the death of his Son, and yet the later theologians who developed the idea that God's justice demands the punishment of death upon sin were "only bringing out the latent presuppositions of St. Paul's thought." [26] Paul never uses ἀντί (instead of) but always ὑπέρ (on behalf of), but the idea of substitution does exist in such

[24] Ibid., pp. 89-90.
[25] Ibid., p. 90.
[26] Ibid., p. 92.

verses as "Him who knew no sin he made to be sin on our behalf; that we might become the righteousness of God in him" (II Cor. 5:21). For this reason he bluntly maintained that it was impossible not only to make these ideas acceptable to the modern mind but also to reconcile them "with the plain teaching of St. Paul's Master and ours." [27]

However, he recognized that within Paul's own religious experience "faith" meant something to the apostle that was very much more than theological or intellectual belief. It implied the identification of the individual believer with the life and death of Christ: to use the phrase which J. S. Stewart took for the title of his book on Paul, it is to be "a man in Christ." The act of justification contained the power not simply to cancel the sin of the past but also to destroy the power of sin within the believer for the future: Paul does not preach a justification by faith without good works. Rashdall thought there was a dichotomy between Paul as a believing Christian and Paul as a rabbinic theologian. He got his theology from the Old Testament, and the apostle's theological theories rested upon his exegesis—in Rashdall's view, faulty exegesis and mistranslation—which he employed in order to reconcile his new Christian experience with the Hebrew religion.[28]

But Rashdall maintained that Paul's later epistles show a quite different development—"The whole development exhibited in these epistles may be summed up by saying that the tendency is toward an insistence upon Christ's work as revelation rather than as retrospective atonement, and upon the moral effects of that revelation rather than upon the juridical acquittal which is effected." [29] If we accept Dean Rashdall's evaluation of Paul's theological development, we are led to believe that for once in the history of religion the old truism "young radicals become old conservatives" was reversed.

In dealing with the teaching of primitive Christianity one of the first things that Rashdall observed was that Paul's views on the Atonement were not taken up by the Church. His racial universalism, his ethical teaching, his views on the Church and its sacraments, his doctrine of the Person of Christ, all these aspects of Paul's theology

[27] Ibid., p. 98.
[28] Ibid., pp. 120-21.
[29] Ibid., p. 143.

had an immediate and lasting effect, but Rashdall declared that Paul's theories regarding the Atonement "were simply left on one side" and that this was partly because they were an innovation that stood apart from the main stream of the Church's tradition.[30]

Dean Rashdall judged the rest of the New Testament by the teaching of Christianity as he has understood it from those Gospel accounts which he was prepared to regard as authentic. He noted that although one might expect the writer to the Hebrews to reproduce the Pauline ideas, that writer does not mention vicarious punishment. Rashdall's attempt to explain away the sacrificial language of the epistle is not very convincing, nor could everyone agree with his claim that "faith" in the epistle has more in common with Philo than with Paul.[31] In the Petrine epistles (on the authorship of which the Dean had considerable doubt) he maintained that the emphasis upon the sufferings of Christ was not necessarily limited to the death of Christ and that they were closer in spirit to Hebrews than to the thought of Paul. In his view the *Pastoral Epistles* have few traces of Pauline language, *James* is a flat contradiction of Paul, the thought in the *Apocalypse* is pre-Pauline, and although the *Johannine Epistles* show Pauline influence in other respects, there is none of Paul's atonement doctrine either in them or in the Apostolic Fathers.

These are the biblical presuppositions upon which he builds his examination of the history of the doctrine in chapters that deal with the Patristic theories, Latin Theology in Augustine, Anselm, and Abelard, Scholasticism, and Luther and the Reformation. In the earlier period he bases a great deal upon Origen, and he says that to turn from Tertullian to Origen "is like emerging from a dimly-lighted Roman catacomb into the brilliant sunshine of a southern noon."[32] He maintained that in those passages where Origen speaks of our Lord's death in the conventional language of sacrifice or as a propitiation for sin, the expressions are "constantly ethicized and rationalized."[33] Origen was to Rashdall the greatest mind and the greatest thinker produced by the patristic age;[34] the Greek Father had "a completer philosophy of redemption than that of any other Christian

---
[30] *Ibid.*, p. 149.
[31] *Ibid.*, p. 162-63.
[32] *Ibid.*, p. 255.
[33] *Ibid.*, p. 263.
[34] *Ibid.*, pp. 256, 272.

Father" because he tried to face the problem of evil. Rashdall declared:

> His whole philosophy is constructed on the basis of an extreme and uncompromising Libertarianism which is sometimes pushed to the point of denying the divine foreknowledge. He is about the most thoroughgoing and consistent free-willer in the whole history of human thought.... Origen sees and admits without the smallest attempt at evasion or concealment that even so the existence of evil implies a limitation of the Creator's power.[35]

This is quoted not to imply that it is either true or false as a judgment on Origen, but because it indicates Dean Rashdall's own criteria of judgment.

The climax, of course, comes with Abelard, for "in Abelard not only the ransom theory but any kind of substitutionary or expiatory atonement is explicitly denied." The efficacy of our Lord's death "is now quite definitely and explicitly explained by its subjective influence upon the mind of the sinner. The voluntary death of the innocent Son of God on man's behalf moves the sinner to gratitude and answering love—and so to consciousness of sin, repentance, amendment." [36] This is the moral theory of atonement that Rashdall wishes to commend to his own day. "At last," he declared, "we have found a theory of the atonement which thoroughly appeals to reason and to conscience." [37] He suggested there was nothing specially original in the idea, since Paul has a good deal of it, the Johannine writings give it its purest expression, and it is repeatedly to be found in the Fathers.

> Whatever else they teach about the death of Christ, they all with one consent teach this—that it was a revelation of the love of God, intended to call forth answering love in man.... Gratitude is the last spark of the divine image to disappear from the soul of man. Gratitude towards a human benefactor is the motive which is most likely to appeal to the soul in which least remains of that image. And when the human benefactor is thought of as the supreme Incarnation of God, gratitude to Christ passes into and becomes indistinguishable from gratitude to the Father whom He reveals.[38]

[35] *Ibid.*, p. 267.
[36] *Ibid.*, p. 358.
[37] *Ibid.*, p. 360.
[38] *Ibid.*, pp. 360-61.

THE ATONEMENT AND THE SACRAMENTS

Taking his stand upon this Abelardian view, Hastings Rashdall sets out his own views in a more systematic form in his final chapter. Since his work is implicitly directed against the "objective" theories in general and the theory of penal substitution in particular, he pays special attention to Dr. Denney's book, *The Death of Christ*, of which more will be said.

Dean Rashdall's strictures against the penal theory are entirely valid at the point where he criticized the relationship between this theory of the Atonement and the doctrine of the Trinity. As a "picture" in which to set the events that led to our redemption, the penal categories may still be defended, but as a "theory"—i.e., as an attempt to provide a comprehensive and exclusive account of how and why the Atonement took place—it has led directly to a false separation between the work of the Persons in the Trinity. Hastings Rashdall rightly protests against this.[39]

He bases his own positive conception of the Incarnation, and hence of the Atonement, upon the progressive revelation of a latent "divinity" within everyone.

> If we can say that in humanity generally there is some revelation of God—a growing, developing, progressive revelation, and a higher degree of such revelation in the heroes, the saints, the prophets, the founders and reformers of great religions, then the idea of an incarnation becomes possible. If we can say that God is to some extent revealed in all men, then it becomes possible to think of Him as making a supreme, culminating, unique revelation of Himself in one human character and life. And such a crowning revelation I believe that the conscience and reason of mankind do discover in the historical Jesus of Nazareth.[40]

Because of this supreme human revelation of God and because it was essential that the identification of himself with man's lot must be complete, Rashdall took up the view (put forward by Bushnell) that God is a suffering God. Writing at the close of the blood bath

---

[39] *Ibid.*, pp. 445-46.

[40] *Ibid.*, pp. 447-48. One may question whether this conception of incarnation did not suffer from the same danger of Arianism that Rashdall rightly discerned in the penal theory of Atonement. Rashdall himself avoided this because God was, to him, not only supremely, but really in the incarnation and suffering of Christ; but others who did not believe in the "passibility" of God would have some difficulty in avoiding a subordinationist conception of Christ's divinity. Furthermore, if the equivalent danger in the penal theory led to tritheism, in the Abelardian theory it leads to pantheism.

of the First World War, when Britain had lost a million young men killed in Flanders, he declared, "A God who could contemplate such a world as ours without suffering would not be a loving God, nor would He be in the least like Christ." [41] We may venture the personal comment that perhaps it is our delicate but wholly inadequate distinctions in thinking about the Godhead that cause the difficulty. God did suffer in Christ, and by the Resurrection and Ascension Christ's suffering is caught up into the very center and being of Godhead. At this point it is truer to face the paradoxes than to try to be too logical. God cannot be other than God in all his plentitude, but God can, and did, suffer in Christ—both truths are part of the Christian revelation, and neither truth must be jettisoned simply because at the moment our minds and hearts are not big enough to understand how they are to be held together.

"The atonement," says Rashdall, "is the very central doctrine of Christianity in so far as it proclaims, and brings home to the heart of man, the supreme Christian truth that God is love, and that love is the most precious thing in human life." [42] One may feel that there is more to be said about it than this, but this at least must be said.

4. Abelardus Recogitans: Robert Franks

Before passing on to a general criticism of the neo-Abelardian position, let us compare the approach that is made to the subject by Principal R. S. Franks. He had published his *History of the Doctrine of the Work of Christ* as early as 1918, but in the Dale Lectures delivered in 1933, he treated the same subject systematically and reasserted his basic position. The high peak of Liberal influence had passed. His reassessment came at a time when, with a reluctant realization of the dangers to peace that were growing in Europe and at the beginning of the neo-orthodox impact from Switzerland, both British theology in general and his own denomination (Congregational) in particular were soon to move away from the subjectivity and too sanguine hopes of theological liberalism. His contribution is significant, therefore, not simply as representing the standpoint of those who had rediscovered Abelard but as one who, having taken

[41] *Ibid.*, p. 453.
[42] *Ibid.*, p. 454.

the Abelardian position, reassessed that position in the face of the theology represented by Karl Barth and Emil Brunner, and within a world that was becoming skeptical of those very values of "love" and "gratitude" on which the Abelardian view rested. It is therefore with the published form of his Dale Lectures that we shall be concerned.

In his preface to this book, *The Atonement* (1934), Franks acknowledged that he and Rashdall defended the same general position but claimed that their metaphysical basis was different. As a philosopher he could not entertain Rashdall's view of the passibility of God, but more generally his criticism of Rashdall is one of method. In Franks's view the former Dean of Carlisle had given too much space to history and too little to systematic construction. Fundamentally his criticism is that Rashdall had not adequately undergirded the Abelardian theory of the Atonement either theologically or philosophically, and therefore, Franks was "unable to accept Dr. Rashdall's treatise as a satisfactory defence of Abelardianism."[43]

He described his own spiritual pilgrimage as having come out of the older fundamentalist evangelicalism, and after breaking with this through the works of Ritschl and Harnack, he had been inspired to try to reach a metaphysical basis for his faith through reading Ernst Troeltsch. Then he had been driven through Schleiermacher via the writings of C. H. Weisse and Karl Heim, to arrive eventually at the medieval scholastics and in particular to his own countryman, Alexander of Hales, who, he says, was "the true progenitor of the type of theology for which I stand."[44] The brief account of his intellectual and spiritual pilgrimage is important since it helps us to understand his mental and religious presuppositions. Franks must have been attracted by the medieval attempt to reconcile Augustinian theology with the rediscovery of Aristotelian philosophy, but because his view of Reason was ultimately derived from the philosophy of the medieval scholastics, he would find it difficult to accept Rashdall's view of a God that suffers.

On the other hand in biblical studies he had the same critical presuppositions as Hastings Rashdall. He found the real center of the Bible's message in the Old Testament prophets and the Synoptic Gospels, at the very heart of which there was the teaching of Jesus.

[43] Franks, *op. cit.* (O.U.P., 1934), pp. xi-xii.
[44] *Ibid.*, p. x.

"We have then," he said, "the teaching of Jesus as our ultimate historical standard for Christianity, since the story can but give weight and body to the teaching, but not affect its principles: we cannot believe that Jesus lived and died on other principles than those on which He taught." [45] He had little sympathy with the new biblical orthodoxy, news of which was just beginning to percolate into the consciousness of British theologians. He regarded Barth's work as a return to the obscurantism and authority of the later Nominalists and twitted Brunner for praising Anselm not for his rationality but for his agreement with Paul, which he said is rather like a politician who is a radical, not because he believes in the principles of radicalism but for the good and solid Conservative reason that his father was a radical before him! [46]

Jesus was to Franks much more than his teaching, and he faced the problems of his position. For this reason he showed some uneasiness in his treatment of the Old Testament, because having demonstrated that ethically and religiously it was the prophetic stream that connected the Old Testament revelation to the teaching of or Lord, it was difficult to explain why this prophetic tradition came to its climax in the incomparable figure of the Suffering Servant in Is. 53, which had been the constant proof-text for the penal theory of the Atonement.[47] One of the differences between Franks and Rashdall is the feeling we have that Franks saw the force of this kind of problem but Rashdall did not.

It was perhaps partly due to the fact that twenty years separate *The Idea of the Atonement in Christian Theology* and Franks's Dale Lectures, and whatever spiritual and intellectual pilgrimage lay behind the latter, the one who delivered them could not help reflecting something of the changing temper of his time. Hastings Rashdall had been conscious of the world suffering that had come to a head in the 1914-1918 war and which made belief in the uniqueness of Christ's sufferings difficult. But when Robert Franks wrote *The Atonement*, he was part of a world in which whispered proofs about the bestialities taking place in Hitler's concentration camps made belief in moral progress virtually impossible, even from behind the

[45] Ibid., p. 33.
[46] Ibid., p. 20.
[47] Ibid., pp. 39-40.

ostrich-like security provided by the North Sea and the English Channel. "We must not," he wrote, "argue from moral progress, since civilizations rise and fall, and progress is annihilated. The nineteenth century believed in progress: but can we believe in progress after the Great War? The century of hope has been succeeded by the century of disillusionment: men now regard the victorians as hopelessly sentimental and idealistic: realism is the order of the day." [48] To Franks this realism was based upon rationality, and religion was nothing if not rational, but it was a moral or rather a religious rationality. He protested against those who disparaged the Abelardian theory of the Atonement as a "moral" theory, since he maintained that it is more religious than moral because it is based on the Divine grace shown by the love of God in Christ. In the same way he argued that it is wrongly called subjective, since although it contains subjective response by the believer, it is a response made to the *objective* fact of God's love demonstrated to us in Jesus Christ.

The way in which he treated his subject was taken directly from Anselm, for although he differed radically from Anselm's premises and conclusions, he regarded the *Cur Deus Homo* as the finest example of systematic theological thinking that has ever been written.[49] It should be remembered that his intention was not to review once more the biblical and historical evidence regarding the Atonement but to put the doctrine and the theory of it that he supported on a more sound metaphysical basis than hitherto. In attempting to give the basis for a Christian metaphysic, he started with the conception of God's changelessness, taking as his philosophical basis the foundation thought of Anselm's ontology, the idea of God as *quo nihil maius cogitari potest*—"than which nothing greater can be conceived." Having reviewed the criticisms of this concept in the writings of Thomas Aquinas and Kant, he arrived at the conclusion that Kant did not destroy the idea but put it on a firmer basis, for "Kant enables us to reach a more definite description of the Absolute as Personal Good Will." [50] It is obviously not possible to do justice to his argument here nor is it particularly germane to our own theme, but this is the starting point he took for his approach to theology and the

---

[48] *Ibid.*, p. 118.
[49] *Ibid.*, pp. 6-7.
[50] *Ibid.*, p. 115.

doctrine of atonement—"this metaphysic of Good Will, regnant in the universe, furnishes the required basis for Christian theology, when we identify the Good Will with the Love of God." [51]

At the same time Franks recognized that no one is ever saved by the ontological argument of Anselm or Kant's revision of it: emotion and not reason is the "spring of action." How then, he asked, do we find God, "not as an inference from the universe, not even as an inference from morality, but as a saving God"? His answer was, as the answer must always be, "through Christ." [52] He then has to go on and speak of the way in which we can apprehend this revelation of God in Christ, and for this he took as his point of departure Schleiermacher's feeling of "dependence." At the end of his argument he is able to say that we must set, against any conception of arbitrary revelation, an intuition of God as Love, "an insight into his character as the highest ethical ideal, and a feeling of complete dependence upon Him for the realization not only of the ethical ideal, but also of all accompanying blessings that our composite nature requires." [53]

The importance of "dependence" as a central concept in his exposition of the Atonement gives the impression that although Franks and Rashdall stood fundamentally for the same Abelardian position, the former had a deeper understanding of the principle of grace and of the work of the Holy Spirit in the dealings of God with men; he gave to both Church and Sacraments a significant place in the plan of salvation.[54] Like McLeod Campbell and Bushnell, Franks saw God's will for us in terms of our obedience within the sonship which he offers us. There is the obedience of the slave and the obedience of the child, and "it is the latter obedience which we owe to God, and which the revelation of His love to us inspires." He spoke of sin as "the rejection of the Divine Love," as "failure to trust and obey God," and he stressed the judgment of love in a way that never once appeared in Rashdall's book.[55] In forgiveness, he reminds us, the initiative is always with God, and the death of Jesus assures us that

---

[51] *Ibid.*, p. 121.
[52] *Ibid.*, pp. 123-24.
[53] *Ibid.*, pp. 131-32.
[54] *Ibid.*, pp. 149-50, 171-73.
[55] *Ibid.*, p. 155.

this initiative has been taken. This is the "objective" element in Franks's view of the Atonement, and it is in this sense that he applied the word "martyr" (μάρτυς) to our Lord—he was witnessing to the love and mercy of God.

Nevertheless, his position is Abelardian. In the last chapter where he examined the historic theories of the Atonement in the light of his previous study, he spoke approvingly of Dale's comment that the historic words—Sacrifice, Ransom, Propitiation—were to be regarded rather as illustrations of the truth about the death of Christ than as the basis for theories. But having said that, he immediately went on to show that no "illustration" was really tenable other than the Abelardian! Several times he gets into trouble with illustrations which are intended to elucidate but often succeed in irritating. In one place he suggested that the Atonement is like the action of doctors or nurses going to work among a plague-ridden people and at last being struck down themselves.[56] If the real plague was sin, then Dr. Franks's illustration obviously will not hold.

Again, he declared that it was not as a penalty that Christ endured the Cross, but "rather as a shepherd endures hardship, exposure, danger, and even death for the sheep. The sheep enjoy their safety because of what the shepherd has endured."[57] But what is the danger from which the sheep are saved? On the showing of writers like Franks and Rashdall there is none. There is no sense of urgency, of a real *salvation*, in the gospel they present, for the illustration of the shepherd is good only if first, the danger can be shown to be urgent and real, and secondly, if it is the shepherd's own action at the cost of his life which *wins* safety for the sheep. If the sheep come to safety simply by imitating his example, there is reason for thinking that they have done a good deal to save themselves. Does the gospel give us such grounds for pelagian pride?

5. Critique of the Modern Abelardians

We are now in a position where we can engage in a more thoroughgoing critique of Abelard's theory as it has appeared in its modern dress. Rashdall and Franks put the coping stone upon the edifice that had been begun by McLeod Campbell and Horace Bushnell, for

[56] *Ibid.*, p. 167.
[57] *Ibid.*, p. 188.

when the earlier writers had re-established the doctrine of the Atonement on the "moral influence" of our Lord, the development of the doctrine simply in terms of example was inevitable. The criticisms that arise do so not because the Abelardian view is false, but because it represents certain aspects of the doctrine as if they were the whole truth. What we offer in criticism is not against the vital truth within the Abelardian position but against the claim of its adherents to express all that needs to be said about atonement. No other theory of Atonement is as exclusive as this one.

1. It has often been pointed out that as a comprehensive theory it takes too cheap a view of both sin and forgiveness. Franks spoke of sin as a "rejection of Divine Love" or as a "failure to trust and obey God," but it is more even than this—it is an *outrage* upon love.[58] It is the sense of the extreme heinousness of sin and of the great cost of forgiveness which is so often missing in the Abelardian position; it may present us with Jesus as a Leader to be followed but it never shows to us the Saving God, who at extreme cost to himself, cancels the sin. It was Horace Bushnell's experience of the wrongs that were done to him which induced him in later years to write the book in which he modified some of his earlier views on forgiveness—because he began to see how difficult forgiveness could be and must be, even for God.[59]

2. The Abelardian theory reveals a deceptive simplicity that can obscure intellectual and moral pride. Does our salvation depend ultimately upon our *understanding* of the teaching of Jesus, or upon simple faith in what he did which is then prepared to be instructed by his Spirit? The Abelardian theologians speak about God's free forgiveness following upon our penitence, but what is the factor in the gospel which in their view brings the individual to the point of repentance? Sometimes they write as if we reach this point because we have at last managed to comprehend the meaning of our Lord's life and teaching, rather than because we have faced what he did to save us from our sin. If it is that, then the gospel is founded upon reason and intelligence rather than upon grace and our response in humility.

[58] T. H. Hughes, *The Atonement: Modern Theories of the Doctrine*, p. 219.
[59] Cf. Cave, op. cit., pp. 222-23.

3. Another aspect of the same problem is seen in the attitude of the neo-Abelardians to biblical interpretation. This is far too great a problem for us to go into very deeply, and we are perhaps still a long way from the final answer, but at any rate we must see the challenge that it sets to our faith. Protestant Christianity must face the fact that just as the Reformation took the Bible out of the exclusive control of clerical scholars and gave it to the people, so the effects of Liberal biblical criticism have been to take the Bible out of the hands of ordinary Christians and put it back into the control of the scholar. In honesty we may not be able to return to the naïve fundamentalism of our fathers, but we must ask ourselves how we can put the Bible back into the hands of those who sit in our pews with the full confidence that they will get its central message of God's redeeming grace in Christ. One of the most great hearted Christians I have known was the Liberal scholar, Dr. C. J. Cadoux, but while we were at college, B. H. Sims of Bristol wrote the following limerick about Dr. Cadoux's attitude to biblical studies:

> I am told that Dr. Cadoux
> Thinks but part of the Bible is troux:
>   Start at Mark, so they say,
>   Read a chapter a day,
> Continue a week, and you're throux!

I am sure this does not do strict justice to Dr. Cadoux's real beliefs in the matter, but it was the impression often given by Liberal scholarship.

The Liberals did not see what this meant—that if the *spiritual* truth of the Bible was always to be dependent upon critical studies, the ordinary Christian could never understand the Bible until he had obtained at least a Ph.D. degree in theology. Simply because the doctrine of our redemption concerns every individual, it cannot rest upon the kind of biblical interpretation that depends ultimately upon critical acumen or technical knowledge. If the gospel is for all men, intellectual or educational advantages may help us to understand it better, but they can never be the basic requirement for understanding it sufficiently to be saved by it and to discover the good life that it offers. Fundamentalism contains tremendous dangers, but Protestantism can never remain content to answer it by putting the Bible exclusively in the hands of "experts."

4. The charge of moral and spiritual pride is even more fundamental. Robert Franks quite rightly protests against the phrase "mere" example that is so often used against the Abelardian position. He does so because the word "mere" implies a minimal standard.[60] But my main protest would be against the very thing for which he is contending, for the underlying idea of "example" implies for me and most men an impossible maximum that they can never achieve—indeed, it implies *the maximum* standard, that of Christ himself. To try by one's own efforts to follow the life of Christ is to see the standards of the Law raised to perfection undreamt by any Hebrew prophet, and before that Personification of the Law I stand condemned in a far deeper and more hopeless sense than those who fell under condemnation from the Law of Moses.

If this is what God offers in Christ, then it is not grace but wholly judgment, and we should be better under the Old Covenant than under the New. As T. O. Wedel poses the question for us, "What can Jesus as mere Master of human perfection really do for you? The Sermon on the Mount as a vision of the Mount Everest of moral striving can beckon to a life of ethical heroism. But woe unto those who drop by the wayside in that upward climb. No mere mortal can endure the consciousness of failure and guilt, unaided, for so long."[61] On the other hand perhaps this is one of the places where complete failure is less to be feared than partial success, for if I am invited to win my own salvation by imitating Christ's goodness, then who can blame me for my modest pride if in struggling to follow, I manage to stumble a few faltering steps of my own. Of all the dangers into which the ancient heresies have led us, perhaps it is Pelagius who in the end brings us quickest to Lucifer's sin.

5. The same kind of criticism can be levelled at the Abelardian writers for their cavalier attitude to Time. Nicholas Berdyaev has pointed to the tendency of a religion of progress to dismiss the past ages as valueless except as instrumental to the ultimate goal of history. "There is no valid ground," he says, "for degrading those generations

---

[60] Franks, op. cit., p. 163.
[61] T. O. Wedel, *The Christianity of Main Street* (New York: Macmillan, 1951), p. 105.

whose lot has been cast among pain and imperfection beneath that whose pre-eminence has been ordained in blessedness and joy. No future perfection can expiate the sufferings of past generations." [62] No theory of Time and History is more likely to make us doubt the very existence of Providence, for a God who refuses himself to past generations, and admits to his favor only the final and perfect product of history, "could only be thought of as a vampire, unjust and pitiless to the vast bulk of mankind." [63]

One of the most irritating characteristics of theologians is the common assumption they make that the full plan of salvation had not been revealed until their own book appeared. It is this kind of overenthusiasm which has been so noticeable in the writings of the modern Abelardians. It is true that both Rashdall and Franks insist that there has been a constant outcropping of the moral influence theory of the Atonement all through the history of the Church, but this was sporadic, and the ethical emphasis was for hundreds of years at a time dominated by theories that appeared to run counter to it. If the different theories of the Atonement had been seen as complementary aspects of the same gospel, one could agree with the Abelardians' contention that the older theories were often terribly faulty and inadequate for the needs of the succeeding generations. But they carry their claims further and assert that no theory other than that which is centered in the influence of our Lord's example can be regarded as in the least consistent with the Gospel of Jesus. We must ask, what about those previous ages? Was our Lord content for the greater part of the Church's history to leave his Church to be built upon ideas of redemption that were so entirely contrary to the gospel he came to reveal?

6. Furthermore, do the moral influence theories adequately explain the miracle by which the Church lives? No doubt the exponents of Abelard felt they had provided sufficient explanation for the miracle of the Church's continued life when they pointed to the fact that the early Apologists and Fathers consistently stressed the ethical effects of Christ's example. But such a reading of early church history bypasses several other facts which need to be considered. It ignores the influence of Paul and the churches founded by those who were

[62] Nicholas Berdyaev, *The Meaning of History* (Bles, 1936), p. 189.
[63] *Ibid.*, p. 193.

influenced by his theology and sacramental teaching; it ignores the fact that the ethical aspect of our Lord's death and passion was not the only aspect which appears in the early Christian writings (e.g., the mystical union with Christ's sacrifice shown in the attitude to martyrdom and the recurring language of sacrifice); it ignores the constant influence within the life of the early church of the reading of Scripture and of the liturgies.

Further, it does not do justice to Christian experience, for several decades of liberal preaching in a Europe that has since been devastated by persecution and war have proved that beyond the incentive of our Lord's example, sinners need to know that he has done something for them which makes a power available for them to tread in his steps. Robert Franks came very near to recognizing this is the stress he puts on the Church and Sacraments at the end of his book, but Hastings Rashdall has very little help for poor sinners like most of us. It may seem to be an unfair comment, but the content of his book keeps pace with its index—it begins with "Abelard" and ends with "Zwingli."

7. Is the revelation of God's love the main reason for the objective work of Jesus Christ? Men need to know not only that God has shown his love and given them an example in Christ, but that Christ has wiped the slate clean, that despite their sin something, independently of them and their attitude, has been done by God in Christ. Moreover, we do not get rid of our sin unless we can know that it has been really forgiven—a forgiveness which goes beyond a mere dismissal of the penalty and which brings about reinstatement and reconciliation with God will be costly to God.

Take the illustration of the love between parent and child, of which theologians are rightly very fond because it is so very near to God's relationship to us, and let us see where it brings us. What is the most thrilling moment of a parent's life? There are obviously many exciting moments—when you see your child as a baby for the first time, when he smiles for the first time, when he speaks his first word, or when he begins to step out on his own. All these are exciting moments, but for the moment of greatest thrill there is a great deal to be said for the time when, suddenly realizing that he loves you, he throws his arms round your neck and says it. That is the kind of response which God wants from us, a love which answers his love. How does it come about;

is it by imitation and example? Yes, partly, but at a far deeper level it comes about because for months and even years the parents have been engaged in countless deeds of love of which the child was not at the time in any way conscious that they were expressions of parental love—actions that have fed, clothed, protected, and disciplined the child from the earliest moment of his life. But gradually it dawns upon the child that these prosaic actions have been the expressions of a very deep love, to which he responds.

Suppose, however, the father had consciously done everything *specifically* to reveal the depth of his own love for the boy, what would have happened then? He would probably have been a spoilt and even a cynical child. In order that the love behind the parent's actions can be felt, the deeds *have* to be indirect expressions of love—the revelation of the parent's love is not their main purpose, it is subordinated to their main concern, which is the well-being of the child. It is because they put the health and safety of the child first, and only because of that, that they do in fact reveal the depth of their love. The same point was made by Robert Dale when he declared that God does not redeem us by revealing his love, but "He reveals His love by redeeming us." [64]

Perhaps this is at the back of what Paul is trying to tell us in Rom. 1:18-20. God has been acting like this for us all the time, but men have refused to recognize the love behind the actions and are now prevented by their cynicism from making the response of love, just as a child who has grown cynical about his parents' love for him will get more cynical and more miserable in his cynicism. We can imagine the kind of situation in which such a son falls upon evil days and finds himself in a position where only his father can save him and at the cost of his own life. If the father truly loves his son, will he take that step of sacrifice primarily in order to reveal his love, or primarily to save his son? Both elements will be in his action, and neither must be denied, but which would be the first in the father's heart? Or, to bring our illustration into line with Christian doctrine, which is the more truly Godlike action, more truly close to the divine humility and complete self-emptying of Christ—that God should come in Christ primarily to reveal his love for me, or that he should

---

[64] Robert Dale, *Christian Doctrine* (Hodder and Stoughton, 1895), p. 221.

primarily come at the expense of his own "life" to save me from the bondage of the living death in which I was held close? That love "without strings attached" reveals the depth of God's concern and love for me as nothing else can, but it presupposes that first he has done something for me that I could not do for myself.

We have said a good deal in criticism of the Abelardian view of the Atonement when its adherents presume to represent it as containing all that needs to be said about the doctrine of our redemption. We have done so deliberately, not because it is any worse than other theories when they make the same mistake, but because it is the theory to which the twentieth century has been most attracted and which we might therefore be tempted to regard as the unofficial dogma of liberal Protestantism. Having said that, let us add that no conception of the Atonement which does not have a central place for the truths that Abelard revealed can be true to the New Testament. We need to see our Lord as the human Ideal and Example, if only to understand how much we stand in need of grace. Measure yourself by the Cross, and see how high you stand.

CHAPTER VI

Reaction and Return

1. Robert Dale Reasserts the Objective Atonement

BETWEEN 1875 AND THE EARLY YEARS OF THE TWENTIETH CENTURY the discussion of the doctrine of the Atonement underwent a definite but almost imperceptible shift in its center of gravity. Up to this time those who had been contending for a reinterpretation of the doctrine in terms of the moral influence of our Lord's death had been able to direct their attack against the archaic ideas and infelicitous modes of expression in which the theologians of former centuries had cast their thought. The Puritan systems of theology had been the classic expression of penal substitution and provided the obvious whipping boy amid the scientific thought of the later nineteenth century. But in 1875 R. W. Dale entered the lists not only to champion an objective view of the Atonement but also specifically to defend the evangelical truths in the theory of penal substitution. It was apparent from the immediate reaction to his book, *The Atonement*, that here was a restatement from which it was possible vigorously to dissent but which it was not possible to ignore. Professor Moberly, for all his criticisms of Dale, declared that Dale's work "has stood, and will stand, as a real and solid contribution to the faith and goodness of his own generation." [1]

Robert Dale was the leading Congregational minister of his time and is one of the greatest representatives of a succession stretching down from Puritan times of ministers who successfully strove to combine theological scholarship with the active claims of a pastoral and pulpit ministry. Invited several times to the principalship of one college or another, Dale remained minister of the church at Carrs Lane, Birmingham, England (1859-95), and from that pulpit exerted a Christian influence not only upon the social reform of his own city

---

[1] Moberly, op. cit., p. 396.

but upon the political and religious life of the nation. At a time when individualism was not encouraging a sense of strong churchmanship, he regarded himself as "the highest of high churchman," and in an age which was beginning to demonstrate a growing distrust of theology, he made no pretense of preaching anything else. He recalls that on one occasion when, as a young man, he was chided by an older minister for preaching doctrinal sermons because the people would not stand it, he had replied, "They will have to stand it." [2] They not only stood it but thrived on it.

His discourses on *Christian Doctrine* are an illustration of the doctrinal fare offered week by week to the Carrs Lane congregation and in them we have a later summary of Dale's view of the Atonement,[3] but his great apologia was *The Atonement*, published in 1875.[4] In these two books Dale is usually regarded as having made a most vigorous defence of the theory of penal substitution, and broadly speaking that is true, for Dale undoubtedly believed that our Lord suffered on the Cross the penalty for our sin—"our sins were laid upon Him as a burden, and that burden He carried up to the Cross on which He died." [5] But even although Dale himself believed that he was defending the old theory, the judgment needs qualification, for there is a great deal of difference between Dale's exposition of penal substitution and that of the seventeenth-century Puritans. This difference is the measure of the extent to which the discussion was to shift its basis during the years that followed *The Atonement*.

Perhaps the first difference we notice between Dale and his theological predecessors is that of the temper in which he wrote. Dale wrote as a man of the nineteenth century who was honestly trying to face the concerns and the doubts of the men and women around him to whom he had to minister, and throughout his writing one has the impression that he was not merely trying to reconcile an outworn theology with a new day but to reveal the relevance of the Christian gospel to the needs of the day in which he lived. He defended the historic theory of the Atonement not because it was old, but because he believed it was relevant. He understood the way in which the rigid

---

[2] *Christian Doctrine*, p. iii.
[3] Hodder and Stoughton, 1894: Lectures X-XII, to which Lectures VIII and IX on "Man" and "Sin" might be regarded as prefatory.
[4] Hodder and Stoughton: "Congregational Union Lecture" for 1875.
[5] *Christian Doctrine*, p. 229.

application of the forensic and penal terms in his doctrine revolted the sensitive conscience. He called such extravagance "the appalling doctrine which enthrones a rigid Justice over the moral universe and denies to Mercy all authority and power." But he is at pains to show that even though we recoil at such a doctrine, we must recognize the truth that it contains, that forgiveness alone does not wholly blot out the penalties that adhere to wrongdoing.[6]

It would be unfair to suggest that the Puritans were as concerned with the doctrine of Atonement as much as they were with the fact of Atonement, since we have seen that there was a deep evangelical strain in their writings. But that which was implicit in the best of the Puritans was made explicit by Dale, namely, that the fact of the Atonement is infinitely more important than any particular theory of it.[7] To Dale all theories of the Atonement are relative and inadequate—to appropriate to ourselves the work of Christ is the vitally important fact for our souls, "then," he says, "although you may be wholly unable to discover any relation between human sin and the Death of Christ and between the Death of Christ and the Divine Forgiveness of sin, you receive the great and awful and glorious Fact of which every doctrine and theory of the Atonement can be nothing more than an inadequate explanation."[8] It is clear that in Dale we have no arid Protestant scholasticism seeking to transpose theory into dogma but a deep pastoral concern to relate the facts of the gospel to the needs of human life and to the conviction of Christian experience.

It is not only in the temper of his writing that Dale differed from the Puritans but also in substance and method. A consideration of the latter may bring to light and illustrate the former. It has been said that Dale inaugurated a new development in the use of the Bible with regard to the doctrine, for instead of quoting isolated passages and texts—on the basis that any text from the Bible is as good as any other—Robert Dale tried to trace the distinctive teaching of the doctrine throughout the New Testament.[9] At the same time Dean Rashdall maintained that the real ground of Dale's belief

---

[6] Ibid., p. 246.
[7] The Atonement, p. 4.
[8] Christian Doctrine, pp. 230-31.
[9] T. H. Hughes, The Atonement: Modern Theories, p. 75.

was the authority of Scripture.[10] It is in the polarity of those judgments that the significance of Robert Dale is to be found.

From the biblical point of view he was a conservative but by no means a fundamentalist, in the somewhat unhappy modern usage of that term. In the 1870's we should hardly expect him to have fathomed all the later results of biblical criticism, but he appears to have accepted at least some of the critical scholarship that was current in his day. He had a very deep sense, however, of the authority of the Bible, and although for his purposes he was unwilling to claim any special authority or inspiration for the apostles,[11] he would have maintained that the tradition of the Church as it is revealed to us throughout the whole of the New Testament is not simply to be discarded because it is church tradition. It means that if Dale was very far from the Puritans in his treatment of the scriptural proof, in his insistence on the *wholeness* of the New Testament witness and to the gospel that is in all Scripture, he is far nearer the biblical scholars of our own day than he was to the extreme liberals who were his contemporaries or who followed him.

In his Introduction to *The Atonement*, having made it quite clear that he regarded all theologies of Atonement as relative—"it is not the doctrine of the Death of Christ that atones for human sin, but the Death itself"[12]—he went on to say that we cannot be neutral between the two great opposing theories—Anselm and Abelard—because whether you believe that there is a direct relationship between Christ's Death and the remission of sins or that the Crucifixion simply demonstrates the supreme appeal of the Divine Love to us, one of these views is implied in our every act of prayer and worship.[13] Dale defined his own intention as that of showing that there is a direct relationship between the Death of Christ and the remission of sins. He proposed to prove this first by establishing the Atonement as a fact and then by going on to try and construct a reasonable theory from the fact. Hence the first six lectures were concerned with reviewing the New Testament evidence for the *fact* of the Atonement (i.e., for believing that the death of our Lord has in some way ob-

---

[10] Rashdall, op. cit., p. 495.
[11] *Christian Doctrine*, p. 224.
[12] *The Atonement*, p. 4.
[13] Ibid., pp. 10-11.

jectively changed our relationship to God and therefore made the remission of sins and reconciliation with him possible). In this part of the book Dale often has insights into his subject that can be still read with profit.

When Hastings Rashdall and Robert Franks claimed that the center of the gospel was to be sought in the teaching of Jesus, they had been simply echoing the ideas put forward by one of Dr. Dale's great contemporaries, Dr. Benjamin Jowett, when he declared:

> It is hard to imagine that there can be any truer expression of the Gospel than the words of Christ himself, or that any truth omitted by Him is essential to the Gospel. "The disciple is not above his master nor the servant greater than his Lord." The philosophy of Plato was not better understood by his followers than by himself, nor can we allow that the Gospel is to be interpreted by the Epistles, or that the Sermon on the Mount is only half Christian, and needs the fuller interpretation or revelation of St. Paul, or the author of the Epistle to the Hebrews.[14]

For Jowett the teaching of Jesus was the heart of the Christian gospel. Dale maintained that the gospel centered in the Person of Christ and not in his teaching. Far more of God, said Dale, was revealed in what our Lord was, in what he did, and in what he suffered than in what he taught. Dale saw nothing strange in the fact that the Church's Faith about our Lord contained elements that were not in our Lord's teaching, because ultimately the gospel was not to be found in the teaching alone but in what Christ was in his own Person, in what he revealed in deeds as well as words. "The real truth," said Dale, "is that while He came to preach the gospel, His chief object in coming was that there might be a gospel to preach.... Even if He had said nothing—and happily He has said much—about the relation of His Death to the guilt and the redemption of the human race, it seems to me that the doctrine of the Atonement developed in the Epistles would be the only satisfactory explanation of some of the most remarkable phenomena recorded in the Four Gospels."[15] From the point of view of his scientific knowledge of biblical scholarship Robert Dale may have been very much a conservative belonging to the later nineteenth century, but we are struck by the modernity of

---

[14] Quoted by Dale from Jowett's *The Epistles of St. Paul;* cf. *ibid.,* p. 93.
[15] *Ibid.,* pp. 46, 49.

his theological understanding of the Bible and in particular by his theological grasp of the person and place of Jesus Christ in the New Testament.

It must, of course, be admitted that in his account of the testimony borne by Jesus himself to his own death, Dale often used material from the Synoptists and the Fourth Gospel which later critics might question as the *ipsissima verba* of our Lord, but that issue would have been more or less irrelevant to him. He would have insisted that the question we have to ask is not the literalist question—whether or not Jesus uttered these words precisely as they are set down— but whether what the Evangelist has written is true to the Spirit and intention of our Lord, true to the inner meaning of his life and death as he revealed it to his chosen and closest associates. Fundamentally, as against the views put forward by Benjamin Jowett, and later by Rashdall and Franks, the issue is this, that if the apostolic record cannot be trusted at the vital point of what is necessary for redemption, then our Lord must have been "the most inefficient of moral teachers." [16]

Because of the centrality of Christ's Person in the biblical record, Dale insisted that our Lord's death could not be regarded simply as a martyrdom. He placed a great deal of stress upon the cry of dereliction from the Cross, for either this must be accepted as the true experience of Jesus Christ—momentarily he was forsaken by God—or else one must be prepared to say that he lost faith at that point. One may feel that this "either-or" is far too simple, and that the alternatives need some qualification, but Dale's insistence upon the reality of the experience behind the cry illustrates one very important difference between his conception of our Lord's "penal" suffering and that of the Calvinists who preceded him. For Dale it was the spiritual anguish and suffering which came to our Lord from the knowledge of the desperate evils of the world that constituted the greatest penalty Christ endured upon the Cross: the accent never fell in Dale's writings upon the physical suffering of the Crucifixion.[17]

Dale continued his search for the New Testament evidence of an objective atonement by a systematic examination of the Gospels, the Petrine, Johannine, and Pauline writings, and—curiously—in the

---
[16] *Ibid.*, p. 105.
[17] *The Atonement*, pp. 58-63.

Epistle of James. His argument from James is such a brilliant piece of reasoning that it deserves to be taken far more seriously than perhaps it has been. He recognized that James has always been a problem because the epistle seems to run counter to the greater part of the New Testament. Liberal theologians prefer to explain away Paul and point out that the whole conception of salvation in James is based upon justification by "works" in flat contradiction to any Pauline or Johannine belief in an objective atonement. Theologians who prefer more traditional views of the Atonement go to the other side of the fence, and becoming Biblical Critics with Martin Luther, are tempted to dismiss the Epistle of James as an epistle of straw.

Dale admitted that the whole emphasis in the epistle is ethical and that there is no mention of any objective atonement through the Cross; but he asks why this is so. What was the particular heresy that James was trying to correct? It seems clear that the Church was having trouble with the appearance of Antinomian Christians who had forced Paul's idea of justification by faith to the point where faith became mere belief and was entirely divorced from the good works which should spring from faith in the gospel. But belief in what? Dale asked, what was the substance of the faith which they regarded as being sufficient to save them without any further reference to good works? Surely, he argued, if the heart of the gospel had been understood by the early church simply in terms of following the teaching of the Man who went about doing good, or if the Cross has been understood simply in terms of offering to us an incentive to live more like Christ, then the Antinomian heresy was the very heresy which could never have arisen. Such a conception of the work of Christ, he said, has many defects:

> But it has one great merit; it is a conception in which the Antinomian heresy can never take root. The weeds as well as the healthy crops show the quality and nature of the soil, and if any theory of the work of Christ renders impossible a heresy which actually arose in the Churches which Apostles founded, this is decisive evidence that the theory is not Apostolic. . . . Salvation must have been represented to them as something else than a change in their personal life and character effected by the revelation of God in Christ, and something else than the natural and necessary result of such a change.[18]

[18] *Ibid.*, pp. 180-81.

In other words the only kind of gospel in the early church which could have made such a heresy possible was one which declared an objective atonement in Christ's death as being in itself the ground of the remission of sins.

Dale buttressed this argument by pointing to the general emphasis of the New Testament upon the events of Good Friday and Easter, and the proportion of space given to those events in all the Gospels—particularly in the Fourth Gospel, which he described as "representative of the highest and most spiritual form of Christian thought." [19] So at the conclusion of his New Testament studies Dale said, "We who confess that the Lord Jesus Christ is God manifest in the flesh, and who receive the Apostles as trustworthy representatives of His teaching, must accept the fact that by His Death He atoned for the sins of men, although we may be unable to construct a theory of the Atonement." [20]

This needs to be underlined, for this is really the position that Dale reached, and it is only when he went on to try and construct a theory to fit the biblical facts that he was led into the contradictions and ambiguities which made Rashdall dismiss him so contemptuously.[21] It has been truly said that as long as Dale is speaking of the fact of the Atonement he is clear and incisive, but when he passes from description of the fact to the construction of a theory, he becomes confused and even contradictory. So for him to argue that the existence of the belief in the penal substitution can only be due to the fact that "the Church received it from the Apostles" and that "the Apostles received it from Christ," [22] is going much further than his own biblical and historical investigation would warrant. As one of the most convinced Congregationalists in the history of that Confession, Dale might have reflected that this argument, or one very similar, could be used to defend episcopacy!

Why is Dale inconsistent and contradictory when he tries to produce a constructive theory of the Atonement, and what is his real problem? He set out with the intention of proving that the Atonement was to be explained in terms of an objective fact which Christ achieved

---

[19] Ibid., p. 156.
[20] Ibid., p. 267.
[21] Infra., p. 203; cf. *The Idea of the Atonement*, p. 495.
[22] *The Atonement*, p. 309.

upon the Cross for us and which was the means whereby sinners could be granted the remission of their sins. Of this objective fact Dale has no shadow of doubt because it was the heart of his own personal religion and pastoral experience. He sincerely believed that this kind of objectivity was to be maintained only in a theory of penal substitution, but he failed to see that this was an intellectual inference drawn from the traditional theology in which he had been schooled and was no necessary part of the salvation which he had experienced in the gospel.

He had begun positively with a thorough New Testament study, which showed that if one takes the New Testament as a whole it is permeated through and through with the recognition that what Christ did upon the Cross was done on account of our sin, and that because of his death we are delivered from the penalty and power of sin.[23] The objective nature of the Atonement *as a fact* stands clear by Dale's examination of the New Testament. However, all which Dale could prove on this basis was that the New Testament recognizes the objective nature of the Atonement as a fact but not any particular theory to explain the fact—certainly not necessarily a theory of penal substitution. Robert Dale's main problem, then, was to reconcile his own conviction with the facts that he was able to establish.

Dale showed that many different ideas were used in which to describe the atonement—"ransom," "sacrifice," "propitiation," and "example"—but he was obviously satisfied with none of the theories that gathered around these ideas in the history of the Church. He insisted that they were illustrations, and he is as critical as any critic in the history of the doctrine in demonstrating the impossibility of employing any of them as the basis of a proved theory of the Atonement. What he said about "ransom" may be taken as an example:

> If the Death of Christ is supposed to receive its full interpretation when described as a Ransom, to whom was the Ransom paid? Was it paid, as some of the Fathers supposed, to the devil? That hypothesis is revolting. Was it paid to God Himself? That hypothesis is incoherent; God Himself provided the Ransom, He could not pay it to Himself. . . . Was it paid by Christ to rescue us from the power of the Father? That hypothesis is intolerable; there is no schism in the Godhead. . . . Was the Ransom paid by the Divine mercy to the Divine justice? That hypothesis is mere rhet-

---

[23] *Ibid.*, p. 298.

oric. Was it paid by God to the ideal Law of Righteousness which we had offended? Criminal law knows nothing of ransoms, and a ransom cannot be paid to an idea.[24]

In the same way he went on to show the objections to a theory based upon the idea of our Lord as a "propitiation" or as a substitute, for such a substitution, he says, "would be contrary to the principle of justice." [25] Here, then, is the real reason for Dale's contradictions and ambiguities. Biblical evidence and pastoral experience convinced him of men's need to rely on an objective atonement centered in the death of Christ, but he could find no theory to do justice to the fact, although he clung to those elements within the theory of penal substitution that seemed to be vital for evangelical religion. Fundamentally, no theory of the Atonement satisfied him. "These illustrations of the nature and effect of the Death of Christ," he wrote, "are illustrations and nothing more. They are analogous to the transcendent fact only at single points. The fact is absolutely unique." [26]

This, then, is Dale's real conclusion, and although he felt impelled to carry on and try to formulate a conception of the Death of Christ which would "naturally account for all these various representations of it," that is where he should have stopped. His persistence produced those embarrassments which led Rashdall to speak of his "constant succession of ambiguities and verbal juggleries." [27] John Oman gets far nearer the mark when he speaks of Dale's "honest blunderings." [28] But when the balance of the ledger is struck Dale's New Testament defense of the objective fact has received and will receive continuing credit over the years. In his attempt to bring the penal theory up to date he failed, but as a work which demonstrates the need for those objective elements in the Atonement for which the penal theory stood, his contribution cannot be ignored. As Sidney Cave observed with great insight, "the book that was intended to conserve the penal theory showed that it could only be defended by its abandonment." [29]

[24] Ibid., p. 357.
[25] Ibid., p. 358.
[26] Ibid.
[27] Rashdall, op. cit., p. 495.
[28] Quoted by Cave, op. cit., p. 227.
[29] Ibid.

At the same time, Dale's reluctance to give up the penal theory must be seen within the ongoing struggle among theologians themselves. Who could tell at that time whether the bitterness of the struggle represented the birthpangs of a new and surer theology, or the death throes of the Faith itself? We have already mentioned Dale's opposition to the liberalism of Dr. Jowett, the Master of Balliol College, Oxford. Jowett was the outstanding Liberal thinker in Britain at that time, a man whose erudition has been justly celebrated in the apocryphal stories that continue to be whispered in the cloisters of Oxford, but who will perhaps live longest in the well-known rhyme:

> First come I, my name is Jowett,
> There's no knowledge but I know it.
> I am Master of this college;
> What I don't know isn't knowledge. (*Balliol Rhymes*)

A redoubtable champion for Liberal thought. To a later generation there is something rather amusing in the fact that such a man should have been the center of an academic *cause célèbre* and hauled before the Vice-Chancellor's court to answer for his advanced views on the inspiration of Holy Scripture. But there was nothing amusing in the incident to the theological protagonists at the time. Moberly is right when he points out that both Jowett and Dale are to be understood only in the light of those things that they are anxious to oppose.[30]

Dale's reaction, although much more judicious than that of the Puritans, must be seen very much in the same way as the reaction of those seventeenth-century Calvinists to the ever-present threat of the old Socinian enemy, for this was the enemy still, and the new liberalism seemed to be its willing handmaid. The Hibbert lecturer for 1883 confidently pointed to the new historical method as a means whereby all the old theological presuppositions would be swept away, for he could "see no evidence that Christ ever intended to teach any dogmatic system of theology at all."[31] We should remember that if we now see such radical thinkers as Frederick Denison Maurice as the

---

[30] Moberly, op. cit., p. 386.
[31] *The Reformation of the Sixteenth Century* (Williams and Norgate, 1883), p. 423. Charles Beard, the lecturer, is not to be confused with the American historian of that name.

precursors of a very different kind of theology, in their day they were regarded with considerable suspicion; Maurice's Unitarian upbringing was something to which the Anglican Church was never fully reconciled. It was in this spirit that Dale attacked the liberalizing views but always reserving his most determined attack against the Unitarian James Martineau, for he insisted that it is impossible "to discuss the Evangelical theory of the Atonement on the Unitarian theory of the Person of Christ." [32]

Dale did not fall into the same trap as some of the earlier Calvinist writers by trying to force too clear a separation between the work of the Three Persons in the Trinity. On the contrary he implicitly shows that the only basis on which the penal categories can be defended, even as an analogy of the truth, was that of the unity of God within the work of redemption. "God Himself," he declared, "in the Person of His Son, has become flesh. There is a wonderful solidarity between Him and the human race. Our sin He could not share; but He came into the dark and awful shadow which sin has cast upon the life of men. How dark the shadow was we never knew until it fell upon His great glory and eclipsed it." [33] It was, then, with a conception of a Trinity in Unity within the work of Redemption that Robert Dale maintained that the Atonement was to be understood only within the context of a full Trinitarian doctrine of the Godhead. Against Martineau's expostulation that such an objective theory involved ideas that were immoral and criminal, he exclaimed, "is there any 'immorality,' any 'crime,' anything to provoke 'a cry of indignant shame,' in the resolve of God himself, in the person of Christ, to endure suffering instead of inflicting it? ... 'Immorality!' It is a most wonderful proof of the infinite love of God. 'Crime!' It is the supreme manifestation of God's moral perfection." [34]

This illustrates the difference between Robert Dale's thought and that of the seventeenth century. The Puritans helped to bring the theory of penal substitution into being in the course of their defence of the doctrine of the Trinity, and some had ended by falling foul of the very errors they had sought to avoid. Dale showed that if the value of objective salvation (for which they had rightly con-

---

[32] *The Atonement*, p. 394.
[33] *Christian Doctrine*, p. 265.
[34] *The Atonement*, p. 396.

tended) was to be defended in such categories, it could be maintained only by a doctrine of God which was Trinity in absolute Unity. And if we think we detect in this passage Dr. Dale the preacher as well as Dale the theologian, we must remember the issues for which he believed he was contending, for he was also speaking as a pastor—one who had had some experience of human need and the cure of souls and who took seriously his pastoral responsibility to maintain and interpret the Church's Faith.

2. James Denney Repeats the Theme

When Dr. James Denney's book, *The Death of Christ*, appeared in 1902, one of its reviewers summarized it by saying that "Dr. Denny does over again, but in his own way and with consummate ability, what Dr. Dale did." This is the measure of its value and perhaps of its limitation. It was described in the same review as "an exceedingly able defence of that doctrine of the Atonement which is known as atonement by substitute." [35] Perhaps one of the chief reasons for its significance is in the fact that whereas Robert Dale's conservative approach to Scripture might be misunderstood as "fundamentalism," no one could make the same mistake about Denney, for it was immediately recognized that his defence of the theory of penal substitution had been carried out "in full view of, and taking well into account, the present position of the Higher Criticism of the New Testament." [36] Indeed, one of the main purposes of James Denney's book was to meet the challenge leveled by biblical criticism at the unity and inspiration of the Bible and to show where the divinely inspired unity of Scripture was to be found. In doing this Denney not only took up and reaffirmed the particular view of the Atonement defended by Dale, but in the course of his study he threw into sharper focus many of the theological implications that were implicit in Robert Dale's basic position. He said many of the same things as Dale, but he said them "with consummate ability."

James Denney (1856-1917) was Professor of New Testament studies (and later Principal) at the United Free Church College (Presbyterian) at Glasgow. He wrote three books on the Atonement, *The Death of Christ* (1902), *The Atonement and the Modern Mind*,

---

[35] David Purves in *The Critical Review* (1902), pp. 45-46.
[36] Ibid., p. 46.

published a year later, and *The Christian Doctrine of Reconciliation*, which appeared in 1917 and may be taken to represent his final reflections on the doctrine. This last work is the book in which he reviewed the historic presentations of the Atonement, but although he may have modified slightly some of his earlier views, in the main it reaffirms the basic positions he had reached when he wrote the former volumes. It is with the two earlier books that we shall concern ourselves not only because they give us the center of his teaching but because in them Denney writes with something of the passion of a prophet. As W. P. Du Bose remarked, "first thoughts have their use and the attraction and advantage of at least a greater freshness and enthusiasm." [37] Furthermore, in his first book, *The Death of Christ*, Denney presents us with the biblical basis for his views and develops the line of New Testament study which has been laid down by Dale. I suppose we can hardly regard it as remarkable that a New Testament scholar should base his investigation of the Atonement in *The Death of Christ* on a systematic examination of the doctrine of the New Testament (with the significant omission of *James*), until we remember that this method had been one of the unique features of Dale's book published twenty-seven years earlier. Both writers were concerned to demonstrate that the unity and inspiration of the New Testament was centered in its soteriology. Denney asserts that the unity of the New Testament is not fortuitous, the books are not held together "simply by the art of the bookbinder," [38] but its unity and its inspiration are seen to be the same thing when "we see that it converges upon and culminates in a divine love bearing the sin of the world." [39] The unity of Scripture is to be found in the Atonement.

Denney thus makes explicit something which is implicit in all Dale's writing on the subject, that the Atonement is the center of the Christian faith and the heart of all Christian theology. The Atonement, Denney said in one of his books, is "Christianity in brief." [40] It is "wrapt up in every truth of the Christian religion," [41] governing the whole realm of Christian doctrine, for when it is given the central

---

[37] *The Soteriology of the New Testament* (New York: The Macmillan Co., 1899), p. v.
[38] *The Death of Christ* (Hodder and Stoughton), p. 3.
[39] *Ibid.*, p. 314.
[40] *The Atonement and the Modern Mind* (Hodder and Stoughton, 1903), p. 2.
[41] *The Death of Christ*, p. 302.

place that Scripture secures for it, it will be seen to be "the proper evangelical foundation for the doctrine of the Person of Christ." [42] Once this is admitted, it must inevitably influence the doctrines of God, the Church, and the Sacraments. So for Denney, as for Dale before him, the unity of Scripture and the center of Christian doctrine is to be found in God's plan of Redemption—Atonement.

This Atonement comes to a head in the death of Christ. "Forgiveness is mediated through Christ," he is fond of saying, "but specifically through his death." [43] It is because he sees the death of Christ as his supreme saving act for man that he can have no traffic with any who would make the Incarnation sufficient cause for our salvation. "If Christ had done less than die for us, therefore—if He had separated from us, or declined to be one with us, in the solemn experience in which the darkness of sin is sounded and all its bitterness tasted,—there would have been no Atonement." [44] Robert Dale had said the same sort of thing, but Denney put the issue even more precisely—Christ's death is "the centre and consummation of His work." [45] It was an assertion of what P. T. Forsyth was to call "the cruciality of the Cross."

At the same time it would be incorrect to suggest that Denney asserted an atonement which centered in the death of Christ without any reference to what happened before or after the Crucifixion. He spoke of the death as the consummation of Christ's life, but it is our Lord himself who is the Atonement or propitiation, and in this total work his life and teaching are included. But Denney avers that this divine life "only enters into the Atonement, and has reconciling power, because it is pervaded from beginning to end by the consciousness of His death." [46] Instead of saying that both the life and death of Jesus contributed to the Atonement—which is true enough—Denney would say that our Lord's consciousness of a vocation that was to be supremely manifested in death was so strong that "we should rather say that His life is part of His death: a deliberate and conscious descent, ever deeper and deeper, into the dark valley where at the last hour

---

[42] *Ibid.*, p. 317.
[43] *The Atonement and the Modern Mind*, pp. 63, 80-81.
[44] *Ibid.*, p. 107.
[45] *The Death of Christ*, p. 9.
[46] *The Atonement and the Modern Mind*, p. 108.

the last reality of sin was to be met and borne." The Passion, he declared, "is our Lord's sublimest action—an action so potent that all His other actions are sublated in it." [47]

Side-by-side with this we must read what Denney said about the Resurrection, for if he thought of the death of Christ as the consummation of our Lord's earthly life, the Resurrection was to him the vindication of all that he achieved for us in both life and death. The Christ who is our Atonement and propitiation is he who died and rose again. "The New Testament preaches a Christ who was dead and is alive, not a Christ who was alive and is dead," and therefore, "to preach the Atonement means not only to preach One who bore our sins in death, but One who by rising again from the dead demonstrated the final defeat of sin, and One who comes in the power of His risen life—which means, in the power of the Atonement accepted by God—to make all who commit themselves to Him in faith partakers in His victory." [48]

It is right that we should put this passage from Denney's *The Atonement and the Modern Mind* against a certain impression gained from *The Death of Christ* that his exposition of the Atonement is too static to be entirely true to the spirit of the New Testament. He put a very great and necessary emphasis upon the work of Christ as a finished work, but in some subtle way we have the impression that in *The Death of Christ* justification and sanctification are very much the same thing precisely because he believed in a finished work of Christ. Perhaps Denney had subconsciously felt that if he gave too great a place for the Atonement as a continuing work of the risen Christ in the believer, he would be opening the way simply to an ethical and subjective conception of the doctrine. However, it must have been clear—and possibly the publication of *The Atonement and the Modern Mind* in 1903 was tacit recognition of the fact—that a doctrine of the Atonement which did not speak of the power of the risen Christ and the work of the Holy Spirit could not imply atonement in its fulness. In his second book Denney corrected the impression he had given in the earlier book, although it is only fair to add that in *The Death of Christ* he had suggested that in the terms "faith" and the Pauline expression "in Christ" we have clues as to

[47] *Ibid.*, p. 109.
[48] *Ibid.*, p. 112.

the terms on which the facts of the Christian Faith, and particularly the death of Christ have their place and effect within the life of men.[49] The power of the Resurrection and the Holy Spirit were implied, although at the time he failed to make their vital place in the Atonement explicit.

His view becomes clearer in what he said in *The Death of Christ* about the Sacraments. He pointed out that according to the rabbinic and apocalyptic writers the food that was to be eaten in the messianic banquet was the Messiah Himself.[50] "There is nothing in Christianity," he said, "more primitive than the Sacraments, and the Sacraments, wherever they exist, are witnesses to the connection between the death of Christ and the forgiveness of sins."[51] Writing of the account of the Sacraments given by Luke in Acts, he said that both Dominical Sacraments were memorials of our Lord's death and that therefore what the Acts has to say about them was not due to any particular sacramentarian tendency in the author, but that Luke simply "brings out the place which the death of Christ had at the basis of the Christian religion, as the condition of the forgiveness of sins, when he gives the sacramental side of Christianity the prominence it has in the early chapters of Acts. From the New Testament point of view, the Sacraments contain the gospel in brief; they contain it in inseparable connection with the death of Jesus; and as long as they hold their place in the Church the saving significance of that death has a witness which it will not be easy to dispute."[52]

We must not be sidetracked into a discussion how far Denney was advocating "mere memorialism." It is more important to see the significance of what he is asserting, for if the sacraments "contain the gospel in brief," then no attenuated doctrine of "mere memorialism" will be adequate for them. This is an extremely important emphasis to which Denney returns when dealing with the place of the Sacraments in Paul, for he declares that "both Sacraments are forms into which we may put as much of the gospel as they will carry; and St. Paul, for his part, practically puts the whole of his gospel into each."[53]

[49] *The Death of Christ*, p. 106.
[50] *Ibid.*, p. 46.
[51] *Ibid.*, p. 84.
[52] *Ibid.*, p. 85.
[53] *Ibid.*, p. 137.

Having given us that vital insight, we wish Denney had gone on to show not only their relation to the death of Christ, but the way in which they assist the Christian to participate in the life of Christ here and now and the assurance they give of a place in the Marriage Supper of the Lamb hereafter. The question we are forced to put is whether the Sacraments are related *only* to something done for believers in the past, or whether through that their witness is not also to a continuing work of reconciliation that will be consummated only at the Resurrection.

Earlier we stressed a good deal the similarities between the treatment of the Atonement by Robert Dale and the treatment by James Denney, but it would be wrong to suggest that the latter's examination of the doctrine was consciously modeled upon that of Dale—far from it. Denney's work was an independent study of the subject which concentrated even more upon the New Testament evidence than Dale, and the different critical presuppositions of the two men prevented any question of imitation. But we may suggest that Denney's defence of the substitutionary theory may have arisen, like Dale's, not only from the fact that they were nurtured in the same Calvinist theology but also because Denney was sensitive at the same point of doctrine as his predecessor. In *The Death of Christ* he pointed quite correctly to the fact that the attack launched by Socinianism against the orthodox faith began historically not with denial of the Incarnation but with denial of the Atonement. He went on to say that "it is with the denial of the Atonement that it always begins anew, and to begin here, is to end, sooner or later, with putting Christ out of the Christian religion altogether." [54] The same point is made in another passage where he declared that, "The process which starts with rejecting the objective Atonement—in other words, the finished work of Christ and the eternal dependence on Him and obligation to Him which this involves—has its inevitable and natural issue in the denial that Christ has any essential place in the Gospel." [55] Like Dale, in stat-

---

[54] *Ibid.*, p. 320.
[55] *Ibid.*, pp. 238-39. Perhaps the same point is illustrated in Dr. J. Scott Lidgett's *The Spiritual Principle of the Atonement* (Kelly, 1898). Scott Lidgett was extremely sensitive to the views of the Unitarian, Dr. Martineau, and although he appears to be defending the theory of penal substitution his main concern is that "objective" elements in the doctrine should not be lost and that any satisfactory statement of the Atonement must be based on adequate doctrines of the Trinity and the Person of

ing this belief he went on to assume that if an "objective Atonement" was to be defended it could only be done in terms of the substitutionary theory.

This fear of letting the thin end of the wedge open the way to Socinianism really determined the attitude of theologians like Dale and Denney toward Liberal theology. For those who understood best the cause for which they were contending, the scientific criticism of Scripture was not so much to be feared, for as Denney pointed out "belief in the inspiration of Scripture is neither the beginning of the Christian life nor the foundation of Christian theology"—it was an end result, a final conclusion which one reached as day-by-day biblical truth was proved by experience.[56] But to the person who believed in the integrated wholeness of Christian doctrine, it was a very different matter when the doctrinal front was attacked, for not much ground could be given there without abandoning the Christian Faith altogether. Doctrine defined the meaning of those truths described in Scripture by which men were saved and by which the Church lived, but the trouble with both sides in the argument was that they tended to identify the imperfect metaphors and images in which doctrine had been traditionally expressed with the apostolic truth for which the doctrine had stood. It was for these reasons that Dale and Denney reacted so vigorously against the moral influence theories of the Atonement. If one believed that these views would inevitably lead to the widespread breakdown of the Church's doctrine, there was matter enough for concern.

One gains the impression, however, that in this concern to defend the historic Faith James Denney either did not understand the moral influence theories or else did not wish to do so. The reviewer of *The Death of Christ* said that the most notable feature of the book was the fact that the penal substitutionary theory of atonement was "vindicated by the author with unique confidence and extraordinary enthusiasm, and without recognizing that the representatives of any other theory have a claim to be heard."[57] This exuberance sometimes gives us the feeling that Denney is not being quite fair to the expon-

---

Christ. He tried to put the elements of "substitution" and "satisfaction" within the revelation of the Fatherhood of God in the life and witness of our Lord.

[56] *The Atonement and the Modern Mind*, p. 9.
[57] Purves, *op. cit*, p. 45.

ents of the moral influence theories, and a good example of the way in which he treated them is to be seen in the following illustration:

> If I were sitting on the end of a pier, on a summer day enjoying the sunshine and the air, and some one came along and jumped into the water and got drowned "to prove his love for me," I should find it quite unintelligible. I might be in much need of love, but an act in no rational relation to any of my necessities could not prove it. But if I had fallen over the pier and were drowning, and some one sprang into the water, and at the cost of making my peril, or what but for him would be my fate, his own, saved me from death, then I should say, "Greater love hath no man than this." I should say it intelligibly, because there would be an intelligible relation between the sacrifice which love made and the necessity from which it redeemed.[58]

Hastings Rashdall made very heavy weather of this when he ponderously suggested that the illustration would better represent the Abelardian view if one were to go to the man at the end of the pier and declare, "To show my love for you, I will allow myself to be thrown into the sea by those who have threatened to do so unless I abandon my work of preaching what I believe to be the truth of God, of preparing the way for His Kingdom and for your admission thereto"![59] If the chief character in this illustration *loves* the one at the end of the pier—and personal love and devotion surely come nearest to the point of the story—such a lugubrious offer as Rashdall suggests might be regarded as equally lunatic and even more unintelligible than if the would-be martyr simply jumped off at the deep end and blew a kiss to his loved one on the way! Rashdall's explanation will not do primarily because the illustration itself is inadequate to describe his view of the Atonement. In using it Denney misrepresented the Abelardian position, since not even the most doctrinaire Abelardian has ever suggested that our Lord committed suicide in order to demonstrate his love for us: Denney's story virtually adds up to this. Denney, and Rashdall, might have remembered that an illustration is not an allegory, and the fundamental criticism is that the example Denney selected to illustrate one aspect of the Atonement

[58] *The Death of Christ*, p. 177.
[59] Rashdall, op. cit., p. 442.

was totally inapplicable to another. Hastings Rashdall, although reluctant to use it, was rather slow in not recognizing this.

This is typical of a certain unwillingness to give the ethical aspect of the Atonement its proper due. After all, the moral influence of Christ's death and the ethical fruits produced in the believer by our Lord's example are not simply a theory to be set against other theories and proved right or wrong, but they are an integral part of Christ's atoning work for us. As against the German theologians—Pfleiderer and Weiss—who had recognized both a juridical and an ethical emphasis in Paul, James Denney is undoubtedly right in maintaining that the apostle's thought had its own unity and coherence in Christian experience. But those whom he was criticizing were just as right in insisting that the ethical element is definitely to be found in Paul's writings (side-by-side with something nearer to Denney's own point of view) and that it must not be ignored.[60] In the same way in appealing to Rom. 5:8 ff., Denney might have given some weight to the fact that the whole passage comes to its focus in verse 10 where the apostle declares, "For if while we were yet sinners we were reconciled to God by the death of his Son, much more, now that we are reconciled, shall we be saved *by his life.*" Undoubtedly the two parts of the passage are related, and this salvation through "his life" was conceived by the apostle as being dependent upon the believer being "reconciled to God by the death of his Son," but the ethical element is there, and one of the ways in which it becomes operative in the believer is by our Lord's example.[61]

How far is it possible, then, to regard Denney's views as a defence of the theory of penal substitution? Denney's reviewer accepted it as such, Denney's theological opponents recognized it as such, and Denney himself thought that is what he was trying to do. He speaks of "the Christ of the substitutionary Atonement."[62] In another place he said that "if Christ died the death in which sin had involved us—if in His death He took the responsibility of our sins upon Himself—no word is equal to this which falls short of what is meant by calling him our substitute."[63] This seems fairly conclusive

---

[60] *The Death of Christ,* pp. 179-86.
[61] Cf. *Ibid.,* p. 178.
[62] *The Atonement and the Modern Mind,* p. 116.
[63] *The Death of Christ,* p. 103.

until it is realized that there is nothing specifically penal about it, and that although he used the language of substitution and sometimes the metaphors, he repudiated just as strongly as Dale the strictly juridical view of the Atonement. In *The Atonement and the Modern Mind*, published a year after the appearance of *The Death of Christ*, he made this personal apologia:

> If one may be excused a personal reference, few things have astonished me more than to be charged with teaching a "forensic" or "legal" or "judicial" doctrine of Atonement, resting, as such a doctrine must do, on a "forensic" or "legal" or "judicial" conception of man's relation to God. ... There is nothing that I should wish to reprobate more whole-heartedly than the conception which is expressed by these words. To say that the relations of God and man are forensic is to say that they are regulated by statute—that sin is a breach of statute—that the sinner is a criminal—and that God adjudicates on him by interpreting the statute in its application to his case. Everybody knows that that is a travesty of the truth.[64]

At the same time Denney held that if the relations of father and son were more adequate than the relations between judge and criminal to describe our relationship with God, the image of "a naughty child before a parent" was just as faulty and defective in describing our position before God as that of a criminal before his judge. Both were illustrations and as illustrations could do no more than approximate to the truth. That for which Denney was contending was virtually the same as that for which Dale had contended before him, to ensure that the objective element—God's own action—in the Atonement, which had been exemplified in the substitutionary view in such a pronounced form, should not be jettisoned in favor of a theory that was wholly concerned with our human subjective responses. It is clear that when Denney thought of the Atonement (at-one-ment), he was thinking of reconciliation, but it was a reconciliation brought about as much by the necessities within God's own nature as by our own sinful need.[65] God acted—that is the constant theme of the Bible of which James Denney persists in reminding us. In commenting upon the views of Seeberg's *Der Tod Christi* he asked, "What is

---

[64] *The Atonement and the Modern Mind*, p. 46.
[65] Cf. *The Christian Doctrine of Reconciliation*.

the means which God takes to secure fellowship with *sinful* men, *i.e.* to act toward them in a way which does justice to Himself?" He gave the answer to his own question, "something has to be *done*, where sinful men are concerned, before fellowship with God can be taken for granted; and that something God actually *does* when He sets forth Christ a propitiation, through faith, in His blood." [66]

It was in this emphasis upon the "doneness" of God's action in Christ that James Denney and Robert Dale made their great contribution to the subject, and in making the contribution they ultimately assist not only our understanding of the doctrine of the Atonement but also help us to see its relation to the Sacraments. That which was done was done by God. Perhaps the weakness of their theological position was that they stopped at this vital point. Their theological strength was that they did not stop before they had reached it.

3. Incarnation as Atonement: the Thought of Westcott, Caird, and Wilson

When Horace Bushnell spoke of an annual harvest of books on the Atonement, he was perhaps exaggerating, but by the end of the nineteenth century this was becoming literal fact. It is clearly impossible in the scope of our present study to deal with all weighty volumes that poured from the presses to add their own contribution to this doctrine. The distinguished American scholar, W. P. Du Bose, in the preface to the second edition of his book, *The Soteriology of the New Testament* (1899), said that when he had first published the work seven years earlier there had been no sign of the great outburst of interest that had since taken place and which was leading to "almost daily" additions to the available literature.[67] He said that this specifically with regard to the Christological problem which provides the main interest in his own book, but he might have said it with equal truth about the doctrine of Atonement itself. Looking back, it is strange to find the British Methodist, J. Scott Lidgett, complaining in 1898 about the comparative neglect of the doctrine in British theology since the appearance of Dale's great work. Within a few years the theological market was flooded with outstanding works on the subject, and since that time the reasonable average of a book a year has been fully

[66] *The Death of Christ*, p. 173.
[67] Du Bose, op. cit., 2nd ed. p. v.

maintained by British theologians! [68] Scott Lidgett's concern and what followed it shows that the Atonement had become the point of doctrine around which British theology was taking its form, because theologians took this as the point where God visibly meets man in the work of Christ and because what happens here governs not only Christian apologetic but the whole of Christian doctrine.

At the same time the theological debate was no longer a clear issue between the satisfaction and penal theories on the one hand and the Abelardian and moral influence theories on the other. For the purposes of classroom classification it may be useful to speak of this as the main division in the theological approach to the problem, but Scott Lidgett's attempt to restate the doctrine by trying to include the satisfactionary and penal ideas within the governing revelation of the Fatherhood of God, Moberly's conception of "vicarious penitence" and his emphasis upon Church and Sacraments, Denney's emphasis upon the completed act of Atonement and upon reconciliation, and even Dale's attempt to relate the rest of his book to the final chapter are all indications of an intense struggle to reinterpret the doctrine.

New theories were springing up to meet the old facts. There was reaction from the old and from the new, and if historical and biblical studies could lead to a return on the one hand to Abelard and the Gospels, they might lead just as easily on the other to the Reformers and Paul. At the end of his book Scott Lidgett reminds us of a whole group of writers who have since been more or less passed over, who in the face of the confusion of ideas were content to assert the Atonement as a fact but declared that its meaning was by the very nature of the fact unknowable.[69] It was a mystery hidden with God himself. If theology was in the last resort unwilling to take that line, it must have been for the good apologetic reason that "blank mystery does not move men, for their faith means insight." [70] God is ultimately unknowable in this life, but that which Jesus Christ has done for us must be capable of being understood to some extent if we are to respond to it. It may be that what is ultimately revealed is the mystery of the fathomless love of God. If that is so, the divine discontent which has urged theologians to challenge the meaning of the doctrine

[68] *The Spiritual Principle of the Atonement* (Kelly, 1898), p. 1.
[69] *Ibid.*, pp. 488-98.
[70] *Ibid.*, p. 498.

of our Redemption suggests that it is the task of theology to obey the call of faith and go out to meet that illimitable love rather than stand hovering faithless on the brink for fear of being lost in it. To change our metaphor and take our lesson from the patriarch, it is only by faithful wrestling with the problems of the faith that we learn the secret of God's name.[71]

There is another stream of thinking, mostly Anglican, which made its appearance about this time and which to some extent stands between the "objective" and "subjective" interpretations of the doctrine. It is represented by those who instead of seeing the Incarnation as the necessary means whereby the Atonement took place once again took up the thought of Athanasius and expressed the Atonement in terms of the Incarnation itself. According to Bishop B. F. Westcott, who was the pioneer of this school of thought at the end of the nineteenth century, the Incarnation is "the central point of our Faith," "the central event in the life of the world, the central truth in the experience of men."[72]

We have already seen that among those who advocated the moral influence theory of our Lord's sacrifice there was already a tendency to stress the implicit sacrifice of the Incarnation over against the explicit sacrifice of the Crucifixion. The heart of a theory of atonement as put forward by Rashdall or Franks, for example, was in showing that the death of Christ presented an example of the same kind of obedience and self-giving that was illustrated throughout our Lord's earthly life. R. C. Moberly had been influenced by Westcott and had stressed incarnation as a vital aspect of atonement. Horace Bushnell had shown the way many years before when he had insisted that Christ's "incarnate appearing was but the necessary outcoming in time of God's eternal love,"[73] but in emphasizing our Lord's complete identity with us Bushnell separated the idea of Incarnation from any doctrine of an Immaculate Conception by insisting that our Lord was born of maculate and not immaculate motherhood. He shared completely our human nature with its entail from Adam.[74] Others who held the moral

---

[71] Gen. 32:24-30.
[72] *The Incarnation: A Revelation of Human Duties* (S.P.C.K., 1892).
[73] *The Vicarious Sacrifice*, p. 260.
[74] *Ibid.*, p. 325.

influence theory stressed the identity between Christ and men to the extent of showing that our Lord was born with a humanity capable of sinning, and that therefore his moral perfection came from his own effort of will. It was his own moral victory in life and not simply due to the uniqueness of his birth. W. P. Du Bose has perhaps put this view in its most challenging form.[75]

It was in the fact of the Incarnation itself that those who followed Bishop Westcott found the Atonement, although Westcott himself never quite expressed it as baldly as that. His view has been described as a "mystical" theory[76] because it has stressed the corporate and representative character of our Lord's work in becoming human, into which we are caught up—"*for ye are all one man in Christ Jesus*," quoted Westcott in *The Victory of the Cross*. He then went on to comment, "not 'one' only in the abstract by acknowledgement of a real fellowship, by the enjoyment of being essentially the same, but one man: one that is, even as the living vine is one with its many branches, one as the living body is one with its many members."[77] On the other hand it should be said that this conception of Christ's representative work has not been any monopoly of Westcott and those who were influenced by him. The distinctive contribution they made was in the close or even complete identification of the Atonement with the Incarnation which led Archdeacon J. M. Wilson to declare, "Let us say boldly that the Incarnation, that is, the life and death of the Christ,—for the life and death were equally necessary—is the identification of the human and divine life. This identification is the Atonement. There is no other."[78]

Although Wilson gave Westcott the credit for bringing this to light and for starting a theological movement in which, he held, the doctrine of the Incarnation was replacing the doctrine of the Atonement, the point of view was more implied than explicitly stated by the Bishop in his writings. In his lectures on the Apostles' Creed, *The Historic Faith*, Westcott cited Phil. 2:8 ff. and Heb. 2:9 and commented, "So He in His humanity—Jesus—accomplished the true destiny of man, and accomplished through suffering the destiny of man fallen."[79]

---

[75] Du Bose, *op. cit.*, p. 147.
[76] Cf. T. H. Hughes, *The Atonement: Modern Theories*, ch. vii.
[77] *The Victory of the Cross* (Macmillan, 1889), p. 41.
[78] *The Gospel of the Atonement* (Macmillan, 1899), p. 89.
[79] *The Historic Faith* (Macmillan, 1883), p. 60.

THE ATONEMENT AND THE SACRAMENTS

Again, pointing to the strong accent of the verbs in the Creed, he said, " 'Conceived, born, suffered, crucified, dead, buried.' Each word marks a crisis in the sacrifice, and helps us to apprehend its completeness." [80] The ideas of incarnation and atonement are held together within the governing conception of our Lord's sacrifice but gradually the predominance of the Incarnation in his thought emerges in the following passage:

> For Christ that lot of man can be briefly summed up in the phrase 'He suffered,' suffered from first to last, even while he grew in favour with God and man, as seeing the disharmony between "His Father" and "His brethren." He suffered and He endured the cross, the uttermost shame of suffering, being made an outcast from His own people who were by calling the people of God: "He was crucified." And in most terrible form He bore the last issue of Sin, though He knew no Sin: "He died." And He received the last tribute of love from friends who had ceased to hope: "He was buried." Step by step we follow the history, and as we reverently ponder it we learn to look at Christ as the One Divine centre of humanity as created: to look to Him as the Redeemer and Restorer of man fallen: we learn to meditate on the Incarnation itself; and on the sorrows by which it was actually encompassed. We learn something of the lesson of Christ's humanity, something of the lesson of Christ's sufferings.[81]

The Incarnation is seen as the sacrificial act which incorporated all that our Lord has done for man's salvation: it is not specifically identified with atonement, but this is implied.

Some of the distinctive features of this position were brought out in the sermons Westcott preached in Hereford Cathedral in Holy Week, 1888, and published as *The Victory of the Cross*.

1. He wished to show first of all "how the fundamental thought of the Gospel that *the Word became flesh* gives a Divine foundation for our belief that duty is the law of the individual life, and solidarity the law of universal life"—in other words, to show the reality and the possibilities of "that perfection of manhood through suffering which Christ has wrought for us." [82] The foundation of the gospel is in the fact that Christ came and was man—that in itself was sufficient. The

---
[80] *Ibid.*, p. 61.
[81] *Ibid.*, p. 61-62.
[82] Westcott, *The Victory of the Cross*, pp. 4-5.

redemption was in his coming because his coming already implied sacrifice. To Westcott sacrifice was the condition of redemption, for he said, the central truth of Christianity was the thought that "whosoever shall seek to gain his life shall lose it, but whosoever shall lose his life shall preserve it." Westcott held the Incarnation and the Atonement together in these two New Testament thoughts, that the Word became flesh and that the Word of God in becoming flesh revealed himself as redeeming sacrifice personified, a Seed that was prepared to fall into the ground and die that it might bring forth much fruit.

2. A second distinctive element in those who follow the "incarnational" view of the Atonement is the *mystique* of humanity's corporate victory in Christ, to which we have alluded but which in their thinking seems to have followed as much if not more from the action of God in Creation as from his action in Redemption—or rather, that the Incarnation, and therefore the redemptive process, was the inevitable outcome of Creation. "The Incarnation," said Westcott, "is to be regarded primarily in the light of the Divine purpose of Creation,—the attainment of the Divine likeness by humanity—and not in the light of man's premature self-assertion." [83] In other words in Westcott's view, it has to be seen in terms of God's eternal purpose for man rather than primarily in terms of what was necessary in order to save man from his sin. He approached this in an intersting way by showing the solidarity of the human race in its achievements and its failures and then pointed to the implications of this in relation to the Incarnation of Jesus Christ. "Christ as the Head of humanity," he said, "was able to bring within the reach of every one who shares His nature the fruits of His perfect obedience, through the energy of the one life by which we all live. His sufferings were not 'outside us.'" [84]

This element was expressed in a certain kind of immanentism in Principal John Caird's Gifford Lectures.[85] Caird, one of two famous brothers who were distinguished theologians of the (Presbyterian) Church of Scotland, shared certain ideas with the Anglican school we have been discussing. He said that the one who was to be the origin of the new life for man must be, not simply a divine spirit, but a spirit

---

[83] *Ibid.* Notice to the 2nd edition (1888), p. ix.
[84] *Ibid.*, p. 80.
[85] *The Fundamental Ideas of Christianity* (Glasgow: Machebose, 1899) Vol. II, Lectures XVI-XX.

that was human, in whom the selfishness that at present separates our souls from God has been destroyed and the nature of man thus brought perfectly in union with the divine. "It is the very central fact of our Christian faith," Caird said, "that once for all it has been realized, and that in the person and life of Christ we can recognize a nature from which every dividing, disturbing element has passed away —a mind that was the pure medium of Infinite Intelligence, a heart that throbbed in perfect unison with Infinite Love, a will that never vibrated by one faintest aberration from the Infinite Will, a human consciousness possessed and suffused by the very spirit and life of the Living God."[86] There is nothing in this with which to quarrel, for it is centered in the work of Christ, but in a passage like the following there is a somewhat vague immanentism which could so easily degenerate into pantheism:

> The Divine Spirit that was embodied in the life of Christ, and which realizes itself in every soul that yields itself to its transforming power, wherever or whenever it takes possession of human spirits, is in essence one and the same in all. The imperative of duty, the presence within our consciousness that speaks to us in the command, "Be true, be just, be good," is not simply a similar presence in your mind and mine, but it is one and the same divine presence in all; and those in every age and country who have responded to it are united together in one undivided confraternity. And as it is one and the same force which binds the atoms of matter together and holds the planets in their orbits, so every pure thought, every holy aspiration, every effort after goodness in the lowliest or loftiest of human spirits, is a manifestation of the same divine principle that dwelt in Christ and was revealed to the world in His life and death.[87]

Westcott would probably not have gone as far as this, for to him the unity that humanity has in Christ is *in* Christ and not simply through him, and he quoted our Lord's own words, "Because I live, ye shall live also. Apart from me ye can do nothing." Nevertheless, there was a tendency in this concentration on the ideas of Creation and Incarnation, and in the mystical approach to our Lord's representative character, for the Christian gospel to become reduced to an immanent

[86] *Ibid.*, p. 171.
[87] *Ibid.*, pp. 252-53.

sense of goodness missing the sharp edge of the gospel—without much reference to the real need that brought Jesus Christ among men.

3. But we must look at the positive side of this, for it came from a Christian humanism that was just beginning to become acutely aware of the place which the brotherhood of man had in the gospel of Jesus and from men who were beginning to look with new understanding, compassion, and penitence upon the human misery and vice close at hand in nineteenth-century industrial Britain. This compassion, centered in the Incarnation which bound the Christian believer close to his fellow man, is very pronounced in Bishop Westcott's writings. One of his shorter books—lectures to the clergy of Durham, his northern industrial diocese—was entitled, *The Incarnation: a revelation of human duties*. It developed with rather more practical insight than one sometimes expects of a distinguished scholar the social and political implications of his favorite doctrine. It reveals throughout a deep Christian concern that the corporate nature of our redemption in Christ, animated by the Spirit that was in Jesus himself, should be given bold social and political expression by all Christian churchmen. "If I am a Christian," he declared, "I must for my own part acknowledge the widest issues of the incarnation and strive to establish them." [88]

This concern may have attracted Archdeacon Wilson to the thought of Bishop Westcott, for the archdeacon was a clergyman in a large industrial diocese beset with desperate social and economic problems. It was in Wilson's Hulsean Lectures of 1898-99, *The Gospel of the Atonement*, that the identification between the Incarnation and the Atonement, hinted at in Westcott, was frankly embraced. "The doctrine of redemption," he said, "is embodied in the words 'Who for us men, and for our salvation, came down from heaven.' He came to make us what God intended us to be. That is all. If I may express in an aphorism which concentrates the leading truth, but will mislead unless read in the light of the qualifications I have stated and implied, the Incarnation is itself the Atonement." [89]

One of J. M. Wilson's most important qualifications is that although in his view the Incarnation constitutes the act of Atonement, the Atonement was completed on the Cross, for even he had to admit

---

[88] Westcott, op. cit., p. 44.
[89] Wilson, op. cit., pp. 87-88.

THE ATONEMENT AND THE SACRAMENTS

that as Christ has made us one with God, "in some way it is the suffering and the death, even more than the life, that has so affected us."[90] Underlying this concentration upon the Incarnation there was that same deep consciousness of human brotherhood that is to be found in Westcott and the same sense of social solidarity. This is the positive aspect of ideas which can be criticized too easily if one forgets the social and historical background out of which they sprang. The sweated millions in the slums of England's northern cities had heard the traditional views of the Atonement preached at them for a very long time and were unmoved, for the Kingdom of Heaven which the preachers offered seemed a long way off, and the factory with its twelve hours a day was very near. Perhaps they needed to be told of a God who was ready to become a carpenter for their sakes, and who could show them the way in which his Kingdom could come on earth and his will be done here, as it is in heaven. On the other hand looking at this from the other side of the "Social Gospel," having seen its great achievements and its desperate failures, we know that though the sense of social and corporate sin can be deep and real, the evil which is hardest to eradicate and most real to the individual is the sin of the individual. No social salvation can finally be much help to me unless it can convince me that God in Christ also came to save me from my sin.

The significance of those who developed an "incarnational" theory of the Atonement is that although they also proclaimed an "objective" atonement, in another sense they stand diametrically opposite to the position of men like Dale and Denney. For the latter the Cross is "crucial," but for Westcott and Wilson the focal point is the crib. James Denney was particularly scathing toward Wilson. Against Wilson's bold claim that the Incarnation is the Atonement, Denney blandly remarked that it was a pity they had had to wait until the end of the nineteenth century before this simple solution had been discovered—a somewhat unfair observation since the idea had not been entirely unknown to Athanasius, the Greek Fathers, and to others in the history of the Church. Denney objected to the shift from Calvary to Bethlehem. He claimed that the theory changed the biblical accent on the moral problem to an accent on metaphysical ones—in Denney's own pungent phrase, "It does not contain a gospel for lost souls, but

[90] *Ibid.*, p. 101.

a philosophy for speculative minds."[91] Finally, pointing to the kind of Christmas festivities presumably enjoyed by episcopalian Sassenachs, he condemned the whole theory as tending to religious sentimentalism.

Whether one agrees or not with the strictures of James Denney, he was right to recognize the seriousness of the challenge to Protestant theology in any attempt to shift the point where God stood revealed to man from Holy Week and Easter to Advent and Christmas. Real issues were being raised in this struggle over the theology of the Incarnation and the Atonement, issues that could have repercussions throughout the whole field of theology, and which held grave implications for the doctrines of Church and Sacraments.

For Denney the real point at which God is revealed to man is upon the Cross: here God in Christ is shown to be a reconciling God. This is something done by God and is entirely due to the Almighty's own initiative in the face of our sin. If this is seen as the center of theology, then it throws its own light back and shows us what God also did at the Incarnation, it reveals the Person of our Lord and the nature of the Holy Trinity itself, and it points forward to its consummation and confirmation in the actions of God in the Resurrection, Ascension, Pentecost, and in the witness of the Church in Word and Sacrament. If the Atonement and the Cross are taken as the center of theology—central not in point of importance but central as the point of God's self-revelation to man—then all God's relationships with men are illumined by this central fact, from Creation to the doctrine of Last Things. The whole panorama of salvation—*Heilsgeschichte*—is seen as one divine action, God touching man in deed—a deed of complete sacrifice, suffering, and brokenness. Whatever the other implications of Bishop Westcott's thought may be, he himself surely had this thought very much to the fore when he wrote of Christ "reigning from the Cross."

Almost the same could be said (and Westcott said it almost exactly the same) for the conception of theology that would put the Incarnation in the central place where Denney would put the Atonement. The difference would not be in any questioning of the facts themselves but in the way in which the Church regarded the facts. Denney had said that the Incarnational theory changed the Bible's emphasis

[91] *The Death of Christ*, p. 326.

upon moral problems to an accent upon metaphysical ones, and although this may be a sweeping statement, it has something of the truth in it. There *is* an important difference of emphasis. For those whose theology centers in Atonement, the figure on the Cross is central, and it is primarily a figure of shame, suffering, and complete sacrifice. This is *also* the figure of innocence, the man who had been tempted in all points as we are yet without sin, whose divinity would rise triumphant. But these are things hidden for the moment and will not be made apparent until the Resurrection. For those whose theology centers in Incarnation, the focus is at the crib, and the figure in the crib is primarily that of the Innocent Babe, born of the Holy Spirit and a spotless Mother. This is *also* the personification of God's humility, and he will become the Man of Sorrows, but that is hidden at this moment and will not be revealed until later. The impression that comes uppermost at his birth is that of humility and of innocence and purity untouched by human sin. The accent is different from that of the Cross, although in both cases what God was doing was essentially the same thing. At Bethlehem the accent is primarily upon God's presence among us—Emmanuel, "God with us"—rather than upon God's decisive action. On the Cross the accent is upon his redeeming action, which only at the Resurrection is revealed as the proof of his sinless presence among us.

What does this matter for the Church and its theology? Perhaps more than we realize. It matters whether the Church thinks of itself primarily as a continuation of the Incarnation or as an extension of the redemptive work of Christ; whether it is captivated by the importance and maintenance of divine innocence and a purity which cannot sin; whether it sees itself first of all as bearing the world's sin and sorrow—becoming "sin" for the sake of the world—with an innocence and purity that cannot be demonstrated or even claimed until it is revealed at the Resurrection. Theologically (and practically) it matters whether in the Eucharist you see the bread and the wine as primarily the vehicles of God's presence in Incarnation, or as the vehicles of God's action in Redemption, whether in taking the bread and the wine you believe you take to yourself the living purity of Christ which will incorporate you into his perfect humanity, or whether these elements are primarily to you the Real Presence in God's atoning action which make you a member incorporate in a body broken and blood that has been shed for the world. These are some of the issues implied and which stem from whichever doctrine the Church places at the center of her theology—Incarnation or Atonement.

4. Forsyth Attempts a Synthesis

"Nothing can arrest the judgment of the Cross, nothing can shake the judgment-seat of Christ. The world gets a long time to pay, but all the accounts are kept—to the uttermost farthing. Lest if anything were forgotten there might be something unforgiven, unredeemed, and unholy still." [92] The words are those of Peter Taylor Forsyth.

It might seem a little unfair to the reader at the end of a chapter already long enough to turn to P. T. Forsyth, but we must do so not only because his thought has direct revelance to the issues raised at the end of the last section, but also because he is the inevitable bridge between this period of "reaction and return" and what may be regarded as the modern period of "post-critical" theology.

Forsyth was another Congregationalist, but when Sir Thomas Browne at the beginning of the *Religio Medici* confessed, "I am of that reformed new-cast Religion, wherein I mislike nothing but the name, of the same belief our Saviour taught, the Apostles disseminated, the Fathers authorized, and the Martyrs confirmed," he could have been writing for Forsyth, for although Forsyth knew precisely where he stood in matters of churchmanship, no man was more conscious that the responsibilities of his calling extended far beyond any narrowly confessional allegiance. As he wrote in the preface to one of his greatest and most influential books, "My position is neither current Anglican nor popular Protestant. I write from the Free Church camp, but not from any recognized Free Church position. . . . The audience is Free Church, but the treatment means to be Great Church." [93]

Born of very poor parents in Aberdeen in 1849, Forsyth eventually won his way to Aberdeen University. The "brilliant academic career," often employed by the writers of obituaries as a banal way of gilding

---

[92] P. T. Forsyth, *The Justification of God*. (London: Independent Press), p. 216.
[93] *The Church and the Sacraments* (Independent Press, 4th Impression, 1953), p. xv.

a mediocre lily could be applied with literal truth in his case, for his distinguished classmate, Robertson Nicoll, described him as "one of the ablest students Aberdeen University ever boasted." While he was at the university, he came very deeply under the influence of the writings of the Anglican, F. D. Maurice, an influence which remained. After a brief time as tutor in classics he went to Göttingen to study under Ritschl and returned first to pursue a short theological course in London and then to enter the ministry. His first two pastorates in Yorkshire and London must have been something of a disappointment to him from the point of view of his relationship to his own denomination, for his radical views were regarded with such suspicion that neither the Yorkshire nor the London Congregational Union appear to have recognized him. It was not until 1901, at the age of 52 and after a distinguished ministry at Cambridge, that he became a "professional theologian" and accepted the principalship of Hackney College, a small struggling denominational college in London. By that time in spite of constant ill-health, he had made his name as a preacher and theologian, and although he died in 1921, today he is regarded by the members of all confessions as one of the most significant figures that have appeared in British theology.

Forsyth could have been to the Anglo-Saxon world what Barth has been for the European continent if that world had been ready to listen. His importance is not in any theological system he has left us, indeed, since the seventeenth century Anglo-Saxons generally have disliked theological "systems." His books are made up of occasional papers, lectures, and sermons, and hardly any of them were written in the first instance to be read. They have all the defects of the prophet who has a prophetic word to say, and who, without caring too much about the scrupulous analysis of future generations, was determined to say it as effectively as possible to his own contemporary situation. Yet there is no British theologian who in the post-war world after 1945 exerted a greater influence upon the theology of his own country than Forsyth, because the word that he said was the word of which we had need.

In many ways the comparison with Karl Barth is striking: both men have been drawn to the arts—Barth finds theology in music and Forsyth found it in painting. In his early career Barth was deeply interested in social and labor questions and so was Forsyth. But perhaps the most striking similarity is that both men came to their views in congregations *as pastors* trying to meet the needs of those to whom they were called to minister—they started as pastors and only became "theologians" in trying to meet the pastoral need.

In his lectures delivered at Yale, published first in 1908 as *Positive Preaching and the Modern Mind*, Forsyth tells us in a passage which has become a classic the course of his own theological conversion.[94] He said that at the beginning he had been mainly interested in the questions of purely scientific criticism, but through pastoral experience he had seen that people were not prepared for the critical questions that the scholars delighted to raise, and that as a pastor he had no right to foist on them his own verdict on questions that so nearly touched their souls. Alongside this pastoral concern Forsyth himself had experienced a theological awakening that almost amounted to a new conversion to the Faith. "It also pleased God," he said, "by the revelation of His holiness and grace, which the great theologians taught me to find in the Bible, to bring home to me my sin in a way that submerged all the school questions in weight, urgency and poignancy. I was turned from a Christian to a believer, from a lover of love to an object of grace. And so, whereas I first thought that what the Churches needed was enlightened instruction and liberal theology, I came to be sure that what they needed was evangelization, in something more than the conventional sense of that word. . . . There was something to be done, I felt, before they could freely handle the work of the scholars on the central positions. And that something was to revive the faith of the Churches in what made them Churches; to turn them from the ill-found sentiment which had sapped faith; to reopen their eyes to the meaning of their own salvation; to rectify their Christian charity by more concern for Christian truth; to banish the amiable religiosity which had taken possession of them in the name of Christian love; and to restore some sense not only of love's severity, but of the unsparing moral mordancy in the Cross and its judgment, which means salvation to the uttermost."

To Forsyth, however, this did not represent any return to the Fundamentalism of a former day. He declared that his faith in the

[94] *Op. cit.* (Hodder and Stoughton), pp. 281 ff.

critical methods, applied to traditional dogma as well as to Scripture, was unchanged, but it was a case of putting theologically first things first. "In most cases the best contribution the preacher can make at present to the new theology is to deepen and clear the old faith." It was "to deepen the old theology by a sympathetic re-interpretation, which pierces farther into its content of revelation, and speaks the old faith in a new tongue." This is sufficient to indicate why P. T. Forsyth, who in point of time now belongs to the past, is the bridge between the thought of the early days of the present century and today. He sounds like our contemporary, for in 1908 he stood where the great weight of European theology now stands.

It is difficult to say what book or books one should select in order to give Forsyth's interpretation of the Atonement, for the two books which we would expect to give the complete picture, *The Cruciality of the Cross* (1909), and *The Work of Christ* (1910), are so clearly lectures prepared under pressure and by no means say all that Forsyth said on the subject. The late Principal Cave, a student and an intimate friend of Forsyth, said that one of the greatest books on the Atonement would have been the book that Forsyth might have written but did not write.[95] Perhaps Albert Peel—who did not share Forsyth's theological position—showed truer insight when he said that Forsyth's conception of the Atonement was stressed in "a remarkable series of volumes." In truth all Forsyth's theological works are books on the Atonement, because the Cross and its meaning are central to all his thought. To give an adequate account of Forsyth's interpretation of the Atonement would demand a systematic exposition of his whole theology, and although to do this in any detail would be well outside the scope of the present study, we must start from the basic presuppositions of his thought and indicate how these views affected his approach to the Atonement.

1. First of all there is the centrality of the Cross. We have it expressed in the title of his address to the International Congregational Council at Edinburgh, 1908, *The Cruciality of the Cross*, or in the opening words to the same Council at Boston in 1899, "The Cross is the final seat of authority, not only for the Church but for all human society."[96] The world power of the gospel, he said in a book written

---

[95] *Congregational Quarterly* (Vol. XXVI, No. 2, April, 1948), p. 119.
[96] Quoted by Cave, *ibid.*, p. 110.

during the 1914-18 war, is due "to its revealing God in action on the Cross." [97] If the idea of atonement had become wrongly superimposed upon the real gospel, "how," he asked, "has the whole Church come totally to misread its creator, and to miss what for Him was central?" [98] Such a misreading as that, which the advocates of the new Liberalism maintained had happened, "is no misprint but a flaw," a fatal misconception and perversion of the gospel, which if it were true "must destroy any belief in the guidance of the Church by the Holy Spirit."

In another work against the popular theology which summarized the gospel of Christ in the parable of the Prodigal Son, Forsyth ironically asked, if that were truly the case, why our Lord did not either consider his mission discharged once he had given this parable to the world, or else go on like John to a ripe old age simply repeating the same truth in many different forms.[99] Forsyth maintained that the Cross is not only the center of history but the very heart of eternity—"The crucifixion, of course," he says, "is a historic fact, but the cross, the Atonement, like the Christ is superhistoric. And it is in this superhistoric consummation—the kingdom in the cross—that many of our finest modern aspirations should come to unity and rest." [100] In a true sense our Lord lived for the Cross—"The Cross was not simply a fate awaiting Christ in the future; it pervaded subliminally His holy Person. He was born for the Cross. It was His genius, His destiny." [101] To this, he maintained, the whole life and witness of the early Church gave testimony, for in the early Church there had been no church history, no tradition of Christian service, no theology on which to rest their faith—they rested it upon Christ and his Cross.[102] These are simply a series of quotations from Forsyth which indicate the "cruciality of the Cross" for his theology. But we need to ask why he found the center of the gospel at this point—how does it become crucial? We discover the answer to that in the things Forsyth has to say about God and about sin.

2. God is holy. It is not simply with love that we have to deal

---

[97] *The Justification of God*, p. 13.
[98] *The Cruciality of the Cross* (Independent Press, 2nd edition, 1948), p. 49.
[99] *The Work of Christ* (Independent Press, 5th Impression, 1952), p. 106.
[100] *The Cruciality of the Cross*, p. 55.
[101] *The Work of Christ*, p. 108.
[102] *Ibid.*, p. 145.

but with *holy* love. God could not ignore sin because God cannot trifle with his own holiness; "He could will nothing against His holy nature, and he could not abolish the judgment bound up with it." But this holiness which interprets and perfects the love of God was not only the starting point of Forsyth's approach to the work of Christ and our redemption, but it was also the basis of his attitude to the Christian ethic, which was involved in that redemption. "There is only one thing," he says, "that can satisfy the holiness of God, and that is holiness—adequate holiness. . . . For the only adequate confession of a holy God is a perfectly holy man." [103] As Forsyth works this out, it has reference not only to the holy obedience of our Lord himself but specific application also to the life to which the Christian is called in him.

3. Sin is sinful: we have to recognize this sinfulness of sin—its depth and our corporate involvement in it. There is no doubt that he saw the 1914-18 war as a judgment upon that sin, and he pointed out how through the years of peace people had been lulled not only to a complacent disregard of the world's moral problem but to the dangerous position where they imagined that "sin" was an idea that was irrelevant to their modern world. "And now," thundered Forsyth, "God enters the pulpit, and preaches in His own way by deeds. And His sermons are long and taxing, and they spoil the dinner. Clearly God's problem with the world is much more serious than we dreamed. We are having a revelation of the awful and desperate nature of evil. The task which the Cross has to meet is something much greater than a pacific, domestic, fraternal type of religion allows us to face." [104] The war in which the nations were then locked simply underlined the nature of human sin and brought home to Forsyth the way in which the totality of world evil must appear in God's sight. "It is impossible," he declared, "that the whole dimensions and heinousness of wickedness, the abysmal perdition of humanity, should be grasped by any created soul. Only the absolutely holy can measure sin or judge it. No individual man has mind enough to grasp the wickedness of a nation, nor heart enough to bewail it—to say nothing of morals enough to master it. None but Christ gauged the sin of Israel. And what are we to say of the sin of the whole race? No

---

[103] *Ibid.*, p. 126.
[104] *The Justification of God*, p. 23.

single soul of us escapes from the evil far enough to gauge it, to judge it, and therefore to destroy it." [105]

Here is the "objective" basis in P. T. Forsyth's attitude to the Atonement, for only God in his holy love could deal with the tragic dilemma of sin. The whole human race was involved in a kingdom of unified evil, and it was to deal once and for all with this domain of corporate, cosmic guilt that Christ came as the Redeemer. "It is not," he declared, "from our moral lapses nor from our individual taint that we are delivered, but from world sin, sin in dominion, sin solidary if not hereditary, yea, from sin which integrates us into a Satanic Kingdom. An event like the war at least aids God's purpose in this, that it shocks and rouses us into some due sense of what evil is, and what a Saviour's task with it is." [106]

4. The Cross is the judgment of this Holy God upon man's sin. Forsyth saw the war as a lesser judgment of God upon the sins of the Western world, but he declared, "The victory in Christ's Cross is greater than that in any possible war. . . . We now live amid the evolution of the final crisis and last judgment of the sempiternal Cross. All the moral judgment moving to effect in the career of souls, societies, and nations is the action of the Cross as the final, crucial, eternal Act of the moral power of the universe." [107] This judgment is to be conceived not as punishment but as redemption—it is redemption because it is judgment, and it could not be redemption without being judgment.

Furthermore, as God himself is the only one who could grasp the situation and was free to act, the work of Christ in atonement is God's initiative and act: "A holy God self-atoned in Christ is the moral center of the sinful world. Our justification by God has its key in God's justification of Himself." [108] If the Cross of Christ could be conceived simply as a great object-lesson for men to understand God's patient and tender mercy toward penitence, then, declared Forsyth, God would be talking and not acting; but in the Cross he acts.[109] The Atonement is the great objective Act of God himself.

When we turn specifically to Forsyth's treatment of the doctrine of

[105] *Ibid.*, p. 26.
[106] *Ibid.*, p. 25.
[107] *Ibid.*, pp. 24, 206.
[108] *Ibid.*, p. 93.
[109] *The Work of Christ*, p. 132.

the Atonement, we are struck by a series of paradoxes which show that it is almost impossible to fit him neatly into any particular category. He has been classified as being an exponent of a form of "satisfaction" theory,[110] but one could with almost equal justification say that he was an exponent of the "patristic" or penal theories, or place him beside McLeod Campbell and R. C. Moberly, or even point to the ethical emphasis as the key to his thought. The one thing we must say is that he stands with Dale and Denney in maintaining the central places of the Atonement in theology and in emphasizing that it was an objective action by God himself. But the paradoxes within his thought prevent us from carrying the classification much further and rather show that Forsyth sifted the different theories in order to discard the dross and discover that which was of value in them all.

1. As a *theory* of the Atonement it is clear that Forsyth rejects the moral influence view because it denied the objective basis that he found at the heart of the doctrine, and because it savored too much of what we might pretend to do for our own salvation instead of our dependence upon God's act in Christ for us. On the other hand far from any intention of disregarding morality and ethics, Forsyth stressed that any doctrine of the Atonement which sought to do justice to the gospel must be basically ethical. Indeed, he claimed that it was his intention to "moralise" theology, and although as Canon J. K. Mozley pointed out no one was less likely to substitute morality for religion, yet "no one was more intent upon the moral character and leanings and issues of all true religion." [111] The ethical concern was demanded by Forsyth's conception of the Holiness of God as a holiness in which we are called in Christ to participate. One of the most distinctive features of Forsyth's thought is the sense of a continuing ethical and regenerative element in the Atonement, for as mankind is solidary in its sin, so he believed, in Christ it is unified in both redemption and regeneration:

> As the very judgment He bore for us is relevant to our sin by His moral solidarity with us, so the value of His work to God includes also that value which it has in acting on us through that same solidarity, and in presenting us to God as the men it makes us to be. He represents before

[110] T. H. Hughes, *The Atonement: Modern Theories*, ad loc.
[111] Preface by J. K. Mozley to *The Church and the Sacraments* (4th Impression, 1953), p. ix.

God not a natural Humanity that produces Him as its spiritual classic, but the new penitent Humanity that His influence creates. . . . Our faith is already present in His oblation.[112]

At this point Forsyth is close to the thought of McLeod Campbell and R. C. Moberly. The whole purpose of the Atonement is moral and ethical, but it is a morality that comes not from ourselves or from our efforts to copy Jesus but from our Lord himself. As he said of Baptism, "We are baptized into His death, and not merely into dying like Him." [113] The new life of obedience in the Cross of Christ is not simply given to our poor faith, but it belongs to Christ, and it is given to us in him.

2. Although he believed that the Cross was a "satisfaction," he rejected Anselm's conception of satisfaction given to God's honor and the legal terms that went with it. He thought in terms of the satisfaction given by Christ to God in his holy obedience to the Father, but he saw the necessity of basing this view of Atonement upon the work of the whole Trinity working in unity:

> Therefore we press the words to their fulness of meaning: "God was in Christ reconciling," not reconciling through Christ, but actually present as Christ reconciling, doing in Christ His own work of reconciliation. It was done by Godhead itself, and not by the Son alone. The old theologians were right when they insisted that the work of redemption was the work of the whole Trinity—Father, Son, and Holy Spirit; as we express it when we baptize into the new life of reconcilement in the threefold name.[114]

So if Forsyth thinks in terms of satisfaction it is not Anselmic satisfaction but is nearer in some respects to "ethical satisfaction," and in the idea of a solidary redemption in Christ, with all that he implied in that of the regeneration and sanctification of the believer, he went beyond Anselm.

3. In the same way although he spoke in terms which suggest the theory of penal substitution, he rejected the post-reformation opposition between justice and mercy, refused utterly to think of the atoning factor as in any sense concentrated in our Lord's actual sufferings, would not use the word "substitution," and would have nothing to

[112] *The Work of Christ*, p. 193-94.
[113] *Ibid.*, pp. 194-95.
[114] *Ibid.*, p. 152.

THE ATONEMENT AND THE SACRAMENTS

do with any idea of our Lord undergoing a punishment on our behalf. His main desire was to redeem such truth as there was in the old theory without wishing to be tied to its terms. Denney had been prepared to use the idea of "substitution" but showed some aversion from the idea "penal." Forsyth on the other hand retained the idea of "penalty" but rejected the idea of substitution, "because substitution does not take account of the moral results on the soul, and for a full account of the cause we must include all the effects. To do justice to the whole of Christ's work we must include the Church, and in justification include sanctification." [115] In the same way, having spoken of the Cross as God's judgment upon sin, he declaimed in trenchant terms against any punitive idea of the Atonement:

> Does that [God's judgment] mean exacting the utmost farthing of penalty, of suffering? Does it mean that in the hour of his Death Christ suffered, compressed into one brief moment, all the pains of hell that the human race deserved. We cannot think about things in that way. God does not work by such equivalents. What is required is not an equivalent penalty, but an adequate confession of His holiness. Let us get rid of that materialist idea of equivalents. What Christ gave to God was not an equivalent penalty, but an adequate confession of God's holiness, rising from amid extreme conditions of sin. God's holiness, then, was so little to be mocked, that He actually took his own judgment to save it. He spared not His own Son—His own self. His severity of conscience became at the same moment our security of salvation. And the more conscience preaches the changelessness of the judging God, the more it preaches the same changelessness in the grace of Christ.[116]

So Christ did not undergo our punishment— if he were innocent, how could he?—but he did, according to Forsyth, undergo our penalty, because, as he explains it, "there is a penalty and a curse for sin; and Christ consented to enter that region. Christ entered voluntarily into the pain and horror which is sin's penalty from God. Christ, by the deep intimacy of his sympathy with men, entered deeply into the blight and judgment which was entailed by man's sin, and which must be entailed by man's sin if God is holy and therefore a

[115] *Ibid.*, p. 182 note.
[116] *Ibid.*, p. 169-70.

judging God."[117] In order to carry through his redeeming work, our Lord had to assume the life and circumstances not only of humanity but of a *sinful* humanity, for the whole world in which we live and the conditions of life that make for suffering and death are an entail from basic disobedience and sin. Jesus Christ consented to enter *that*, and in that sense he carries our *penalty* but not our *punishment*.

4. We also see Forsyth reviewing the theories that had been put forward in his own day. He pointed out, in common with most critics of the views of McLeod Campbell and Moberly, that our Lord's sinlessness prevented him from being able to make any confession or penitence for the human sin he had not committed. Yet he insisted that there was confession in our Lord's work of Atonement. The great work of Christ was not so much to confess human sin, "but to confess something greater, namely, God's holiness in his judgment upon sin. His confession, indeed, was not in so many words, but in a far more mighty way, by act and deed of life and death. The great confession is not by word of mouth—it is by the life, in the sense, not of mere conduct, but in the great personal sense in which life contains conduct and transcends death. Christ confessed not merely human sin—which in a certain sense, indeed, He could not do—but He confessed God's holiness in reacting mortally against human sin, in cursing human sin, in judging it to its very death."[118] This kept the idea of Christ's confession to God on our behalf but lifted it to a different level from that at which McLeod Campbell and R. C. Moberly had left it.

5. A similar attitude is shown in Forsyth's relation to the ancient "classic" or "dramatic" theory of Irenaeus and the early Fathers. In so far as it was conceived in terms of a payment being made to the powers of darkness, Forsyth rejected it, but he took up the unitary conception which Irenaeus had of the human race and made it the very foundation of his own understanding of Christ's work. His writings are full of the imagery of the cosmic Christ's victory over the powers of darkness: Christ faced sin as its destroyer.[119]

The work of Christ was thus in the same act triumphant on evil, satisfying to the heart of God, and creative to the conscience of man by virtue of

---
[117] *Ibid.*, p. 147. Cf. Bushnell, *supra*, p. 153.
[118] *Ibid.*, pp. 149-50.
[119] *Ibid.*, p. 184.

his solidarity with God on the one side, and on the other with the race. He subdued Satan, rejoiced the Father, and set up in Humanity the kingdom—all in one supreme and consummate act of His own person. He destroyed the kingdom of evil, not by way of preparation for the kingdom of God, but by actually establishing God's kingdom in the heart of it. And He rejoiced, filled, and satisfied the heart of God, not by a statutory obedience, or by one private to Himself, which spectacle disposed God to bless and sanctify man; but by presenting in the compendious compass of His own person a humanity presanctified by the irresistible power of His own timeless work.[120]

If you study the passage just quoted, you will see that there are the three old and familiar aspects of the Atonement. First, its triumphant aspect—the defeat of the powers of evil that was characteristic of the patristic theories. Second, its satisfactory aspect—the way in which God himself was "satisfied" and glorified by what happened in the Cross, which involves the best of all that Anselm and his followers tried to say. Third, its regenerative aspect—which is essentially moral and ethical in its intention and result.[121]

6. This ethical emphasis, which in Forsyth's theology is derived ultimately from the Holiness of God, is concerned with the regeneration of the redeemed community, but this has a double aspect—relating to the past in what Denney called the "finished" work of Christ, and relating to the present and the future through the continuing work of the risen Christ in the power of the Holy Spirit. That which relates to the past is caught up in the representative work of our Lord in the Atonement. Forsyth preferred the word "Representative" to "Substitution" for reasons that we have already seen, but he is not very enamored of either, because he complains that even "Representative" suggests far too much the idea of a "spiritual protagonist" who draws his power and authority democratically from those he represents, instead of our Lord's actual relationship to us which "is royal and not elective." [122] He prefers to use the word "Surety" to describe the place which Christ takes for us before the Father—he guarantees in prospect humanity's offering of holy obedience by his own offering of holy obedience. The Atonement comes

[120] *Ibid.*, pp. 224-25.
[121] Cf. *ibid.*, pp. 199-200.
[122] *Ibid.*, p. 210.

into being through an ethical principle and has the ethics of holiness as its consummation, but it is God's ethic of holiness and not ours. "It is not as Christ is in us that we are saved," said Forsyth, "but as we are in Christ." [123] We are caught up in the atoning work of Christ.

We can follow the ethical theme in his thought in four steps. First, only holy obedience can atone, because only holy obedience can satisfy the holiness of God; [124] secondly, the center of this atoning work is in the obedience, and not the suffering that is involved—or as Forsyth expressed it, the principle of atonement is not obedient suffering but suffering obedience; [125] thirdly, "Christ's holiness is the satisfying thing to God, because it is not only the means but also the anticipation of our holiness, because it carries all our future holiness latent in it and to God's eye patent"; [126] fourthly, through faith Christ's holiness is created by God Himself within us, for "if holiness can be satisfied with nothing but holiness it can only be with a holiness which itself creates." [127]

There can be no ethics without grace. This is the theme of the regenerative aspect of the Atonement and is Forsyth's view par excellence. In particular it stresses the place of the Church and Sacraments. Forsyth spoke of depending upon the power of the Cross daily, and this constant reliance upon the Cross is at the heart of his view of the Church's witness and function. Just as Christ is to be seen not as humanity's paragon but as God's gift and action in redemption, so the Church is not a voluntary society of the like-minded but a gift and act of God for the sanctification of its members and the redemption of the world. In his saving act, declared Forsyth, our Lord became so much at one with the race that the new humanity which he established "arises in history as the company of those who answer and seal His incarnate act with their faith." [128] But Forsyth maintained that the Church finds its center in Christ's Atonement rather than in his Incarnation, for it is only by the experience of redemption that it has any knowledge of what the Incarnation means.[129]

[123] *Ibid.*, p. 215.
[124] *Ibid.*, p. 203.
[125] *Ibid.*, p. 205.
[126] *Ibid.*, p. 208.
[127] *Ibid.*
[128] *Ibid.*, p. 227 note.
[129] *The Church and the Sacraments*, p. 83.

THE ATONEMENT AND THE SACRAMENTS

This has an inevitable application to our understanding of the Sacraments, for he said, "it is a step too logical and inevitable from the Church as the prolongation of the Incarnation to the Eucharist as a prolongation of the Atonement, and to the treatment of it as a sacrifice offered instead of the acceptance, from a present Christ's hands, of His offering once for all." [130] It is obvious that what Forsyth feared was any idea of the Eucharist as a recurring mactation of Christ's Body, such as that which generally prevailed in the medieval Church. Nevertheless, he maintained that the Sacraments must be centered in the Atonement and declared that one of the most laudable features of the Roman Catholic Mass is that "it keeps the rite in the closest connection with the sacrifice of Christ and the virtue of His Cross." [131] He held that the Protestant understanding of the Sacraments centers in the divine *action* within them, which represents the atoning action of our Lord—"the breaking rather than the bread, the outpouring rather than the wine," and so too with Baptism it is "in the significance of the Church's act in close and organic connection with Christ's historic Act and Gift." [132]

Bearing in mind the place which the Cross and the Atonement have in P. T. Forsyth's theology—they are God's own act in Christ for our redemption—in reference to the Sacraments he ultimately brings us to this point, "the essence of the Sacrament in the Church is the common act, the act of the community inhabited by the 'common person' of Christ, therefore Christ's act detailed by Him. That is where its connection with the Cross resided—in Christ's act of donation. But in that act as real act and not pictorial. It was a real assignment, and not exhibition. It was a symbol which not only showed or commemorated, but *did* something, effected something, conveyed something. It made over Christ's death to His own." [133] Forsyth brings Protestant theology to its ultimate sacramental principle—to Sacraments centering in God's Act within the Church, to the constant action of the Living Christ in the midst of those who have been and are being redeemed by the great Act of Christ, Crucified and Risen.

---

[130] *Ibid.*
[131] *Ibid.*, p. 291.
[132] *Ibid.*, p. 235; cf. p. 234.
[133] *Ibid.*, p. 237.

CHAPTER VII

Present Trends

AS FAR AS I KNOW, THE CATALOG HAS NEVER BEEN REGARDED AS A serious art form, but there are two things to be said in its favor—first, one can be sure that all the classic styles will be well marked and reasonably well described, and secondly, it is always possible to discard those items which are of no interest to oneself.

Up to the present the "catalog" method has almost necessarily been the approach we have employed in order to review the field of Christian thought on the Atonement, but we now enter an area where this becomes markedly more difficult. Books on the Atonement continue to appear with bewildering regularity from British presses, and if their appearance cannot be described as a flood, it has been a very reasonable stream.[1] At the same time it is clear that the discussion is becoming international and promises to become increasingly so as theological interest from many sides seems to concentrate upon the doctrine. This surely was to be expected, for it would have been strange if the revival of biblical theology had resulted in the rediscovery of the central place of the person and message of Jesus Christ, without coming to its focus in the Atonement where both person and message stand clear. However, in our attempt to delineate modern trends, we still have to face the marked predominance of British books, and we must inevitably be selective, although it would be a reckless man indeed who would try to forecast what will be the ultimate priority in which history will arrange them. We shall not try to do that. What is more important for our purpose is to see if these more recent works manifest any common characteristics, any trend in thinking and feeling which promises deeper insight

---

[1] A recent American author, writing of Post-Reformation theories, mentioned nearly twenty British writers in a total of about twenty-five cited; and of the non-British writers, the only post-Reformation writers to whom he gives much more than a mention are Grotius and Aulén. William J. Wolf, *No Cross, No Crown* (Garden City: Doubleday, 1957) pp. 109-128.

and wider agreement in the Church's understanding of the work of her redemption.

But first there are two historical questions which should remind us that theology does not come to birth in a historical vacuum. First, let us see something of the theological climate in which the modern debate has been taking place in Britain, and then let us try to see the relationship of American theology to this doctrine as the discussion becomes more general.

1. The Post-War Climate in British Theology

The last theologian in point of time whose books we have considered in any detail was R. S. Franks writing in the early 1930's. Yet in reading the theological books published at that time by those who shared his general perspective, one is conscious that they belong to an entirely different theological climate from our own.

Certainly it must be admitted that the Anglo-Saxon nations have not reflected this change in climate in such a pronounced way as countries in continental Europe. Nevertheless, I think we can discern three major factors which have radically changed and are continuing to change theological thought and the ecclesiastical patterns with which theological ideas are so largely bound up. What follows then is particularly directed to an understanding of the theological climate in one country, but the discerning reader will recognize for himself the parallel factors, which to a greater or lesser extent have produced similar changes of climate in both continental Europe and America.

1. It is worth recalling that Robert Franks had spoken of the nineteenth century as a century of hope which had been succeeded by a century of disillusionment and realism. This change in temper was not due to any single event but has been a process extending over a generation in which Franks and his contemporaries were themselves playing their part, although it was brought to focus in the *terminus a quo* and *terminus ad quem* of the whole period—the wars of 1914-18 and 1939-45, which did more than anything else to empty the prosperous churches and destroy the easy optimism in which Victorian and Edwardian religion had been able to nestle so securely.

Beyond the wars themselves, however, we must take into account their aftermath in Britain's altered world position and the disillusion that has accompanied it, for any student of historical theology who attempted to review the theological trends of the postwar years without giving full weight to the characteristic disillusionment would be sadly lacking in psychological perception. A whole complex of events and reactions were responsible for producing something like a national mood of disenchantment and disgruntlement, in the face of which the deification of humanity and a doctrine of inevitable progress became entirely irrelevant.

Perhaps at its most fundamental level, this disenchantment was concerned with humanity itself, for prior to 1914 many of the most sensitive European thinkers had based their hope upon one or another form of humanitarianism. The hope was so well established in Britain that it continued almost up to 1939 in the expectation that as the League of Nations eradicated the means of war, so the achievement of Socialist ideals (British pattern) would destroy its economic and social causes. Events proved the contrary. In Germany the Labor movement proved itself impotent to curb the rise of National Socialism, and incidents such as the National Strike in 1928, the unofficial strikes in the years following 1945, and the attitude of the Soviet block in the United Nations revealed that the Labor movement could become simply another form of the old power complex. This had underlined the earlier failure of the League of Nations.

This is closely related to one other important factor which helped to condition the national mood since the end of World War II, for we must add to this *mélange* of disappointed national hopes and humanist aspirations the growing consciousness of the misbegotten twin horrors of our age—the rise of the totalitarian state and the possibility of scientific annihilation. We must understand the disillusionment of a people which tried hard to keep a blind eye turned toward what was happening to Jews and other political undesirables in Hitler's Germany, and which has tried hard not to believe its own fears about what has been happening in Siberia or China. We must also give full weight to the psychological effect of the bombing of Hiroshima and Nagasaki in the very year that was to have been the beginning of a new hope and the knowledge that it was done by "our side" in which we had our share. This has left a scar on the Anglo-Saxon soul which will last very long in the folk memory of our peoples.

And if that sounds pathological, perhaps the condition is precisely that. It means that our spiritual trouble is too deep-seated to be dealt with by a brotherly bedside manner and the injunction to "Cheer up! because things are getting better every day." In the face of bombing, the threat of invasion, the shortages and restrictions of wartime, and the alternative terrors of the post-war world, a religion based on noble principles and liberal ideals without any reference to the corporate guilt of the race and without any certainty of a grace far greater than our human possibilities was no longer relevant to the Church or the society in which it was placed.

Before even the First World War broke upon a startled Europe, P. T. Forsyth had discerned that the signs of the times spelt doom to our comfortable religiosity and flaccid theology. The chastening events of this century are leading his countrymen to an honest, if belated, appreciation of the fact that in him we had a prophet who understood our condition and faithfully uttered God's Word to it. We have had to learn "the hard way" that when God enters the pulpit, "He preaches in His own way by deeds."

2. On the other hand if biblical and theological renewal was partly demanded by the spiritual and psychological needs of the time, it was also largely an independent development and has been in itself a direct cause of the present theological trends. Up to 1939, the works of Karl Barth were criticized but usually left unread. Nevertheless, theologians could not indefinitely neglect the new thought that was coming from Europe, which reflected the bitterness of a struggle deeper than the Anglo-Saxon churches had ever been called upon to face. If "continental theology" could say a sustaining word to the Confessing Church in Germany, or to the persecuted churches of Occupied Europe, then it had something to say to the disillusionment of England's lost securities and to the aftermath of her outworn prides.

Of the continental theologians probably Emil Brunner exerted the most widespread influence because more of his books were translated, and he was therefore more widely read. But it should be emphasized that although Britain did not ultimately ignore what was going on in Europe, her own theological development was advanced by having second thoughts in the realm of biblical studies. Biblical scholarship itself, quite independently of any national mood or international situation, was beginning to force the theologians to question the extreme Liberal presuppositions. The 1930's and '40's saw a tremendous output of exact Bible scholarship from British scholars whose work, while accepting the premises of biblical criticism, often ended by criticizing the more radical critics. One cannot discount the new influence from the European mainland, but the significant fact was that it fell into soil which had been prepared not only by events but also by the most recent trends in biblical scholarship. This meant that the new theology could grow up and flourish, but it also meant that it was bound to undergo the subtle changes indigenous to the theological soil and climate of Britain.

3. A further major influence has been the growing consciousness of the Ecumenical Movement. Judged in terms of actual reunion, the results of that movement in Britain, despite the general involvement of British Churches in its conferences and machinery, have been extremely modest. Except for individual congregations or small unions affecting a comparatively small number of Christians, church reunion in Britain has been limited strictly to the confessional boundaries— the union within Scottish Presbyterianism in 1929 and within British Methodism in 1931. Although with "conversations" between Anglicans and Presbyterians on one hand and Anglicans and Methodists on the other, a new spirit may have arrived.

But anyone tempted to regard the present results as negligible needs to reflect upon the strength of theological and ecclesiastical tradition in the British Isles and upon the fact that the rival Confessions are indigenous to the soil of that country and have grown up on the scene of their historic differences: they are not a missionary import.[2] Taking a larger view of the Ecumenical Movement, however, those who know the situation realize that it has resulted in a complete revolution in the temper and attitude of the churches to each other, and that over the past forty or fifty years a new attitude of confidence and respect has shown itself which would have been unthinkable at the beginning of the century. This new relationship, partly the result of the Ecumenical Movement in its organized forms and partly itself a contributory cause of that movement, has meant that ecclesiastically and theologically the churches have had a more direct influence upon each other. The accent upon churchmanship, liturgy and sacra-

---

[2] On this I may be permitted to refer the reader to my article "British Churches and the Ecumenical Future" (*Ecumenical Review*, Jan., 1956), pp. 178-87.

ments of the Anglican Oxford Movement, have not been without marked effect upon the Church of Scotland and the English Free Churches, first of all in strong reaction and then, when the dust had died down, in a more positive self-criticism and acceptance of the challenge that it offered to their own theology. Similarly, the understanding which the nonepiscopal churches have of the place of the laity within the structure of the church, the work of their biblical scholars and even their conception of the ministry has not been without its effect upon the Anglican Church. The twentieth-century English bishop is not often to be identified with the nineteenth-century prelate, whatever the die-hards on either side might wish to believe. The importance of this and the point at which the significance of the Ecumenical Movement is brought to a focus is in the fact that Anglican theologians have taken seriously what their nonepiscopal colleagues have had to say about the Atonement, while the latter have had to listen to what Anglicans have said about the Church and Sacraments. The fact that these concerns are now taken with a new seriousness by all denominations is in large measure due to an ecumenism which has taught us the depth of Christian conviction and the strength of theological integrity represented on both sides.

So in our consideration of modern trends we have to take into account the time in which the literature has been written. We must recognize the unconscious spiritual needs and moral climate of a people whose Christian faith had become lost in the native fog and whose ideals had turned gray and chilly. Within this sense of disillusion we must understand the significance both of the prophetic word uttered by post-critical biblical theology and of the movement of the Spirit that declared the churches' "togetherness" in Christ—a togetherness that arose not only from a need to draw the family together in the face of a hostile or indifferent environment but also from the recognition that in the name of theological truth each Church had its own positive contribution to make.

2. The Atonement and American Theology

What about American theology in relation to this discussion on the doctrine of Atonement? Obviously it would be untrue to suggest that no important books on the subject have appeared since the publication of Horace Bushnell's *Forgiveness and Law*, or that American theology does not find its Protestant center in the doctrine. Yet I suggest that after Bushnell's last book on the subject, American theology turned aside to deal with other theological imperatives that were clamoring for attention.

This is clearly an area in which the stranger ought to tread warily, but I think the fact can be substantiated if it is compared to the theological interest in the subject before Bushnell with that which has been shown since. Before Horace Bushnell caused the thoroughgoing break with Calvinist orthodoxy, American theologians concentrated on the doctrine of Atonement to the same extent and in very much the same way as their counterparts in Britain, except that there seems to have been a certain concentration upon the Governmental theory. Whether this can be traced to the influence of Arminianism (Grotius) or not, one cannot say. Perhaps it was more the outcome of the Great Awakening and the evangelical need to present a less dour gospel than that of rigid penal substitution backed by a narrow doctrine of Election. Certainly most people traced it to Jonathan Edwards, although it seems just as likely to have originated with his bosom friend Samuel Hopkins.[3] Bushnell clearly regarded the theory as very little different and certainly no more acceptable than the orthodox theory of penal substitution and called it a "most sorry theologic invention."[4] By the middle of the nineteenth century there also seems to have been a considerable amount of interest in the questions of the passibility of God, whether or not Christ suffered in respect of his human nature alone, and whether the Atonement provided free grace for all—indications that others besides Bushnell were becoming embarrassed with the implications of Calvinist orthodoxy.[5]

[3] Bushnell draws attention to it in *The Vicarious Sacrifice*, p. 306. Cf. *Forgiveness and Law*, pp. 145-46. Cf. *The Atonement: Discourses and Treatises by Edwards, Smalley, Maxcy, Emmons, Griffin, Burge, and Weeks*, with an Introductory Essay on "The Rise of the Edwardian Theory of Atonement" by Edwards A. Park of Andover Seminary (Boston: Congregational Publishing Society, 1859).

[4] *Forgiveness and Law*, p. 146.

[5] E.g., the discussion on the subject initiated in *The Sufferings of Christ*, (New York: Harper Bros., 1845) by "A Layman" (George Griffin) and replied to by Bennett Tyler of Hartford, *The Sufferings of Christ Confined to His Human Nature*, (Hartford: D. R. Woodford, 1847). Also the American reprint of Thos. Jenkyn, *The Extent of the Atonement* (Boston: Gould and Lincoln, 1859).

But after Bushnell's writings the interest seems to have waned, or rather removed itself to other issues. One has the feeling that although this central pulse is there and gives vitality to all that is being said theologically, its function remains hidden because the attention is concentrated elsewhere. Occasionally a book appeared to defend the older theory of Atonement, like J. B. Remensnyder's *The Atonement and Modern Thought* (1905), or an attempt was made to draw out the truths in all the theories, as in Henry Van Dyke's *The Gospel for a World of Sin*. The best American work on the doctrine from the liberal period is probably A. C. Knudson's *The Doctrine of Redemption* (1933),[6] for it sets the death of Christ within the whole action and purpose of God for man's redemption, but it appears as if the author's main interest was in the exposition of Christian Doctrine in terms of philosophical personalism. This vitiates the work, for the philosophical presuppositions prevented the writer from attributing any good to the objective theories of atonement, whether as "theories" or as descriptive figures. The case was argued persuasively and with great breadth of learning, but one's final estimate of the book must inevitably depend upon the degree to which the philosophical basis is accepted.

One book stands out in the earlier period as one of the most significant restatements of doctrine in its day, and this is W. P. Du Bose's *The Soteriology of the New Testament* (1892). But although Du Bose was professedly writing on the Atonement, we have the impression that his real interest was in the Christological problem. It is true that the doctrine of Atonement is involved in this—we cannot separate the two doctrines—but because of the interest of Du Bose in the two natures of Christ's person, we feel that he was interested in the Atonement only derivatively. It may be important later to consider why this should be so.

If we feel that American theologians have been writing to some extent without a sense of inner necessity in their treatment of the Atonement, we sense also that this has arisen not so much from any failure on the part of the writers themselves but because the gaze of American theology as such is focussed elsewhere. The problem

[6] New York: Abingdon. Cf. also *The Atonement in Modern Religious Thought* (New York: Wittaker, 1901), a symposium of seventeen writers (of which eleven were British!).

why this should be so may appear to lie rather to the side of our subject, but it can nevertheless help us to understand the contemporary way of thinking. What happened that changed the course of American theology after the time of Bushnell and caused it to concentrate on new and more immediate problems?

This is one of those historical questions on which it is undoubtedly easier to hazard brilliant guesses than to establish sure proofs. Clearly we must look for the answer not in those theological trends which America shared with Britain and the continent of Europe but in a set of historical circumstances that were absolutely and distinctively American, which could have forced American theology to separate itself from the problems that concerned Europe and to pioneer its own path. In the very forefront of the historical events which were distinctively America's own experience and which have made the nation of today, there were two—the settlement of the frontiers that gave national strength and the Civil War that re-emphasized national unity.

One can say little about the theological results of the latter, except to offer the suggestion that churches in the South may have become more firmly entrenched in biblical and theological conservatism at least in partial reaction to the liberalism of the northern universities. However one regards the results of this for American theology, we would be blind not to see that in terms of the country's evangelical need the preaching that arose from this theology cannot be dismissed lightly.

The results of the settlement of the frontiers, I believe, were more widespread and perhaps offer more in the way of historical evidence. The earlier colonial settlers had been contained to a large extent by the area between the Allegheny Mountains and the sea, and within that comparatively confined space they had managed to reproduce many of the patterns of the old society from which they had come—predominantly the patterns of Britain and the British. Therefore, to some extent they maintained the illusion of being a transplanted "European" community. But we have to take into account the phenomenal influx of immigrants from the time of the 1846 Irish potato famine and the revolutionary troubles in Europe of 1848 onward through the century. The consequent rise in population and the rapid taming of the frontier was wild and uncivilized. Those who wrested a livelihood out of the wilderness lived very close to the simple issues of life and death. They lived within a context where the moral and religious sanctions of European civilization appeared to be remote and irrelevant. As America girded herself to meet the needs of her rapidly expanding polyglot population and to the face the task of taming the almost illimitable wilderness to the west, the problems that would most occupy the churches were bound to be increasingly the practical and existential problems of carrying the gospel westward and of establishing a basis for Christian ethics. The problem of evangelism was no longer that of reviving a comparatively stable and sophisticated community but of preaching to Indians who had never heard the gospel and to a mixed bag of immigrant humanity that had come to America largely in order to escape "civilization."

In this situation we notice two related but almost contrary trends. In the first place we notice that it was largely the churches which were not afraid to preach the older theories of Atonement with clearcut issues in soteriology and ethics which had the greatest missionary zeal and evangelical success. It has always been admitted that the theory of penal substitution "preaches" well, and its success on the frontier is probably due principally to the fact that those who preached it spoke directly about sin and grace to men who knew themselves to be sinners in need of grace. This evangelical need, stimulated by recurrent religious revivals that had a strong moral emphasis, would be enough to arrest any radical reinterpretation of the Atonement among large sections of American Protestantism. As has been suggested, the Civil War itself may have strengthened the conservatism of a trend inherent in the biblicism and revivals of Anglo-Saxon Protestantism.

In the second place, however, some dim consciousness of the greatness of the national experiment in which they were engaged brought a sense of restlessness and dissatisfaction with the old orthodoxies among Americans: the very readiness to experiment and to try the "new thing" would send many into radical liberalism. As America began to settle down to the emerging pattern of her new nationhood and to become a nation-continent populated by a multi-racial society, those who had been most affected by theological liberalism—the theological leadership of the nation—were inevitably preoccupied with the questions posed by America's own problems and with the sciences that could best solve them—sociology and psychology. Christian ethics became the branch of theology which could speak most directly to the concrete situation, and the new sciences were radically applied to the claims of theology.

I suggest that the result of these emphases, at work in the situation as the problems of American society and of the twentieth century coincided, has been a concentration upon the doctrine of man. I submit that these factors, if they do not entirely explain the difference of emphasis between American and British theology after the time of Horace Bushnell, must certainly have played an important part in defining the path that theology has taken on the American continent.

Nor is this intended to be an oblique way of suggesting that American theology has concentrated upon secondary issues. Within her own situation there can be no doubt that for America during the first half of the twentieth century the doctrine of man has been the doctrine of primary importance, and it is in this area of the Christian faith that she has most to give to the Church Universal. The point is very strikingly illustrated by the fact that the doctrine of man has had a central place in the theology of those who have been the prophetic voices during this century, and in the fact that many of these theologians came to their present emphasis upon Christian doctrine through social ethics, or through the practical application of social ethics within a pastorate in an industrialized society.

We see this new concern with the doctrine of man (and with those parts of Christian doctrine which touch it most closely) emerging as we read W. P. Du Bose's *The Soteriology of the New Testament*. His subject is the doctrine of Salvation, but the emphasis is upon the fact that it is the Salvation of Man, and throughout his book everything is brought to the bar of humanity. Right at the beginning he says that if Christianity "addresses itself to just the evils which exist in our condition and provide just the goods that are necessary for our spiritual completion, our moral perfection, and our actual satisfaction, then it is true." [7] The final test is the human one, for "though human nature or imagination can as yet form no complete theory of Salvation, yet common sense and experience, and such knowledge as through these we have of ourselves, will enable us to sit in judgment upon such theories of it as are presented to us, and

---

[7] Du Bose, op. cit., p. 6.

in the end to accept what *is* true and reject what is false in them." [8]

Of course, this trend had already been indicated by Bushnell in the subtitle of *Forgiveness and Law*—"Grounded in Principles interpreted by Human Analogies." Its dangers are obvious, in that it could so easily degenerate into a vague humanism or to the deification of human endeavor. Yet it arose out of a real concern about man and his nature. This is why Du Bose's work really finds its center in Christology and in the relationship between the divine and the human natures in the life of Christ. More than half his book is devoted to this, and one feels that beyond his wrestling with this problem, he is wrestling not only with its implications for our salvation but also with implications for the actual and potential qualities of man. "I have taken," he said, "the position that if the whole nature, the proper destination and the actual condition of humanity were perfectly known to us, a perfect theory of human salvation could be constructed by us *a priori*. . . . Given what our evil is and what our good would be, we could deduce what our Salvation must be." [9]

In some ways this concentration upon the anthropological issues and in the Incarnation brings Du Bose very near Bishop Westcott and J. M. Wilson—as might be expected, since of all the British writers these represent the group whose concept of Salvation arose most directly out of a social concern—but Du Bose pushes the identity with us of our Lord in his humanity to its ultimate limit. For him Christ's humanity did not only come from maculate motherhood (as, indeed, Bushnell believed), but it was itself capable of sin. The moral perfection of Jesus Christ came from his own will and victory and not simply from the accident of his birth. "If He was man," declared Du Bose, "then He not only ate and drank, and walked and talked, but He knew and thought, and felt and willed, and believed and prayed, and needed and received grace, and grew in knowledge of the Father and in consciousness of Himself, and realized His divine Sonship, and incarnated spiritually and morally as well as physically the Eternal Logos—*all as man*, and just as all men are called to do the same in Him." [10] It was in this sense that *his* victory was our victory. Although this represented the *life* of Christ as a real atonement,

[8] *Ibid.*, p. 8. (The italics are mine.)
[9] *Ibid.*, p. 16.
[10] *Ibid.*, p. 147.

it went off somewhat at a tangent from those who would identify the Atonement with the very act of Incarnation, for according to such a view, the real victory in our Lord (and therefore the real Atonement) took place within the achievement of his earthly life and not simply in the fact that he assumed human flesh.[11] The importance of such a view for the doctrine of man may be readily understood.

Whatever has been the necessary concentration of American theology upon the doctrine of man, the result seems to have been to emphasize the final centrality of the work of Christ. Reinhold Niebuhr puts Atonement at the very center of his understanding of Western culture and civilization,[12] and Paul Tillich—who for his influence upon contemporary American thought must be counted more American than European—finds that the doctrines of the Living God and the Atonement coincide.[13] When one reads such statements by leading theologians in America and remembers that a similar concentration upon the work of Christ has developed from the Christologically oriented theology of the European mainland, one realizes that the discussion is now international and likely to become increasingly so. This new approach of American theology is perhaps signalized by the appearance of recent books like John Knox's New Testament study, *The Death of Christ* (1958), and William J. Wolf's *No Cross, No Crown* (1957). The latter book, although it starts very fundamentally from the anthropological basis of man's needs,[14] goes on to emphasize the extent of the ecumenical consensus. If this means that we can now expect American contributions on the Atonement on the basis of insights gained from the study of doctrine of man, the result can only mean real ecumenical enrichment to our understanding of the redemption wrought by Christ.

3. Three Formative Theologians:
Gustaf Aulén, Bishop Hicks, and Vincent Taylor

One of the books which has profoundly influenced all recent thinking about the Atonement, and which not only reflects the changing

---

[11] T. H. Hughes, op. cit., p. 147.
[12] The Gifford Lectures, *The Nature and Destiny of Man* (New York: Scribners, 1942-43.) II, 211-12.
[13] *Existence and the Christ*, (Systematic Theology II, Chicago: University of Chicago Press, 1957), p. 175.
[14] Wolf, op. cit. Cf. such sections as "Security and Salvation," and "Triumph over Meaninglessness," p. 159-60.

need of its generation but also illustrates the international character of the most recent discussion, is a book by the Swedish theologian Gustaf Aulén, to which we have referred already. It is *Den kristna försoningstanken*, which appeared in English under the title *Christus Victor* in 1931. This title is significant, for it won attention at a time when men were conscious of the towering threat of Nazism and Fascism in Europe, and when the gathering storm of the Second World War and the revelation of man's potential bestiality in such horrors as Belsen and Buchenwald showed us something of the corporate nature of sin—the desperate power of an Evil far bigger than that of the individual sinner, in which our little sins are all involved. Men were more conscious than they had been for a hundred years of facing the immense power of "the Enemy," and it is worth noting that when the World Council of Christian Youth met in Amsterdam under the very shadow of war in 1939, it was under this slogan, "Christus Victor." This declaration of the Church's faith in the work and power of Christ, which had been born within the early Church through the fires of martyrdom, became real once more in a world where the possibility of martyrdom for the Faith entered again to shatter the easy optimism and complacency to which we had become accustomed.

We have already said something of Aulén's distinctive contribution in referring to Martin Luther. Until his book appeared, the real contest regarding the Atonement had been considered to be between Anselm and Abelard. Aulén exploded that. He pointed out that the theologians of the eighteenth and nineteenth centuries had been so preoccupied with attacking the theology of the seventeenth century that they had often been confused the "ransom theory" of the early Fathers with what he calls Anselm's "Latin theory," and that one of the reasons why neither the followers of Anselm nor the Abelardians were prepared to take this "patristic" or "classic" theory seriously was that it had never been formulated in detail as a *theory*. He claimed that he was not putting forward his own idea of the Atonement but simply bringing to light the idea of the doctrine that had governed the theological thinking and liturgical life of the Church during the first nine hundred years of its history, and that this patristic motif of our Lord's victory over sin, the flesh, death, and the devil had been recaptured and revived by Martin Luther. He maintained that although the later Reformers did not follow Luther at this point, the significance of what Luther had done should not be ignored in our estimate of the Reformation itself, for "It now becomes more impossible than ever," he declared, "to treat the Reformation as a revolt against the Catholic Church of Christ. The claim of the evangelical confessions, especially the Augsburg Confession, to represent an evangelical catholicism had in reality a firmer foundation of truth than the Reformers themselves understood." [15]

We must also thank Aulén, however, for stressing that we ought to think not of "theories" but in terms of a motif, a theme, an idea. He helped to free theology from the bondage of having to find a comprehensive explanation of something that is essentially inexplicable. He admitted that the imagery used by Luther and the Fathers is foreign and coarse to modern people, but he brings out four distinctive features of the patristic theme:[16]

1. "However crude the form, the endeavor is to show that God does not stand, as it were, outside the drama that is being played out, but Himself takes part in it, and attains His purpose by internal, not external means; He overcomes evil, not by an an almighty fiat, but by putting in something of His own, through a Divine self-oblation." [17]

2. The deception of the devil is not meant to be taken literally but is used to convey the idea that God acts in a manner that is in accordance with his own just nature—in a way that is "fitting" by making the punishment suit the crime.[18]

3. The patristic theme has been criticized for its dualism, but this dualism simply holds the two parts of a paradox in tension—that the "enemy" has certain "rights" over man by reason of our voluntary sinning, but that he is at the same time an enemy. Aulén suggests that this is not "immoral," as Rashdall would have it. If the Fathers are to be blamed, they are not to be blamed on this count, but "rather because they never fully dared to trust themselves to maintain and assert clearly both sides of the case; to assert at one and the same time

---

[15] Aulén, op. cit., pp. 30-31. Used by permission of S.P.C.K. and The Macmillan Company.
[16] Ibid., pp. 70-71.
[17] Ibid.
[18] Ibid., p. 70; cf. p. 44.

that the devil is God's enemy, and that he is also the executant of God's judgment." [19]

4. Aulén says that "behind all the seemingly fantastic speculation lies the thought that the power of evil ultimately overreaches itself when it comes in conflict with the power of good, with God Himself. It loses the battle at the moment when it seems to be victorious." [20]

So if Aulén revives the ransom theory, it is always with the insistence that types and pictures that it employs are not to be regarded as arguments within a theory but simply dramatic symbols within what is essentially an analogy or parable. He declares at the end of his book that if the classic idea of the Atonement again resumes its leading place in theology, it will probably not go back to precisely the same forms of expression that it used in the past, "its revival will not consist in a putting back of the clock." But "we shall hear again the tremendous paradoxes: that God, the all-ruler, the Infinite, yet accepts the lowliness of the Incarnation; we shall hear again the old realistic message of the conflict of God with the dark, hostile forces of evil, and His victory over them by the Divine self-sacrifice; above all, we shall hear again the note of triumph." [21] These were the classic themes which an enervated theology desperately needed to hear.

Throughout *Christus Victor*, we can discern certain basic presuppositions. First, Aulén insists upon the centrality of the Atonement within Christian thought because as a doctrine "it is directly related to the nature of God," but he would maintain equally strongly its vital connection with the Incarnation. Finally, he emphasizes that the redemption of man depends entirely upon God's initiative—it is a movement in the first place of God to man and not vice versa. For these reasons he struck the right note for later themes. Not everyone could accept his thesis fully, but many later writers have shown themselves to have been deeply influenced by his views, notably Sydney Cave,[22] Vincent Taylor,[23] Leonard Hodgson, and Donald Baillie.[24]

---

[19] Ibid., p. 71.
[20] Ibid., p. 71.
[21] Ibid., p. 176.
[22] Cave, op. cit., pp. 157-58, 255-57.
[23] *Jesus and His Sacrifice* (Macmillan and Company Ltd., St. Martin's Press, Inc., and The Macmillan Company of Canada, 1937), p. 261.
[24] Hodgson, *The Doctrine of the Atonement* (New York: Scribners, 1951), pp. 146-48; Donald Baillie, *God Was in Christ* (New York: Scribners, 1948), p. 200.

Aulén not only revived the note of victory in the ancient images, but he liberated theology from the categories of logic and unimaginative rationality in which the doctrine of the Atonement had often been incarcerated and showed that the Church has been most reasonable and most logical when it has expressed the drama of the work of Christ in the pictures and images of drama itself. He re-emphasized what Dale and Denney had unconsciously revealed, that the fact of the Atonement is ultimate and that our theories about it are relative. For these reasons and because of the importance of the dramatic images employed by the early Church, no one who has written about the doctrine in recent years could afford to ignore what Aulén has had to say.

If *Christus Victor* sounded the challenge of the gospel in the face of totalitarianism and a continent marching into war, *The Fulness of Sacrifice* (1930), published by the late Bishop of Lincoln, F. C. N. Hicks, illustrated the growing ecumenical recognition that the fulness of the Church has yet to be realized. Bishop Hicks admitted that the whole study arose for him out of his participation in the Faith and Order Movement, and his book defines its goal in the last chapter where he brings to a head the ecumenical issues raised by the study and indicates a possible line of advance.

The book also makes explicit something which has been implicit throughout our own historical survey of the doctrine of the Atonement, and which has been becoming more and more open. Namely, the intimate relationship between this doctrine and the Sacraments —particularly with the Sacrament of the Lord's Supper or Eucharist. It shows us the lines that we have been tracing are beginning to converge. Although Hicks wrote from an Anglican position that was sometimes too self-consciously set over against the presuppositions of Protestant biblical scholarship, he nevertheless represented fully the ecumenical concern. If Aulén spoke to the world of new paganisms, Hicks reflected the growing ecumenical conscience in the Church.

He argues that religion is a way of life. We may not be able to apply to primitive religion all the terms that Thomas Hobbes applied to the life of natural man, but Hicks certainly agrees with Hobbes that it was "poor, nasty, brutish." There was a good deal in the early religions that was nonmoral, even downright immoral. But later religion may have gained all the ethical and spiritual principles of which earlier religion was totally ignorant and still have lost the direct relationship with life which was at the center of religious experience for primitive man; for religion, he maintained, "is a life: a way of living. It rests, not upon abstract definitions, but upon a felt contact between man and God." [25] Referring to Lev. 17:11, he argues that this was particularly thrown into relief by the sacrificial cultus in primitive religions, since the blood of the victim was always identified with the victim's life, and it was this life principle which became available in the sacrifice to the one who brought his offering. Dr. Hicks is not the first to point out this relationship between the blood and the life of the sacrificial victim, for McLeod Campbell, Bushnell, and Bishop Westcott had made the same identification many years before,[26] but Hicks is certainly the first in the twentieth century situation to bring the idea out of cold storage and make its application clear.[27] Hicks also emphasizes that sacrifice means cost, and that there can be no real sacrifice without cost. In the Old Testament the sacrificial animals were domestic animals, creatures upon whom the owner had spent some care and attention and which were therefore closely bound up with his common life. Since cost is the essential element in

---

[25] S.P.C.K., p. 26. Quotations are from the 3rd edition of 1946.

[26] Cf. McLeod Campbell, *The Nature of the Atonement*, ch. viii; Bushnell, *Forgiveness and Law*, pp. 66-72; Westcott, The Historic Faith, note viii "The Blood of Christ" pp. 237-44; cf. Hicks, *The Fulness of Sacrifice*, pp. 12, 34-37.

[27] It was to be expected that the publication of the thesis "the blood is the Life" would produce reactions from those who feared that the old evangelical faith was being supplanted by a new theology centered in ethics alone. One good statement from this point of view is that of Leon Morris of Australia, in "The Blood, Life or Death" (*Christianity Today*, March 17, 1958), pp. 6-7. The question must ultimately be resolved by the exegetes, but I do not believe Bishop Hicks's case has been disproved. Certainly we must agree with Dr. Morris that from the biblical evidence the "blood" means not simply "life," but "life yielded up in death," just as we should have to insist that it also implies life given and received through the sacrifice of death. But we cannot go on to say that "it is the termination of life, the *infliction* of death that atones" (op. cit., p. 7). There is no justification for selecting the idea of the *infliction* of death as central to our Lord's sacrifice, however much we may agree that the Death itself is the central and integral means by which his life is offered for us and to us. Certainly we should agree that it is the pouring out of Christ's Life in Death which atones, but essential here is the fact that such a *life* was poured out to this extent for us, not simply the fact that the physical life of Jesus came to an end. The true significance of the Death which he died is to be discovered only through the Life which he lived, and in which, through the Resurrection, he invites us to share.

all sacrifice, there was a sense in which the one who offered a sacrifice offered himself.[28]

Like Aulén, Hicks reflects something of the changing temper of theology in the '30's in his emphasis upon the divine initiative and the "givenness" of the Christian faith. It comes out particularly clearly when he describes the contrast between the Hebraic and Greek ideas of God. The Greeks had reached their monotheism through philosophy, and God was always to them in some sense their own discovery, whereas the Hebrew prophet was always conscious that he was simply fulfilling "the inherited tradition of the race"—God was given, revealed to Israel, and he could not be "discovered." [29] In this revelation both the prophetic witness and the sacrificial cultus had their part to play, and over against those Liberal Protestants who disparaged the latter in order to emphasize the spiritual and ethical aspects of the former, Hicks takes the view that the two movements were complementary.

He made an extremely significant contribution when he demonstrated that all ethical and spiritual advances in the Hebrew religion had been accompanied by corresponding losses. For example if God's ethical nature was to be revealed, human sacrifice clearly had to go, but it meant that the cost of sacrifice could never be made as clearly again. Similarly, although the Deuteronomic reform removed the worst abuses of the local sanctuaries, it could not help removing also the intimacy and spontaneity of the local festivals: "with the new holiness there came, in sacrificial worship, a new futility." [30] This shows that the very virtues of the Hebrew faith should have inevitably driven Israel to the place where it recognized the insufficiency of its own religion. In a real sense the success of Hebrew religion spelt both its own failure and its consummation in our Lord.

Bishop Hicks carried these ideas into his examination of the New Testament. During his ministry our Lord had stressed not only repentance and forgiveness but also the divine initiative and cost in the parables of the Lost Sheep, the Lost Coin, and the Prodigal Son. Zacchaeus was saved, but he did not save himself, for he could not have been saved unless our Lord had been willing to take the initia-

---

[28] Hicks, op. cit., p. 24.
[29] Ibid., pp. 29-31.
[30] Ibid., p. 119.

tive by breaking through convention and entering the publican's home. The same kind of cost was involved in our Lord's death, for "death, voluntarily accepted that life may be formed, is at once the secret of His Kingship, and the revelation of the Father's character and will; and it is so because it is the way in which He seeks and saves His sheep and His treasure." [31] This is the meaning of our Lord's sacrifice.

Perhaps Bishop Hicks overstresses our Lord's continuity with all that had gone before in the history and religion of Israel and underestimates the sharp criticisms Jesus made of the public order and hierarchy of Hebrew religion—the note of discontinuity that cannot be explained away. But developing his previous examination of the sacrificial system of the Old Testament which had been his starting-point, he makes the valid point that the gospel emphasizes the essential meaning of sacrifice when it stresses that in the death of Christ the life of the sacrificial Victim is not ended. That Life was surrendered in order that it might be accepted, and in its acceptance be raised beyond the limitations of mortality into full communion with God in heaven: "He enters into our own self. It is Life given, broken, and surrendered; so transformed as to be universally accessible; that can enter into any life that has caught His spirit, has surrendered itself, allowed itself by dedication to be transformed, and so entering can become a part of each life and the common possession of all." [32] In support of his view he shows that our Lord refrained from using sacrificial language until the institution of the Last Supper, (i.e., not until his own final sacrifice was imminent and he wished to establish its meaning in a living act that would continue in the Church).

This means that the Cross is not to be regarded as the total sacrifice of Christ, but his sacrifice includes the Cross together with both his sacrificial life on earth and his priestly intercession. Hicks here reaches the heart of his thesis and the link that he wished to establish between the Atonement and the Sacraments. He contends that the Church made a fundamental error in identifying sacrifice with death instead of with life, for the Cross is decisive in the conflict between right and wrong. Once the conception of sacrifice is concentrated

[31] Ibid., p. 151.
[32] Ibid., p. 184.

exclusively upon the Death then the Cross becomes an Altar and loyalty to the Cross seems to exclude any continuing sacrifice beyond it. On the other hand Bishop Hicks maintains that if the blood of the Victim meant life—life poured out that it might become available to those for whom the sacrifice was offered—then the death is crucial, not as an end in itself, but as the means whereby this total and continuing sacrifice is effected: "nowhere," he declares, "either in the Synoptic Gospels, or in the rest of the New Testament, is the death regarded as an end in itself. Christ dies in order that He may live." [33]

In the last part of his book Hicks relates his study of sacrifice in the Old and New Testaments to the doctrine of the Eucharist, for it is clear that he is working toward the view that the Life of Christ that was given to us in the death of the Cross is made available to us particularly in the bread and wine of the Sacrament. He shows that there are three necessary aspects of sacrifice which must find their place in any adequate exposition of the Eucharist—an ethical element ("I will have mercy and not sacrifice"), an evangelical element ("Christ was once offered"), and a catholic element ("this our sacrifice of praise and thanksgiving"). Although he does not draw out the parallels himself, it is of some interest to notice that Dr. Hicks's three aspects of the Eucharist correspond with the subjective, objective, and incarnational views of the Atonement.

The significance and intention of his book are made clear in the view that it has been the mistaken emphasis of the Medieval Church upon the death of Christ, as being the sum of our Lord's sacrifice, which has made all these emphases necessary in order to safeguard the full gospel. Whether we stand in a catholic or an evangelical tradition, we can therefore look back with pride upon the witness of our spiritual ancestors, because they were contending for real issues, but the contemporary emphasis upon the ethical aspect is needed to supplement the other two.[34] He suggests that although the New Testament and the early Church had proclaimed the whole work of Christ as our Lord's sacrifice, the change which had come about was related to a debased understanding of the Eucharist that developed when the Church emerged from being a persecuted minority to become a

[33] *Ibid.*, p. 242.
[34] *Ibid.*, pp. 333-50.

state-recognized and popular institution. At that time it had been forced to receive large numbers of new converts into membership without adequate instruction and at a time when there was no general contact with either the pagan or the Jewish sacrificial systems. The identification of the death of Christ as his total act of sacrifice had developed until by the time of the Reformation the equation, sacrifice=death, had become universally accepted.[35] Hicks maintained that because this equation had been already made, the Reformers were entirely right to protest against the tendency of Medieval Catholicism to turn the Mass into a new and repeatable sacrifice (i.e., crucifixion) of our Lord, and to insist that he had died once and for all time upon the Cross. Therefore the equation, sacrifice=death, has also led to a proper revulsion against any conception of the Eucharist which thinks of the bread and wine of the Sacrament as becoming again the material Body and Blood of our Lord as he was before his death. On the other hand, Hicks argues, if the Sacrament is seen in its fullness, "the Body and Blood of the Eucharist are the Body and Blood of the glorified, not the crucified, Christ. They cannot be material. They belong to the time when 'it was spirit,' because Jesus has been glorified. The reasons for the old protest go, and with them all reasons for explaining away the full reality of the Eucharistic Body and Blood." [36]

This is a valiant attempt to find a synthesis for the ecumenical problem of the Eucharist, and we should not ignore the fact that the approach was significantly made through the idea of sacrifice and the doctrine of Atonement. But Bishop Hicks was altogether too sanguine if he thought that by stating the problem in these terms he could win a ready and universal acceptance of his views and resolve forthwith the eucharistic controversy. His book exudes something of the spirit of optimistic eclecticism that was in evidence during the Faith and Order conferences prior to Lund—to an extent that would not win much support today. We consider ourselves to be much wiser and more realistic, and any suggestion that everyone is right is apt to start ugly whispers of syncretism. On the other hand as far as any solution to the ecumenical problem is concerned, we are much more at an impasse, and we have to ask ourselves if Hicks's eucharistic con-

[35] *Ibid.*, pp. 302-3, 311.
[36] *Ibid.*, p. 347.

tentions have been given the attention they deserve, for they do warrant deep and serious consideration. And perhaps none should consider them more deeply and more seriously than those who, on account of their historic protests, are least inclined to admit in the Lord's Supper any conception of Real Presence at all.

It is always dangerous to try to assess the work of an author in his own lifetime, and this must be particularly true of the work of the Methodist scholar, Vincent Taylor, on the Atonement, because one can never be quite sure that he has produced his last word on the subject! After producing his famous trilogy on the biblical basis of the doctrine, *Jesus and his Sacrifice* (Macmillan, 1937), *The Atonement and New Testament Teaching* (Epworth, 1940), and *Forgiveness and Reconciliation* (Macmillan, 1941), he has recently returned to the same theme over a gap of sixteen years in *The Cross of Christ* (Macmillan, 1957). And yet we must pay serious attention to Vincent Taylor's work not merely because it illustrates the remaining important influence in the three that we noted earlier in contemporary theological trends—the emphasis upon sound biblical scholarship and Bible-centered theology—but because his work brings together so many different strands and illustrates the modern attempt to find a synthesis.

First of all he is concerned with a return to the biblical evidence, and with biblical evidence critically examined and theologically understood. For him theology is not only a legitimate sphere of interest for the technical New Testament scholar, but one which he should not abdicate to anyone else.[37] Biblical truth and not human reflection is the *fons et origo* of theology. Hence in *Jesus and His Sacrifice* Vincent Taylor examined the Old Testament background to the "self-consciousness" of our Lord about his own saving work, and in particular the place of such Hebraic concepts as the Kingdom of God, the Messianic Hope, the Suffering Servant, and the underlying ideas of Sacrifice in the Passion sayings of the Gospels. In *The Atonement in New Testament Teaching* he extended his study of the Atonement to the early Christian preaching and to the rest of the New Testament, and in *Forgiveness and Reconciliation* he took up two fundamental New Testament ideas and subjected them to the

---

[37] Taylor, *Forgiveness and Reconciliation*. Reprint of 2nd edition (1956), p. viii.

same kind of thoroughgoing analysis by showing their New Testament relationship to the themes of Justification, Sanctification, and hence Atonement. These three books add up to a fundamental biblical examination of the doctrine that has certainly not been equalled in English and is not likely to be excelled.

At the same time Vincent Taylor's work draws together many different aspects of the doctrine and illustrates the modern attempt to find a synthesis. This is perhaps illustrated in a tendency to overclassify the contributory aspects of the doctrine in *The Atonement in New Testament Teaching*,[38] and it is seen in the clear influence both of Aulén's *Christus Victor* and Bishop Hicks's *The Fulness of Sacrifice* upon his thinking.[39] It has been demonstrated most impressively in his firm contention that the doctrine must be seen in its entirety, as an organic whole.[40]

It is not an assessment of Vincent Taylor's theology which is required or which will be attempted, but rather a synopsis of certain conclusions regarding the doctrine of Atonement that he reached as a result of his biblical studies.

1. In the first place he asserts that the unity of purpose between Jesus and God the Father was so strong that it must necessarily exclude any idea of vindictive punishment. God is the moving cause of redemption and in it gives free course to his love. In this doctrine the unity of the Godhead is at stake, for just as "nothing less than the Catholic doctrine of Christ's Person is the necessary foundation for the message of the Cross," [41] so he maintains that the basis for a

---

[38] In distinguishing fourteen elements regarding the doctrine of the Atonement in the New Testament, Vincent Taylor admits that his classification suggests a precision greater than that of the New Testament writings themselves. This is so, for it is to be doubted whether one can distinguish so clearly, for example, between the "vicarious" and "representative" aspects of Christ's work, or between the sacrificial and eucharistic elements (does Hebrews with its thirteen references to the idea of sacrifice have nothing to say about the Eucharist?). On the other hand the clear analysis which Vincent Taylor has given us does enable us to see the varied ideas which went into the New Testament doctrine of Atonement, and such an analysis was indispensable before any synthesis could be attempted.

[39] In his view Aulén was entirely vindicated by the New Testament (*Jesus and His Sacrifice*, p. 261) and although he went beyond Hicks, he was clearly at one with the Bishop in his emphasis upon the sacrificial idea, upon the identification of "blood" with the release of life, upon the connection of sacrifice with the Eucharist, and in the ecumenical concern. Cf. *ibid.*, p. 296, *The Atonement in New Testament Teaching*, pp. 195, 215.

[40] *Ibid.*, p. 184.
[41] *Ibid.*, p. 173.

full theology of our Lord's sacrificial ministry "can be nothing less than the doctrine of Trinity in unity." [42]

2. In thinking of his Passion as the active fulfillment of his messianic vocation which would bring in the Kingdom, Jesus not only brought certain spiritual truths to light but fulfilled them in his own person. In this fulfillment our Lord thought of himself in relationship to the Servant prophecies as having a vocation of representative and vicarious suffering. Vincent Taylor holds that the New Testament comes very close to, without actually crossing into a doctrine of substitution, and that Pauline theology came within "a hair's breadth" of it,[43] but although we cannot summarize the New Testament in terms of "substitution," there is in the relationship to the Suffering Servant prophecies a substitutionary aspect to our Lord's sacrifice. On the other hand this aspect is thrown entirely out of focus if it is not seen in relation to a faith-union between our Lord and his followers so close and intimate that more and more his offering becomes their own.[44]

3. Having ruled out any idea of a vindictive punishment and having declared that the New Testament does not quite give its weight to an outright substitutionary theory, Vincent Taylor maintains that "it is impossible to think of the suffering of Jesus Himself as anything else but penal suffering." It is clear that here he is tacitly making the same distinction between "penal" and "penalty" that Forsyth had made earlier, for he says:

> Jesus entered into the blight and judgment which rest upon sin, and bore its shame and desolation upon His heart. Because He loved men so greatly He became one with them, entering into the situation in which they stood, sharing the pain of their disobedience, and feeling the pressure of their sins. Such suffering is penal because it is the fruit of the judgment which rests on sin.[45]

4. Although we cannot say from a study of the New Testament that Christ died solely in order that sins might be remitted, his death must include the forgiveness of sins. We can say that the death of Christ was not a necessary condition whereby God was enabled to

---

[42] *Ibid.*, p. 211.
[43] *Ibid.*, pp. 197-98.
[44] *Jesus and His Sacrifice*, p. 282.
[45] *Ibid.*, p. 290.

forgive us our sins, but that does not mean that there is no connection between the forgiveness of sins and the Atonement.[46] Indeed, although Jesus himself did not demand faith in his atoning death, the early Church rightly understood the implications of the gospel in this way, because to them faith in Christ and in his saving work were one and the same.[47]

Taking up the conception of our Lord's obedience which had been stressed by earlier writers, he declares that in the first place the self-offering of Jesus is to be seen in his perfect obedience to the Father. Secondly, this self-offering must be seen in terms of a perfect submission to God's judgment upon sin. And thirdly, employing the ideas of McLeod Campbell and R. C. Moberly, he maintains that it was the expression of our Lord's perfect confession and penitence for the sins of men,[48] for he asserts that although Campbell and Moberly's ideas of the Atonement are not to be found explicitly stated in the New Testament, they are to be allowed as legitimate inferences from the New Testament because they ultimately depend on the idea of sacrifice.[49] Here he is quite clearly trying to sift that which is of value in the views which had already been put forward, and to move toward a doctrine which will have the unity and wholeness that he feels should properly belong to it.

However, Vincent Taylor is not simply concerned to find a New Testament explanation for what Christ *did*, he is also very much concerned to show how men are enabled to participate in the redemptive power of our Lord's self-offering through faith-union with him. This leads him inevitably to devote a good deal of attention to the Sacraments, particularly the Lord's Supper. Although there is a distinction between faith-union as it is expressed in Paul's writings and sacramental communion, he insists that it is impossible to differentiate absolutely between the two.[50] He maintains that theology is not building upon an unsure foundation when it finds in the Eucharist a permanent way by which men may have participation in the self-offering of Jesus. In his examination of the Passion Sayings themselves, he comes to the conclusion that to eat the bread and to drink the wine "is to

---
[46] *Forgiveness and Reconciliation*, pp. 27-28.
[47] *Jesus and His Sacrifice*, pp. 291-92.
[48] Ibid., pp. 307-11.
[49] *The Atonement in N. T. Teaching* (London: Epworth Press), p. 176; cf. p. 200.
[50] *Jesus and His Sacrifice*, p. 292.

participate in the surrendered life and to appropriate its consecrating power. The elements are both symbols and media and derive this significance from the word of Jesus Himself."[51] He stresses the divinely "social" aspect of the Eucharist, and because our relationship with Christ inevitably involves our relationship to our fellows,[52] insisted that the Eucharist must be the center of all corporate worship:

> Once this truth is grasped, the Eucharist is seen from a new angle; it cannot lie at the circumference of Christian worship, but must stand at the centre, as a means whereby man approaches God and appropriates the blessings of Christ's self-offering.... This perception means that no modern presentation of the doctrine of the Atonement is likely to be satisfactory which ignores, or deals imperfectly with, the doctrine of the Eucharist. The Eucharist falls within the orbit of the Atonement alike by reason of the teaching of Jesus and of the life and experience of the Church.[53]

In another place he cites a well known passage from Karl Barth to emphasize the same sacramental center to worship.[54] But it should be noted that Vincent Taylor's emphasis upon sacramental communion is not magical, aesthetic, or even mystical, but *ethical*—it is a means of participating in and becoming identified with the atoning life of Christ. Although all theories of the Atonement are good in their way and provide scope for the exercise of Christian faith, he declares that "it may be doubted if any of them supplies so full an opportunity for its ethical and devotional expression as one founded on the sacrificial principle, just because it is of its essence that the worshipper should identify himself with that which he offers to God."[55] It is this sacrificial principle that Vincent Taylor discovered at the heart of the Sacrament.

In *The Atonement in New Testament Teaching* Vincent Taylor describes a threefold aspect of the doctrine—it is Vicarious ("He died for me"); it is Representative, in our Lord's obedience, in his submis-

---

[51] *Ibid.*, p. 267.
[52] *Ibid.*, p. 231; cf. *The Atonement in N.T. Teaching*, p. 169-70., *Forgiveness and Reconciliation*, pp. 127 ff.
[53] *Jesus and His Sacrifice*, p. 322.
[54] *The Atonement in N.T. Teaching*, p. 207; cf. Barth, *The Knowledge of God and the Service of God* (Gifford Lectures, 1937-38), p. 211.
[55] *Jesus and His Sacrifice*, p. 317.

sion to judgment upon sin, and in his "penitence" for human sin; it is Sacrificial. We appropriate our Lord's redeeming work through faith, through the Sacraments, and through our identity with Christ both in suffering and in our response to life. Vincent Taylor declared that the best New Testament word to describe the purpose of the Atonement is Reconciliation.[56] If one could summarize his understanding of the Atonement in a single word it would be in this root meaning of the word atonement itself—"at-one-ment." And the sacrificial category "is peculiarly suitable for this doctrinal presentation because, in the use of the term 'blood,' it suggests the thought of life, dedicated, offered, transformed, and open to our spiritual appropriation, and because in its basal suggestion of an offering which the worshipper may make his own, it supplies a religious pattern for the needs of thought, devotional culture, worship and service."[57] For this reason he holds that even if there is need in the future to reinterpret the doctrine radically, the fundamental values of the sacrificial concept will have to be maintained.

It has been said that the closer we draw to the Atonement, the nearer we shall be to each other, and in the theological studies of a Lutheran like Aulén, an Anglican like Bishop Hicks, and a Methodist like Vincent Taylor, we see the truth of this being made manifest. They simply underline the fact that in striving to reach the heart of the Atonement, we find ourselves worshiping at the same place, eating the same Bread, and drinking from the same Cup.

4. An International Discussion: Emil Brunner and Donald Baillie

We have quite clearly arrived at the point of the contemporary discussion, regarding which we have not the historical perspective to go into any detail, but side-by-side with the three influences that have helped to determine the nature of that discussion and which have been illustrated in Aulén, Hicks, and Vincent Taylor, we must also have noticed in their writings two other common characteristics. The first is the impact of "neo-orthodox" continental theology, which played into Britain's own biblical renewal, helped to stimulate it and draw out its theological implications, and which as it became better understood provided an anvil upon which the Anglo-Saxon world

---
[56] *The Atonement in N.T. Teaching*, p. 191 (cf. p. 182).
[57] *Ibid.*, p. 198; cf. pp. 184-85.

could try the metal of its own theology. The English-speaking world has had its own theology and its own history of development, but perhaps we are conscious as never before that we can no more live in theological isolation from other countries and confessions than we can withdraw nationally behind the illusory security of an English Channel or a Monroe Doctrine. From 1939 onward the names of Barth and Brunner began to appear in something more than the footnotes of British books, and although a few years ago it was still possible for one Oxford professor of theology to suggest that their theology might be compared with the escapism of Buddhism and another to describe Brunner as a Lutheran, at least during the 1939-45 war they began to be given the serious consideration that their views merited.

The second characteristic is the search for a synthesis. Not only has this been dictated by a growing ecumenical consciousness, but even more by the realization that no one theory can hope to represent adequately the mystery of the Atonement. The seriousness of the challenge made by the moral influence theories upon the traditional forms of the doctrine, the vital theological basis of the "objective" theories, the rediscovery of the "dramatic" categories in the ransom theories, the biblical evidence for the sacrificial concept—all these elements were seen to be indispensable to any true interpretation of the doctrine and forced theologians back to the truth that in this sphere of Christian doctrine the answer was not to be found in a simple "either-or." The search for a synthesis is not for reasons of synthesis itself or because scholars despaired of finding their anwer in a more unitive form, but it was rather because biblical and theological seriousness compelled them to recognize that all the past theories were at one point or another contending for truths that were to be found in Scripture itself.

The influence of continental theology upon the doctrine of the Atonement became particularly noticeable with the appearance of Emil Brunner's *Der Mittler* (*The Mediator*) in English in 1934. Brunner's book is not a treatment of the Atonement as such but of Christology—indeed, it might well have taken as its sub-title the title of one of Forsyth's best known works, "The Person and Place of Jesus Christ"—but no book on such a subject could fail to say a great deal about the saving work of our Lord. There are many things in

The Mediator which made the English world sit up and listen, and it underlined many of the truths toward which British theology itself had been moving. It came at a time when people were beginning to be ready to listen.

It was clear that although Brunner's approach was from the doctrine of the Incarnation which he regarded as the fundamental Christian truth,[58] the only Incarnation which he was concerned to expound was one which was entered by our Lord with the intention and the purpose of the Cross as its goal—theology was for him as for Luther, *theologia crucis*. Taking his stand with the Reformers he declared that "He who understands the Cross aright . . . understands the Bible, he understands Jesus Christ," [59] and it had been that fundamental conviction that had through the years driven the theologians about whom we have been writing forward again and again to wrestle with the doctrine of the Atonement. As Brunner spoke of the Incarnation in this way as God's act for the redemption of man, people began to be reminded of the forgotten accents of Dale, Denney, and Forsyth. Wrote Brunner:

> His Passion and Death is not significant as a moral test which He endured successfully—as an ethical event—but as a divine deed and a divine revelation, as a "Messianic event." It does not merely give Him the right to be called the Redeemer, it constitutes Him as the Redeemer. Only thus can we understand the meaning of His sacrifice. It is the personal entrance into a necessity which existed in the presence of God and for His sake; it means making His own the Divine Will of revelation and of atonement, with the inclusion of this negative element of the suffering of death as expiation. It is "obedience"—not in the general ethical sense, but in the specifically Christian sense, in the sense peculiar to the Messiah, that obedience suggested by Paul's often quoted phrase, according to which the *whole* life of Christ is conceived from the point of view of obedience in suffering.[60]

The Mediator is important because of the reaction it produced. In a book like Donald Baillie's *God Was in Christ* (1948), for example, we

---

[58] E. T. by Olive Wyon. From *The Mediator* by Emil Brunner. Copyright, 1947, by W. L. Jenkins, the Westminster Press and the Lutterworth Press. Used by permission, p. 403.
[59] *Ibid.*, p. 435.
[60] *Ibid.*, pp. 500-501.

see how far British theology had moved during the war—there are deep points of difference with Brunner, but there are equally significant points of fundamental agreement.

Here I must be allowed to bring a footnote into the text. A fairly recent article in *The Christian Century* proposed to "de-mythologize" the term "neo-orthodoxy" and pointed out that the representative thinkers of this movement in America, while sharing certain critical attitudes to the former Liberal categories of inevitable progress and optimism about man, in reality hold radically different theological points of view.[61] The same, of course, would be true of Britain or the European continent. Not only have we the sharp differences between Barth and Brunner, or between them and Bultmann, or between all three of them and many of the super-confessionalists, but in Britain, at least, one would have to number within that movement neo-Thomists as well as "Barthians" or "neo-Calvinists." The writer of the article, however, went on to describe the common emphases of the movement in America and suggested that there was nothing in these specific positions that were common to all that was distinctively Christian. Whether this is a valid judgment about the American scene those who are competent will be able to judge, but this would be wholly untrue for Britain and the Continent, for the one characteristic par excellence of the theological renewal on the eastern side of the Atlantic is precisely its christocentricity, its insistence that since God acted in Christ, all true faith and all true theology start at this point. I make this digression because this is the point which stands clear as common ground between Brunner's *The Mediator* and Baillie's *God Was in Christ*.

I regard the late D. M. Baillie as a representative British theologian, for at the time when he wrote, he undoubtedly stood in the front rank of British theology, and his position defines the place where the great bulk of British theology still stands. He wrote in obvious appreciation of Brunner's *The Mediator*,[62] but at the same time he was deeply critical of the theological trend on the Continent because he had the impression that continental theologians were ready to by-pass the question of historicity in the life of Christ and that they

---

[61] Sydney E. Ahlstrom, "Neo-Orthodoxy Demythologized," *The Christian Century*, May 22, 1957, pp. 649 ff.
[62] Baillie, op. cit. (New York: Scribners), p. 34.

regarded the historical problems connected with the Gospel records as irrelevant. Brunner and his colleagues were "not concerned with the Jesus of history . . . but with the Jesus Christ of personal testimony, who is the real Christ." [63] He says with a good deal of justice that a continental visitor to Britain would be shocked on two counts about the theology he would find there—he would be shocked at the "conservatism" regarding historical criticism and by the "modernism" of the doctrinal theology. At the same time to Anglo-Saxons the continental theology sometimes seems to be "a curious synthesis of dogmatism and scepticism." From this we might imagine that the differences between the theology of Britain and the Continent were far more radical than in fact they are. Baillie makes it quite clear that "the Jesus of history" he is speaking about is by no means to be confused with "the Jesus of history" according to the presuppositions of T. R. Glover and the Liberal school in which he had stood.[64] Baillie did not believe that by cool detached criticism we could finally arrive at an authentic portrait of our Lord, but he maintained that we ought to discover by historical means all we could about that life and character of the One, in the events of whose life the Christian gospel was constituted and whose character had led the New Testament writers to interpret those events doctrinally. If we say that the historical is irrelevant, are we not ignoring the fact that the Word became flesh, and the fact that God's plan of salvation was *revealed* in Christ? [65] This accent of British theology upon the historicity of the events described in the gospel record—the fact that in Christ God *revealed* himself —remains one of its most distinctive elements. Canon Leonard Hodgson has pointed out that the inclusion of the historical material in the creed is criticized because it requires faith at a point where certainty is extremely difficult to obtain, and to include such things in the creed perhaps puts our faith at the mercy of "chance discoveries." [66] But to deny the historical element would be to deny the faith, and Baillie would go on to argue that for theology to ignore the historical task of testing and verifying where possible those crucial events would amount to an abdication of its proper function.

[63] *Ibid.*, p. 35.
[64] *The Jesus of History* (S.C.M., 1917).
[65] *Op. cit.*, pp. 48 ff.
[66] Hodgson, *op. cit.* (New York: Scribners), p. 121.

Yet Baillie stands uncompromisingly with Barth and Brunner rather than with the earlier Liberals. He is conscious that he is carrying on the war on two fronts, for he is as anxious as the continental theologians to explode the presumptuous claims of the Liberals about the "historical Jesus." However, he is also at pains to preserve (against what he calls the modern "Logotheism") the Liberal contention that Christ was a real historical person with a life and character that can be studied similar to that of any other historical person. We must not imagine that this historical study can give us the whole truth about Jesus Christ, but it must not be ignored, for what was revealed in his life, death, and character to the writers of the New Testament is important not as the revelation of "the Jesus of History" but as the revelation of God incarnate. *Therefore,* history matters. For the rest Baillie stood very much with the continental theologians. His Christology and soteriology are not less centered than Barth's and Brunner's in the divine initiative. No less than theirs his theology is based upon the frank dialectic of apparently irreducible paradoxes, and at the very center of all his theology we find the paradox of grace which he uses as the key to unlock the meaning of our Lord's Incarnation and Atonement. To Donald Baillie the Incarnation was demonstrated in the paradox of a Person who could win the confession made by Peter at Caesarea Philippi, and at the same time declare that it was not he himself who spoke but that the Father was speaking through him and that without the Father he could do nothing. This points on to the continuing paradox of grace in the Christian life whereby the saints who have won the greatest moral victories in Christ's name have insistently declared "It is not I but Christ." But it also points back to the eternal purpose and intention of God himself, who loves mankind so dearly and hates his sin so completely that at one and the same time he demands absolute obedience and provides that obedience in the work of Christ and the action of the Holy Spirit. Grace is the root paradox because it is the very spring of God's purpose for us.

Logically at this point Baillie's ideas lead to an idea of kenosis—not indeed in the sense of divine limitation, an idea which he resolutely rejects as inadequate to the Incarnation—but as a positive concept, an eternal outpouring of God himself in Creation, Incarnation, and Redemption, eternally an expression of God's grace and beatitude in the Trinity. Baillie did not develop his ideas to this point, but if he had, it would have implied an idea of *kenosis* which would perhaps have been more akin to Orthodox thought than the kenotic theories of Protestantism that he is at pains to reject.

Because he found the center of theology in the paradox of grace and because it implied this eternal outpouring of God himself, the center of his doctrine is in the work of Atonement. His book simply re-emphasizes the fact (as does *The Mediator*) that Incarnation and Atonement are inseparably linked together, and that in speaking of either, we are speaking of one movement in history—the atoning Incarnation, the Incarnate Atonement. It is a movement; it is an action of God in history for the redemption of man—a redemption that was implicit in the outpouring of God in Creation. Indeed, what is being emphasized is not only the indissoluble link between the doctrines of Atonement and Incarnation but their unity with all Christian doctrine—Baillie and Brunner are added testimonies to the growing cloud of modern witnesses that all Christian doctrine is a unity.

This is perhaps a natural corollary to expect from the search for a synthesis, for if Atonement is an action taken by God himself, we cannot ignore its implications both for the doctrine of the Person of our Lord and for the doctrine of the Trinity. Just as if we are to take the sacrificial and ethical aspects of the Atonement seriously, we cannot ignore what they imply for the work of the Holy Spirit in the Church and through the Sacraments. So we could go on: from an examination of this doctrine of our Lord's redeeming work we find ourselves faced with the Christian faith in its wholeness. Perhaps he intended it to be like that.

5. Toward an Ecumenical Consensus

The demand for a doctrine of the Atonement that is in the fullest sense catholic by doing justice to all the biblical concepts must be stressed as one of the most striking characteristics of recent books and as an illustration of a growing consensus. It has been pointed out that there are many theories but no one theory can claim to have the official *imprimatur* of the Church,[67] and Oliver Chase Quick, in setting

---

[67] *Ibid.*, p. 13. Cf. the passage from W. P. Du Bose, quoted *infra*, pp. 280-81. Also see this statement by Karl Barth, "Do not confuse my theory of reconciliation with the thing itself. All theories of reconciliation can be but pointers." *Dogmatics in Outline* (S.C.M., 1949), p. 116. E.T. by G. T. Thomson.

forth a view in which he tried to reconcile the moral, dramatic, juridical, and sacrificial theories, declared that no theory or any number of theories could be sufficient to express the fulness of the doctrine.[68] Although modern writers are no less critical of former theories than the writers of the past (e.g., both Quick and Hodgson are deeply critical of certain parts of Aulén's work), they recognize the value in all the views that have been put forward. Usually their own distinctive contributions are not in promoting new "white hopes" that will knock the other theories out of the ring but in attempts to find the true scriptural principle that will reconcile the doctrine's different aspects. It is in the true succession to Forsyth, even as he—perhaps without recognizing it—was in the succession of Thomas Aquinas.

Does the modern consensus go any further than this? Are we able to find any other common characteristics beyond the desire to bring together the best elements in all previous theories on the subject? We can, but there is no clear unanimity yet on the biblical principle that can affect this synthesis of the doctrine, although a number of writers find it in the sacrificial obedience of our Lord, but to illustrate the variety of thinking, we might take three recent Anglican writers as examples. O. C. Quick emphasizes the New Society which God creates through the Atonement—"the Gospel of the New World"—as the reconciling principle;[69] Leonard Hodgson sees the Atonement as God's action to defeat evil and his call to the Church to engage in the same self-giving, while H. A. Hodges finds the principle in the sacrifice of our Lord's obedience and concentrates on correcting protestant errors in the conception of "'Justification by Faith."[70] Yet all three writers take the best of the former theories into their accounts of the doctrine and are concerned with presenting the doctrine in its wholeness.

This is the common ground whether written from a "protestant" or a "catholic" point of view, but beyond this there are other characteristics which can be traced within all recent writing on the Atonement.

1. The chief feature of the theological renewal in Europe is its christocentric nature, but we must be clear what we mean by their "christocentricity." It is certainly not to be understood as an exclu-

---

[68] Quick, *Doctrines of the Creed* (Nisbet, 1938; 5th Impression, 1954), p. 222.
[69] *The Gospel of the New World* (Nisbet, 1944).
[70] *The Pattern of Atonement* (S.C.M. 1955).

sive concentration upon the purely human aspects of our Lord's nature, in the way which Hodges applies the term to certain movements in medieval Catholic devotion or to certain circles of post-Reformation Protestantism.[71] To speak of the modern writers as "christocentric" means not that they are "Jesus centered" but "Christ centered." That is, they put at the center of their theology the full doctrines of our Lord's Person and of the Incarnation, and they do so not for the sake of appearing "orthodox" but because they recognize that nothing less than the Church's full doctrine will do justice to the facts which the Atonement sets forth. This is true of all the modern British writers—as true for a high Anglican like Professor Hodges as for a Methodist like Vincent Taylor.[72]

2. Another aspect of this emphasis upon a full Christology is the note of victory. "He reigns from this Tree," declares Dr. J. S. Whale,[73] and almost all the recent writers emphasize that the Atonement is not limited to the Crucifixion but is caught up into the Resurrection and the Ascension and is effectively active at the heart of Church's life on earth and of our Lord's Priestly intercession at God's Right Hand. When Oliver Quick speaks of the sacramental character of the Resurrection and Ascension of our Lord, he is really speaking of the connection that these aspects of our Lord's ministry have with Christ's work of Redemption.[74] This leads straight into the recognition of the relationship between this victorious Atonement to the Sacraments of the Church, for in the Sacraments—and particularly in the Eucharist, as the Eastern Church has always maintained—the whole drama of our redemption is present in what has been well described as "the eternal simultaneity of heaven." [75]

3. The Atonement centers in action—God's action and initiative. We shall not be surprised to hear a good continental Reformed theologian like Emil Brunner declaiming that "the doctrine of the Atonement is not a 'theory of sacrifice,' but it is the unveiling of our guilt in its truly fatal character, and of the incomprehensible Act of Grace by which God has taken our part." [76] Nor will we think it too

---

[71] Ibid., p. 48.
[72] Cf. also J. S. Whale, chs. iv and v in *Christian Doctrine* (C.U.P., 1942).
[73] Ibid., p. 87. Cf. Westcott, quoted supra, p. 225.
[74] *The Christian Sacraments* (Nisbet, 1927, 10th impression, 1948), p. 93.
[75] Nathaniel Micklem in *Christian Worship* (O.U.P., 1936), p. 256.
[76] Brunner, op. cit., pp. 599-600.

remarkable that Karl Barth should declare, "In the sense of the Apostolic witness the Crucifixion of Jesus Christ is the concrete deed and action of God Himself," and he develops this in a way which makes Christ fully our substitute.[77] We shall not be too surprised to hear the Scots Presbyterian, Donald Baillie, speaking of God expiating our sins as only God could do and of a Christology centering in the divine initiative,[78] and we would expect to find one of Forsyth's fellow-confessionalists like J. S. Whale announcing in Forsythian terms that "His Passion is Action."[79] But the point is made no less clearly by Anglicans, like Leonard Hodgson who says that "Christianity proclaims a God who acts,"[80] and by O. C. Quick who describes the Atonement as "the Sacrament of God's power in act."[81] "In the whole process of our redemption," writes Professor Hodges, "it is He who takes the initiative and retains it throughout."[82] The same point is made by William J. Wolf, who of all recent writers on the Atonement, has had most insight into the nature of the new ecumenical consensus. For, "the work of atonement is, throughout, the expression of God's holy love. It is love that leads the Father to beget the Son, in the fullness of time to be born as a humble man, and to pour out his life in sacrificial self-giving. It is holy love again after his death and resurrection that causes him to send the Holy Spirit to lead men to respond to his saving work for them. Each person of the Trinity is involved in the work of atonement, although it naturally centers in the person and work of the God-man."[83]

4. This last quotation brings to the fore a further aspect of the doctrine where there appears to be growing unanimity—the fact that the doctrine of Atonement cannot be separated from the other main doctrines of the Christian faith. First, as Brunner declared, "The Incarnation and the Cross form an indissoluble unity,"[84] for if the objective element in the Atonement is indispensable, then the work

---

[77] Barth, op. cit. (London: S.C.M. Press, publishers—Alec R. Allinson, U. S. distributors), p. 116. Although Barth conceives of Christ as our substitute, he does not, however, think of the infliction of the Cross as a punishment by the Father upon the Son—because he emphasizes that God acts on the Cross. Ibid.
[78] Baillie, op. cit., pp. 65, 199.
[79] Whale, op. cit., p. 87.
[80] Hodgson, op. cit., p. 122.
[81] Quick, The Christian Sacraments, p. 93.
[82] Hodges, op. cit., p. 58.
[83] Wolf, op. cit., p. 186.
[84] Brunner, op. cit., p. 492.

of Christ in redemption cannot be considered apart from the whole divine action whereby the Word became flesh and dwelt among us. "It is essential to the Christian faith to believe that Jesus of Nazareth was incarnate God," [85] and one could go on to show that far from it leading to any attempt to over-emphasize the Cross at the expense of our Lord's birth, the struggle to understand more profoundly the meaning of the Atonement forced the theologians to take the Incarnation more seriously. Where a man has seen most deeply into the meaning of the Cross, he would stand with Father Georges Florovsky when he quotes the bold phrase of Gregory Nazianus, "we needed an Incarnate God; God put to death, that we might live," or with Karl Barth in his insistence that we can only understand the Incarnation and the Atonement through each other.[86] Equally, the Atonement cannot be separated from a doctrine of the Trinity, for if in the terms of Baillie's title the center of that great act of God in Incarnation and redemption was in the fact that God was in Christ, then the theologian cannot avoid saying something about the doctrine of God. "Father and Son," writes H. A. Hodges, "are at one in all things. It is the Father who sends the Son to be the Saviour of the world." [87] "Our Redemption," writes N. Micklem, "is the work of the whole Trinity." [88] If the Atonement is above all things God's own act, then there can be no false dichotomy between the Persons of the Godhead in that redeeming act. If this is true, we must realize the implications for the inner life of the Trinity itself in its relationship to the Atonement when we make such a statement as "in Jesus Christ Punisher and Punished are one." [89]

5. Although no modern writer regards the moral influence theories as in themselves adequate for the doctrine in its wholeness, there is nevertheless a strong desire to do justice to the ethical aspects of our redemption. When Bishop Hicks wrote *The Fulness of Sacrifice* in 1930, the influence of the neo-Abelardian thinkers was strong enough to be in his mind when he suggested that concentration upon ethics

---

[85] Hodgson, op. cit., pp. 137-38.
[86] Georges Florovsky, "On the Tree of the Cross" in *St. Vladimir's Seminary Quarterly* (New York, 1953, Vol. I, Nos. 3 and 4), p. 13; Karl Barth, *Dogmatics in Outline*, p. 114.
[87] Hodges, op. cit., p. 51.
[88] Micklem, *The Doctrine of Our Redemption* (Eyre and Spottiswoode, 1943), p. 96.
[89] Hodgson, op. cit., p. 78.

would be the great contemporary contribution to the doctrine. But Canon J. K. Mozley has made the suggestion, which is at first sight somewhat surprising, that one of Forsyth's great contributions to our understanding of Atonement was his determination to ethicize it. No one was less likely to substitute morality for religion,[90] and this fact should give us cause enough to ponder on the real springs of the contemporary interest in ethics. Forsyth's concern was to ethicize the doctrine itself, to bring out the fact that the doctrine of the Atonement must be consistent with the holiness of the righteous God revealed in the Bible, and from this it followed that the individual's response to the gospel in personal ethics and in sacramental communion finds its source in the holiness of God revealed upon the Cross. Among the modern writers the link between Atonement, ethics, and Sacrament is to be found not only in Forsyth and Bishop Hicks but in all those who have seriously tried to incorporate the sacrificial concepts into their doctrine of Atonement. If "the blood is the life" poured out to death, then the life of Christ is made available to us by faith and by drinking the cup that he was prepared to drink.

6. This last point illustrates the one which is to follow. While modern writers try to do justice to all previous theories, there is a noticeable tendency to put the sacrificial categories at the center of the doctrine as those which can be theologically the most helpful for our own generation.[91] We might cite as an example the words of Vincent Taylor quoted earlier,[92] or the fact that Donald Baillie discovers his most telling evidence for the cost of forgiveness in Atonement in the sacrificial system, or the contribution of Hicks in bringing the Old Testament sacrifices into the foreground of our thought regarding the sacrifice of our Lord and the acknowledgment of his work

---

[90] In his preface to the post-war editions of Forsyth's *The Church and the Sacraments* (Independent Press), pp. viii-ix. Cf. also Canon Mozely's discussion of Forsyth in *The Doctrine of Atonement* (New York: Scribners, 1916), pp. 182-83.

[91] William Wolf seriously questions this, and on good grounds. "The sacrificial theory," he says, "labors under a severe apologetic handicap that is not always appreciated by technical scholars. Modern man finds the background of the sacrificial theory wholly uncongenial. For him sacrifice is obscured by popular misconceptions. One cannot so rest the preaching of the Cross upon the sacrificial theory that the preaching must always be preceded by a series of archaeological addresses on the background of sacrifice, Plainly if this theory is to be helpful it must be able to disentangle the essential significance of sacrifice perhaps in terms of "costly act" and "divine suffering" from the strange trappings of forgotten rituals." *No Cross, No Crown*, p. 124.

[92] Supra, pp. 267-68, cf. note 55.

THE ATONEMENT AND THE SACRAMENTS

in writers like Vincent Taylor, Baillie, and Whale. The fundamental importance of the ideas drawn from the biblical sacrifices is that they are taken from no one part of the Bible and from no one writer—they emphasize the unity of Scripture's testimony, and they demonstrate the consummation of Israel's historic worship in the sacrifice of her Messiah upon the Cross.

7. The note of cosmic redemption is very strongly heard, not only in its relationship to a future eschatology but also to ethics and in relation to the continuing work of the Church for the redemption of the world here and now. The words attributed to the great Jesuit missionary, Francis Xavier, find their way into many protestant hymn books today,[93] and there has been a growing belief that if the sole object of the gospel is individual salvation and the assurance it gives "me" that "I" am saved, it would be difficult to think of this as salvation at all. Nathaniel Micklem at the end of *The Doctrine of Our Redemption* (which was written in the middle of World War II) asks, in effect, if heaven could be heaven if with it there were the consciousness that other souls remain outside the scope of God's grace and the power of Christ's redeeming blood.[94] Hodgson raises the issue in a slightly different form in a chapter on "Creation and Redemption," and this theme may be said to be the central motif of Oliver Quick's *The Gospel of the New World*. It may be described as an eschatological emphasis, as long as we do not falsely limit that term to some ever receding future state, for the modern British writers, partly no doubt under the influence of C. H. Dodd's studies, insist that the gospel also brings the eschaton into the world now. The redemption of society is just as much the concern of the Church in the present as it will become its glory and proof of its faithfulness in the final end of time.

8. Finally, there is the emphasis which it has been the special task of this present work to point out and underline, the recognition that the doctrine of the Atonement is directly related to the Dominical Sacraments and especially to the Sacrament of the Lord's Supper. When an Orthodox theologian like Georges Florovsky describes the

---

[93] I refer to the verses of a well known hymn attributed to Xavier, translated by Edward Caswall, and quoted *infra*, p. 379.

[94] Micklem, *op. cit.*, pp. 95-96. Dr. Micklem does not explicitly pose the question in this way, but his meaning is implicit.

Eucharist as the Sacrament of Redemption,[95] we must be careful not to read into that description a purely Protestant understanding of what "Redemption" means, but bearing in mind the different confessional interpretations at this point, we have seen the same concern to link the Sacraments with the doctrine of Redemption in writers like Forsyth, Vincent Taylor, and Bishop Hicks. Whatever our confessional allegiance, the Sacraments have become more and more for us the central expression of the redeeming work of Christ in the life of the Church. In the water of Baptism or at the table of the Lord's Supper, God's saving Act in all its victory, in all its objective "once-for-all" reality is brought into direct relation with our ethical response and with the Church's eschatological hope and present task.

"In the long experience of the Church," writes Dr. Whale, "this faith-union with the Redeemer is no formal possibility; it becomes a living reality through sacramental communion with him. At the Holy Table the remembered words and deeds of Jesus, as set forth in the pages of the Gospels, become the real presence of the Lord. Believers have fellowship with him, with one another, and with the great unseen company of the redeemed on earth and in heaven, through the communion of the Body and Blood of Christ. This is the end, use and effect of the Sacrament; it sets forth the means of grace and the hope of glory." [96] This is not the place to discuss this particular view of the Sacrament, but if we may shift the horizon from Britain for a moment and see this consensus in something more like its true ecumenical dimensions, we can see that from the Anglo-Catholic Hodges to the Reformed Karl Barth, and from the Methodist Vincent Taylor to the Russian Orthodox Georges Florovsky there is fundamental agreement in placing the sacraments at the center of Christian worship as sacraments of Redemption. If the Church is "first and always the Eucharistic fellowship," [97] it is so because it is first always the redeemed community. This recognition is one of the most striking features of recent thought on the doctrine of our Redemption. Why it should be so, what it means, and what it may imply it will be our task in the third part of this book to try to expound.

[95] "On the Tree of the Cross," *St. Vladimir's Seminary Quarterly*, p. 32.
[96] Whale, op. cit., p. 90.
[97] Bishop Stephen Neill in an article "Christian Society and the Church," *Episcopal Church News* (February 21, 1954), p. 31.

CHAPTER VIII

Future Problems

HERE THE PATH DIVIDES. IN THE THIRD PART OF THIS BOOK I SHALL direct attention to the Sacraments in order to see them in the light of what has been written about the Atonement. This is the point to which I have been working. But before we turn specifically to this, let us travel a little way along the other path that needs to be explored. Let us look at the Atonement in relationship to the other doctrines of the Christian Faith, although we must recognize that we can but discern the outlines of future theological inquiry.

1. Incarnation and the Church

We must start with the Incarnation. In an earlier chapter I have already hinted at the importance of the relationship between the Incarnation and the Atonement.[1] It must be clear that the doctrine of the Incarnation becomes an ecumenical issue of the highest importance in its relationship with the doctrine of the Church, for "Catholic"[2] teaching believes, with a good deal of biblical justification, that if the Church is the Body of Christ, then she is also, by implication, the extension of his Incarnation in Time. It has become increasingly obvious that if Protestants are going to take the Pauline image with proper seriousness, if indeed the image is anything more than a mere figure of speech, any doctrine of the Church which describes the Church principally in terms of a human voluntary society is totally inadequate. We have to face the plain issue that according to the New Testament the visible Church itself is an indispensable and in-

---

[1] *Supra*, pp. 225-27.
[2] I put the word in quotation marks, first, because it is a word which should never be mortgaged to any one branch of the Christian Church, and secondly, because when I speak of "Catholic" theology I include the theology of the Eastern Orthodox Churches and those sympathetic tendencies which are to be found within Anglicanism and continental Protestantism.

tegral part of God's act of Redemption. But the problem becomes acute between Protestant and "Catholic" when, arguing from this link between the Incarnation and the Church, the further step is taken to identify the institutional Church with our Lord's sinlessness, and by that means to claim sinlessness and infallibility for a particular institutional Church as his Body. Many of those who argue from the "Catholic" position boldly make this claim, maintaining that although Christians may sin, the Church cannot sin precisely because it is his body in the world. Protestant theology on the other hand has been properly hesitant to take this step, not always because it has been unwilling to take the Pauline image seriously, but because it has been all too conscious of the fact that, whatever may be said of the *Una Sancta* as it is known to God, churches in their representative words and actions (and not merely individuals) reveal sin. It has been this consciousness of the mixed character of the Church—not only as sharing with its Lord a nature that is at once human and divine, but also of having within it wheat and tares, New Adam and Old Adam—that has led to Protestant reserve in making the identification between the Incarnation and the Church as its visible extension in time.

Leaving aside the way in which Pietism turned the distinction between a "visible" and "invisible" Church to fit its theology of the "new birth" and the "twice born," it must be clear that the original distinction of the Reformers—who were surely following Augustine—was made simply to bring the note of realism into our thinking about the Church as *it is*, the frank recognition that it is a fallacy and almost a blasphemy for any instituted Church to represent itself as sinless or infallible. On the other hand the distinction has confused the issue by creating a false dichotomy between the Church as a visible institution—apparently the only church known to the New Testament—and what is assumed to be the "true" or invisible Church of the Elect that is known to God alone. The continuing ecumenical discussion, and not least the biblical renewal which has inspired it, has been teaching us that the distinction between the "visible" and "invisible" Church is often misleading, and that Protestants have frankly to accept the fact that the Church was instituted as a visible living community of flesh and blood and that *as such* it is the Body of Christ, the vehicle of his Spirit, and the continuation of his incarnate life.

Our problem is to accept the biblical picture without falling into the idolatry of equating Christ's own sinless perfection with actions undertaken by a Church that through its members may be fallible, imperfect, and sinful. If we hold such a high New Testament doctrine of the Church, how are we to explain the Church's official attitudes of institutional conservatism, evangelical lethargy, and fratricidal persecution? The criterion which our Lord gave us for judging the prophets that would profess to come in his name was "by their fruits ye shall know them" (Matt. 7:15-20), and although it is a dangerous standard to apply by reason of the spiritual pride, it sometimes produces in the one who so judges, it has our Lord's own warrant. We have every right to expect that those branches of the Church which claim exclusively to be "the Church" should possess above all others the fruits of the Spirit (Gal. 5:22-23). They should be more zealous in evangelism, more faithful in life and doctrine, and more loving toward all men than those who do not measure up to their own doctrinal, hierarchical, or liturgical pattern of Christian orthodoxy. If there is any longer any real protest in Protestantism, this is it. It is one which "Catholics" have consistently tried to evade, for if our Lord applied this standard to the prophets who would arise in his name, how much more applicable it is to the societies that profess to be his Body. If the Protestant distinction between a "visible" and "invisible" church is not ultimately convincing, neither is the "Catholic" casuistry which tries to distinguish between what the Church does (which is held to be perfect) and the actions of its responsible members (which may be sinful).

Here I suggest that the way forward may be in a deeper understanding of the relationship between Incarnation and Atonement. In this respect to ask whether theology starts with Atonement or with Incarnation becomes not a question of academic hairsplitting but a question of great importance in the Church's understanding of itself and of its function in the world. It is not a question of rating one doctrine higher than another but of trying to find the true point of contact between God and man—where God is *revealed* to man. "Catholic" theology seems to find this point in the Incarnation, and there have been some who have suggested that the Atonement was simply the inevitable fulfillment of the Incarnation. Protestant theology questions this. It has unconsciously been impressed by the hiddenness of the glory and perfection of God in Christ until the events of Good Friday and Easter Sunday spelled out the meaning of his birth and life. In the words of one of Isaac Watts's finest passion hymns:

> But in the grace that rescued man,
>   His brightest form of glory shines;
> Here, on the cross, 'tis fairest drawn
>   In precious blood, and crimson lines.
>
> Here His whole Name appears complete:
>   Nor wit can guess, nor reason prove,
> Which of the letters best is writ,
>   The power, the wisdom, or the love.

Protestant theology has, therefore, tended to set forth the Atonement as the starting point of theology, because it is the point where the veil disappears from the face of God and where man as he is faces God as he is. To insist on this is not to denigrate the Incarnation to a position of lesser importance in Christian doctrine—indeed it must be clear from the theologians we have already quoted that unless the full miracle and mystery of the Incarnation is understood in its magnitude as God's own act, the Atonement itself becomes irrelevant. It is to insist that the Incarnation did not take place as an end in itself but for the purpose of Redemption—i.e., the Incarnation took place so that God's eternal and sacrificing love would be revealed, to achieve reconciliation between man and God, and to open to man the possibility of entering into the life of Christ. In winning this for man Christ's human body upon the Cross was not "perfect" as the world would recognize perfection. To the eye of faith it may be recognized as perfect in suffering, perfect for the task to which it had been born, but at the same time it was lacerated, broken, and given over to death. Furthermore, we read in the Scriptures passages that we would never dare apply to Jesus Christ on our own authority, that he "his own self bare our sins in his own body on the tree" (I Pet. 2:24), that he was "being made a curse for us" (Gal. 3:13), and that "he hath made him to be sin for us, who knew no sin" (II Cor. 5:21). Whatever else these and similar passages may mean, they surely mean that upon the Cross our Lord bore within his own wounds, within the suffering and mortality of his body, the results of our sin, and that in hanging upon the Cross he seemed to accept and actually accepted the sentence and curse of sin for us.

Therefore, if the purpose of our Lord's Incarnation were wholly redemptive and if his perfection and glory were in some sense hidden until the revelation of that supreme purpose at the Resurrection, should we not expect the same to be true of the Church if she is in any sense an extension of his incarnation? Is participation in the incarnate life of our Lord something to be claimed by the Church in terms of divine sinlessness or asserted in terms of infallibility? Or on the contrary is it something which can be revealed only in brokenness, by becoming perfect herself in suffering, in obedient sacrifice for the redemption of the world? Obviously both Incarnation and Atonement must have their place in our thinking about the Church if the Church is the Body of Christ, for they can never be separated. But the perfection of his incarnate life, or for that matter the glory of his risen life, are not honors to be claimed as a right even by the Church. If the Church as an institution, or its representative spokesmen make such claims on its behalf, then they are demonstrating a spirit that is fundamentally contrary to that of the Lord they profess to serve, who, although he was in the form of God, did not regard equality with God as a prize to be grabbed but emptied himself: taking the form of a servant he was made in the likeness of men, and being found in the form of man, he humbled himself and became obedient unto death, even the death of the Cross (Phil. 2:6-8). To claim a part in his Incarnation or glory *as a right*, far from being a manifestation and proof of the Church's purity and holiness, might become nothing less than the sin of Lucifer. The Church *is* part of his life, incarnate and glorified, but how that is so and why it should be so is a hidden mystery of grace that can be revealed by God alone and will probably not be revealed until the Resurrection of all things. The Church has it as a gift, but she cannot claim it as a right. The one thing she can and must claim in order to reveal and fulfill her vocation is her share in the atoning purpose of the Incarnation. She can be his Body in that, and only as she is faithful in that will it be manifest to men that she is born "not of blood, nor of the will of the flesh, nor of the will of man, but of God" (John 1:13).

The same idea may be followed through in the Old Testament parallels, and if the story of the People of God—the Church—begins with the call of Abraham, these parallels are not to be disregarded. Was Israel's true vocation messianic, or was it to be seen in terms of the Suffering Servant? Obviously both, but it was ultimately revealed to be truly Messianic only as it was lived in terms of the Suffering Servant of Yahweh. This example of obedient service was ultimately revealed as Israel's true glory and the proof that she was indeed the People of God. It seems clear that Hebrew prophets no less than Protestant theologians were exercised about the question of the "true" Israel as distinguished from the actual Israel. In the doctrine of the Remnant they seem virtually to have arrived at a theory of the "visible" and "invisible" Israel. Even so, it was to Israel as a visible people that the covenant promises were made, and when our Lord accepted his vocation in Baptism, lived and suffered, he did so as a Jew, the visible representative of a recognizable race. As Christians we claim that the promises to Israel are fulfilled in Christ, but the fact remains that there were promises made to Israel and it was to Israel that they were first fulfilled. God does not turn his back on the people who bear his name. At the same time Israel remained the People of God but was always the People of God under judgment, and never more so than when her Representative and Messiah hung upon the Cross. It is the same with the Church. Through the blood of Christ's atoning death she is spotless and holy in the sight of God, but here on earth she herself is under the judgment of the Cross. Even as her Lord most truly revealed the lineaments of his incarnate divinity in submitting to the judgment of the Cross, perhaps the Church will reveal her own divine origin and nature most clearly as she pays less attention to claims of divine perfection and is content to reveal in her own members the broken Body of her redeeming Lord.

2. "He hath made him to be sin for us, who knew no sin"

It may well be, therefore, that we shall be forced to re-examine the doctrine of the Atonement precisely because we have arrived at an

THE ATONEMENT AND THE SACRAMENTS

impasse regarding the doctrine of the Church and its relation to the Incarnation. If this is so, theology will have to give more attention to what the Bible says about our Lord *really* taking upon himself our sin, for it is clear that however we interpret the scripture passages, Christ does take our actual sins upon his own broken body within the sins of the Church's membership.

This introduces a further problem which is ultimately concerned with the relationship between the Atonement and the doctrines of the Person of Christ and the Trinity. What does it mean that Jesus Christ was "made to be sin" for us? When we consider the Atonement as a cosmic event and its relation to the whole of creation, we are brought face to face with the problem of evil in its totality and not simply with the problem of human sin. We are forced to ask again the perennial questions of theology, what is evil, why does it exist?—evil, not simply as human sin and its evil consequences, but all the evil that seems to have existed prior to human sin and which appears to exist now independently of it—the ugliness, the waste, the blind chance, and the suffering. In particular we are faced with the problem of death—not simply the death of human beings which might be explained as the result of their sin, but the death which holds the whole cosmic order within its grasp, from the red suns spinning their way into the uncomprehending wastes of space to the dried leaf spinning its way to the ground. Questions are raised here which are fundamental to any full understanding of the Atonement just as they are fundamental to our understanding of the nature of God. The problem of evil appears to be so much greater and more complex than sin and the sinner, which although it is the issue in its most acute form, is still only a part of it. Who bears ultimate responsibilty for the existence of evil? A good deal may be explained by some theory such as a precosmic fall, but even supposing it approximates to the truth, we still face the fact that in granting rational beings the freedom of choice to do good or evil, God deliberately accepted the risk of sin and all its evil entail—he consciously permitted the possibility of evil. In the Book of Job Lucifer is God's agent for evil to chastise Job, but he is *God's* agent for evil just as Pharaoh or Nebuchadnezzar were agents of his chastisement at other periods of Israel's history. This may be typically Hebraic anthropomorphism, but we cannot avoid the conclusion that in the creation of a universe in which free beings might exist, God accepts ultimate responsibility for the existence of evil.[3]

What has this to do with what Jesus did upon the Cross? Obviously it has a great deal to do with the cosmic nature of Redemption, but more specifically it has a very close relationship to the way God in Christ bore our sin.

This has two aspects—relating to Jesus as Man, and relating to Jesus as God. In the first it raises the question how far our Lord was by his birth brought under the conditions of that evil legacy that is the common lot of humanity, "original sin." When the Church has put forward the sinlessness of Mary in an attempt to safeguard the "perfect" humanity of our Lord, did it defend or jeopardize the reality of his humanity? Has it actually defended his sinless purity at the expense of making him a Docetic Christ who by his birth must have been totally removed from the most desperate actuality of human life? How can we say that Jesus undertook our life as a man, if by the very perfection of his parenthood—divine and human—he could not really be touched by the temptations of our common lot? Despite the way in which these questions are phrased, I do not pose them with the intention of implying easy answers but simply to ask that in issues which so vitally affect the Church's apologetic, the questions themselves should not be foreclosed because of dogmas that are, in any case, debatable on biblical grounds. Certainly we can be sure of our Lord's actual sinlessness—the evidence of those who knew him best is unanimous at that point. But some of our Lord's own words in the Gospels force us to look at the relation between his sinlessness and his birth with critical frankness—"Why callest thou me good? There is none good but one, that is, God" (Mark 10:18). Such words, uttered in the full knowledge of his own personal innocence before God, may also carry within them the consciousness of an identity with man much closer than the dogma of an Immaculate Conception seems to allow. If our Lord carried within his own person something of the *inherited* guilt of the race, then there is a real sense in which he who knew no

---

[3] The ideas in this section were set down some years before I read William J. Wolf's *No Cross, No Crown*, but our independent studies of the Atonement would appear to have brought us to a very similar focus at this point. Cf. "The 'Necessity' of the Cross" *op. cit.*, pp. 200-203.

sin became sin for us. "Holiness," writes Canon J. E. Fison, "is achieved not by separation from sin, but by vicarious identification with it." [4]

The second aspect relates to Jesus Christ as God. By raising the question how far God accepts responsibility for the existence of evil, it reveals something of the involvement of the whole Trinity in the work of redemption. Sin, says Emil Brunner, means making man supreme—it is the claim of man that he is God. In the Cross man faced God and God faced man, and the Crucifixion brought to a head the great indictment that humanity makes against its Creator, that he is finally responsible for the evil of man's lot and the sinfulness of his nature. We have it expressed in the bitter words of Edward Fitzgerald in *Omar Khayyam*:

> O Thou, who didst with pitfall and with gin
> Beset the Road I was to wander in,
>   Thou wilt not with Predestined and Evil round
> Enmesh, and then impute my Fall to Sin!
>
> Oh Thou, who Man of baser Earth didst make,
> And even with Paradise didst devise the Snake:
>   For all the Sin wherewith the Face of Man
> Is blackened—Man's forgiveness give—and take!

It is as if man at the Crucifixion uttered sentence and exacted the execution of his presumptuous demand, which was the abdication and capital punishment of God himself, and the recognition that human power, human decision, human standards, and human verdicts are the only ultimate authority: that man is really God. The Crucifixion was, in Dorothy Sayers' phrase, "the execution of God" for the sins of the world, man exacting from God the penalty for the world and its evil. The old ransom theories thought of the Atonement in terms of the debt for sin being paid to the devil; the satisfaction theories explained it as penal suffering inflicted to satisfy God's justice. But to give a content to the Atonement that every generation can understand (and to get nearer to the Passion narratives), we should perhaps think of it

---

[4] J. E. Fison, *The Blessing of the Holy Spirit* (Longmans, 1950), p. 110.

as a penalty or debt *demanded by and paid to man*. That measures the enormity of the deed that was perpetrated by our Lord's accusers, but it is also the measure of the goodness that was prepared to pay the price. The miracle of miracles is that in Christ God meets the charge that man makes against him and proves its falsity in the very act of taking the judgment for human sin upon himself. Here we are in the realm of pure grace.

3. "Ye shall be as gods"

Contrary to the appearances, the evil of the world does not exist in its own right but only in a perverted consciousness—a Cartesian egocentric consciousness—which is not willing to accept the world as God has given it but wants to use that world as the empire of its own supremacy, and which, therefore, turns the material world into an instrument of its own rebellion. The primeval evils that appear to exist outside man did not exist as evils until there was a consciousness which put itself in the center of existence, and by judging all events and circumstances of the natural order with reference *to itself* and its own experience, claimed to define the distinction between what is good and what is evil. This is the heart of the original temptation in Gen. 3:5. On the other hand God permitted that possibility by granting man the use of reason and a free will, and in doing so our Creator accepted final responsibility for evil. But in the Cross he does three things which turn the tables on man's indictment. First, he reveals in the Person of Christ his own nature of compassionate and sacrificial love, demonstrates the injustice of man's charge, and delivers judgment upon those who had elected themselves to be his judges. Secondly, his action in Christ is the immeasurable measure of his eternal purpose and love toward man. Thirdly and perhaps the deepest paradox of all, in this great Act of Reconciliation he throws open to penitent mankind *by grace* the very possibility that idolatrous mankind claimed *as a right*—namely, the possibility of becoming "as Gods," of being united to him and sharing in the divine life. The irresponsible and blasphemous attempt of mankind to assert its own divinity, which is dramatized for us in the stories of the Fall and the Tower of Babel, and which culminates in the still more blasphemous assault of heaven at the Crucifixion, is revealed at the Cross to be what it is. But in the same divine Act, that which men had tried to win by pride and force, God freely offers to them through faith in Christ's saving work and life in his redeeming Spirit. The serpent in the Garden had offered to Adam and Eve the bait "ye shall be as gods" through the power that comes from knowledge. God, in the passion and exaltation of Christ and in the regenerating work of the Holy Spirit, turns the diabolic temptation into a divine promise and shows us that the key to unlock that heaven is not power that comes from omnipotence or omniscience but obedience in a love which forgives its enemies by loving them to the Cross and beyond.

The essential quality in God's grace is this quality of illimitable self-outpouring which in human terms we must describe as "sacrificial" but which in its divine aspect is so much more than that term can imply—God doing infinitely more than is necessary and doing it because it was his nature to do it. It is not *kenosis* in the sense of self-limitation, but it is *kenosis* as the superabundant and inevitable outpouring of the Divine Nature—God giving himself up to us completely in Creation, Providence, Redemption, and Regeneration. That is grace, and here the whole Godhead is at work in the "sacrificial" self-giving. Here too the events of the Passion and Resurrection of our Lord must be seen in relation to his total life and teaching, for the teaching of Jesus is important not only because it sets out the standard of God's ethical demand upon man but more because of what it tells us about himself. It has often been pointed out that if the Sermon on the Mount were simply God's moral claim against men, it would be nothing less than a continuation of the bondage of the Law—the Mosaic Law carried to the "nth" degree—setting its own seal to the indictment against man by establishing beyond all refutation his utter inability to get near God's righteous demands. Look, however, at the Sermon on the Mount from the point of view of what it tells us about God—indeed, see it in the light of what he *is* at that very moment doing in Christ—turning the other cheek, going the extra mile, forgiving not seven times but seventy times seven. These things are the pattern of the divine life translated for us into human terms. This shows the natural man what his claim "to be as God" really means in terms of holiness. "Here His whole name appears complete"—he goes the extra mile, he turns the other cheek, he forgives to the point of death and beyond, he bows to the indictment that man utters and pays the price that his bitterness demands, not because it is a just sentence and still less because man has passed the sentence and issued the demand, but because his nature is pure grace. And in the final miracle of that grace, he turns the gibbet into a throne and the crown of thorns into a crown of glory, not only for himself, but for any one of his accusers who in penitence and faith is willing to accept his love.

PART III

Treasure in Earthen Vessels

CHAPTER IX

The Atonement and the Sacraments

GEORGE NATHANIEL CURZON, THAT "MOST SUPERIOR PERSON," ONCE spoke approvingly of "the intelligent anticipation of events before they occur." I hope the anticipation of certain conclusions from our historical study of the Atonement has been intelligent, for we must now revert to things we have touched upon in the last chapter. We do so primarily in order that the issues in the ecumenical conversation between "Protestant" and "Catholic" may be thrown into clearer relief. What follows arises simply from the desire to assist in that clarification—particularly to help those Protestants and Catholics alike who, amid the many voices with which the churches of the Reformation seem to speak, sometimes despair of any basic Protestant position.

1. Where Christian Theology Begins

We have stressed the unity of all Christian doctrine, and it may be taken as axiomatic that if the doctrine of the Atonement is studied in isolation from the rest of the Christian faith there is inevitable distortion. However, precisely because Christian doctrine is a unity, it is vitally important to recognize the proper center from which we start, and I believe this need to find a focus has driven evangelical Christianity in all ages to place its central emphasis upon the climactic historical movement which gathers up the Incarnation and the Atonement into one great Act of God. We start from God in Christ. This must be the starting point of theology, the place at which God touches us most directly and obviously.

It is when we go further to try to find the central focus and motive within that historic revelation that there is a sharp difference of emphasis. If it is possible to generalize at this point, I believe that the main emphasis in Catholic theology, following such Fathers as Athanasius, has been to find its center—the point of contact between God and man—in the Incarnation, so that what happened upon the Cross and in the Resurrection was the inevitable result of the event which began in the self-emptying of the Word of God to take upon himself human flesh. God had already determined to demonstrate his love for man by becoming incarnate, and in the midst of a world permeated by evil, it was therefore inevitable that he would live such a life, die such a death, and vindicate his goodness by rising triumphant. This view is illustrated when a modern Anglo-Catholic writer like Fr. E. L. Mascall, who bluntly asks whether Lady Day ought not to displace Good Friday as the high point in the Church's commemoration of Redemption.[1] It presupposes the priority of the Incarnation in Christian doctrine, whereas our previous study has shown that Protestant theology has found its center of gravity in the Atonement. There has always been a deep suspicion on the part of Puritans lest the unmitigated joy of Advent and the temptation to sentimentalize Christmas should obscure the meaning of Christ's coming revealed in Good Friday and Easter. Although the protest has led to excesses—even the semi-pagan expedient of glorifying the "New Year"—yet the real point in the protest needs to be recognized. I submit that these differences of emphasis between Catholic and Protestant need to be appreciated in our understanding of each other, because they have led to important differences in the doctrines of Church and Sacraments.

If we are right to suggest that Protestantism puts the Atonement at the center of its theology, what are the grounds for that position? Surely *prima facie* there is more to be said for the Incarnation or the Annunciation of Mary as the starting point of Christian faith, for can we escape from the fact that the historic point of contact between God and man was the actual moment when the Word became flesh and dwelt among us? Yet *is* this the whole truth? We must not be misled by the fact that the Incarnation was the first direct "physical" contact between God and man, and that this priority in point of time makes it the beginning of the Gospels. Of course the Atonement could not have taken place without the coming of our Lord in human flesh—there is an indivisibility about the two doctrines which must never be threatened—and yet the Protestant, in fidelity to the scrip-

[1] *Christ, the Christian and the Church* (Longmans, Green & Co., 1946), p. 69. Lady Day is the Feast of the Annunciation, March 25th.

tural evidence, cannot accept the Incarnation as so clearly and manifestly the actual place of meeting between God's grace and man's need that it constitutes in itself all that was necessary for Atonement. It is the beginning of God's movement into history *to reconcile*—the Gospels start with the announcement that Jesus was born in Bethlehem of Judaea in the reign of Caesar Augustus—but he was born to be the Lamb of God. We must put the redemptive work of the Cross within the total context of the birth, life, teaching, and resurrection of our Lord, for that redemptive work includes all the divine outpouring from the moment when Mary conceived by the Holy Ghost. But we must remember that the Incarnation itself took place within a context, the context of Israel's preparation and of the predetermined purpose of Almighty God to redeem the human race: Christ is the Lamb slain from the foundation of the world. Therefore, we do not think in terms of a prior event in time but rather in terms of a prior and active purpose—God's "Word"—in eternity. In maintaining the interdependence of Incarnation and Atonement as one historic movement due to one divine initiative, Protestant theology declares that the Incarnation took place because of and within the purpose of God's atoning grace. The point is very simply illustrated by the Christmas tree around which our family gathered at Christmas. It was a good straight tree, and it bore as many decorations and colored lights as any, but its base was firmly set in a wooden cross. So it is in our understanding of the Incarnation of our Lord: it took place within the setting of the cross.

Perhaps we can best make the point, however, by reference to the Bible story itself, by contrasting the "hiddenness" of God's deed at Bethlehem with the revelation of what happened when the work of Redemption was complete. At the time of our Lord's birth we are told of certain groups of people who recognized in the Infant Jesus the Messiah of God. But they came to this recognition either by way of a particular revelation, or because they had been granted special insight into the purpose of God. So, in the traditional accounts of the Nativity, it was revealed to Mary by the angel Gabriel who it was that should be born of her, and both Zacharias in the Temple and the shepherds in the fields had the news of the Infant Saviour revealed to them by special messengers of God. To Joseph it came in a dream, the Magi were guided by a star and by their understanding of the ancient signs, while Simeon and Anna were typical of those who in every age had been waiting and looking for the consolation of Israel, people of simple but deep and expectant insight into the purposes of God. This was prepared soil. The Gospel accounts emphasize that at the time of his birth, it was *not* generally obvious to people who he was and what he had come to do—it was revealed only to the few. In the words of Charles Wesley's most beloved Christmas hymn, "Veiled in flesh the Godhead see."

Even so, if we look at the special revelations that were granted to those who move across the scene of the Nativity, or to the words that the tradition of the Church has attributed to them, we see that the gospel writers put the coming of Jesus fully within God's redemptive purpose. "Thou shalt call his name *Jesus*,[2] for he shall *save* his people from their sins" (the angel to Joseph; cf. also the Annunciation, Luke 1:31); "He hath holpen his servant Israel in the remembrance of his mercy" (the Magnificat); "Blessed be the Lord God of Israel, for he hath *visited* and *redeemed* his people" (Benedictus; cf. also the rest of the Benedictus); "For unto you is born this day in the city of David a *Saviour*, which is *Christ the Lord*" (the angel to the shepherds); "For mine eyes have seen thy *salvation* which thou hast prepared before the face of all people" (Nunc Dimittis). Written into his birth there is the purpose of redemption, but the revelation is given only to the few: God's Word to the world has yet to be made explicit.

It was made more explicit but not fully so at the Cross, even although what was done was certainly done in the full view of everyone. It was not until after the Resurrection and Pentecost that the full meaning of what had happened in their midst made its full impact upon men's hearts. But at the Cross the work begins to be explicit—"It is finished." Those who realized the truth at Calvary were very different from the devout hearts of those who rejoiced at his birth, and in the confessions of the dying thief and the Roman centurion, and even in the unconscious prophecy of Caiaphas (John 28:14), there was recognition of what this deed was to mean for the salvation of men. This became far clearer after the Resurrection when the presence of the Risen Christ demonstrated to the disciples

---

[2] Matt. 1:21. Jesus the Greek form of the Hebrew name "Joshua." The name seems to mean "Jah is salvation," hence a Deliverer sent by God.

the meaning of his suffering (cf. Luke 24:25 ff.) and when the gift of the Holy Spirit sent the apostles out into the world to preach the Good News. It was the gospel of the Crucified and Risen Christ which was the center of their message, and in their evangelism this proved to be the place where every man had to react in either faith or rejection.

It is at this point that theology meets apologetic. The Atonement is the starting point of theology because this is where God is revealed to men as he is and the Christian faith is presented to the world in its simple starkness. For the first task of theology is to make that manifestation of God's redeeming purpose in the Cross and Resurrection relevant to our contemporaries, to make it real and apparent to the workmen who, as I wrote this, were digging the hole for a drain outside. We may speak of "apologetic" in this sense not as making the gospel easier but as making it clearer—not to minimize its challenge but to make its challenge fully explicit. This is the vital task of apologetic properly conceived. If theology fails at this point, or worse still if it ignores it, we might very well question what it has to do with the gospel of Jesus Christ. Here is our starting point. By all means let us see the Cross and Resurrection within the setting of our Lord's birth and his total life and teaching, but let it also be with the realization that his Incarnation—birth, life, teaching, death, resurrection, and ascension—took place within the context of God's eternal and prevenient purpose for the salvation of men, and that his purpose was Reconciliation—Atonement—between himself and men through the outpouring of himself to death in Christ.

2. Themes and Theories

A further aspect of our study which is of considerable significance at a different ecumenical level is the mutual relationship between the theology of the Church and the historical context in which it made its appearance. The Church can congratulate itself that although there are many theologies of the Atonement no one of them "can claim to be the official doctrine of the Church." [3] Even the sacrificial imagery, or the great "dramatic" representation of the work of Christ in terms of his victory over sin, death, and the devil, which can prove their

---

[3] Hodgson, op. cit., p. 13.

venerable antiquity in the New Testament and in the thought of the early Church, are themselves only images and symbols. We can say much the same about all the images and theories that have been used to explain the doctrine in the history of the Church, for many of them can claim to have a biblical basis, and they have all been relevant to the day in which they first appeared. As such they still have relevance for us in our attempts to interpret the truth, but they need to supplement and correct each other, and none of them can claim to be complete in an exclusive way.

Moreover they underline the need for theology to interpret Christian doctrine in terms that will be understood within its own generation. Dr. Hicks was probably right in thinking that in taking over the sacrificial categories, the New Testament writers took over the images of the Hebrew sacrificial system, and that these images served the Church's purpose for as long as there was living contact with and understanding of the meaning of sacrifice. It is of some importance to note that the Atonement was expounded to the early church's converts in the sacrificial categories which both Jew and Gentile quite naturally expected to find at the center of true religion. It is equally significant to notice that as the relevance of the sacrificial concepts waned the place was taken by the idea of "ransom." This was the time when the membership of the Church was largely made up of the slaves and dispossessed classes of the world, and when the fact of slavery was the dominant feature in the social and economic structure of the society in which the Church had to make its witness—a time when it was always possible for a free man, by ill fortune or bad management, by defeat in war or deception at home, to find not only that his property had vanished, but also that he had mortgaged the freedom of himself and his family. Whether as a free man, a freed man, or a slave a man in these centuries understood the meaning of "ransom" because slavery was an inescapable fact, and therefore, no better figure for those times could have been used in which to describe what God had achieved for man in Jesus Christ.

As we move on to the time of Anselm, the metaphor has changed even as the times had changed. When he speaks in terms of "satisfaction" given to God's "honor," he is using the picture forms of the medieval feudal society with its close connection with the ideas and language of chivalry. The conceptions of satisfaction and honor were of the very warp and woof of feudal society, and Anselm's underlying thought of dishonor done to God by man in his sin has to be understood in terms of the horror that the medieval man had of breaking the oath of fealty he owed to his liege lord, and of the state of outlawry which was its punishment. In his description of the Atonement Anselm used the conceptions that were an integral part of the society in which he lived. The same is true to a greater or lesser extent of the other medieval theologians—the influence of the idea of romantic love upon Abelard at the beginning of the age of chivalry, or Aquinas' desire to find a comprehensive consensus of doctrine that would buttress his attempt to sum up all theology, and which was itself a reflection of the greatest single factor of the western world at that time, the comprehensive dominion and unity of Church and Empire over all medieval life and thought.

At the time of the Reformation there was a new consciousness of the Bible, and this may be responsible for the reappearance of the "ransom" theory that we find in Luther and of the sacrificial imagery that we find in Calvin. But side-by-side with these ideas the penal emphasis developed, and it was this conception which eventually captured the imaginations of men. We have already indicated some of the reasons why this may have happened, but we have to recognize that the penal emphasis was taken up at a time when, with the breakdown of feudalism, the individual was conscious that the national state had taken the place of the feudal overlord and the idea of impersonal justice took the place of the personal oath of fealty. In the administration of justice the state not only had the function of punishing wrong-doers as a dissuasive against crime but also the duty of inflicting upon the criminal the punishment that society demanded.

Furthermore, we can see that this new national consciousness itself was responsible for the next step in human relationships—the beginnings of international law—which is personified for us not only in the person and work of Hugo Grotius but just as significantly in his Rectoral theory of Atonement. Incidentally, it should be noted that in some sense Grotius was before his time, for nations were not yet ready to accept the idea of international law in any but a very limited sense. It was the penal theory, with its accent upon the individual's responsibility to the arbitrary State, that dominated the theology of the next two hundred years. It was not until the beginning of the nineteenth century that the Rectoral theory began to be taken up once more, when men began to be interested not so much in the punitive rights of the state but in the manifestation of Justice for its own sake.

So one can pass on to nineteenth-century liberalism and the moral influence theory, and to the particular way in which that rediscovery of Abelard was asserted in the responsibility of the individual for his own salvation. Remember the tremendously vigorous spirit of Individualism in that virile century, when nothing seemed impossible to the human spirit, and you will see how the moral influence theories that were put forward draw from ideas that are expressed not only in Darwin's theory of evolution or John Stuart Mill's utilitarian philosophy, but more existentially, perhaps, in Samuel Smiles' *Self Help*. In the nineteenth century this was the measure of a man's possibility and of his dignity in the world, in the universe, and before God.

For these reasons if for no others, we ought to give full value to the social, political, and cultural factors which are influencing our own thinking today—the revived sense of corporate humanity which the late Wendell Willkie expressed in his *One World* animates our thinking in the West and drives us back to the ancient pictures that were used to express this idea in previous ages. We also belong to our environment. The advent of the completely unscrupulous totalitarian state on the one hand and the possibility of cosmic catastrophe by total war on the other makes many of us much more ready than our immediate forefathers to think in terms of sin and salvation that is racial and solidary. In our choice of biblical imagery, in our accent upon the concepts used by the Fathers, and even in our demand for objectivity in doctrine, Church, and Sacraments, we are just as much the creatures of our own day as our forbears were of theirs, desperately seeking as they did to take the assurance of Christ's atoning work to ourselves and commend it to our fellows. This does not invalidate the images but simply puts them into perspective. On the other hand we need to remember that if these are the distinctive accents of the West, they are not necessarily the terms in which the East or the South can accept the gospel, for while the western world in watching the dissolution of its old imperialisms calls for "one world," new nationalisms are arising in Asia and Africa which may have a very different theme. It is therefore necessary to enter a caveat at this point and stress the urgency with which churches in these continents should be encouraged to produce theologians who can interpret the work of Christ for their own lands and circumstances.

In the light of this there are two things that I would wish to re-iterate in summary about this historical review of the doctrine of the Atonement. First, that, in recognizing the influence of non-theological factors upon the different forms of that doctrine, we must see the theological images as belonging very largely to the historical context in which they appeared: they are all relative and partial. It has not been a strength but a mortal danger when theologians have tried to make one of the pictures the final criterion. Important and relevant though each theory has been for its age, it is not within the spiritual competence of the theologian to interpret this particular doctrine in a form that will stand for all time. Other doctrines may be given classical expression by the Church, but if the doctrine of the Atonement is the point where theology becomes apologetic (in the sense in which we have used the term), the forms in which it is expressed can never be fixed. The *fact* of the Atonement is unalterable, but the images must always remain flexible—not in order to conform to the spirit of the age and present the gospel in the way men find pleasant or attractive, but in order to stab their hearts awake and present the scandal of the Cross to each succeeding age in its sharpest form. The American theologian W. P. Du Bose very wisely made this point when he observed:

> The mind of the Church, while it has been made up from the beginning and has undergone no change as to the fact of Salvation in Christ and the essential contents of that fact, has by no means been always one with itself in its theoretical or speculative explanation of the fact. Or rather, we should say, perhaps, that the Church as such has not and cannot have such an explanation. The Church holds facts which never change; it cannot hold opinions which must be and ought to be always changing.[4]

As we look at history we cannot help feeling that Providence has been mightily at work, for despite the fact that the categories of the Ransom theory dominated theology for almost a millenium and sat-

---

[4] Du Bose, *op. cit.*, pp. 18-19.

isfaction theories for a further eight hundred years, no one theory has ever been universally accepted by the Church. Perhaps one of the fortunate by-products of our "unhappy divisions" has been the fact that since the time of the great Councils there has been no universally accepted vehicle by which such universal acceptance of a single theory could be imposed. By the grace of God the ecumenical concern of our modern time has arisen when, by reason of our historical studies, the Church appreciates the danger and is less likely to allow such imposition than in former times. This doctrine, so vital to evangelism can never be confined to symbols that are static.

The second point to be reiterated is the positive side of this same truth, the necessity for an ongoing work of theology, not only in selecting what is of value in the past theories but also in recasting the truth of the doctrine in the best forms for each generation. This is an ongoing work and responsibility. The theories put forward by the theologians of the past may have been deficient in many respects, and their picture forms may have contained regrettable aberrations, but unconsciously this was the work they were doing. We are beginning to see now what our forefathers in the faith were less ready to admit, that in every restatement of the doctrine there were grains of eternal truth to be winnowed from the perishable husks of theological imagery. The ephemeral nature of theologizing has always been difficult for the theologian himself to concede, for whether it is Anselm or Horace Bushnell, Athanasius, or James Denney, Peter Abelard or Robert Dale, he has usually been too preoccupied in backing his own theory against all other contenders to recognize clearly either the truth in their view or that which was transitory in his own. The work of description must go on, even although we know we are using pictures and symbols which, however apt at the time, are of limited relevance and will be discarded like those that have preceded them. The theologian is always in the difficulty of knowing that he must use thought forms that are faulty and incomplete to describe an action by God in history which can never finally be subject to human analysis and clarification. We theologize about the Atonement always with the prayer that God will use our imperfect images to speak his living word in Christ to our generation, that he will baptize our pictures and symbols with his own Spirit of Truth.

3. The Divine Drama

At this point there is a question which demands an answer. Although the Church has become tied to no particular theory of the Atonement as its official doctrine, we know that at different periods in her history her theologians have very heavily weighted the scales in favor of one theory or another. If there has been no official doctrine of Atonement that could claim to be the ultimate test of orthodoxy, there have been plenty of semi-official doctrines which have been regarded as the measure of theological respectability, and through the conservatism or lethargy of theologians and clergy these doctrines have retained their prestige long after their relevance has passed away. What happened to the Church, represented by the ordinary Christian, during those periods when currently held theories of the Atonement were hopelessly antiquated and inadequate? Can we suggest that because of bad theology nobody for hundreds of years was able to have any true idea of the atoning work of Christ, or that through these years the Church was hopelessly corrupt? Let us not minimize the effects of bad theology and antiquated ideas upon the life of the Church, but obviously we cannot make any such sweeping assertions. There is abundant evidence of a countless number of believers who have entered into the meaning of the Cross in every age, even at the times when the theological schools have been at their lowest spiritual ebb. Why was this so, and where has been the safeguard that has kept the Church true to the historic faith during such times?

Some years ago when I was minister of a church in England one of the congregational discussion groups called me in to help them on a problem. Through the winter they had been studying a certain book under the guidance of one of the church's very gifted laymen, and in considering the doctrine of the Atonement the members of the group had decided that no one of the many theories was really adequate to their need or to meet the challenge of the world in which they lived. In trying to meet the question I was forced to ask myself the question I have tried to pose above—was it not strange that our Lord had apparently left us without any descriptive explanation of this doctrine? Did he leave the ages of subsequent history without any picture, any principle of explanation? This is probably the question that has been at the back of the minds of all the theologians who have wrestled with the doctrine to find a unifying principle or metaphor. Granted that this wrestling must go on, and granted that this is a challenge that theology must never shirk, yet is it reasonable to suppose that our Lord would leave the faithful entirely to themselves with no help in understanding his atoning work? Does he leave us at this point, literally, to work out the terms of our own salvation?

With these questions unresolved in my mind I went to my group of church members without much hope of being able to help them. Out of my own concern and uncertainty I began to speak to them, and we began to review again the images that have been used to describe the Atonement in the Bible and in the history of the Church. We had not been doing this for very long before I realized that we were speaking not specifically about the doctrine at all but that we were really expounding the Sacraments that our Lord gave us—Baptism and the Lord's Supper. All the ideas and illustrations which were able to make the doctrine of our Redemption understandable and relevant to this little group of Christians were to be found here in the Sacraments that were performed almost week by week in the public worship of their own church. Our Lord did not leave us without a sign, for he gave us these dramatic symbols of what he has done for us, which have been present in the Church throughout its history, to help and to guide the faithful in their understanding of the truth about his death and resurrection and its application to them. As they take these to their comfort, they appropriate their meaning. Here are the symbols of God's action in bringing about our redemption, which even when theology had gone hopelessly astray were always present in the continuing life of the Church to remind God's people of the meaning for them of the saving work of Christ.

We can come to the same truth in another way. Throughout our historical study we notice increasing agreement that revelation is given to us in acts rather than in words [5]—or rather that the Word of God is supremely demonstrated in a redemptive Act. If this divine action is at the heart of the gospel, then in interpreting it we are in the realm of epic and drama rather than of definition and formula, the realm of worship rather than that of pure theology. This suggests that the dramatic action of Christian worship is an indis-

[5] Leonard Hodgson, *The Doctrine of the Trinity* (1944), p. 14.

pensable commentary upon all that the Church believes about God's action for us in Christ. In a unique way this is true of the Dominical Sacraments, because they are the symbols that Christ himself has given us, and in a special sense true of the Lord's Supper because it is at the heart of the continuing worship of the Church. So the Anglican theologian, Canon Hodgson, says of the Atonement that "however much we may be helped by considerations drawn from battlefields, law-courts, or elsewhere, it is in the sphere of religious worship that God in Christ is most directly revealed to His disciples. . . . It is no accident that their first interpretation of what He had done was in terms of the Temple worship and sacrifice.[6] So the Methodist scholar Vincent Taylor declares that "no modern presentation of the doctrine of the Atonement is likely to be satisfactory which ignores, or deals imperfectly with, the doctrine of the Eucharist," for "the Eucharist falls within the orbit of the Atonement alike by reason of the teaching of Jesus and of the life and experience of the Church."[7] They are our contemporaries who are simply echoing what was said many years ago by the Congregationalist P. T. Forsyth, when he declared that what elevates the Lord's Supper from the mysteries is the eternal nature of Christ's moral act of sacrifice. "It is the unique idea of atonement that makes the difference, God's atonement of Himself in Christ. . . . The evangelists say that the rite was the eating and drinking of Christ *through the agency of* bread and wine. These were the handled elements, what was enjoyed was Christ's person, but His person as centring in the wondrous Act of regenerating grace in His death."[8] In the Lord's Supper we have a dramatic proclamation of what happened to him, and because of that what happens to the Christian now: not simply what happened to Jesus but also what happens *in* Christ.

If there is at the heart of the Sacraments this declaration of Christ's saving act, then Protestant Christians who know something about their atonement-centered theology and value it should be the most sacramental of all Christians. These sacramental implications of Protestant faith were fully worked out by Forsyth:

[6] Hodgson, *The Doctrine of the Atonement*, p. 148.
[7] Taylor, *Jesus and His Sacrifice*, p. 322.
[8] *The Church and the Sacraments*, pp. 263-64.

THE ATONEMENT AND THE SACRAMENTS

God offers Himself. He makes the sacrifice. He did in Christ, and He always does. In prayer we go to God, in Sacrament He comes to us. The Sacrament is not an occasion of offering even ourselves to God, nor chiefly of our presenting Christ's offering; but it is an occasion of God in Christ offering, giving Himself anew to us in His Church. In this respect you may perceive that the Sacrament is really more akin to preaching, than to prayer; it is God offering Himself more than it is we inviting Him, or approaching Him . . . *idem effectus verbi et ritus*. The word and the rite do the same thing.[9]

If this firm evangelical conception of the Sacraments had been the basis of Protestant practice since the Reformation, there would be no need to worry either about the place of the Sacraments in the life and worship of our churches or about our theologies of the Atonement. But we have to admit that Protestants have often set up the Word over against the Sacrament, and this has resulted not only in the Sacraments becoming mere appendages to the preaching service but also in debased ideas of Atonement. H. A. Hodges argues with some justification that whatever aberrations have appeared in the theories of the Atonement as advanced by Catholic theologians, they have always been under the correction of regular sacramental practice, and that it is "where the eucharist has been neglected, or where a minimizing doctrine of it has prevailed, that the doctrine of the Atonement too has taken on a meagre and ill-proportioned and often misleading form." [10] His criticism is just.

On the other hand we are not all able to feel quite so satisfied as Hodges about "Catholic" interpretations of the Atonement. It is true that in "Catholic" churches the liturgical life of the Church has been present to supplement and correct perverse or uncertain theologies, but we notice certain features within the liturgical traditions that give us cause to hesitate. First, we notice that, although a fixed liturgical tradition *ought* to be a great safeguard of the faith, the great Symbol that interprets the work of Christ to each succeeding generation, liturgies like theologies change slowly but surely—not always for the

---
[9] *Ibid.*, pp. 238-39.
[10] Hodges, *op. cit.*, p. 59. The same point is made by Father Jarrett-Kerr when he says that it is "only a sacramental Catholicism that puts the Atonement concretely, immediately, scandalously, into every moment of time, through the Mass." Cf. also his citation from Fr. Victor White; Martin Jarrett-Kerr C.R., *The Atonement in Our Time* (New York: Morehouse-Gorham, 1953) pp. 153-54.

better. In this development the evangelical truths of the Sacrament have often been overlaid and hidden, so that although the essential truth is there in the action of the liturgy, its relation to the living gospel of Jesus Christ becomes obscure. When this has happened, it becomes far harder to bring the practice of the Church back to the path from which she has strayed than is the case when her worship is cast in simpler and more flexible forms. That does not mean that the so-called "extempore" forms of worship do not become just as fixed and (in their individualism) far more arid than the liturgies of the ancient churches. Anyone who has ministered for any length of time in one of the "free" churches knows that although in theory the form of worship is free, in practice it conforms to a general pattern in which monotony can be only too often mistaken for simplicity. Nevertheless, with all the obvious defects the churches that are free to experiment in their worship are not so likely to fall into the error of idolizing the form of worship, and whether they avail themselves of the opportunity or not, they are not prevented by any concept of ecclesiastical infallibility from changing the form when they are in error. On the other side, whatever the beauty, dignity, and content of liturgical worship, all the elements—good and bad—which over the years have been built into the structure are more or less permanent, and liturgical reform becomes extremely difficult, as we see illustrated in the hard work which such movements have had in certain communions.

This carries with it the corollary that the effectiveness of the Sacraments in proclaiming and interpreting the drama of the gospel will be very seriously qualified if the Church follows a sacramental practice in which the Atonement is not at its very center. Here too we have questions to put to those in the "Catholic" position. The Atonement could never be entirely excluded from Catholic thought— even as the Sacraments could never entirely disappear from Protestant worship as long as Atonement held a central place in its theology. But as we have indicated previously, there are reasons for thinking that the Atonement has sometimes taken second place to the Incarnation in Catholic theology. When faith and devotion are thus concentrated upon, the fact that the Son of God became Man, rather than upon what happened to that Man and how God achieved our salvation through what happened to that Man, then in sacramental theology the elements themselves, like the flesh, become more important than what is done to them and through them. This is the point at which the difference between the two theologies throws light upon our different sacramental practice. It is an issue to which we shall have to speak again when we deal with the Holy Communion of the Lord's Supper. At this stage having raised it we can leave it. But while stressing the vital importance of the Sacraments in the continuing life of the Church, we shall insist with equal determination that if theology needs the corrective of sacramental life, the liturgical practice of the Church needs the corrective of a theology centered in Christ's redeeming work.

The conclusion is this. Both Christian theology and the Church's life of worship center in the redeeming work of God in Christ and for this reason the Sacraments "cannot lie at the circumference of Christian worship but must stand at the centre, as a means whereby man approaches God and appropriates the blessings of Christ's self-offering." [11] The Eucharist is "the real centre of the Church's common and social life," [12] and when Protestants have taken the doctrine of the Atonement seriously they have found it necessary to reassert the centrality of the Sacrament. The Sacraments, however, are in that relationship to Christian worship not for aesthetic reasons and still less for reasons of sentimental piety or conservative "orthodoxy," but because here the Church stands again in the presence of Christ's great redemptive work—we stand again as witnesses to God's great Act in Christ for our salvation which he represents to the Church.

Some time ago a young Greek Orthodox theologian declared in a sermon at the Ecumenical Institute that in "trying to meet the modern man we are tempted to try and put this foolishness, the Cross, into a wisdom of our own." That is the constant temptation of the theologian simply because the problem of communicating the gospel, of effective apologetic, is laid upon his conscience by the Church. There is only one safeguard, which Eastern Orthodoxy understands perhaps better than any Church, that the theologian, not only for the sake of his own soul but also for the sake of fidelity to the work of theology, must stand fully within the sacramental life of the Church. There in penitence he can receive those eternal symbols in which our

---

[11] Taylor, *Jesus and His Sacrifice*, p. 322.
[12] Forsyth, *The Church and the Sacraments*, p. 260.

Lord himself chose to express his redemptive work. When this happens, then liturgy corrects theology and worship becomes the confirmation of the Church's faith.

4. The Deeds of the Living Christ

We must carry our thinking about the Sacraments further. They are dramatic symbols of the gospel, but they are more than that, for "a Sacrament is as much more than a symbol as a symbol is more than a memorial." [13] As symbols of Redemption they are effective as parables in action, but if they are no more than that we are still far short of what the New Testament teaches and the faith of the Church confirms. The crucified and risen Christ comes to us in the Sacraments. If the Reformers firmly set themselves against the idea of transubstantiation and what appeared to be the magical features of the Roman Mass, we still find in them a doctrine of the Sacraments that is a very long way from the "mere memorialism" of recent Modernism. Baptism and the Lord's Supper to them were not merely ordinances in which the Church carries out certain divinely appointed rites and subjectively appropriates by her own faith certain spiritual lessons. Whatever the differences in the eucharistic controversies of the sixteenth century, Luther, Calvin, and Zwingli,[14] were agreed in maintaining that Christ is effectively mediated to us in the Sacrament.

If, however, the center of theology is God's redemptive work in Christ, then in the Sacraments he must come to us in like kind, and just as the Church is an extension of that redemptive action in the world, so the Sacraments are an extension of that redemptive action in the Church. The Redeemer comes to us in the Sacraments and not primarily by the action of our faith, but by his own divine initiative. The Church's faith is operative in the Sacraments, and they become ineffective ceremonies or simple magic if we deny it, but the great fact with which we have to reckon in the water of Baptism or around the Lord's Table is not our own faith but his faithfulness. In a passage on the Eucharist which has been very often quoted, P. T. Forsyth declared, "It is not an hour of instruction but of communion. It is an act, not a lesson; and it is not a spectacle or a

---

[13] *Ibid.*, p. 229.
[14] Cf. the chapter by C. J. Cadoux in *Christian Worship*, especially p. 147.

ceremony. It does something. It is *opus operatum*. More, it is an act of the Church more than of the individual. Further still, it is an act created by the eternal Act of Christ which made and makes the Church. At the last it is the Act of Christ present in the Church, which does not so much live as Christ lives in it. It is Christ's act offering Himself to men rather than the act of the Church offering Christ to God." [15] I believe this is the historic Protestant view, although in many quarters Protestantism has strayed from it. Nevertheless, I believe this position is nearest to those biblical insights that were granted to the Reformation, and that those who have understood the insights best would stand with Forsyth. If this is so, then ultimately the issue between Catholic and Protestant is not *whether* our Lord comes to us in the Sacraments but *how*.

Not by Transubstantiation as it has been defined and expounded in Catholic theology—not by a total identification of the consecrated bread and wine with the material Body and Blood of Christ himself. To take this view is a misunderstanding of the Incarnation and of the use to which flesh and blood was put in the Incarnation. It leads to a material and even mechanistic view of the Sacrament, which is just as much in error as the spirituality that ignores the use which God constantly makes of material things as means of grace. During his ministry, and particularly at the end of his ministry, our Lord very carefully avoided giving any cause for the development of a "Jesus cult," a new religion that would be inspired and nourished by the worship of his bodily form. There was some danger of that at the time when he was transfigured before his disciples. At once Peter wanted to stay on the mountain top and erect three tabernacles (shrines?)—one for Jesus and one each for the prophets who had appeared with him. Here might have been the beginning of a new cult which would have degenerated into the idolatry of our Lord's physical form just as surely as the worship of Yahweh had been perverted into the idolatry of the golden calf. Jesus killed it before it was born. He forbade the disciples to tell anyone about the incident until after the Resurrection—until after his bodily presence was taken from them—and straightway he led them down the mountain to witness the meaning of the Transfiguration in action, in the cure of the

---

[15] Forsyth, *op. cit.*, p. 229.

epileptic boy (Mark 9:2 ff.; Matt. 17:2 ff.). The religion that he was to inaugurate would not be the mystical worship of his physical form but devotion to his Person in a different sense. It would be devotion to, and participation in his living Spirit as it works through human flesh and as it is actively engaged and made manifest in dealing with the world's spiritual sickness and insanity. What Canon J. E. Fison has said about Hebrew religion is essentially true of all biblical religion, "there may be transfiguration: there can be no transubstantiation." [16]

The same is made even clearer in the Resurrection accounts. The center of the doubt of Thomas was that he wanted something that he could touch and handle before he would believe. As we read the stories of how Jesus came to the disciples after the first Easter, we find that there is very rarely any suggestion of an immediate glad recognition and reunion. More often we read of an initial hesitance and even an inexplicable failure to recognize the Risen Lord, as if our Lord were gradually weaning his followers away from their devotion to the physical form they had known and loved and preparing them to recognize him in a different way. After Mary Magdalene had finished talking to the two men in white at the sepulcher, we are told that she turned round and saw Jesus, but "knew not that it was Jesus." Jesus asked her why she was crying and whom she was seeking, and she, "supposing him to have been the gardener," begged him to tell her where her Lord was laid. It was only after the Risen Jesus had uttered her name in his own characteristic way that she recognized who it was by her side (John 20:1 ff.). Is her failure to recognize the Lord to be put down to grief or to the morning mist? Or was her Master trying to lead the passionate and devoted Mary to a worship that was deeper than she could ever give to the form she knew, however sacred his physical appearance might be to her? "Touch me not."

There is the interesting account in John 21, ending with Peter's commission, of how Jesus met some of his disciples by the lake of Galilee. It is particularly interesting because it is so similar in many details to a story that occurs in the fifth chapter of Luke, when at the very beginning of our Lord's ministry Peter had cried, "Depart from me, for I am a sinful man, O Lord!" and when Jesus, by means of the

---

[16] Fison, *The Blessing of the Holy Spirit*, p. 72.

miracle of the draught of fishes had gone on to show the disciples their apostolic vocation to become fishers of men. It may be that the miracle is a "doublet," but it may be that it is not, and that the Fourth Evangelist had a very good reason for including it in his account of the last days of our Lord on earth. He significantly places it after the Resurrection, and he tells us how, as on the former occasion, the diciples had fished in the lake all night without any success. In the morning Jesus stood and hailed them from the shore, but "the disciples knew not that it was Jesus." It was only after the miracle took place—to reaffirm their vocation after their doubts and denials?—that John said to Peter, "It is the Lord!" It was something that happened, something that Jesus *did* and which was characteristic of him which brought the cry of recognition. To what, then, is one to attribute their failure to recognize him earlier—to their own doubt or a sea vapor? Or was Jesus Christ leading them on to recognize that in their future evangelism he would be just as effectively and miraculously by their side as he had been in the days by Galilee?

Perhaps the best example of all is that of the two disciples who walked to the village Emmaus on the first Easter Sunday (Luke 24:13-35) and were discussing the events of the past few terrible days. "And it came to pass, while they communed together, that Jesus himself drew near, and went with them. But their eyes were holden that they should not know Him." They did not know him even though he was by their side, even though they were discussing the events of his own death, even though he expounded the Scriptures to show that the Christ had to suffer and then be glorified. Was it that even as disillusionment had clamped down upon their hearts the oncoming dusk clouded their eyes? It was not until they had reached the village, invited him to be their guest, and sit down to share their evening meal with them that suddenly they recognized him in a characteristic and pregnant gesture: "And it came to pass, when he had sat down with them to meat, he took bread, and blessed it, and brake, and gave to them. And their eyes were opened and they knew him."

All these incidents illustrate the fact that after the Resurrection the eyes of the disciples were directed away from the actual flesh and blood of our Lord's bodily form toward that which it had enshrined and of which it had been the Living Vehicle. They were dissuaded, almost against their will, from identifying absolutely his material form with that Living Spirit, which was now to be with them always, even to the end of time. And they were shown that this presence of the Glorified Christ would be revealed to them supremely in action. But the physical element was not spiritualized away—it was still vitally important as the necessary vehicle of an action. For the key to all these incidents is in action—action which is characteristic of Jesus Christ. This is the revelation of his living presence in the Sacraments of the Church—through the active working of the Holy Spirit Jesus Christ may come to us and to others in many different ways, but he comes to us supremely in this. I belong to a Christian confession which has experienced its full share of subjectivity in the interpretation of the Sacraments, and we have needed to be reminded that "it belongs to our tradition and to the truth of the Gospel to lay all the stress upon the action of the living God. It is God who calls and regenerates, He who comes and gives himself to us. His action is first and last." [17] But this is the emphasis of no one confession or Christian tradition but of the Bible itself, for God is revealed in action that is at one and the same time redemptive and creative. In the prophetic symbolism of the Old Testament prophets we see that when they uttered his word to the nation, that Word of the Lord was already active and bringing to pass the will of God in history. His Word is an active Word which does things and which can be recognized in the things it does.

So God in the Sacraments represents to the Church his own dramatic intervention into history for the redemption of the world, and his presence in the crucified and glorified Christ is revealed within the Church in the breaking of Bread. To quote Nathaniel Micklem, "the Sacraments derive their whole meaning from the redeeming Work of Christ. It is action which they symbolize and convey. The essence of the Sacrament, therefore, is action, not species." [18] There we are presented with a summary of what I believe the Protestant tradition has always been trying to say about the Sacraments when it has been most true to its own scriptural origins. This is the center of a doctrine of the Real Presence. It is a position which is based not

---

[17] Nathaniel Micklem, *Christian Worship* (London: Oxford University Press, 1954), p. 243.
[18] *Ibid.*, p. 245.

upon *a priori* arguments from a given historical theology, but it is essentially based upon the Bible's revelation of that redemptive Action of Almighty God begun in Israel's history and consummated in Jesus Christ. And it has been confirmed in the experience of all those who under the shadow of the Cross have been washed by water and the Spirit, and who have received at his hands the broken Body and the shed Blood of his atoning sacrifice.

CHAPTER X

Baptism

1. Ecumenical Problems of Baptism

EACH OF THE DOMINICAL SACRAMENTS IN ITS OWN WAY PROVIDES AN illustration of the unity and division of the Church at their deepest level. In a profound sense the fact that they are generally accepted and practiced by almost every Christian confession that claims to be a "Church" is a witness to our essential unity in Christ. In an equally profound sense the fact that the Churches do not recognize as valid the way in which these Sacraments are received and practiced by other churches is an acknowledgment of tragic disunity.

Baptism is recognized as the rite of initiation into the Christian Church by all who accept the Christian Sacraments, and its importance to the unity of Christians is seen in the fact that the great majority of Catholics and Protestants—where the cleavages appear greatest in almost every other aspect of faith and practice—recognize each other's baptism.[1] On the other hand some of the most adamantine questions that divide the churches have their focus in this Sacrament. There is first the issue between those who practice the Baptism of infants and those who require "believer's Baptism," which separates the Baptists and Disciples of Christ from the other branches of the Church. But beyond this issue and the part which personal faith plays in Christian Baptism, there is the equally intransigent problem of the theological meaning of Baptism—disagreement about what is actually effected in the Sacrament—and here the lines cross and recross the old pattern of the traditional "Baptist versus Paedo-Baptist" controversy.

One of the most important points of departure is between those who hold a strict theory of baptismal regeneration and those—

---

[1] The most striking exceptions are the Orthodox, who often require re-baptism for converts from Protestantism and the stricter Baptist Churches which require Believer's Baptism on the part of all their members.

whether Baptist or Paedo-Baptist—who do not. On the one side are ranged strict "Catholics" and some strict Baptists, and on the other side, together with some Baptists of more liberal principle, there are the majority of Protestants who, from the standpoint of a theology based on faith, find it difficult to reconcile a doctrine of baptismal regeneration with their actual practice of infant Baptism. For some the rite of Baptism itself constitutes entry into membership of the Church; it is the guarantee of salvation and mediates the Holy Spirit's presence. Others, while believing that Baptism is the sign and seal of these benefits, insist that before the benefits can be realized the promises of Baptism must be fulfilled in the faith of the believer. This broadly describes two positions, but between the foci there are many variants.

The division over the meaning of Baptism is coming more and more into the foreground as churches move out of their isolation. It is at the center of the practical issue of proselytism that has been raised now at the ecumenical level by reason of the new status in which "Free" Churches and "State" Churches, Protestants and Orthodox, find themselves as partners in the Ecumenical Movement. There has always been tension when evangelical missions have entered areas governed by strong State churches, where to be a member of the nation is normally regarded as implying membership of the national church and the right of Baptism into that church. The real center of tension, however, is a radical difference of attitude to Baptism—between churches which believe that Baptism as an infant into the *volkskirche* puts the indelible stamp of that church upon the individual for life, and churches which believe that the rite of Baptism means nothing of itself without personal faith. Evangelicals moving into countries where practically the whole population has received Christian Baptism and presumably should have received the gift of the Holy Spirit, without apparently being expected to receive any of the distinctive *charismata* in private or public morals that go with it, have often jumped to the conclusion that these people needed the gospel and have forthwith proceeded to make converts! They have acted on the principle that where a man's eternal life is at stake it is better to act first and theologize later. In this, however, their religious instinct and even their motivation has often been better than their theology. This has been true on the issue of baptism itself, for in their anxiety to uphold the New Testament primacy of faith in Christ, they have often been forced into suggesting that Baptism into Christ is unimportant or irrelevant. The New Testament position would appear to be different, for if it asserts the primacy of faith, it asserts with equal clarity the importance of faith's Sacrament. The basic theological ground for carrying the gospel to those whose church has never brought its members' Baptism to the bar of personal faith, ought to be not because baptism means so little, but because it means so much.

In baptism Christ brings his promise of Redemption and a new life in his Resurrection, but if this promise has been sealed to us in the water of Baptism and we, either by our own ignorance and folly or by the laxity and failure of our ministers and priests, turn our backs upon its implications, then it becomes to us a Sacrament of judgment. Just as Christ was the Judgment of God to those who rejected him, so our Baptism can be our judgment: grace can do no other than to judge where it does not convert. Let us admit that mission churches have often been more concerned with building up new parishes of their own than in helping to revitalize the indigenous national church. But it should be said on the other side that those nationally large churches that have been content to baptize infants into the faith without ever bothering to bring them later to the point of a personal confession of faith might very well thank God if others try to do with their "members" what they have failed to do. The pastoral concern of the Christian priest or minister ought surely not to be less than that of the ancient Hebrew prophet (Ezek. 3:17-21; 33:7-16).

If, however, the Ecumenical Movement is bringing Baptism into the center of theological discussion, the Sacrament has been a long time arriving there. This is due not only to the reluctance of many to face what is regarded as an extremely dangerous issue but perhaps equally to the fact that the numerically largest and evangelically the most successful branch of the Baptist churches (the Southern Baptist Convention) has not yet seen fit to risk its beliefs in the open ecumenical arena. Until that position is changed, the Baptist issue will never receive the attention that is due to it. On the other hand although one senses the reluctance of churches radically to change their attitude to Baptism and although all the newly sponsored official "enquiries" and reports are less likely to advance Godly revolution than to justify once more "historic" positions, one also senses beneath the surface a very deep and widespread uneasiness about the present practice of Baptism in most churches. Whatever the official attitude of the confessions there has been a very remarkable revival of interest in Baptism on the part of the theologians, and it has resulted in a discussion that is both ecumenical and international. Indeed, the major contributions have come not from the Anglo-Saxon Churches of Baptist belief and practice but first from national Churches on the Continent of Europe and then from the Established Churches in Britain.

It is with this background to remind us of the ecumenical nature of the problems associated with it that we turn to the Sacrament of Baptism.

2. The New Testament Dilemma

The perplexity of the Church regarding Baptism is not only by reason of the apparent dichotomy between the practice of the Church in the New Testament and the Church's continuous practice of infant Baptism since roughly the third century A.D., but also because when we address ourselves to the question what Baptism means, there is a good deal in the New Testament which seems to pull in different directions.

When one has made the most of such "proofs" as the Philippian gaoler's very convenient family in Acts 6:33, there is almost no hint of evidence for any practice of infant baptism in the New Testament. It has been admitted, even by some who maintain the validity of infant baptism, that this mode of baptism may have been expressly excluded by I Cor. 7:14—presumably because Paul believed that the children of a believing parent were already in a special relationship to God, and Paul's omission to mention Baptism in this passage is a pointer that it was not used in such cases.[2] There may be a significant parallel in what the apostle felt about the circumcision of Jewish believers. He was charged at Jerusalem with having urged Jewish converts to forsake the law of Moses, "telling them not to circumcize their children or observe the customs" (Acts 21:21). Possibly there was no truth in the charge, but there is enough to show that Paul

---

[2] E.g., P. T. Forsyth, *The Church and the Sacraments*, p. 211.

believed that grace abrogated the provisions of the Law for the families of Jews and Gentiles alike. Was that in his view because the children of Christian parents had been baptized "into the Name," or simply because of the faith of the parents?

We do not know the answer, and we are not likely to discover it, for if Paul's principle of *sola fide* appears on one side, the common practice of being baptized for the dead which is mentioned in I Cor. 15:29 appears on the other. Furthermore, over against the overwhelming evidence that Baptism in the New Testament was given to believers and the very meager evidence for any parallel practice of infant Baptism, we have to accept the fact that there is no trace at all of children who have been brought up in Christian homes being baptized as adults. Oscar Cullman maintains that this is even worse attested than infant Baptism "and indeed lacks any kind of proof." [3]

There is, however, another tension regarding Baptism in the New Testament, which is at a somewhat deeper level, and which becomes most marked in the teaching of Paul. Both the missionary situation in which the early Church came into existence and the accent upon confession of faith in the Baptism of its converts demanded the primacy of faith and the development of a theology founded upon that primacy. There is a good deal in Paul's life and teaching to support this. He reminds the Christians at Rome how Abraham's faith was counted to him for righteousness for believing the promise of God and says that in the same way it will be counted to us "who believe on him who was raised from the dead, who was put to death for our trespasses and raised for our justification. Therefore," he continues, "since we are justified by faith, we have peace with God through our Lord Jesus Christ," (Rom. 5:23). In the same way writing to the Galatians, he reminds them that a man is not justified by the works of the law, "but through faith in Jesus Christ." [4] We seem to have here a faith-centered theology that could not leave room for any rite, even the rite of Baptism, to rival it as the ground of salvation. Perhaps the most telling passage in this respect is Paul's personal affirmation to the Church at Corinth that he had baptized very few converts, be-

---

[3] Oscar Cullman, *Baptism in the New Testament*, E.T. of *Die Tauflehre des neuen Testaments* by J. K. S. Reid (S.C.M. first published in English 1950, 5th Impression, 1956), p. 26.
[4] Gal. 2:16. Cf. 3:24; Rom. 3:28; Phil. 3:7-11.

cause "Christ did not send me to baptize but to preach the gospel," (I Cor. 1:17). These instances and many others could be cited which point in one direction, to the absolute primacy of faith in the thought of Paul as that which justifies a believer before God. By implication such a view would appear to relegate Baptism to only symbolic importance in the life of the believer.

But the evidence is by no means all on one side as H. T. Andrews showed in the chapter he contributed to Forsyth's *The Church and the Sacraments*. The chapter reflects the scholarship of the period when it was written, but I believe modern New Testament research would strengthen rather than weaken Andrews' conclusion that "the sacramental principle is a vital element in the teaching of St. Paul." [5] He cited some significant examples regarding Baptism—the verse in the first epistle to the Corinthians, for example, where Paul reminds his readers that the kingdom of God was not for idol worshipers, or immoral persons, or thieves or drunkards, concluding "such were some of you. But you were washed, you were sanctified, you were justified in the name of the Lord Jesus and in the Spirit of our God" (I Cor. 6:11). It is suggested that the best commentary for "you were washed" is to be found in the story of Paul's own conversion where Ananias exhorted the young Saul to "rise and be baptized, and wash away your sins, calling upon his [Christ's] name" (Acts 20:16). Andrews added the comment that to describe such a "washing" in Baptism as simply a symbol of conversion would rob it of all its force.[6] He also pointed to the practice of being baptized for the dead (cf. I Cor. 15:29) and asked how that could have grown up unless "baptism was believed to confer some spiritual endowment which could not be obtained in any other way." [7] His main argument, however, is based upon the passage in Ephesians, where Paul reminded his readers that "there is one body and one Spirit, just as you were called to one hope that belongs to your call, one Lord, one faith, one baptism, one God and Father of all, who is above all and through all," (Eph. 4:4-6). Andrews asked why Paul gave Baptism such an important place in the progression of spiritual realities if he regarded it of only secondary importance, particularly since both the Eucha-

---

[5] H. T. Andrews, *The Church and the Sacraments*, p. 154.
[6] *Ibid.*, p. 159.
[7] *Ibid.*

rist and the Apostolate were omitted. The clearest and "most incontrovertible statement" is to be found in the twenty-sixth verse of chapter five when the apostle speaks of our Lord loving the Church and giving himself up for her "that he might sanctify her, having cleansed her by the washing of water with the word, that the church might be presented before him in splendor, without spot or wrinkle or any such thing, that she might be holy and without blemish." Such passages preclude us from interpreting the more general statements of Paul—"baptized into Christ," baptized "into one body"—in merely a symbolic sense, and the writer submitted that in their light "it is very hard to resist the conclusion (however little we may like it) that if the Epistles of St. Paul do not enunciate the ecclesiastical doctrine of Baptismal Regeneration, they at any rate approximate very closely to it." But always in our consideration of the meaning of Baptism in the New Testament there is the significant difference that "there is no shred of real proof that baptism was ever administered to infants in the Apostolic age." [8]

These illustrations are quoted because they are examples of the kind of problems that every honest scholar—Baptist and Paedo-Baptist alike—is likely to discover for himself when he goes to the New Testament and allows it to judge the present practice of his church. It is a dilemma which perhaps cannot finally be solved until, as Andrews pointed out, we have settled the prior issue: where do we find the seat of final authority for the Christian faith.

3. The Place of Baptism in Christian Worship

On the other hand although the debate about the mode and meaning of Baptism continues, there seems to have been a growing sense of agreement among scholars regarding its essential meaning and its place in the life of the Church. This has been in large measure due to the revival of Bible-centered theology and to the fact—to which H. T. Andrews alluded—that the place of the Sacrament in the life of the Apostolic Church becomes the more inescapable the more seriously we are prepared to take the New Testament writings themselves. If one is prepared to discount the Epistles as secondary scripture, then it may be possible to relegate the sacramental issues to a secondary

[8] *Ibid.*, p. 160.

place in theology but if not then these issues are forced into the foreground of the Church's thinking about its life and witness. Although Anglo-Saxon writers have made very valuable contributions to this aspect of the problem, undoubtedly the pace has been set by Karl Barth. We must return to consider the meaning of Baptism at greater length, but at this stage we note that his views have had the very important practical effect of bringing the sacrament of Baptism once more into the center of the Church's worship.

Baptism, declares Barth, is "indirectly and mediately a free word and act of Jesus Christ Himself"; even as the Church does not gather herself but is gathered by her Lord, so the Church did not invent Baptism, but administers it as it has been instituted by her Lord. It is Christ himself who "makes water-baptism powerful for repentance and the forgiveness of sins. He who needed not these things, submitted himself to them, thereby setting forth both what happened on Golgotha and also what happened on Easter morning, thus declaring His solidarity with sinners. Baptism was thereby made a living and expressive representation of Christ's high-priestly death and resurrection." [9] Barth maintains that Baptism, in common with the other dominical Sacrament is administered by the Church, within the structure of its worship and together with the faithful preaching of the Word. In his Gifford lectures he pleads for the re-establishment of the Sacraments at the center of Reformed worship. "Would the sermon not be delivered and listened to quite differently," he asks, "if everything outwardly and visibly began with baptism and moved towards the Lord's Supper? . . . The hearing of the Word of God forms the real action of the Church and in the last resort everything depends on its taking place around the centre characterised by the two sacraments." [10]

The practical implication of Barth's christocentric theology is thus to assert the Sacraments at the center of Reformed worship—"in principle baptism cannot be tolerated as a private act or a family festival. In principle it can only be celebrated within the framework of

---

[9] *The Teaching of the Church Regarding Baptism*, E.T. of *Die kirchliche Lehre von der Taufe* by E. A. Payne (S.C.M., 1948), p. 17-18.
[10] Karl Barth, *The Knowledge of God and the Service of God*, E.T. of *Gotteserkenntnis und Gottesdienst* by J. L. M. Haire and Ian Henderson (Hodder and Stoughton, 1933; 3rd Impression 1955), pp. 211-12.

the public worship of God." [11] In this way the weight of Barth's authority has been added to an independent trend in Britain which had already been begun in the writings of Denney and Forsyth. This trend, which has had a steady and increasing influence since the '30's of this century, has produced something like a liturgical revival in the reformed churches of Britain. It is a revival of concern about the Church's worship that has been actuated not by aesthetic or even strictly liturgical considerations—still less from a desire to copy the sacramental practices of Anglicans or Roman Catholics—but by the theological concern to reveal and express the gospel at the heart of all worship. As a recent American observer of this trend in Britain has written, what the leaders of the movement regard as essential "is the formal expression in Christian worship of the dependence of the preached Word and the Sacraments upon the Gospel." [12]

In this trend Baptism has its place. "Baptism," wrote Forsyth, "as a Sacrament of the Church is an act of the Church"; like the Lord's Supper it declares and enacts the whole Gospel.[13] Therefore, it implies the participation of the whole congregation of the Church within the context of worship and the preaching of God's Word. The reaction has been entirely away from any suggestion that this is a rite which may be administered at the minister's discretion or in private family parties. It is the Church's Sacrament and as such is to be administered normally only in the context of public worship, or at least in the presence of the Church's accredited representatives. In support of this one can cite a post-war and widely used service book for ministers prepared by a younger group of English Congregationalists, which echoes Forsyth when it declares that "the right and duty of administering the sacraments belongs to the whole church; therefore, save for urgent reasons, Baptism is always to be performed in the church"; and they go on to show that by "the church" they in-

---

[11] *The Teaching of the Church Regarding Baptism*, p. 32.

[12] John W. Grant, *Free Churchmanship in England 1870-1940* (Independent Press, n.d.), ch. vii, and especially pp. 325-40. Grant could have made even more than he has done of the liturgical repercussions of the theological revival (especially in Methodism), and to be a complete picture of the movement in Britain his account would need to be supplemented by an account of similar movements in Scotland (e.g., in the distinctive emphases of the Iona Community and the writings of W. D. Maxwell) and in the Anglican Church (e.g., the work of Dom Gregory Dix and such expressions as the Parish Communion movement).

[13] *The Church and the Sacraments*, pp. 187, 191.

tend not merely the church building but the context of public worship.[14] There is some evidence for thinking that this kind of Free Church and Reformed reaction has not been without its effect upon the attitude of thoughtful Anglicans. The practical issue of this concern about the place of the Sacrament in the worship of the Church has been that although one has the impression that Barth's views have yet to be implemented in the Reformed worship of large areas of Europe, the central place of the Sacraments in the worship of the Church is already largely accepted in Britain.

4. Jesus and His Baptism

It will be seen that we have not been able to speak of the place which Baptism should occupy in worship without touching upon its meaning, and if it can be said that there has been drawing together in the understanding of its essential meaning, it must not be imagined that this problem has been forthwith resolved. Indeed, although certain basic agreements have been reached by some theologians across the theological and confessional frontiers, even the arrival at those agreements has been attended by the revelation of deep divisions. It is with humility in the face of the unresolved conflicts that we approach the question of the meaning.

If Baptism is a sacramental representation of the redemptive act of God in the work of Jesus Christ, it is first to that total work and ministry of our Lord that we must look in order to discover its meaning. The ministry of our Lord was initiated by his Baptism. But ought we to start here or at his circumcision? Jesus was circumcised in the manner required of all Jewish males, and in that way he became a full member of the Jewish nation and people. This is where our problem begins, for was his later ministry a radical break with the past or a fulfillment of it? Obviously that is not the right way to state the question, for it was both—it was the fulfillment of Israel's history and the divine promises made to her, but it was also in the same act the creation of a "New Israel" on a new basis that implied the abrogation of much that was regarded as indispensable within the Jewish religion. Yet Jesus was circumcised, and although it is impossible to distinguish between the religious and the civil implications of the

---

[14] *A Book of Public Worship* (ed. John Huxtable, John Marsh, Romilly Micklem, James Todd; O.U.P., 1948, 2nd ed. 1949), p. xvii.

rite, Oscar Cullman is surely right to insist that the essence of the rite of circumcision was not reception into the Jewish nation but reception into the covenant.[15] To be circumcised was to be made one with the people of God and an inheritor of both the promises and the responsibilities. Therefore, although there was in our Lord's ministry a real element of discontinuity with the past, a sense in which his ministry and mission was "wholly other" than what had gone before, the break did not come at this point. Our Lord seems rather to have accepted the implications of his own circumcision by accepting his own ministry as a fulfillment of his membership in the people of God. Perhaps the most important element of "wholly otherness" which he gave to that mission was in the totally different content that he gave to it. To use an idea of which Canon J. E. Fison is fond, and which I believe is both true and helpful, the new quality that our Lord gave to the mission of Israel is in the fact that he "transfigured" it. This was something "wholly other" if you like, but it was not radically different in the sense of being any deflection of God's purpose for Israel but the raising of that purpose to a height far beyond human imagination and even beyond prophetic insight.

The fact that Jesus was circumcised in the manner that was common to all Jewish males must not be regarded simply as an accident of his birth. It had its place in the purpose of God—as significant a place as the choice of Mary as his mother and the Jewish nation as his people. Yet we cannot imagine that our Lord as a baby willed to be circumcised. It was a responsibility which his human parents out of the fullness of their own faith and piety undertook for him. In doing this they may have been doing no more than that which was the normal practice of all good Jews, and yet in a deep sense by that action they were committing him to all that followed in his earthly life, because he and he alone could comprehend the true vocation of Israel and would stand before God and the world as its Representative. His parents did this for him, and yet in the final issue they could not accept responsibility for the way in which he accepted that vocation. Only he finally could take responsibility for that, and it had to be an action of his own free choice. So in the circumcision of Christ we see the finger of God's choice laid upon him without his

---

[15] *Op. cit.*, p. 58.

own conscious assent, and yet at the Baptism we see our Lord consciously and willingly undertaking the vocation for which his circumcision had marked him. The Circumcision would have meant nothing apart from the Baptism, and yet without the choice implied in the Circumcision the Baptism would have lost its specific reference to Israel.

This is a necessary preface to our consideration of the Baptism of Jesus. It has been pointed out that the Baptism which John proclaimed at Jordan had its own roots in the Baptism of proselytes that was practiced by the Jews at that time. It is evident that proselytes were both baptized and circumcised and that the two ceremonies applied both to adults and children, but that proselyte baptism was a requirement for those who wished to enter the Jewish nation and was applicable to gentiles alone. A Baptist scholar, Neville Clark, has suggested that John the Baptist's daring innovation "lay in his assertion that the qualification for membership of the true Israel was ethical not racial; and that the apostate nation, thus standing in the same position as the gentiles it despised, must undergo the rite of incorporation." [16] John's Baptism was therefore one of "repentance for the forgiveness of sins" (Mark 14:36; Matt. 26:39; Luke 22:42; John 28:11), but it was also set fully within the immediate prospect of a messianic eschatology, for the one who would come after John would baptize with the Holy Spirit and with fire (Mark 1:7-8; Matt. 3-11; Luke 3:16; John 1:26-27, 33).

The first thing we notice is that the Baptism of Jesus is extremely well attested, occurring in all four of the Gospels, which is in itself a sufficient witness not simply to the historic fact, but just as significantly to the importance which the evangelists placed upon the fact in interpreting the life of Christ. But the question immediately arises why Jesus submitted to this Baptism, since we believe that he could have felt no need of repentance. I believe Neville Clark is right when he refers us to our Lord's reply to John, "Let it be so now, for thus it is fitting for us to fulfill all righteousness," and finds in this a direct recognition of the parallel with the Servant of Yahweh.[17] This would be fully in line with the rest of our Lord's life and particularly with

---

[16] *An Approach to the Theology of the Sacraments* (Naperville: Allenson, 1956), p. 12, Vol. 17 of *Studies in Biblical Theology*.
[17] Ibid., p. 13.

the evidence of how he approached his Passion. In other words it is suggested that at the Baptism, our Lord interpreted and accepted the messianic vocation in the light of the Servant conception and received confirmation of that mission in like terms both in the actualized descent of the Holy Spirit and in the Voice which declared, "Thou art my beloved Son, [ὁ ἀγαπητός] with thee I am well pleased." In fact it is not impossible that the parallelism could be carried even further in terms of the messianic Psalm 2, "Thou art my Son; this day have I begotten thee" (Ps. 2:7). The messianic conception, however, is very clearly interpreted in a special way which refers directly to sacrifice. In the Fourth Gospel John the Baptist is represented as openly acknowledging this aspect of our Lord's vocation in the salutation, "Behold the Lamb of God!" It is perhaps relatively unimportant whether there is a direct connection between this phrase and the Servant conception or not, for the important thing to notice is that this construction was certainly put upon it by the author of the Gospel, writing as he did on "the other side" of the Resurrection and interpreting our Lord's life in the light of Good Friday and Easter.

Cullman is surely right in bringing the Baptism of Jesus into direct relation to two other important passages in the Gospels where our Lord himself related the idea of Baptism specifically to his Passion (Mark 10:38; Luke 12:50).[18] On the first occasion the mother of James and John came to Jesus and asked him the modest favor of granting her sons the chief seats on his right hand and left hand when he had come to his kingdom! Jesus turned to the two young men and told them, "You do not know what you are asking. Are you able to drink the cup that I drink, or be baptized with the baptism with which I am baptized?" They replied, "We are able," and Jesus said to them, "The cup that I drink you will drink, and with the baptism with which I am baptized, you will be baptized; but to sit at my right hand or at my left hand is not mine to grant, but it is for the ones for whom it has been prepared." (Matt. 20:20-28.) The significance of this particular passage is in the fact that the sacramental imagery of both the cup and of Baptism are used together, and they refer quite obviously to the Cross and Passion—or rather, to his whole life of sacrifice up to, including, and culminating in the Cross and Passion. Even if the

---

[18] Cullman, op. cit., pp. 19-20.

figures that are used here could be open to other interpretations, they become quite explicit when taken in conjunction with the use of the same imagery elsewhere. There is the quite unambiguous use of the term "cup" in the stories of the Passion in the Garden, and precisely the same import is given to the term "Baptism" in the second of the crucial passages (Luke 12:50), when our Lord declared, "I have a baptism to be baptized with; and how am I constrained until it is accomplished!" We cannot believe this was other than his Passion and the Cross.

This was the "Baptism" of Jesus. It was his whole work of salvation that would reach its climax and entire fulfillment in all that was to come to him through his death and Resurrection. Yet if this is so, it must throw back its meaning to the Baptism that he underwent in Jordan at the hands of John the Baptist, for that Baptism with its voluntary choice of the Servant's messianic rôle and its divine acknowledgment could not mean anything other than this. However, if this is the meaning of the Baptism in Jordan, we must give full weight to the element of our Lord's voluntary choice in that act, for no one, not even God the Father, could take responsibility for that decision on behalf of the human Jesus: Christ's Sonship was recognized and acknowledged in the very freedom of his willingness to be the Son. His paternity and patrimony were made evident by the nature of his act. If at the circumcision the action of our Lord's human parents brought him within the framework of the Old Covenant so that, being who he was, he could not avoid becoming the True Israel and the Inheritor of its glory and mission, then we must give equal weight to the fact that at his Baptism he voluntarily undertook these obligations with all that they might imply. The ultimate mystery of the relation between election and free choice is here, and neither element can be discarded without making Jesus Christ less than he was. If this is true, then the circumcision and the Baptism of our Lord are complementary aspects of the same event.

On the other hand the actual Baptism in Jordan has three distinctive and important emphases. First, there was our Lord's voluntary acceptance of his destiny—his destiny was accepted not as a "fate" but as a call, a vocation to "fulfil all righteousness" with all that this might imply. Secondly, in the voice from heaven and the descent of the Holy Spirit there was the recognition by God himself not only of the selection of Jesus for the rôle he was to play but also of our Lord's willingness to accept that rôle. Thirdly, there is the recognition that Christ's messianic ministry was to be interpreted in terms of the Suffering Servant and the way of sacrifice: the Cross was written into the Baptism by all the actors in that story. Oscar Cullman may identify the Cross with the Baptism too far, so that for him they tend to become a single event, yet we must agree that "the Baptism of Jesus points forward to the end, to the climax of His life, the Cross, in which alone all Baptism will find its fulfilment." [19] Neville Clark, from a Baptist point of view, says essentially the same when he declares that in the last resort and on the deepest level, the Baptism is the Cross, for at Jordan "Jesus received his calling as the Servant of the Lord, accepted his vocation of redemption through suffering, acknowledged his baptism in terms of the cross." [20]

The force of this is driven home by the absence of any distinctive form of Baptism for his adherents during the course of our Lord's ministry. In the one passage where he is reported to have baptized, the Evangelist was apparently relying upon some envious hearsay on the part of John's disciples, and a few verses later he categorically withdraws his previous statement and declares that it was only our Lord's disciples who baptized. This unwillingness of Jesus to baptize his followers has, I believe, to be seen at a far deeper level than merely an unwillingness to reduplicate what John the Baptist was doing—it has to be seen in the light of his total vocation. The baptism that he will offer to men is radically different from that of John, for in him the *eschaton* toward which John pointed has already arrived, the kingdom has come on earth as it is in heaven, and men are going to be invited to be baptized into that kingdom by the same baptism that he himself has received. They could not know the meaning of baptism until they had seen the Cross. The answer given by our Lord to James and John is of the essence of what Christian Baptism was to mean: they would be baptized by the same baptism that Jesus himself has accepted. Objectively they would receive the sign of something done by him on their behalf, but its meaning would become real to them only as subjectively they identified themselves with this objective sacrifice. So before they offered to take that step, it was well that they should

---
[19] *Ibid.*, p. 19.
[20] Clark, *op. cit.*, p. 18 (also p. 16).

reflect upon what it was for which they were asking—"Are you able to drink the cup that I drink, or be baptized with the baptism with which I am baptized?" No man could be expected to undergo such a baptism without undertaking it by his own free consent.

Such examples as we read in the Gospels of the disciples undertaking the responsibility of baptizing others seem to have come rather from the previous association with John than from any express command of our Lord (John 3:22-4:6). And we notice that Baptism formed no part of the charge given to the Twelve and the Seventy (Luke 9:1-6; 10:1-24; cf. Matt. 10:1-42). In view of the other New Testament passages where the idea of Baptism is explicitly linked with the whole of our Lord's atoning work, it seems clear that he had this special reason for abstaining from baptizing during his ministry. It would certainly be wrong to assume that because he did not baptize he regarded Baptism as having no relevance to his proclamation of the Kingdom—that would be too violent a contradiction from his readiness to undergo the Baptism of John—but rather does it seem as if Jesus was waiting to give his own content to what Baptism into his name should mean, a significance that could be won for the Sacrament only by his Cross and Resurrection. The true parallel is perhaps to be found in the fact that Bishop Hicks drew to our notice, that Jesus did not use any sacrificial language until the Lord's Supper when he could see the path ahead and was resolved to go to the end.[21] As with the eucharistic meal, so with Baptism, he wanted the meaning of these ordinances to be fully centered in his redeeming death and in actions that would help the true meaning to live on in the life of the Church. Whether one regards the last few verses of Matthew's Gospel (28:18-20) as the verbal command of Christ or not, it is very significant that when the Evangelist came to the point of expressing the last command of our Lord to his apostolate, the commission to baptize was put into the mouth of the *glorified* Christ. The command to baptize came on "the yonder side" of Easter, presumably because only after Easter could the early Church be expected to understand what it meant, and the Sacrament came into the practice of the Church only after the Crucifixion, Easter, and Pentecost had given the Sacrament the fullness of its meaning. Cullman maintains that the Cross

---

[21] Supra, p. 260.

of Christ was a "general baptism" undertaken by Christ on our behalf, and in his emphasis upon the prevenient grace of God he perhaps fails sufficiently to see that this "Baptism" of our Lord unto death involves not merely the Cross but the whole of Christ's redeeming work.[22] Neville Clark has a more comprehensive view and surely one which is nearer to the New Testament, when he insists that

> baptism is not in the last resort baptism into the death of Christ but baptism into Christ, the incarnate, crucified, risen and ascended Redeemer. In baptism the disciple enters into the whole redemptive action of his Lord, so that what was once done representatively for him may now be done in actuality in him; he is incorporated in order that he may be crucified.[23]

5. The New Testament Testimony

Many of the things about which we have been speaking are brought out in the practice of the early Church in the Book of the Acts. God's choice of the believer and the sense of personal commitment are both to be found there without any feeling of incongruity, just as we find there all the signs that were present at our Lord's own Baptism. The Sacrament in Acts has at its heart faith centered in the death and Resurrection of Jesus Christ, Baptism by water, and a new covenant between God and men that is ratified in the seal of the Spirit. The Church's Baptism took over the "general baptism" of our Lord's atoning work but with certain special emphases that were due to the fact that those who entered into the Baptism were sinners in need of cleansing before they could become the sons of God by adoption. For this reason it was bound to retain the element of repentance that had been in John's baptizing, and whereas Christ himself had been able to accept the purpose of God directly, the Baptism of the new convert could only be baptism "into the Name"—i.e., the saving purpose—of Jesus Christ himself. The believer was baptized into Christ, but this meant far more than the intellectual acceptance of what Jesus had done, for by the power of the Holy Spirit it implied for the believer the acceptance *for himself* of the Baptism that Christ had undergone. Perhaps we can see the issues in their sharpest form if we

---

[22] Cullman, op. cit., pp. 32-33.
[23] Clark, op. cit., p. 31.

look at them in terms of a series of relationships, almost of paradoxes or tensions, in which they were understood and experienced by the early Church.

1. We see that faith in the atoning work of Christ implied the action of Baptism by water, but we also see that Baptism by water implied *faith* in Christ's atoning work. This holds together at the sacramental level very much what Dietrich Bonhoeffer has tried to make us hold together at the ethical level—the fact that only the one who believes is truly obedient, and that only the one who is obedient truly believes. So the external work (or in sacramental terms, the rite) is a necessary demonstration of the internal gift, just as much as it is true to say that the internal gift must be present if the external rite is to have any Christian meaning.[24] Bonhoeffer showed that we needed to relearn this elementary truth of Christian discipleship, but what is seen in Bonhoeffer in ethical terms is very closely related to what we need also to learn in sacramental terms. Indeed, it holds the key to any proper ethical understanding of the Sacraments. On the other hand the earliest followers would have been totally unable to understand any dichotomy between the two elements of the gospel that are being held in tension. Just as faith and obedience (works!) were aspects of the same total commitment to their Lord, so faith and Baptism would have been seen in the same light.

When the Ethiopian heard the Word proclaimed through Philip, expounding the work of Christ through the prophecy of the fifty-third chapter of Isaiah, he believed, but he asked, "What is to prevent my being baptized?" and he was granted baptism through his faith in Christ (Acts 8:26-39). The eunuch, as one who was prevented by the Jewish Law from ever being able to receive the baptism and circumcision of Judaism, understood that Baptism was no mere dispensable sign of his own faith, but it was the gift of God, which sealed to him the promises, and as such it was to be received gladly as an incredible privilege of grace.[25] At the same time, the early Church

[24] Bonhoeffer, op. cit., pp. 56 ff. E.T. by R. H. Fuller.
[25] I do not feel commentaries give sufficient weight to the fact that the man was a eunuch, and this gives an added significance to the fact that he was reading Isa. 53. To get something of the sense of community in suffering which drew him to Christ, read Isa. 53:2-3, 8, 10. The eunuch's loneliness must have been all the more poignant if—as it appears he was—he had been drawn to the Hebrew faith only to discover his sexual status prevented him forever from identifying himself with the people of God.

would have found it impossible to conceive Baptism without faith, for faith in Christ was the only ground upon which Baptism appears to have been granted. If the "general baptism" undertaken by our Lord demands no response, then the rite of baptism itself might be all that was necessary for salvation, but this would make faith an optional extra in the gospel. According to the New Testament it was not the rite itself which saved a person: both faith and Baptism were expected of the convert.

2. There is a very close and reciprocal relationship between the Baptism of water and the Baptism of the Holy Spirit, but although the relationship is close and interpenetrating, there is nothing automatic or rigid in the relationship. The New Testament neither suggests that all those who have been baptized with water have been baptized with the Holy Ghost, nor does it suggest that those who show the fruits of the Spirit should thereby ignore Baptism by water. In the significant case of Pentecost itself there is no mention of the Baptism of the Apostles or of those who were already followers of Jesus. The feet washing incident, Pentecost, or both may correspond to the later Baptism of believers in the case of the apostles, but we cannot be dogmatic on the point, for there is no clear evidence that the apostles, or even the wider circle of disciples and women, ever underwent a form of Christian Baptism other than the Baptism of John. On the other hand we find that the disciples of John whom Apollos discovered at Corinth were baptized into the name of the Lord Jesus, even although they had previously been baptized according to the Baptism of John (Acts 18:24–19:7). We are left to infer that this re-baptism, with the laying on of hands by Paul, brought about the blessing of the Holy Spirit. The Holy Spirit seems to have been given sometimes upon the laying on of hands by an apostle (Acts 8:17) and sometimes not (Acts 4:31). It usually followed Baptism by water, but on at least one occasion it came simply when those who were present heard the Word of God preached (Acts 10:44).

We see that although there is a close relationship between Baptism, the gift of the Spirit, and the apostolic laying on of hands, there is nothing fixed or inevitable in the relationship. One thing, however, ought to be stressed, that even when the Holy Spirit fell upon those who heard the Word but who were not yet baptized, Baptism was not disregarded. The Jewish Christians who were present at Caesarea when Peter preached to Cornelius and his fellow gentiles were amazed, not so much that the Holy Spirit had come to those who were as yet unbaptized, but that it should have come to gentiles (Acts 10: 45-6). Nevertheless, they did not dispense with Baptism by water— they did not argue that because these people already had the gift of the Holy Spirit, Baptism was unnecessary. Seen from one point of view, Cornelius and his friends already *had* the promise of God, and the fact that this promise had been received was an indication of their faith. Yet Peter's question was not "Do these people need to be baptized, since they have already received the Holy Spirit just as we have?" but it was, "Can anyone forbid water for baptizing these people who have received the Holy Spirit just as we have?" (Acts 10:46.) What had baptism to offer to these converts, for the promise from God was already theirs? Clearly, Baptism was regarded as a privilege, and what was necessary was the opportunity for these men to demonstrate their own identity with the atoning work of Christ and with the redeemed community. Here is the obverse side of Baptism, demonstrated in the Baptism of our Lord himself, which accepts God's Election and vocation in the power and gift of the Spirit, and which also publicly becomes identified with that purpose in order to "fulfil all righteousness."

3. This introduces the third set of contrasting relationships regarding Baptism in the early Church. Baptism implies the identity of the believer with the redeeming work of Christ, and equally, such a willingness to become identified with Christ implies Baptism. This becomes more pronounced in the Pauline epistles, but it is present also in Acts in the readiness of the members of the infant Church to face martyrdom, and not least in the life and witness of Paul himself.

At this point we cannot avoid considering the ethical implications of Baptism and their relationship to the gift of the Holy Spirt, for "there is no real meaning in Baptism, however impressive Christ may be, if He be not regenerative, if it means that we are to be but moved by the Spirit, and not born again." [26] One of the most disconcerting elements in the New Testament epistles is the way in which, after a particularly high sounding piece of theology about the Atonement or

---

[26] Forsyth, The Church and the Sacraments, p. 190.

the Sacraments, the writers often appear immediately to plunge into bathos by dealing with extremely practical and mundane matters of simple morality. We may remember that the same feature is to be detected in the writings of the Apostolic Fathers. But we must see how this progression from high theology to practical ethics was made and try to understand what it implies for the writer about the doctrine or Sacrament about which he is writing. Peter, having pointed to the eight people who were saved "through water" in the ark of Noah, says, "Baptism, which corresponds to this, now saves you, not as the removal of dirt from the body but as an appeal [interrogation, questioning] for a clear conscience through the resurrection of Jesus Christ" (I Pet. 3:21). Let us underline the fact that to the apostle Baptism is *not* "as the removal of dirt from the body" but as an appeal to God through the Resurrection of Christ. This does not mean that the idea of purification through washing was absent from Peter's conception of Baptism, but it does mean that it was made very much subordinate to its dynamic character—going down into death with Christ and rising in newness of life. Christian Baptism effects not simply cleansing—here it is in contrast to John's Baptism—but regeneration through faith in the redeeming work of Christ. "Since therefore Christ suffered in the flesh, arm yourselves with the same thought, for whoever has suffered in the flesh has ceased from sin, so as to live for the rest of the time in the flesh no longer by human passions but by the will of God" (I Pet. 4:1-2). Obviously this was written with the immediate threat of persecution in mind, but let us mark well the integral relationship in the writer's mind between these three things—Baptism, faith in the death and resurrection of our Lord, and regeneration to positive Christian virtue. The center of it will be found in the Christian's identity with his Lord.

This sense of identity with the redeeming work of Christ, of being crucified to the old self and of living in the power of the Resurrection, is particularly central in the thought of Paul—"I have been crucified with Christ; it is no longer I who live, but Christ who lives in me; and the life I now live in the flesh I live by faith in the Son of God, who loved me and gave himself for me" (Gal. 2:20). This he says with respect to faith—it is a faith-union in the sacrifice of our Lord—just as later in the same epistle, after reminding his readers that circumcision and uncircumcision can no longer be of any use to them but only faith which works through love, he goes on to declare that "those who belong to Christ Jesus have crucified the flesh with its passions and desires": to live by the Spirit is to walk by the Spirit (Gal. 5:26-27; 5:6).

At the same time the startling thing about Paul is that he speaks in precisely equal terms about Baptism. To the Church at Rome he writes that those who have been baptized into Christ Jesus were baptized into his death. "We were buried therefore by him by baptism into death, so that as Christ was raised from the dead by the glory of the Father, we too might walk in newness of life" (Rom. 6:3-5). The same thought is repeated in the epistle to the Colossians, where he tells the Church that its members have been circumcised with a circumcision not made with hands, and goes on to declare, "You were buried with him in baptism, in which you were also raised with him through faith in the working of God, who raised him from the dead" (Col. 2:11-12). The passage is very important because this is where Paul goes on to speak of the Atonement itself, of the cancelling of "the bond that stood against us," and of God's triumph in our Lord over the principalities and powers (Col. 2:13-15). If Paul speaks of our union in the death and resurrection of Christ by faith in the same way as he speaks about our participation in our Lord's death and resurrection by Baptism, then it is clear that in the mind of Paul faith and Baptism are so closely related as to be virtually indistinguishable. He could not separate them, because if faith was the basic presupposition for Baptism, to be baptized was to demonstrate and to claim the promises of faith.

Paul shows us the center of the Sacrament as that which is at the same time the center of our faith—the mighty act of God in the death and resurrection of Jesus Christ and his gift of new life in his Holy Spirit, the same Holy Spirit that inspired him "to suffer and to die." We are cleansed, we are plunged beneath the flood of the outpoured life of the Son of God that was given for us in pure grace. If "the blood is the life," then in the truest and most reverend sense our sins are "covered" by that blood of the New Covenant, we are immersed in that outpouring of life which went down into death that it might, by fulfilling all righteousness, raise us to its own quality of life eternal. It is worth reminding ourselves that this conception of Baptism is maintained by the eastern Orthodox Churches in the immersion of infants, while the Church of Ethiopia traditionally identifies the water of Baptism with the water which flowed from our Lord's side at the Crucifixion—a direct reference in the Sacrament to the atoning work of Christ.

However, in the atoning act of God we have our part, for even as we willingly take to ourselves the promises guaranteed to us by his deed, so he grants us his Spirit that by his mighty power we become "at one" with him both in sharing his glory and in our willingness to share in this generous outpouring of life and love for the redemption of the world. As our Lord's voluntary action and God's almighty purpose in him were shown to be one at his Baptism, so in our baptism God's act in Christ and our response in the Spirit of Christ should be one. There should be no false opposition between "objective" and "subjective" here.

6. Mode and Meaning

If there has, however, been some consensus among theologians regarding the essential meaning of Baptism and more readiness to assert its biblical relation to the atoning work of Christ, the end result seems to drive them sharply apart on the question of mode. It may be that in certain quarters this question is not as acute as it has been formerly,[27] but wherever there has been an attempt to grapple with the biblical meaning of the Sacrament it has had to be seriously reviewed. This is at least in part due to the fact that the common form of the Sacrament in the sprinkling of infants appears to many serious thinkers to be a wholly inadequate vehicle for a full doctrine of the Sacrament, and as a sacramental act it stands in very pale contrast to the Pauline imagery and the practice of the early Church. In the *Didache*, for example, the churches are directed wherever possible to baptize converts in running water, but if that is impossible for practical reasons, the candidate is at least to have water poured over the head three times "in the name of the Father, and of the Son, and of the Holy Spirit": the action with water is not minimized but is an integral part of the Sacrament. For the same reason, perhaps, it is clear from the official Anglican report, *Baptism Today*, that an appreciable minority of opinion within the Church of England advocates baptismal reform

---

[27] Among the groups that studied "Baptism" in preparation for the Oberlin "Faith and Order" Conference in 1957, it was reported that in America the question of mode was lessening as a point of contention.

in that Church along the lines of believers' Baptism.[28] The most significant attack, however, on the generally accepted position of those who baptize infants has come from the great Reformed theologian, Karl Barth. When Barth's brief monograph, *Die Kirchliche Lehre von der Taufe*, appeared, Oscar Cullman (his colleague and on this matter his most doughty opponent) declared that certainly no more fundamental defense of believers' Baptism had ever appeared, even from the ranks of the important Baptist churches of the Anglo-Saxon world.[29]

The central issue in the modern reassessment of Baptism is the same as it has always been—the place that the faith and personal commitment of the recipient should have in a Sacrament that is admittedly the Sacrament of initiation into the Christian Church. This has become acute with the realization that the presuppositions on which the *Volkskirche* principle was adopted in Europe no longer apply in a secularized western society. Against the traditional view Barth bluntly declares that "Neither by exegesis nor from the nature of the case can it be established that the baptized person can be merely a passive instrument. Rather it may be shown, by exegesis and from the nature of the case, that in this action the baptized is an active partner and that at whatever state of life he may be, plainly no *infans* [infant] can be such a person." [30] Or in another place he declares, "Baptism is in the New Testament in every case the indispensable answer to an unavoidable question by a man who has come to faith. . . . In the sphere of the New Testament one is not brought to baptism; one comes to baptism." [31]

Clearly, this is a central issue around which much of the baptismal controversy revolves, but it is clear from Barth that beyond this we cannot relegate the question of the mode of Baptism to a place of irrelevance since the manner in which Baptism is conducted is so intimately tied up with the meaning of the Sacrament. Barth speaks scathingly of those whose sole concern regarding the validity of the Sacrament seems to be in assuring themselves that at least the head of the candidate has been wetted with real water! [32] The issue goes deep, for fundamentally we must ask whether the Sacrament is to have an

---

[28] Church of England Publications, 1946, pp. 28-29.
[29] Cullman, *Baptism in the N.T.*, p. 8.
[30] E.T. *The Teaching of the Church Regarding Baptism*, p. 41.
[31] *Ibid.*, p. 42.
[32] *Ibid.*, p. 37.

active form that is equal to its doctrinal content. If the grace of God is revealed sacramentally in action, then to curtail the action within the active form—much more to change it—runs the serious risk of obscuring the essential gospel that is at the heart of the Sacrament. This is the real issue in the question of mode.

Historically, Baptists have maintained that only the action of total immersion as it appears to have been practiced in New Testament times is fully adequate to the content of Baptism as it is presented to us by Paul in Rom. 6, and the practice seems to have been revived in the 1640's for this reason. The first of the Baptist Confessions to prescribe this mode of Baptism was the Particular Baptist Confession of 1644, which lays down its principles in this respect very clearly:

> The way and manner of the dispensing of this Ordinance the Scripture holds out to be dipping or plunging the whole body under water; it being a sign, must answer the thing signified, which are these: first, the washing the whole soul in the blood of Christ; secondly, that interest the Saints have in the death, burial, and resurrection; thirdly, together with the confirmation of our faith, that as certainly as the body is buried under water, and riseth again, so certainly shall the bodies of the Saints be raised by the power of Christ, in the day of resurrection, to reign with Christ.[33]

I do not think we should expect these early Baptists to have been more spiritually minded than other Puritans and Separatists of their time, and undoubtedly through their adoption of this particular mode there runs a very strong streak of biblical literalism. On the other hand in contrast to many modern Baptists, we find that the subjective element—"the confirmation of our faith"—is certainly not given the primacy of place in their conception of the Sacrament, but that the whole action is seen by them as a dramatic representation of the believer faced with the complete work of Christ for his salvation. As the late H. Wheeler Robinson, one of the most perceptive of Baptist leaders, has insisted, the Sacrament of Christian Baptism is an acted creed, for by it the members of the Church "are repeatedly brought face to face with the facts of the death and resurrection as the salient

---

[33] Quoted by H. Wheeler Robinson in *Baptist Principles* (Carey Kingsgate, 1925, 4th ed. 1955), p. 65. I acknowledge my debt to J. D. Hughey, Jr., of the Baptist Seminary at Rüschlikon for directing me to this confession and to other Baptist literature on the subject.

articles of their faith—an epitomized 'Apostles' Creed," [34] The mode of Baptism, then, is not simply a question of whether or not it is necessary slavishly to follow the same form of Baptism that appears in the New Testament, but it is whether any other form but the one described in the New Testament can safeguard the essential meaning of the Sacrament or adequately contain the doctrinal implications that the New Testament writers found in it. John Wesley is reputed to have made himself unpopular with the mothers of Georgia when he insisted that their babies should be totally immersed, but in that he may have had better theological than psychological insight!

On the other hand to see the force of these arguments and even to concede as much does not necessarily mean that we can accept the present-day Baptist position "lock, stock and barrel." Cullman, although he may not touch Barth's basic appeal to the New Testament, nevertheless shows that in certain important respects that evidence cuts across modern Baptist assumptions.[35] When we have given full weight to Barth's suggestion that the churches' fidelity to infant Baptism is in large measure due to their tenaciously holding to the *Volkskirche* principle, this still does not explain why Congregationalists and Methodists—churches which grew up in protest to that idea, which have traditionally appealed to the New Testament as the rule of faith and practice—have been equally loath to give up the practice of infant Baptism.[36] If we are honestly to face the dilemma of the Church in the baptism controversy, we must see that all the arguments are not all on one side. We must review what can be said in favor of infant Baptism, reminding ourselves that Jesus Christ himself was received into the covenant of the people of God by an analogous rite of circumcision.

In the first place perhaps one of the most important reasons that have kept Congregationalists and Methodists faithful to the mode that has become traditional has been a very real fear of what is implied in the Anabaptist practice of rebaptizing those who have already undergone a form of Baptism as infants. Karl Barth, while writing in

---

[34] H. Wheeler Robinson, *The Life and Faith of the Baptists* (Kingsgate, 1927; rev. ed. 1946), p. 80.

[35] Cf. *supra*, p. 323.

[36] It should be remembered that although Congregationalists became a kind of national church in Massachusetts and Connecticut, they had already taken a stand on this issue either as a Separatists or as non-conforming Puritans in England.

the most forthright terms in favor of believers' Baptism, has no stomach for "deplorable sectarian re-baptism," for in his view, "no rejection of the order and practice of baptism through the fault of the Church, or through the fault or lack on the part of the candidate, can make the baptism of a person, once it has been performed, ineffective and therefore invalid, or can lead to or justify a call to re-baptism according to a better order and practice." [37] One wishes that he had expanded his views at this point, but presumably he takes his stand on the Einmaligkeit—the "once-for-all-ness"—of that Act of God which Baptism proclaims. Taking the same view, one might wish to push it further and insist that however defective the present practice of the churches may be, to require rebaptism is virtually to believe that the effectiveness of that which the Sacrament represents depends ultimately upon the correct ritual actions of men rather than upon God's act in free grace. This is no excuse for the churches to continue to administer a Sacrament defectively, but ultimately what God declares in his act is of primary importance. Just as this is made effective for us once through the one Act in Christ, so it is sealed to us in time through the ministrations of the one Sacrament. Without developing the point at great length, there is legitimate fear that the rebaptism of those who have been baptized in infancy implies that infant Baptism is invalid. Therefore, the Churches which practise such rebaptism unchurch well over 90 per cent of modern professing Christians and considerably more than that percentage of the baptized Christians of the past. It is the fundamental difference at this point between the Reformers who thought of their work as the Church's reformation and the Anabaptists who implied the re-formation of the Church.

The second, and the positive theological reason for infant Baptism, is to be sought in those New Testament passages that deal with the Atonement. It is concerned with "the free antecedent grace of God" in our redemption, the child's entry into God's covenant of grace which exists for him before his birth, and into the full understanding of which he can only grow by knowledge and faith. Barth remarked upon the curious fact that the Reformers themselves did not make anything of this argument, but whether they did or not, if it is con-

---

[37] Barth, *The Teaching of the Church Regarding Baptism*, p. 35; cf. ibid., pp. 36, 56-58.

sistent with the gospel, it is not to be ignored. It is the plea that what is done in Baptism is done already by God's grace for the child without his knowledge, without his consent, and without his faith. Cullman declares that

> Church Baptism would acquire a fundamentally different character from that of the general baptism accomplished by Jesus at Golgotha, if God's operation were dependent upon the human acts of faith and confession, while in fact the deepest significance of the atonement is precisely that it is accomplished without any kind of co-operation, and even against the will, against the knowledge, against faith of those for whom it is effective.[38]

Although this does not wholly meet the other claims that can be put forward from the New Testament, it *is* a New Testament principle which cannot be declared sacramentally by any means other than by *infant* Baptism. It is the declaration *in action* that God receives the child into the eternal covenant that has been prepared for it. Independent of whether that child ultimately ratifies the covenant by faith or not, independent of whether in the course of time he grows up to be a saint or an infidel, a believer, or a heretic, the Church declares in this act that the Son of God came into the world in great humility, lived, suffered, died, and rose again, and that he did all this in order that *this* little scrap of humanity might have the promise of eternal life.

There is a hymn by the eighteenth-century essayist, Joseph Addison, that describes something of the grace which is here expressed in the Sacrament:

> When all Thy mercies, O my God,
>   My rising soul surveys,
> Transported with the view, I'm lost
>   In wonder, love, and praise.
>
> Unnumbered comforts to my soul
>   Thy tender care bestowed,
> Before my infant heart conceived
>   From whom those comforts flowed.

[38] Cullman, op. cit., pp. 32-33.

"Before my infant heart conceived"—that is why it is done. The words of the late B. L. Manning express the real issue for which those who practice infant Baptism are contending

Baptism is not dedication. In baptism the main thing is not what men do, but what God has done. It a sign that Christ claims all men as His own and that He has redeemed them to a new way of life. That is why we baptize children. We do not baptize them because we or they have faith... We do not baptize them in order to make them children of God... We baptize them because they are already God's... The water of baptism declares that they are already entitled to all God's mercies to men in the passion of Christ.[39]

It is the sign that "God shows his love for us in that while we were yet sinners Christ died for us" (Rom. 5:8), that as the Lord said to Jeremiah in the Old Testament, "Before I formed you in the womb I knew you, and before you were born I consecrated you." Even so we are the people of his choice and sealed in the blood of his Son by a deed. Just as the circumcision of Christ brought him into the old covenant of the people of God, a covenant which in his Baptism he took up voluntarily by becoming the Servant of the Lord and the single Representative of the New Israel of God, so in Baptism God's covenant and call are sealed to the child.

If this is the main theological ground for the Baptism of infants, it explains to some extent why the practice is held so tenaciously. It involves a gospel principle which we are reluctant to give up. It has been pointed out that there are difficulties and dangers in the position,[40] and it is difficult to see how one can apply a rigid theory of baptismal regeneration when the basis of Baptism has been changed—albeit for New Testament reasons—from the ground on which Baptism was granted in the New Testament. Certainly it is hard to see how that regeneration, carrying with it the blessing of the Holy Spirit, can become operative until faith is consciously accepted by the child. The need for the church which practices infant Baptism to see that confirmation is a serious matter of *faith* and not a simple matter of matriculation into the communicant membership upon assent to a

---

[39] B. L. Manning, *Why Not Abandon the Church?* (London: Independent Press), p. 47. Cited in *A Book of Public Worship*, p. xvii.

[40] Barth, *op. cit.*, p. 52.

minimum of instruction can hardly be emphasized too strongly. As Barth says, it "cries aloud."

7. The Exclusive Modes

If we accept the logic of the last section we appear to be completely at an impasse, because although it can be shown that the two modes emphasize complementary aspects of the gospel, in the present practice of the churches they must be mutually exclusive. The churches cannot, therefore, get beyond this point unless they are frankly willing to recognize the dilemma and to re-examine the Sacrament with a view to regaining the wholeness of its theological meaning rather than to justify one or the other aspect of it. In particular Christians must recognize the mutual exclusiveness of the different modes, which precludes a complete understanding of the Sacrament to us all because of the very incompleteness of our own sacramental experience.

At the moment there is a blank before the eyes of the paedo-baptist churches which prevents them from seeing that in their present mode a tremendously important area of sacramental experience has been lost to them, and that it is principally in the significant area where the New Testament view of Baptism brings home the grace of God to the believer in terms of the cost of his discipleship—"Ye shall indeed drink of my cup, and be baptized with the baptism with which I am baptized." It is worth noting that the Roman Catholic Church, for all those features of its sacramental doctrine that seem to cut across the New Testament view, still holds the belief that side-by-side with normal churchly Baptism, and equally valid, there can exist the true Baptism of blood in martyrdom. The question this raises is whether the identity of the believer with Christ is something to be made explicit only for the few who are martyred, or whether it should be found at the center of the Baptism of every member of the Church. There is something like a conspiracy of blindness in the way in which the theologians in all confessions who are the most anxious to understand and develop the meaning of the Sacraments will take the sacramental ideas of Paul (which implied conversion, the significant imagery of believers' Baptism and faith-union with Christ) and apply them without any further comment to the practice of infant Baptism where none of these most vitally important factors are in the least operative. Indeed, Cullman's identification of Baptism with the Cross of Christ almost makes nonsense of the gospel if it is joined sacramentally to an act in which the identity of the believer in that Cross by faith is not made explicit. Too often the jump is quite easily and casually made from the Pauline language about dying and rising with Christ (in Rom. 6) where personal commitment is implied throughout, and the case of the infant who is baptized by sprinkling and who owes his Baptism to the faith or whim of his parents or more often to the accident of his birth in a "Christian" country where social convention expects it. There is something vaguely dishonest about this cavalier treatment of the New Testament.

On the other hand Baptist writers often too easily assume that because they have almost a monopoly of the New Testament evidence that they have necessarily a monopoly of the truth about the Sacrament. Often we have the uncomfortable impression that the actual letter of the New Testament is being kept at the expense of the Spirit, and that in the demand for New Testament norms there is not so much a concern to find the sacramental form that will do justice to New Testament theology, as a return to the kind of biblicism that precludes all theological wrestling and often all thought. Furthermore, those who should have been the highest of high churchmen with regard to this Sacrament have often gloried in their willingness to deny it any sacramental content, so that one has often been tempted to say, "if it means only this much, why bother?" An over-concentration on the manward and subjective aspects of Baptism has so often justified the strictures that have been leveled against Baptists, and they have too often demonstrated the need of that for which H. Wheeler Robinson called in his time—an "Oxford Movement" of their own order. Wheeler Robinson was not afraid to press for a new understanding of baptismal grace among Baptists, but he understood the "blind spots" of his own confessionalists. "The reaction from a false doctrine of divine grace in baptism has made them suspicious even of the genuine sacramentarianism of the New Testament," and he added the comment, "We have been saying *believers'* baptism so emphatically that we have failed, or at least are failing now, to say with anything like equal emphasis, believers' *baptism*, i.e., the entrance of believers into a life of supernatural powers." [41]

[41] *The Life and Faith of the Baptists*, p. 146.

When one has passed one's criticism of both sides in the controversy, the root problem remains that of the mutual exclusivity of the two modes. If I am baptized as a baby, then unless I become a Baptist as a convert, I am inevitably denied the right of affirming God's action for me by going through the waters of Baptism as a believer. It cannot be my experience sacramentally, and nothing but that sacramental act can give it to me. On the other hand if my parents refuse to have me baptized as an infant in order to give me the right of a believer's Baptism, then within modern western society that Sacrament will almost inevitably be concentrated upon personal witness and my individual faith rather than upon God's prevenient grace and mercy. This is particularly true of children born into Christian homes, for the sense of miraculous election which converts in the early Church must have had, and which may be experienced by a modern convert from paganism, cannot be present in the same measure for a young person whose whole heredity and environment have been Christian, and whose entry into the Church has progressed along the normal lines of the Christianized churchgoing society into which he was born. It will be difficult for such a person on reaching years of decision not to make his decision to join a particular church very much as he exercises his rights as a citizen to join a political party. If infant Baptism in western society has tended to become a superstitious or meaningless rite, believers' Baptism in the same society emphasizes the voluntary element to an alarming degree. Infant Baptism in such a society can have real evangelical content if the churches are alive to their responsibilties, for at the time of confirmation I can by faith consciously take hold of that which I am now able to realize was done for me as an act of unasked, unlimited, and unmerited grace. But this understanding of the gospel can be mediated sacramentally only if the individual has been baptized before he was ever conscious of what was done.

This then is the dilemma. The modes are mutually exclusive, and by the very nature of the case we are always on "the other side" of the baptismal controversy. Neither side can really understand the other because it has not shared the same sacramental experience, and both sides are suspicious of each other because although we may be prepared to risk much for the cause of ecumenism, we dare not risk that which gets so close to that which we have experienced in Christ.

At the same time if we are prepared to look at both sides objectively and assess their positive content, we find that they are expressing sacramentally complementary emphases in the Gospel. Infant "dedication" in Baptist churches and "Confirmation" or some similar rite in paedo-baptist churches are both a recognition of this, although neither of the supplementary expedients we have adopted can take the place of that which should be done by water and the Spirit. To realize the fullness of its faith within this Sacrament, it seems as if the Church needs both rites.

8. Toward Sacramental Fullness in Jesus Christ

Instead of arguing from either the Church of the New Testament or from church tradition we should perhaps do better to go back to the example of the life of our Lord himself, for we can explain away neither his circumcision nor his Baptism by John in Jordan. Strictly speaking neither was necessary either to incorporate Jesus into God's People or to symbolize the acceptance of his messianic task. Yet although of all men born he might most justifiably have excused himself from "mere" rites, he underwent both. By Baptism he did not deny his circumcision—he accepted it. The circumcision of Jesus pointed backward to God's choice of a people for himself, to the deliverance at the Red Sea and to the selection of the saving remnant. It pointed forward to the time when our Lord would stand upon the banks of Jordan and consciously accept the implications of a greater Baptism that only he could undergo. The Baptism pointed backward to the meaning of the circumcision, and it cast its image forward to Calvary and beyond. But in undertaking this at the hands of John our Lord revealed that Baptism, as he understood it, has at its heart not only fulfillment by the Cross but also acceptance of the Cross. For us, then, there can be no full comprehension of its meaning—indeed, no real salvation—without the willingness in this act to take up our own cross and follow him. "If I do not wash you, you have no part in me" (John 13:8). The whole point of this rebuke to Peter on the night of our Lord's betrayal was that Peter needed to learn the very lesson of humility that Jesus was giving him at that moment, for his remark to Jesus, "You shall never wash my feet," demonstrated a subtle sense of pride. If Peter could not accept the humility in our Lord's action, he would never understand the nature of the royal service offered by his Master, and if he mistook the meaning of that, how could he be expected to follow? In our interpretation of the incident we quite rightly put the accent upon Christ's action—"If *I* do not wash you." In the shadow of the Cross that is right, but we must see equally in this rebuke and in the whole of the incident of the feet washing something of the nature of what being "washed" meant for the disciples. In the light of that example they were not likely to misunderstand the ethical overtones—to be washed by him was certainly to be made clean by his own act on the Cross, but it was also to be made *clean* with the same kind of cleanness with which he appeared before God and men: "I have given you an example, that you also should do as I have done to you" (John 13:15). Commitment with its ethical implications cannot be charmed out of the gospel of salvation in favor of any formal acceptance of the Church's requirements, whether such compliance is conceived as a ritual requirement in a Sacrament or as an intellectual requirement in the formal demand for "faith." To be a Christian means to be committed to Christ, and that in turn means to be committed to his Cross. There is no escape from what the gospel means, for it is written into the New Testament meaning of both faith and Sacrament.[42]

At the same time the very consciousness that we cannot walk this path alone forces us to claim the promise of Pentecost. The gift of the Spirit is obviously related to our Lord's Baptism, although we should notice that it was prefigured at the Circumcision in the joyful recognition by Simeon and Anna, who were themselves in possession of the Spirit (Luke 2:25, 36). Nevertheless, we might ask when the Holy Spirit was given to Jesus. Are we to assume from his Baptism that the Spirit was not with him when he insisted on doing his Father's business at Jerusalem at the age of twelve, or during the thirty years at Nazareth that he grew in favor with God and man? Obviously not;

---

[42] It is clear that πίστις—faith—undergoes a change between the time of the Pauline epistles and the epistle of James. I would maintain that in the greater part of the New Testament, however, and particularly in the writings of Paul and the Evangelists, "faith" means not only assent to the historical veracity of the gospel but the readiness to trust oneself in life and death to that Truth. This is the kind of meaning which gave content to the early baptismal statement "Jesus is Lord." As a creedal statement (i.e., as a statement of "the Faith") it left a great deal unsaid, but as a statement of *faith* (i.e., of personal trust) it said all that could be said, for it implied the commitment of the whole person to Jesus Christ.

and yet at the Baptism the Holy Spirit came upon him in a special way, in a way that had particular reference to the Messianic and priestly call that he *in that* act had accepted. The vocation was present at the very beginning of his life, as all those who surround the scene of the Nativity recognized, but now at the Baptism his vocation becomes sacramentally entered, and to meet the need of this hour the Holy Spirit (who had also been present from the first) is sacramentally given. The importance of this for us is that if all these aspects of the Circumcision and Baptism of our Lord are to be expressed sacramentally within the Church, it means that only a sacramental action that is analogous to *both* modes of Baptism as they are practiced at the present can carry the fullness of meaning that should be incorporated into the one Sacrament of Baptism.

In what follows in this chapter I am conscious that the suggestions offered may go further than theological prudence would seem to dictate. Yet I believe that it is only by a readiness to look again at the full meaning of Baptism in the New Testament that we shall be properly equipped to face the ecumenical problems that have arisen in connection with this Sacrament. It carries with it the corollary that perhaps only in readiness to expose themselves in a radical and honest reassessment will theologians begin to contribute seriously to that aspect of the problem. Therefore, what follows should be accepted not as evincing any desire to be "radical" for its own sake, still less as offering any blueprint of a solution, but as a fresh attempt to think through the ecumenical problem of Baptism not from the old premises but from the point where we ask what is the positive biblical content that this Sacrament ought to carry within the Christian Church.

Baptism represents to us the work of God for our salvation, which was prepared for us before we had ever heard the Gospel and responded to it. It is a salvation into which we are called but which we need to take to ourselves in such a way that we understand it is a promise for us only as humbly and in faith we identify ourselves with our Lord's sacrifice: the only Baptism in the Church is a Baptism to witness, to *marturia*. Indeed, one of the present day challenges that should give us cause to question our normal ecclesiastical practice is the realization that for the ordinary faithful member of the Church, Baptism should have far more the meaning of "ordination" into the priesthood of all believers.[43] Perhaps as our recognition of the "laity" as the People of God grows deeper, the Church may begin to recognize ordination and the confirmation of Baptism rather as parallel orders within its ministry than as grades in a hierarchical progression. In most churches Baptism and confirmation are regarded as two separate acts. Whereas if we believe that Baptism should bring together in a sacramental form all the wealth of meaning that should be associated with an individual's entry into the Church, Baptism and confirmation should be regarded as one Sacrament and essentially one act. When we see an infant baptized and when we see the same child finally grow up to accept his Christian vocation as a believer in a public confession of faith, we see two different aspects of one and the same event: it is one Sacrament completed in two parts—two actions in time but one action in eternity. We are usually too obsessed with the time factor, which cannot be significant to God at all. Infant Baptism needs a form of confirmation which is integral to the Sacrament of Baptism itself, and which is not a sort of optional extra for those who want to demonstrate their active identification with the fellowship of the Church. Can the Body of Christ claim as full members those who (although baptized) have no intention to be his disciples, who may in fact be apostates from the Baptism they have undergone as infants? True, Christ and the Church have a particular claim upon them to become members by reason of their Baptism, just as our Lord as Messiah had a claim upon the whole Jewish nation by reason of its circumcision and commitment to the Law. But such a deed performed in infancy and followed by no subsequent act of volition can no more make a baptized individual into a disciple of Jesus Christ than circumcision could make the Jew a member of the New Israel in Christ. One may "belong" to the Church in the sense that by the act of Baptism in infancy the Church has set Christ's claim and promise upon the individual; one may "belong" to Christ in the sense that he died to save all men, but one cannot belong to him in the sense of being "in Christ" and of being in his Body without some measure of active faith. Let the churches be clear when they speak of "members" whether they mean those who happen to have been baptized by them in infancy or those who have made some sign of their

---

[43] A concept which is becoming increasingly prominent in the Studies of the Department of the Laity of the World Council of Churches.

discipleship. For the sake of honesty let us not be afraid of making this distinction, and let those who befog the issue by insisting that the New Testament knows nothing of any distinction between a "visible" and "invisible" Church (which is true) reflect upon the fact that the New Testament knows nothing of any infant Baptism (which is equally true). To try to identify the Visible Church (i.e., the only Church known to the New Testament) with those who have been baptized on the basis of a Baptism so radically different from that of the New Testament indicates mental and spiritual lacunae of very serious proportions.

There is a psychological aspect of the problem here which is too often disregarded. Baptism and membership of the Church is made too easy when it demands nothing on the part of the recipient. Perhaps there is no psychological need as deep in the western world as the need for commitment, the desire to find something *worth* the sacrifice of life and heart. One of the most significant of the "angry young men" who have written in Britain since the war, wrote recently that "to reject or avoid commitment is a disease which runs through English society like a rust in wheat." [44] Bonhoeffer indicated much the same attitude in the German society for which he wrote in *The Cost of Discipleship* and illustrated it in the popular demand for "easy grace." One of the most pathetic needs of the western democracies in the face of totalitarian ideologies is simply the need to be committed. I am not arguing for just any kind of commitment—that may be good enough for political purposes—but I am arguing for commitment to Christ within his Church. The question then is whether the Church should pander to the general cowardice or make its sacramental demands upon the believers truly symbolic of the total commitment that Christ makes upon us.

This raises the important questions of the nature and mode of baptismal confirmation—if the Baptism that an individual has undergone as an infant is to be confirmed, should it be confirmed in the easiest, the least demanding way, or should it be confirmed in an action which conveys the terms of the Baptism? At this point, the point of commitment, the New Testament meaning of membership in the Church should surely be conveyed sacramentally by going down one-

---

[44] Leslie Paul, author of *The Angry Young Man*, writing in *The Christian Newsletter*, Oct., 1957, p. 17.

self into the waters and experiencing what it means as a baptized convert to be buried with Christ and raised with him into newness of life. A similar case could be made out for actualizing the sacramental gift of the Holy Spirit by the Laying on of Hands. Are our sacramental actions *big* enough to proclaim the meaning of Baptism? This is not a question whether or not the Holy Spirit has already been active in the believer before the action—the question is much more improper and irrelevant than to ask whether a young man loved his fiancée before he gave her the engagement ring—but it is a question of the means that are adequate to proclaim the gospel, what action best conveys this sacramental grace. Those who question the need of any such action on the ground that the Holy Spirit is always available to the believer might ask why the early Church found any need for it. They might also ask themselves why the Spirit came to Jesus sacramentally at the Baptism when that Holy Spirit was already so clearly his. In so many things we are tempted to use our "faith" in Jesus and our liberty in the gospel to assert our freedom from discipleship and to justify a fundamental unwillingness to follow him in humility. If the early Church discovered that the gift of the Holy Spirit was conveyed sacramentally by the Laying on of Hands, we should ask whether in discarding the form we have lost something of the grace.

What we are concerned with here is not with what makes the confirmation of Baptism valid or invalid—obviously a church may have all the forms and still miss the meaning—but whether the forms we do have are adequate to convey sacramentally the proclamation of the gospel in its wholeness. If we go back to the New Testament actions, it is not because these are necessarily the only forms for the Church, but because the New Testament must clearly be the norm for the Church. If the New Testament *meaning* of baptism is to be retained, the sacramental action of the Church today must at least be as adequate to that meaning as the sacramental action within the New Testament itself. Our Lord used water, bread, and wine for these purposes and used them in a certain way. We have to ask whether the way in which we use these chosen vehicles of grace can convey the full and proper meaning of his act.

Only by striving to achieve fullness in the Sacrament of Baptism can the Church hope to surmount the impasse of the present situation and find unity. I plead for a form of baptismal confirmation that will fully bring home the meaning of Baptism. We must ask the churches to put the question to themselves—how much of the gospel have they mortgaged in their readiness to give up the symbolism of immersion? I would ask the churches to consider a view of the Sacrament that would include the "baptism" of infants followed by confirmation of believers by immersion, not as constituting two Baptisms, still less as a form of anabaptism, but as constituting one act, one sacrament in time—the Sacrament of Baptism by water and the Spirit. The Church should comprehend both actions as complementary halves of the same Sacrament. This would presuppose, of course, that both those who have been "baptized" as infants and those who have not would undergo the same act in public confession of their faith, but that whereas in the case of the former the action would be acknowledged by the Church in the words of confirmation, in the case of the latter it would be solemnized as believer's Baptism. In both cases, however, the ratification of baptismal vows would be undertaken in the New Testament act of immersion as being the action which carries within it the fulness of what the Sacrament should mean to the believer. And following upon this action of personal commitment in faith, it would seem that the sacramental gift of the Holy Spirit by the Laying on of Hands and the reception of the fully baptized member at the Sacrament of the Lord's Supper would be the logical churchly consequences. "Here we offer and present unto Thee ourselves, our souls and our bodies, to be a reasonable, holy and living sacrifice." The two Sacraments point toward each other as they both express the same living gospel, and they meet at the point of God's act in Christ and our commitment to him.

Let us, however, beware of our limitations. Any sacramental reform, however ritually adequate or theologically satisfying, cannot take the place of the gospel itself and will turn sour if it is used as a new measurement of exclusivity and orthodoxy, for the gospel is always more generous than either our theologies or the ecclesiastical forms in which we seek to express them. If such reform is desirable, it is not from any literal (i.e., ritual) attitude toward the sacramental forms employed in New Testament times, but because the Sacraments of the Church should have forms adequate to their meaning if they are to proclaim the gospel of Jesus Christ. The suggestions above are put forward in order simply to call into question in as clear a way as possible our ecclesiastical prejudices about the Sacrament and our conventional methods of approaching the baptismal controversy. They are offered in the conviction that it is only as we think of winning back for the churches the wholeness of Baptism's meaning that we shall begin to surmount the ecumenical impasse of the two mutually exclusive modes that divide the churches at present. Until that time we are all the poorer; and perhaps there are none so poor as those who argue, with the church at Laodicea, that they are rich and have need of nothing.

CHAPTER XI

The Lord's Supper

1. The Bread of Life

WE HAVE ARRIVED AT THE LORD'S SUPPER, BUT WHO IS ADEQUATE TO write about it? No writer can plumb the depths or ascend the heights of the Sacrament that stands at the center of Christian worship. All our deepest insights and most enlightened perceptions are but flashes from the surface of its meaning. One is aware of so much more that should have been said. What is offered in these pages is offered with the consciousness that we have presented only certain limited aspects of the Sacrament, and if different insights have been granted to other confessions, this is a matter not for the envy that would disparage but for the envy that would "covet earnestly the best gifts." In this, as in so many things, we are often nearer the truth in what we assert than in what we deny.

I start from what some people will regard as a rather curious place. Robert Browne's little book, *A Booke which sheweth the Life and Manners of all true Christians*, is one of the important trilogy that was published from his exile at Middleburgh in 1582, in which the principles of the "gathered church" were first presented in a systematic form to the modern world. Those who know anything of the subsequent history of English Separatism, or of the churches which have taken a good deal of their doctrine of the Church from Browne, would hardly expect to find a very high doctrine of Sacraments, and yet a comparison of *A Booke which sheweth* with the views of the author's spiritual descendants shows how far they have descended: "The Lord's Supper," declared Browne, "is a Sacrament or mark of the apparent Church, sealing unto us by the breaking and eating of bread and drinking the Cup in one holy communion, and by the word accordingly preached, that we are happily redeemed by the breaking of the body and shedding of the blood of Christ Jesus, and we thereby grow into one body, and church, in one communion of graces, whereof Christ is the head, to keep and seek agreement under one law and government in all thankfulness and holy obedience." [1] To Browne the Sacrament of the Lord's Supper was certainly not a dispensable rite but was an essential mark of the Church. Moreover, in this view it had a clear and essential relationship both to the preaching of God's Word and to the life and discipline of the Church. The most significant aspect of this passage, however, is the unmistakable relationship which the writer maintains between the action within the Sacrament and the action of Christ in our redemption. The Supper, "by the breaking and eating of bread and drinking the Cup," seals to us the fact that "we are happily redeemed by the breaking of the body and shedding of the blood of Christ Jesus."

This is the position which we have reached. Baptism and the Lord's Supper bring to us sacramentally in deeds God's action in Christ for our redemption. In the words of Neville Clark both sacraments are extensions of the Atonement: "both are concerned with incorporation into Christ, with death and resurrection; both are made powerful by the operation of the Holy Spirit; both stand under the sign of the cross; both are sacraments of inaugurated eschatology." [2] In the sacraments the Risen Christ takes us to the center of his redeeming act and reveals its meaning in the action of sacred drama. As Robert Browne went on to say about the Lord's Supper, "The spiritual use and feeding of the body and blood of Christ, is an applying of his whole work of our redemption by that outward sign, to feel effectually the remedy of our miseries by that partaking and growing together in one body of Christ and spiritual communion." [3] Within the Sacrament the meaning of our salvation is mediated by Christ in and through the corporate action of the Church.

In this mediation the Eucharist, or Lord's Supper, has a special place by reason of its place at the center of the Church's worship. Baptism has particular reference to the individual in one decisive and unrepeatable act of God's grace, but the Lord's Supper is a repeated and continual Sacrament of grace to us at the heart of the congregation's corporate worship, and as Canon O. C. Quick reminds us, its

---

[1] Robert Browne, *A Booke which sheweth the Life and Manners of all true Christians*, sec. 59. Cf. secs. 59-63.
[2] Neville Clark, op. cit., p. 83.
[3] Browne, op. cit., sec. 62.

virtue is in its repetition.[4] Where it has not had the central place that is its due, the worship and even the theology of churches have suffered, as we have already admitted. But we have also recognized that the growing understanding of the Atonement's central place in biblical theology has led us to see the connection of this doctrine with the Sacraments in the New Testament. It forces us to take seriously the place of the Lord's Supper in the life of the early Church.

The Bible shows us that the Eucharist speaks to us of God's action in redemption. Whichever account of the Last Supper is preferred, nothing can take from it the importance that it obviously had both for the evangelists and for Paul in the story of our Lord's ministry, and nothing can rob it of its significance as the Last Supper of our Lord. The words of the Institution may be turned into a beautiful allegory if they are to be seen only in the light of what our Lord said about the Bread of Life in the sixth chapter of John's Gospel, and if that could be done without any reference to the crucifixion. But the Institution cannot be considered independently of the crucifixion, for that which gives the Supper its primary significance is its intimate relation to the death and resurrection of our Lord. Just as we have to see the reference to the "Baptism" with which our Lord said he would be baptized in the light of the sacrifice in his passion and death, so also we must see the reference to the "cup" which he said he would have to drink in the light of that cup which he took in the Upper Room, and with the illuminating reflection within it of the cup which a few hours later in the garden he prayed with tears that he might be allowed to forgo.

To see the same truth with regard to the bread which he broke at the Last Supper—it is not the Bread of Life discourse in John 6 which interprets his breaking the bread at the Supper, but rather the revelation of "the breaking of the body" upon the cross which throws its light back and illumines his words and actions both at the Supper and in the discourse in the sixth chapter of John's Gospel. This is indicated in the Bread of Life discourse itself. Although it arose directly out of the miracle of the feeding of the multitude—which may clearly be interpreted sacramentally—it was not in the first instance sacramental but ethical, or rather it was sacramental only because it was primarily concerned with the ethics of his complete and perfect sac-

[4] O. C. Quick, *The Christian Sacraments*, p. 186.

rifice. Behind the miracle and behind all the subsequent discussion with those who sought him at Capernaum, there was the most pointed contrast between the materialistic greed of those who simply wanted him to provide them with another free meal and the meaning of his own life. It was the issue of the first temptation over again.

> Truly, truly, I say to you, he who believes has eternal life. I am the bread of life. Your fathers ate the manna in the wilderness, and they died. This is the bread which comes down from heaven, that a man may eat of it and not die. I am the living bread which came down from heaven; if any one eats of this bread, he will live for ever; and the bread which I shall give for the life of the world is my flesh.

The Jews then disputed among themselves, saying, "How can this man give us his flesh to eat?" So Jesus said to them:

> Truly, truly, I say unto you, unless you eat the flesh of the Son of man and drink his blood, you have no life in you; he who eats my flesh and drinks my blood has eternal life, and I will raise him up at the last day. For my flesh is food indeed, and my blood is drink indeed. He who eats my flesh and drinks my blood abides in me, and I in him. As the living Father sent me, and I live because of the Father, so he who eats me will live because of me. This is the bread which came down from heaven, not such as the fathers ate and died; he who eats this bread will live for ever. (John 6:52-58, R.S.V.)

To eat his flesh and drink his blood was not to be thought of materialistically or ritualistically, for the miraculous benefits it conveyed were not to be conceived as an end in themselves—to eat and drink of him was directed solely toward the attainment of eternal life. And eternal life has a clear ethical content in the Gospels: it would have been granted to the rich young ruler if he had been prepared to accept the sacrifice that our Lord demanded (Matt. 19:16; Mark 10:17; Luke 18:18); it was the basic desire of the lawyer who asked to be told who his neighbor was, and to whom in reply Jesus told the story of the Good Samaritan (Luke 10:25); it was the promised reward of the disciples who had left everything to follow him (Mark 10:30). More particularly in the Fourth Gospel eternal life was related in a very special way to our Lord's hour of his "glory," and it was in full view of his approaching death that he declared, "He who loves his life loses it, and he who hates his life in this world will keep it for eternal life" (John 12:25). In all these instances the path to eternal life is sacrifice, and it is a sacrifice which is above all things ethical in the demand of an absolute denial of self. This is what the life of Jesus supremely made manifest before men. It was ethical in the sense that it actualized the Law at a level that had never before been seen. The cross revealed a paradox, for on the one hand it carried this ethical standard to its highest point of achievement, and on the other hand it miraculously opened the way whereby men could follow. Whatever else our Lord's words about eating his flesh and drinking his blood must mean, they must mean this: it is the cross and the ethic of the cross that ultimately interpret the discourse on the Bread of Life, and if it can be interpreted sacramentally, it is to be interpreted sacramentally only through the cross.

To Jesus himself the incentive for his own life of sacrifice was sufficiently clear, for what the eating of his flesh and the drinking of his blood would mean to others, the perfect obedience that he could give to his Father meant to him. O. C. Quick gives us the salutary reminder that when it comes to the question of ultimate priority, "the glory of God must always be placed before the edification, or even the redemption, of man." [5] Not that we should imagine any false separation between God's glory and man's redemption in the life of our Lord, for we cannot doubt that for Jesus Christ both were caught up into God's almighty purpose within his own life and death. Nevertheless, the final goal of our Lord's life was the glory of his Father: "I have food to eat of which you do not know. . . . My food is to do the will of him who sent me, and to accomplish his work" (John 4:32, 34). What the "Bread of Life" is to man, the will of the Father was to him. Yet from first to last the will of God for Jesus Christ was to redeem fallen humanity, and this involved a life of sacrifice over which there was always the shadow of a cross. To eat of his flesh and to drink of his blood cannot mean less than to participate in this.

These ideas find some of their most pointed expression in John's Gospel. The evangelist does not supplement the synoptists with a variety of fresh incidents from the life of Jesus with a view to starting

---

[5] *Ibid.*, p. 197.

new church traditions (the feet washing incident at the Last Supper may be an exception), but he directs his energies toward helping his readers to understand the inner meaning of our Lord's life and death. Whether it is in the Bread of Life Discourse, the raising of Lazarus, or in the very great proportion of material that he devotes to the last week of our Lord's life (chapters twelve to twenty-one), one is conscious that the events of the Passion, Crucifixion, and Resurrection offer the key to all the evangelist is saying. If full value is given to the place which the Passion and the events leading up to the Passion occupy in the gospel, it is difficult to agree with the suggestion that the cross and the historic element play a less significant part in John than in Paul.[6] It may be that the events are overlaid by the themes of the discourses, but the Gospel as a whole is clearly centered in an interpretation of the life and mission of Jesus Christ by a disciple who stood on the other side of the cross and resurrection, and who sees everything that Jesus said and did in the light of those climactic events.

2. Prefigured Sacraments in Paul

A Protestant is not likely to miss the evangelical place of faith in the writings of Paul but is more likely to disregard his sacramental and ethical emphases. But as we have already seen, profession of the Christian Faith had very definite sacramental associations in the mind of the apostle. He could hardly have written as he did about the abrogation of circumcision and the Jewish ritual by grace if circumcision and the forms of the ancient religion had not formerly meant a great deal to him. His words must be read not as those of one who was indifferent to the ritual of the Law against which he argued, but as one who had cared intensely. They are testimony not to indifference but to the intensity and reality of his conversion.

He seems to have seen all Hebrew religion as under the prefigured images of Baptism and the Lord's Supper. "I want you to know, brethren," he writes to the Corinthians, "that our fathers were all under the cloud, and all passed through the sea, and all were baptized into Moses in the cloud and in the sea, and all ate the same supernatural food and all drank the same supernatural drink. For they drank from the supernatural Rock which followed them, and the Rock

---

[6] Yngve Brilioth, *Eucharistic Faith and Practice, Evangelical and Catholic* (S.P.C.K., 1930), E.T. by A. G. Hebert, S.S.M., p. 35.

was Christ." (I Cor. 10:1-4, R.S.V.) We are at once struck by the sacramental way in which Paul interprets the life of Israel in the wilderness and by the fact that he obviously has Christian Baptism and the Eucharist in mind. Perhaps the most immediately impressive evidence to his high sacramental doctrine is that he seems to equate the cloud (the Spirit?) and the passage of the Red Sea (water?) with Baptism "into Moses." There is sufficient evidence in the Old Testament to show that the deliverance at the Red Sea was regarded by the Israelites as *the* great act of redemption which made them God's people, and here Paul appears to be equating that event not with *faith* in the cross and resurrection but with *Baptism* into the cross and resurrection.[7] Similarly with regard to the Eucharist, there is the reference to "supernatural" food (the manna), and it is clear from the parallelism of the passage that if Paul thought this about the manna of the wilderness, he thought in similar terms of the bread of the Eucharist. The wine of the Lord's Supper is clearly identified with the water that flowed from the rock in the desert, and Paul bluntly says that the Rock from which it flowed was Christ. We may try to explain away the images by saying that he meant them in only a figurative and mystical sense, but can we be so sure? Would that be true to the thought and temper of an apostle who had been so dramatically converted from Judaism, and who found types and figures for Christ all through the Old Testament?

On the other hand Paul's apparent sacramentalism is not the whole story, for although he shows that the Israelites were held within the sanctity of these Old Testament "sacraments," "nevertheless," he says, "with most of them God was not pleased; for they were overthrown in the wilderness" (I Cor. 10:5). Immediately he goes on to tell the church at Corinth that these events were warnings for them all not to desire the same evil things that the Israelites did. He warns the members of the church not to be idolators, or to be immoral, or to put God to the test, or to be grumblers like the Children of Israel, for the implication is that God will punish them as he punished the

---

[7] Cf. Ps. 106. Reflection, of course, will reveal that the deliverance at the Red Sea confirmed the Israelites as the People of God. They had already been the chosen people for a very long time, although they had not known it, and they themselves had proved their choice by following Moses out of Egypt. All this was recognized in the folk lore of the nation in the stories of the patriarchs; nevertheless, it is clear that the Hebrews regarded the deliverance at the Red Sea as the "crucial" deliverance of their nation.

Israelites. Sacraments do not dispense with the ethics that come from faith, and to be under sacramental grace is not to be made immune from punishment and even rejection by God. In the thought of Paul judgment is but the obverse side of grace, and the greater the gift of sacramental grace, the greater is the judgment of the Sacraments upon those who ignore or abuse them. This means that the grace of the Sacraments has a direct reference to the way in which Christians should live: it confirms and strengthens, or *judges*, the ethic of the disciple, it does not supplant it. Just as the Bread of Life discourse has a clear ethical reference, so the parallelism which Paul uses here emphasizes the ethical nature of our calling as God's people.

We should remember that throughout this chapter (I Cor. 10) Paul is taking up the practical moral question that had been raised in chapter eight, whether Christians ought to eat meat which had been offered to idols in the temples. His teaching about the Lord's Supper is actually incidental to his main theme, and perhaps for that reason it carries more weight. He says that the illustration of Israel's failure ought to make Christians the more careful. He continues:

> Therefore my beloved, shun the worship of idols. I speak as to sensible men; judge for yourselves what I say. The cup of blessing which we bless, is it not a participation in the blood of Christ? The bread which we break, is it not a participation in the body of Christ? Because there is one loaf, we who are many are one body, for we all partake of the same loaf. Consider the practice of Israel; are not those who eat the sacrifices partners in the altar? What do I imply then? That the food offered to idols is anything, or that an idol is anything? No, I imply that what pagans sacrifice they offer to demons and not to God. I do not want you to be partners with demons. You cannot drink the cup of the Lord and the cup of demons. You cannot partake of the table of the Lord and the table of demons.
> (I Cor. 10:14-21.)

Again we find the sacramental emphasis, for to eat the bread and drink the cup of the Lord's Supper is to participate in the body and blood of Christ in such a way as to become partners with Christ. If one takes the whole context in which Paul is writing, it seems that behind his thought is the idea of the intimate and integral partnership between husband and wife as the kind of relationship that exists between the god and the worshiper. The practical moral problems with which the apostle deals in this epistle and the sacramental understanding which he had of the human body have a direct relationship to what he says about the Christian sacraments (cf. I Cor. 6:12-20; 7:1-15). This kind of union which exists in marriage illustrates the closeness and intimacy of the spiritual union between Christ and the Church, particularly in the Communion of the Lord's Supper.

In the eleventh chapter this thought is maintained when he discusses the way in which the members of the church at Corinth profaned the Eucharist by their unseemly behavior, and he gives us the words of the Institution of the Lord's Supper. It is perhaps worth noting in passing that this appears to be one of the two traditions within the life of the infant Church which are so crucial to its faith that the apostle does not trust his own words but repeats the evidence in the verbal form in which he had received it (cf. I Cor. 11:23; 15:1-3 ff.). We must look at the actual words of the Institution in more detail later, but at this point we should notice the observation that Paul adds to his account of the Supper. Whoever eats the bread or drinks the cup in an unworthy manner is, in his view, guilty of profaning the body and blood of the Lord, and for this reason "Let a man examine himself, and so eat of the bread and drink of the cup. For any one who eats and drinks without discerning the body eats and drinks judgment upon himself." (I Cor. 11:28-29.) Then he makes the curious comment, "That is why many of you are weak and ill, and some have died. But if we judged ourselves truly, we should not be judged." (I Cor. 11:30-31.) It suggests that Paul's sacramentalism went far enough for him to believe that the Eucharist carried within it a miraculous power strong enough to destroy those who abused it. To the apostle grace always became judgment in very concrete and even material ways for the spiritually undiscerning (cf. Acts 12:4-12). At the same time we have to recognize that the reason for this judgment existed not so much in the disregard of a required ritual but in the flagrant abuse of elementary Christian moral standards. The basis of these standards, as in other areas of life and action, was no longer in the Law but in the grace of God revealed within the events of the gospel: "For as often as you eat this bread and drink this cup, you proclaim the Lord's death until he comes." The ethical emphasis centered in the cross reappears just at the moment when we begin to suspect that the apostle is making the Sacrament the focus and *sine qua* non of the gospel. Paul's sacramentalism has to be seen alongside his ethical emphasis. Nevertheless, although we cannot push Paul's thought thus far, there is enough to show that to him the Eucharist was far more than mere memorialism.

3. Memorial and Act

Are we justified in speaking of "mere" memorial? It is in Paul's account of the Sacrament that he emphasizes the words "Do this in remembrance (ἀνάμνησις) of me." Bishop Brilioth reminds us that this emphasis upon the Lord's Supper as a memorial to Christ represented the vital historical element in the Sacrament that was in clear contrast to the heathen mysteries, in which there was no attempt to relate the rite to any historical event.[8] The Lord's Supper *is* a memorial, and like Jacob's pillar set up at Bethel or the twelve stones planted by Joshua after the passage over Jordan, it is the existing witness in the present to the historicity of something that happened in the past. The thought behind this remembrance is concrete and Hebraic.

Bishop Brilioth, indeed, maintains that by his repetition of the words "Do this in remembrance of me," Paul lays more emphasis upon the death of Christ and the historic element in the Eucharist than is to be found in the synoptists, and "it is the Pauline account which shows most clearly the centre round which the still fluid eucharistic ideas of the primitive church were more and more to gather."[9] That center is the atoning death of Christ, for in the teaching of the great Apostle to the gentiles, as often as this holy Supper takes place, the Church proclaims the death of her Lord, until he comes again.

But the memorialism in Paul's understanding of the Eucharist must not be confused with the memorialism of our own day. It may, on the contrary, have a good deal to do with the exalted view he took of the Sacrament. It has been pointed out that we must not imagine that "memory" and "remembrance" mean to us exactly what they meant to the Jew, for behind "remembrance" in the New Testament there is the Hebrew word zakar, which has all the concreteness of Hebrew thought within it. It is the same word that was used by the woman of Zarephath on the death of her son when she charged Elijah, "You

[8] Brilioth, op. cit., p. 34.
[9] Ibid., p. 35.

have come to me to bring my sin to remembrance, and to cause the death of my son!" (I Kings 17:18.) [10] There is very much more in this word than the simple action of recalling to mind something that has happened—it is calling an event back to life, the action of bringing an event out of the past into the present. This is not "mere memorialism" in the weakened sense we have come to know it. If this is the meaning of the remembrance of our word in the Eucharist, it has less to do with pious memories than with the "Real Presence," for if in this sense we do this in remembrance of him, we bring the event which we remember out of the past and make it effective—re-present it—in the present by dramatic action.

The importance of action within the Eucharist as a continuation of the mighty acts of God, and especially of his redeeming action in Jesus Christ our Lord, may provide us with a clue to understanding the Protestant experience of the presence of Christ in the Lord's Supper. Donald Baillie pointed out that although the supper is indeed a sacrament of the Real Presence, it also belongs to a situation in which we are and yet are not in the presence of our Lord. In the Sacrament we stand "between a memory and a hope," for our Lord's presence with us is not in the same mode as it was with the disciples in the Upper Room in the days of his flesh, nor is it yet of the same reality as that which we shall realize at the marriage supper of the Lamb.[11]

On the other hand, although it is of the essential nature of the Eucharist both to look backward to our Lord in the flesh and forward to the consummation of his reign, it is impossible to separate his presence from our present experience. We are reminded once again of the well-known passage from C. H. Dodd, in which he says that within the Eucharist, "the Church perpetually reconstitutes the crisis in which the Kingdom of God came in history. . . . At each Eucharist we are there—we are in the night in which He was betrayed, at Golgotha, before the empty tomb on Easter day, and in the upper room where He appeared; and we are at the moment of His coming, with

---

[10] I owe this thought and the illustration, together with a great deal more, to the former principal of Mansfield College, Oxford, Nathaniel Micklem, whom I remember expounding this theme in his lectures during the last war. Recently I have been intrigued to see the same argument, together with the same old Testament illustration, in Neville Clark's *An Approach to the Theology of the Sacraments*, p. 62. Doubtless there is a common source! For a bibliographical note on the subject see Clark, ibid., note 2.

[11] *The Theology of the Sacraments* (Faber, 1957), pp. 102-3.

angels and archangels and all the company of heaven, in the twinkling of an eye at the last trump." [12] There *is* a present experience of Christ, and although it may be "bound up with a corporate memory of real events," it is certainly not limited to that.

The key to our understanding of it seems to be in the very *action* of the Eucharist itself, and we appear to be driven to this conclusion the more surely as we discover the center of our theology in the action of God who in Christ is reconciling the world to himself. "It is that act," said Forsyth, "and not the element that contains Christ and appropriates His Act.... To confess a Saviour and a salvation is not saying something, nor thinking, but doing. It is the Church rising with its Lord to the height of action—active reception of His gift who is acting in its midst with the utmost that God could do.... The holy sacrament is the sacrament of the holiest act and not simply of a most sacred essence or even presence." [13] Sacraments, writes a more modern theologian of the same confession, are "the acts of Christ in and through His Church; they are Calvary, as it were, projected into later time and brought personally home to the recipient." [14]

Perhaps this agreement is not so remarkable, but it should be compared with the words of certain Anglicans—Canon O. C. Quick for example—"at every point of the Eucharistic action the whole Christ is present in that through which He acts; and that through which He acts is at every point His Body as the instrument and expression of His will." The remarkable thing about this passage is not that it sounds suspiciously "catholic," but that it should be so pronouncedly protestant in its emphasis not upon the essence of the elements but upon what God is *doing* through them. Indeed, Quick held that the presence of Christ is not to be sought in the elements as material things, "but as they are within the process of a certain action which takes them up into itself, uses them as its instruments, and expresses itself in them." [15] Equally striking is the evidence supplied by Dom Gregory Dix, who against the tendency in western Christianity to think of the Eucharist primarily as something *said*—"to say mass"— remarked that before the fourth century the Church thought of the

---

[12] *The Apostolic Preaching and Its Developments* (Hodder and Stoughton, 1936; 2nd ed., 1944), p. 94.
[13] P. T. Forsyth, *The Church and the Sacraments*, pp. 237, 274, 197.
[14] Nathaniel Micklem, *What Is the Faith?* (Hodder and Stoughton, 1936), p. 205.
[15] O. C. Quick, *The Christian Sacraments*, pp. 224, 225.

rite primarily as something to be *done*.[16] He said that this essential action within the Eucharist is "of necessity and by intention a corporate action—"*Do this* (*poieite*, plural). The blessed Bread is *broken* that it may be *shared*, and 'we being many' made 'one Body'; the blessed Cup is *delivered* that it may be a '*partaking* of the Blood of Christ.' It is of the deepest meaning of the rite that those who take part are thereby united indissolubly with one another and with all who are Christ's, 'because' (*hoti*) each is thereby united with Him, and through Him with the Father, with whom He is One." [17] Dom Gregory italicized certain words in this passage to demonstrate the corporateness of the action—in itself a very important point—but with very little change in his italics we could illustrate equally well the importance of the simple fact that *action* is the center, they are *verbs*, and the Supper has its focus in things that we *do* together and in the name of Christ.

But it is primarily not our action but his. We are given a command —"Do this" (imperative)—but we obey that command because of the One who gives it. Ultimately we follow his action because it *is* his action at the Last Supper, and because he revealed its meaning in the events that followed. The chief actor of the drama is always God in Christ: God in Christ who first took the initiative for our salvation by humbling himself, taking the form of a servant, and pouring out his life to the death of the Cross; God in Christ triumphant over sin, death, and the devil in the Resurrection; God in Christ risen and glorified, making himself available to us by the power of the Holy Spirit; God in Christ present with us in this eucharistic act in the "eternal simultaneity of heaven"; God in Christ made actual among us, as by *his own* action the purpose of his redeeming act is made real in our midst.

4. Incarnation and the Real Presence

The application of this to what we have said previously about theologies centered in incarnation and theologies centered in atonement will be fairly obvious. To state the issue in terms that may be too clear to be entirely just but which I submit are still generally true, a theology that centers in the Incarnation will tend to interpret the

---

[16] *The Shape of the Liturgy* (Dacre Press, 2nd ed. and 6th impression, 1954), p. 12.
[17] *Ibid.*, p. 1.

Eucharist as another form in which Christ's body is extended physically in time, and will concentrate upon the bread and wine as another physical manifestation of his presence within the elements of sacrament. On the other hand those who find the center of their theology in the Atonement will regard what Christ *does* through his body as more important than the nature of the physical essence. If they think of the Sacraments as a continuation of our Lord's ministry, it will be as a continuation of our Lord's kerygmatic and redeeming ministry—his reconciling action. The Eucharist itself will be seen as a divine event, a continuation of the μεγαλεῖα, the "mighty acts" of God which are the Bible's theme. In the Lord's Supper such a theology will stress not so much the physical essence of the elements but what is being accomplished by God in and through them.

That is not to say that the physical substance of the bread and wine is irrelevant. Just as the Atonement could not have taken place had not "the Word became flesh and dwelt among us," so the great deed of God in Christ could not be mediated to us in the Sacrament without the agency of bread and wine. Bread and wine, the staple diet for life in the time of our Lord, are the necessary means whereby we receive the Bread of Life and the Wine of the True Vine, the staple diet of the soul. But these material elements must never be so emphasized that they are regarded as carrying within themselves, per se, salvation. The truth of Christ comes to us in "earthen vessels," and the earthen vessels are sanctified and made holy through that of which they are the vehicle, but they must never be equated with it or regarded as its equal. The Incarnation does not of itself save us, for as we have seen, it is one of the paradoxes of the gospel that if Christ had left this earth without undergoing the death of the Cross, his incarnate life would have been not salvation but the great indictment. So with the elements: yes, they are indispensable because they show us that God did not save man by denying the physical nature of creation but by affirming it, by appropriating it to himself and using it as the means of achieving his highest purpose. But this creation still stands under the Cross, and the glory it has is the glory of the divine life that is enacted in its midst.

In the Roman Catholic theory of Transubstantiation there is a real attempt to assert that the divine life of Christ makes use of the physical nature of the world God created. We would agree with Canon

Quick when he says that in so far as it does this the Roman doctrine is to be commended, but that "in so far as it tends to make men venerate some material object as embodying deity . . . it is certainly to be repudiated." [18] We can say that in asserting a "Real Presence" within the divine action of the Eucharist—"this is my body which is *broken. . . . Do* this in remembrance of me"—the Protestant recognizes the essential place of the bread and the wine as much as the Catholic. In the Incarnation the flesh was made the means of divine grace, and in becoming the perfect vehicle it became perfect in its obedience and self-oblation: God sanctifies and uses material things as channels of his grace. But he does not deify them. This must be at the back of our thinking whenever we consider the ecumenical problem of eucharistic theology between Catholic and Protestant.

Does the experience of the Living Christ in the Communion of the Lord's Supper enable the Protestant to move any nearer to the Catholic without ultimately denying the "once for all time" character of our Lord's sacrifice upon Calvary? We recall that Bishop Hicks made a serious attempt to resolve the Catholic-Protestant dilemma when he insisted that "the Body and the Blood of the Eucharist are the Body and the Blood of the glorified, not the crucified Christ. They cannot be material. They belong to the time when "it was Spirit." [19] This is a valuable suggestion which seems to avoid the element of magic implied in the change of substance, and instead we are presented with a miracle of grace in the triumph of Christ's finished work. On the other hand the bishop overlooked the importance of our Lord's *action* in the Atonement and within the Eucharist. From the Protestant side of the fence it must be insisted that if the elements are made "His body and blood," they can be so constituted only by his divine act, and it is his action alone which can make them so. His action is primary. If the sacraments are a dramatic "preaching" of the Word of God—we *proclaim* the Lord's death until he comes—then it must always be "the breaking rather than the bread, and the outpouring rather than the wine." [20] If we receive them as his body and his blood, we can do so only because of what his deed has made them. Word

---

[18] Quick, The Christian Sacraments, p. 195.
[19] The Fulness of Sacrifice, p. 347.
[20] P. T. Forsyth, *The Church and the Sacraments*, p. 234.

and Sacrament declare the same thing, that God is reconciling the world to himself, and because of that it is through his deed of reconciliation that his presence becomes known to us and his glory is revealed among us.

No realist—not even a Christian realist full of faith—could confidently assert when or even whether the bitter issues between the Catholic and Protestant doctrines of the Eucharist will be reconciled in this life. But if reconciliation is to come, perhaps it will be possible only as all Christians seek to deepen their own experience of Jesus Christ and recognize themselves as the objects of his grace. O. C. Quick reminds us that whatever have been the abuses of the Roman Catholic Mass, the theory of the Mass "has always associated Christ's presence with a definite action." [21] That is true—and it is a fact which should give us hope—but when it has been done in so literal a manner as to suggest that each celebration of the Mass is a new immolation of our Lord, the Protestant has no option than to reject it as rivaling the unique sacrifice of Christ for us at Calvary.

At the same time, the Roman Catholic Mass and the Orthodox Liturgy do have their historic origin in that act of Christ, and if we all go to the source of our worship, we cannot but find ourselves closer to each other. Let us take courage in that hope.

5. The Institution of the Last Supper

We suggested earlier that the doctrine of the Atonement has been represented to the Church in each generation within the action of the Eucharist. If this is so, we must ask what aspects of the doctrine are to be found within the Sacrament. To answer this we cannot go to any particular liturgy as the norm, but we must look for the essential elements of the doctrine within the Institution of the Supper itself:

> For I have received of the Lord that which also I delivered unto you, That the Lord Jesus, the same night in which he was betrayed *took bread*: and when he *had given thanks*, he *brake* it, and said, *Take, eat*: this *is* my body, which *is* broken for you: this *do* in remembrance [i.e., for the "bringing back"] of me. After the same manner also he *took* the cup, when he had *supped, saying,* This cup *is* the new testament in my blood:

---

[21] Quick, op. cit., p. 220.

this *do* ye, as oft as ye *drink* it, in remembrance of me. For as often as ye *eat* this bread, and *drink* this cup, ye *do* shew the Lord's death till he come. (I Cor. 11:23-26. K.J.V.)

In these three verses there are no less than twenty-two verbs, and the passage includes as we have seen, the double use of the word "remembrance" which has the force of a very definite action. Jesus is the central, indeed the only, character, and what happened is specifically related to a certain time. It was "the same night that he was betrayed" —what happened at the Supper has its special significance by reason of the time when it took place.

In the compressed lines of the Institution we seem to have a summary of the plan of redemption. Our Lord "took bread" just as in the Incarnation by becoming man he took flesh; he gave thanks just as his whole life was an act of praise and thanksgiving to God; when that thanksgiving was complete, he broke the bread. He broke the bread: it was an act of his own volition. The Fourth Evangelist surely represents the spirit of our Lord's sacrifice perfectly when he puts into the mouth of Jesus the words, "For this reason the Father loves me, because I lay down my life, that I may take it again. No one takes it from me, but I lay it down of my own accord. I have power to lay it down, and I have power to take it again." (John 10:17-18. R.S.V.) Then he took the cup when he had supped. We know something of what that cup represented to him: it was the cup of sacrifice; a cup of sacrifice which he could not take unless he was prepared to fill it with his own life blood poured out in obedience to the Father's will, so that he could hand the same cup to the men who were with him. What this cup contains is the new testament, the new covenant, which can be taken only as it is shared in his blood. There is no other "new covenant"—this is the covenant of which the prophet had spoken when he recorded God's promise to Israel.

> Behold, the days are coming, says the Lord, when I will make a new covenant with the house of Israel and the house of Judah. . . . I will put my law within them, and I will write it upon their hearts; and I will be their God, and they shall be my people. And no longer shall each man teach his neighbor and each his brother, saying, "Know the Lord," for they shall all know me, from the least of them to the greatest, says the Lord;

for I will forgive their iniquity, and I will remember their sin no more.
(Jer. 31:31-34. R.S.V.)

This covenant held the promise not only of the forgiveness of sins and reinstatement as God's people but also the hope of a spiritual and ethical renewal because God's will would be established in the very heart of man. This was now to be sealed in the Blood of Christ. He offers *this* bread and *this* cup to the disciples and tells them to do this in remembrance of him, to do these things in order to bring him and his saving deed out of the past into actual present. For as they eat this bread and drink this cup they will show forth his death. We are reminded of how Paul in the previous chapter (I Cor. 10:17) told the members of the church at Corinth that they are all of a piece in the same loaf, being members of the same Body.[22] They partook of the broken Body of Christ even as they partook of the bread, but as they did so, they themselves became the Body and the loaf within the world: "as often as ye eat this bread, and drink this cup, *ye do shew* [or proclaim] the Lord's death"—God in Christ reconciling the world to himself *through the Church*. There is an ancient prayer of the *Didache* (perpetuated in the Order for the Lord's Supper of the Reformed Church of France) which retains something of this thought when it prays that as the piece of bread was scattered over the hills (in the wheat) and was brought together and made one, so may the Church be reunited from all corners of the earth into God's Kingdom. But in the Institution and in Paul's thought the accent is upon the Church becoming the loaf, the body of Christ, *within* the world—the Church proclaims the Lord's death by what its members are doing. Ignatius had used the same imagery in this sense as he went on his way to martyrdom.[23]

This they were to continue to do "until He comes." The Church is a Church in waiting for its Lord and for the consummation of all things in his Kingdom. At this point it is either Paul or the early Church which is adding the comment, but whichever it is, the comment is being added from the other side of the Cross and Resurrection. Whoever is speaking is speaking after the Crucifixion, Resurrection, As-

---
[22] At this point I have preferred the rendering of the K.J.V., the English R.V., and James Moffatt to that of the R.S.V., Weymouth, and the English R.V. Margin.
[23] Cf. supra, p. 42.

cension, and Pentecost had revealed the full meaning and glory of the life and death of our Lord. The great drama of redemption is caught up in the participation of the Church and the anticipation of its part in the Marriage Supper of the Lamb. Now they participated in the brokenness of the bread and the bitterness of the cup, but it was not for ever—the end was sure, and it was to be consummated in the triumphal coming of Christ in the glory and power of his Kingdom.

Here within a brief compass in the Institution of the Supper the whole panorama of redemption is set out. It sends shafts of light back into the Old Testament promises, and through all the different aspects of our Lord's work and ministry it points onward to the consummation; one act of God given to us for our salvation represented now by Christ in the midst of his people. This is even more pronounced in the full movement of the Eucharist, and whenever one has gathered with the Lord's people in faith, the believer is caught up in a Christian experience that transcends time, whether the service is in the gorgeously ornate Liturgy of the eastern Orthodox churches, or in the simple dignity of the Lord's Supper with Baptists or the Disciples of Christ.

At the end of his most illuminating essay on the Sacraments, Nathaniel Micklem has described what I have been trying to say in a passage that deserves to become a classic. It is quoted in full because I could not equal it:

According to the ancient use the minister at the Sacrament cries, "Up with your hearts!" and the people respond, "We lift them up unto the Lord." From that moment it is conceived that the heavens are opened, and the Church on earth gathers with the Church in heaven—"therefore with angels and archangels and all the company of heaven we laud and magnify thy glorious Name." So, too, time is, as it were, rolled up, and that which in ordinary human experience we know as successive is seen in the eternal simultaneity of heaven. From the blood of Abel shed at the foundation of the world, through the sacrifice of Abraham on Mt. Moriah to the Holy Nativity of Jesus Christ, Immanuel, His sacred Passion, His Resurrection in victory, His triumphs in the Church, His coming again in power and great glory—the whole drama of Redemption is, as it were, present together before our eyes as visibly occurrent, and the promise of our own inheritance is sealed by the Lord Himself upon our wondering hearts.[24]

I can only add the testimony, "Amen!"

6. Ethics and the Eucharist: the Challenge of the Cross

There is a somewhat hackneyed story about a Salvation Army lassie who is supposed to have approached a bishop in a train with the question, "Sir, are you saved?" According to the story the bishop was a New Testament scholar of some eminence, and in his answer he gave his questioner a Greek lesson on the passive tenses of σώξω (to save)—"Now tell me precisely what you mean, my dear, 'have been saved,' 'am being saved,' or 'will be saved'?" If the Atonement is to mean anything to us, it must mean all these things, and if the Eucharist represents to us the meaning of the Atonement, we ought to expect to find in it all these different aspects of the work of salvation.

What about "the present tense" in the plan of salvation? Granted that Peter Abelard is not the whole gospel. Where is that for which he contended represented in the Eucharist; how does the vitally important personal identification of ourselves with Christ's sacrifice take place in the Sacrament in such a way that the meaning of our commitment to him is made plain? I shall devote the remaining part of this chapter to this aspect because of its importance to contemporary apologetic. It is clear that as we take the bread and wine we take to ourselves the assurance of what Christ's death achieved *for* us, but how does it become the kind of food that produces action *in* us? It feeds our faith, but is it really spiritual food unless it produces in the believer a response in life?

It may be that the religious needs of modern people go much deeper than ethics, that to try and summarize the gospel in terms of "doing good" and the Golden Rule is the great temptation of today. But there can be no doubt that this is the point where the Christian gospel offers its challenge in its most uncompromising and clearly understood terms. Edward Caswall's translation of the Latin hymn (which we would like to think was written by that most Christian Jesuit, Francis Xavier) exactly reflects the spirit of many modern

---

[24] Nathaniel Micklem in *Christian Worship*, p. 255.

would-be Christians, who are far less impressed with the personal alternatives of heaven or hell hereafter than with the challenge of the life of Jesus here and now:

> My God, I love Thee, not because
> I hope for heaven thereby,
> Nor yet because, if I love not,
> I must forever die.
>
> Thou, O my Jesus, Thou didst me
> Upon the Cross embrace;
> For me didst bear the nails and spear,
> And manifold disgrace;
>
> Then why, O blessed Jesus Christ,
> Should I not love Thee well?
> Not for the sake of winning heaven,
> Nor of escaping hell;
>
> Not with the hope of gaining aught,
> Not seeking a reward;
> But as Thyself hast lovèd me,
> O ever-loving Lord.

That seems to many to be a far nobler attitude in the face of Christ's sacrifice than the morbid preoccupation of so-called saints in former ages with their own salvation, for how can a real follower of Jesus Christ rest satisfied in heaven while one of God's children remains damned without? The modern emphasis upon Redemption that is cosmic and racial is intimately related to ethics, for many of our most sensitive contemporaries are, *for ethical reasons*, not interested in winning for themselves a salvation that is individual and solitary. The late Donald Baillie demonstrated this when he wrote, "A man can't save himself alone—because then he wouldn't be saved from selfishness, and if you're not saved from selfishness you're not saved at all in any sense that Christ would care for." [25]

This means not less ethical conscience but more. There are few people as unlovely as the typical "Lady Bountiful" (British version)

---

[25] "A Man's Life," sermon published posthumously in *The British Weekly*, Dec. 5, 1957, p. 20.

or "Do-Gooder" (American version), whose benefactions are first and last either the guarantee of their own salvation or an advertisement of their own sanctity. The modern skeptic has little use for either. In the same sermon, Donald Baillie showed the vast gulf that exists between the person who is entirely motivated with the desire to guarantee his own salvation and the kind of life that should be a result of the gospel. Of the former he says that our Lord "certainly didn't mean anything as narrow and self centred. He meant something far bigger—I might almost say more reckless—than that . . . the only way really to gain and keep and save one's soul, one's chance, is to pour it out, bravely, nobly, unselfishly, lovingly—in fact, to lose it—not to be afraid to lose it. Then you'll find it." The only ethics in the Christian gospel are those of a Man who poured out his life on a cross for others, in obedience to God. The ethical challenge of our Lord in seeking those who were lost at the expense of his own life is something that all men can understand: it is the point where the Christian faith is most clearly understood by the modern world but where traditional theories of the Atonement appear to be utterly irrelevant and unreal.

Unfortunately, it elicits admiration rather than imitation. It remains an ideal without often being accepted as a possibility for life, because our contemporaries do not see that beyond any question of personal salvation, it is only faith in an objective work of Christ upon the Cross which can make discipleship possible. We are within the dilemma of the strength and weakness of the Abelardian position. It has always been strong in its call to men to adventure with the divine Hero, but it has always been weak because it has never shown men how they are to get the strength to reach anywhere near his standard. We are called to be little Christs, but although the spirit may be willing enough, the flesh is always too weak.

Even so that ethical call remains. We certainly err very greatly if we take the Great Assize, the Sermon on the Mount, or the parable of the Good Samaritan as our summary of the gospel. But it is certain that we err even more fundamentally if by an emphasis upon sound doctrine, ecclesiastical order, or correct liturgical and sacramental life we ignore the fact that faith in Christ is directed toward a life given in love to the world. As the pattern of our Lord's own life and sacrifice became clearer to the disciples, this calling was given a new content by the Cross. The disciples left their homes to follow him, but a day came when Jesus called them together and declared, "If any man would come after me, let him deny himself, and take up his cross, and follow me." (Mark 8:34-35; Matt. 16:24-25; Luke 9:23-24.) For whoever was intent upon saving his life would be the one to lose it, and the one who was willing to give up his life for the sake of Jesus and the gospel would be the one who would find his life and save it. Salvation was to be found in a new quality of life that could be gained only by way of the Cross and all that the Cross implied. This is the great truth for which all the best that is, in the moral influence theories of the Atonement, has been contending, and it is the ultimate fact from which many people would willingly escape by means of any kind of "objectivity" they can find, whether in doctrine, church, or sacrament. "The supreme art of the devil," said Horace Bushnell, in a quotation we cited earlier, "never invented a greater mischief to be done, or a theft more nearly amounting to the stealing of the cross itself, than filching away thus, from the followers of Christ, the conviction that they are thoroughly to partake the sacrifice of their Master."

The trouble with the modern "pagan" is that he shows every evidence of having a split mind in the face of the challenge of Christ. On the one side he is often far too honest to accept salvation by means of "easy grace," and he admits he is fascinated by the Figure on the Cross. On the other he shies away from the challenge because the ideal is too high, and he is all too conscious of his own moral limitations. The gospel that he needs is a gospel that, in meeting his weakness with God's grace, does not avoid the ethics of the Cross but shows him how he too can be given the power to meet the ethical challenge of Calvary.

7. Ethics and the Eucharist: the Response of Faith

This is the doctrine of Atonement which the Church needs to preach, and this is the doctrine which we should discover at the heart of the Eucharist. As we give thanks in the great prayer of thanksgiving for our Lord's triumph not only upon the cross but also in his life, his resurrection, and ascension to God's right hand, as the bread is broken and the wine poured out, we have unfolded before us the objective fact of what he did for us and the prospective promise of salvation at the end of time: "We have an advocate with the Father,

Jesus Christ the righteous." (I John 2:1.) As we receive the bread and wine, we take to ourselves the fact that he did this for us, and nothing can change or modify the fact that it was for us that he did it.

But like the doctrine of the Atonement itself, the Sacraments emphasize the Christian's commitment to his Lord. Both Sacraments are full of the ethics of the Cross, not in the sense of offering simply an incentive to imitate Jesus Christ as best we can, but in the sense of offering us the means whereby we can do it. For at the center of that ethical impulse, indeed paradoxically at the very apex of ethical achievement, there is the grace which makes it possible, the Cross itself. Only by throwing ourselves on God's mercy before that do we receive the grace in faith that makes discipleship possible: the end of our proud hopes is literally the beginning of God's miracle in us.

This was made explicit when the mother of James and John came to Jesus and interceded for her sons. She did not know what she was asking for them then, although she may have guessed when, on the night of the Crucifixion, she ministered to the broken body of the Lord. But Jesus himself had known what it implied—"Are you able to drink the cup that I am to drink?" It was not simply the cup of suffering for its own sake, but it was the cup of obedience to God voluntarily taken. It was a cup of obedience that might involve suffering, but which certainly involved sacrifice—a life poured out that it might be given to men for their redemption and given back to God as a sacrifice of perfect obedience to his divine will.

The ethical aspect of the Eucharist is in the fact that the cup of our Lord's sacrifice is offered to men that it might be taken and shared in like kind. When Peter declared to our Lord, "You shall never wash my feet," Jesus replied, "If I do not wash you, you have no part in me." (John 13:8.) In view of the fact that this took place on the night of betrayal, we cannot take it as simply a reference to the necessity of the ritual act of Baptism. We must interpret it in the light of that baptism that our Lord was about to undergo on the Cross; for Peter needed to be washed by that, not only in the sense of needing this to be done for him, but equally in the sense of being washed from his sin into the sacrifice of his Lord. The incident is parallel to the occasion when Jesus told the Jews that they could not have life within them unless they were prepared to eat the flesh and drink the blood of the Son of Man (John 6:53). Again this passage may be interpreted sacramentally as an indirect reference to the Eucharist, but surely it is a reference to the Eucharist only as the Supper proclaims the meaning of his sacrifice. It is his sacrifice which saves them, not the rite, and the importance of the rite is only as it sets forth what he did and enables us to take its redeeming work to ourselves.

To take Christ's work to ourselves is an essential part of the plan of salvation. The giving and receiving of the bread and wine in the Lord's Supper is as essential a part of the action of the Sacrament as the breaking of bread, and the ethical call is within that action. As members receive the broken bread and poured-out wine, they clearly receive the assurance of that Atonement which their Lord effected for them in his broken body and poured out blood: certainly we also take to ourselves that objective and historic fact which nothing can change. But reflect upon the fact that when members of the early Church received the broken bread and the poured-out wine, they took to themselves not only the bread but its brokenness, not only the wine but its "poured-outness," and in that action the martyr Church pledged its faith in its Lord.

For the early Christians, redemption was not simply something in the past that had been achieved (however great), nor something in the future that would be consummated (however glorious), for it was part of present experience as each member kept tryst with his Lord in bread that had been broken and wine that had been freely poured. It is broken bread and poured-out wine which the Church takes to herself in the Sacrament of the Lord's Supper. That is, it is bread and wine in which God is doing something in like kind to that which he did for our salvation in his Son Jesus Christ. But "we must be broken ere we deeply bless." [26] This brokenness of the bread and libation of the wine is accepted with the bread and the wine by the Church, not simply as the representation of an event that happened sometime in history on her behalf, but as an event that is by God's action of giving it and her action of receiving it, brought out of the past into the living present. This is a sacrifice in which she herself participates as the Body of Christ in the world, by coming under the same obedience

---

[26] P. T. Forsyth, *The Church and the Sacraments*, p. 239.

and by taking to herself her Lord's brokenness and voluntary outpouring for the redemption of the world.

As the apostles and destined martyrs of the early Church took this Sacrament, how else could they understand the cup of sacrifice, how else can we explain the link between liturgy and the highest point of ethical sacrifice in martyrdom within the early writings, how else could the Sacrament speak to those who knew that at any moment they might be called upon to follow their Lord literally to the Cross? This was the "here and now" meaning of salvation for them. But here too was the grace which made the sacrifice possible. Within the sacramental life of the Church they became, in Paul's phrase, crucified with Christ that they might live. Yet it was not they who now lived, but Christ himself lived in them that he might through them redeem the world. To live in this way was not to pretend to any quality of life achieved by one's own efforts, but it was to live in the Cross—it was, again in one of Paul's most daring phrases, to fill up what was lacking in the suffering of Christ.

This ethical commitment to Christ, which is based not upon our efforts to imitate him but upon our acceptance of his grace towards us in the Cross, is to be found throughout the New Testament. We can see it all through the epistles in the identification which is drawn between the sufferings of the saints and the suffering of our Lord.[27] We can see it in our Lord's own pledge at the Last Supper not to drink of the fruit of the vine until he should drink it new in his Father's kingdom.[28] For what could this "fruit of the vine" be but the fruits of his sacrifice—the obedient sacrifice of the Church in like kind to that which he was about to offer? We see it in the very nature of "faith" in the Gospels and in the writings of Paul as something which demands active response to that which Christ does for us. And although the trials amid which the New Testament writers lived give to their sacrifice an existential quality that we find it difficult to enter fully by reason of the changed circumstances, we cannot doubt that the Church is called to work out what this obedience means in terms of her own present life.

Within the Sacrament of his Body and his Blood Jesus does not simply meet our need to know that he has won our salvation for us,

---

[27] Cf. II Cor. 1:5-7; Phil. 3:10; Heb. 2:10; I Pet. 4:13.
[28] Mark 14:25; Matt. 26:29; Luke 22:18.

but in meeting the need he gives us the earnest of salvation in food that makes us a living part of him. As the broken bread is handed to us, and as we are offered the poured-out wine, we are called to enter the brokenness and self-oblation of the One on whom we have based our assurance. To feed on him means this. This is the ethical, cross-centered call to sacrifice within the Eucharist, to take to ourselves not only his Body but its brokenness, not only his Blood but its libation. It means that if the Churches of the Reformation, by the centrality of the Atonement in their theology, ought to have been the most sacramental of all Christians, then we can say just as emphatically that "Catholics" by their emphasis upon the sacraments ought to have been the most insistent upon Christian discipleship. If we have both failed, it is because we have too often misunderstood the very things that we have professed to value most highly.

Some time ago I came upon a short verse which seemed to summarize what we have been trying to say:

> My life must be Christ's broken bread,
> My love His outpoured wine,
> A cup o'erfilled, a table spread
> Beneath His name and Sign,
> That other souls, refreshed and fed,
> May share His life through mine.[29]

This verse does not come out of the experience of one of the great sacramental churches. It was written by General Albert E. Orsborn of the Salvation Army—a Christian body that does not have regular sacraments but which has had a magnificent record of sacrificial obedience in the spirit of our Lord. By no means does it represent all there is within the Sacrament when I take the bread and drink from the cup. But if I have all other insights and this is lacking, I am nothing. It may well be that before we can come to the plenitude of the Church's sacramental experience those of us who have professed to love and cherish Baptism and the Lord's Supper will have to go in penitence to bodies like the Salvation Army and the Society of Friends to teach us what the Sacraments should mean in terms of Christian humility, obedience, and sacrifice. For to partake of the

---

[29] *Salvation Army Songs*, Gen. Albert E. Orsborn. Copyright—The Salvation Army (1954), No. 462. Used by permission.

broken bread should include willingness to accept his brokenness, and to drink the cup that he offers us should include willingness to sip from the cup he tasted in Gethsemane and which he drained to the dregs on the cross.

8. Epilogue—or Prologue?

As we come to the end of this study of the Atonement and the Sacraments, it is appropriate that we should look forward in the light of our subject to the Church's mission, for the point at which the Church clarifies the meaning of Atonement for herself is only to set the stage for her missionary task. The task of translating all that we have been saying into effective apologetic has yet to be undertaken. Perhaps the essential point that we would make about the Atonement in relation to the Church's mission is the simple fact that when Jesus came among us to live and die, God became a missionary to men. Christ's redeeming work is God's mission to the world, and the Church is called to participate in a redemptive and missionary task of the same kind. Her essential task within the world is this missionary task, but because it is missionary it must be redemptive with the same outpouring of life and love that was demonstrated in her Lord. If in this last part of our book we have stressed the ethical aspect of commitment in both the doctrine and the Sacraments it is simply to demonstrate that it is part of the essential character of both. It is only a part. God's act is at the center, and ethics, even the ethics of a cross-centered commitment, are at the periphery, but as the Church goes out into the world this action by the Church in the spirit of her Lord is at every part *all round* the periphery and not simply in nicely selected segments of it.

Men fail miserably when they try to follow the ethical standards of Jesus without recognizing that they are in need of grace and forgiveness. But there is an attitude which is equally dangerous—dangerous because it simply supplants the sin of pride for that of selfishness—when "Christians" are content to accept the assurance of God's act in Christ as the guarantee of their own salvation without recognizing any call to discipleship and service. If the Church's mission is the redemptive mission to the world initiated by God in Christ, we need both the assurance and the commitment.

THE LORD'S SUPPER

At Christmas the churches in Indonesia hold a special celebration[30] which seems to bring us to our proper focus. Each member gathered in the church holds a candle, and at a given point in the service—"Arise, shine; for thy light is come!"—they light their candles at a large central candle. This represents the Incarnation, the advent of Jesus at Bethlehem, and the worshipers kneel in a large circle around the crib to symbolize the world's homage to the Christ of God. Later in the service the whole congregation, with their lighted candles, forms a large cross to remind themselves that the purpose of the Incarnation was for sacrifice and Atonement. Then at the end of their worship they go out with the lights they have taken from that central "Light of the World" to light up the blackness of the world outside. There are several suggestive points to this piece of dramatic symbolism, but one of the deepest truths it portrays is the fact that Christians are not only under the Cross but *in* it, not merely claiming the benefits and promises of Christ's redeeming work but sharing in its sacrifice and glory. Having recognized that, as his disciples they can go out to take the light they have received from him into the world.

And as we leave our place at the Lord's Table, we go out not only in the strength of the Cross but also in its commitment, "For as often as you eat this bread and drink the cup, you proclaim the Lord's death until he comes."

---

[30] I am indebted to Pastor Hans-Ruedi Weber, formerly of Indonesia, now of Geneva, for this illustration.

Index

of

Subjects and Proper Names

Abbot, Archbishop George, 117
Abel, 377
Abelard, Peter, 80-85, 115, 146, 166, 168, 170, 178, 179
"Abelardian" Theory of Atonement. See Atonement, Moral Influence theory
Abraham, 323, 377
Adam
  disobedience of, 99
  fall of, 49
  the "First Adam," 49
  the "Second Adam." See Jesus Christ; Paul
Alexander of Hales, 182
Ames, William, 116
Ananias, 324
Anabaptists, 114, 344, 345
Andrews, H. T., 324, 325
Anna, 300, 352
Anselm, 48, 65-80, 103, 115, 150, 184; see also Atonement
Antinomian (ism), 200
Apologetic, 31, 66, 67, 70, 75, 122, 217, 301
Apostles' Creed, 107
Aquinas, Thomas, 85-90, 184
Arian (ism), 78, 139
Arminius (Arminianism), 114-16, 126, 135, 136, 247
Athanasius, 57-60, 218, 224
Atonement
  birth of the word, 20-23
  definition of, 18, 19
  in English versions of the Bible, 23-26
Atonement theories
  Moral Influence (Abelardian or Exemplarist), 38, 80-85, 147, 150, 154, 160, 165, 168, 170, 179, 184, 187, 190, 214
  Mystical, 63n., 86, 219
  Penal Substitutionary, 92-97, 98-109, 116, 119, 120, 126, 129, 135, 139, 151, 163, 180, 195, 212, 214
  Ransom (Patristic or Classic), 44, 47-53, 54, 62, 74, 86, 94, 95, 104-5, 109, 111, 145, 151
  Rectoral, 116, 182, 303, 304; see also Grotius
  Sacrificial, 103, 145, 159, 257-63, 263-68, 278-79, 302
  Satisfaction (Anselmian or Latin), 48, 66-80, 103, 151, 254

Augsburg Confession, 110, 116, 255
Augustine, 57, 60, 61, 178
Augustus Caesar, 299
Aulen, Gustaf, 62, 76, 78, 94, 254-57

Baillie, Donald, 256, 270-74, 277, 369, 379, 380
Baptism, 32, 88, 165, 308, 319-58
Baptismal Regeneration, 325
Barth, Karl, 182, 183, 228, 244, 267, 277, 278, 326, 342, 344, 345, 348
Baur, F. C., 140
Believers Baptism, Chapter X, *passim*
Berdyaev, N., 189
Bernard, 84
Biddle, John, 125-26
Blood (of Christ), 44, 144-46
Body of Christ. See Church and Lord's Supper
Bogue, David, 138
Bonhoeffer, Dietrich, 158, 336
Brilioth, Yngve, 368
Browne, Robert, 359, 360
Brunner, Emil, 182-83, 244, 269
Bultmann, Rudolf, 170
Bushnell, Horace, 46, 127, 149-61, 166, 168, 218, 247

Caiaphas, 95
Caird, John B., 221
Calvin, John, 97-109
Calvinism, 127, 128, 130, 135-40, 143, 247
Campbell, McLeod, 127, 140-49
Carey, William, 138
Cave, Sidney, 97, 203, 230, 256
Church, 43, 88, 185, 191, 239, 282-87
Clark, Neville, 330, 335
Classic Theory of Atonement. See Atonement theories
Clement of Alexandria, 47-48
Clement of Rome, 37
Communication, 30
Confirmation, 351
Cornelius, 338
Creation, 38, 50, 221, 222, 273
Cromwell, Oliver, 124-25
Cullman, Oscar, 329, 331, 333, 334, 344, 348
Curzon, George Nathaniel, 297

Dale, Robert, 162-63, 192, 194-206, 224
Darwin, Charles, 140, 304
David, 44
Deism, 139

INDEX

Denney, James, 162, 206-16, 224-25, 248, 252
Didache, 36, 341
Dix, Dom Gregory, 370
Dodd, C. H., 280, 369
Du Bose, W. P., 207, 216, 248, 252

Eastern Orthodoxy, 312, 340
Ecumenical Movement, 245-46, 320-21
Edwards, Jonathan, 127-31
Election (doctrine of), 115-16, 126, 135, 137-38, 247
Elijah, 368
Eliot, John, 137
Eucharist. See Lord's Supper
Evangelical, 122; see also Apologetic
Eve, 49, 292
Exemplarist Theory of Atonement. See Atonement theories, Moral Influence
Expiation, 27, 28, 29, 105, 116, 174

Fison, J. E., 290, 329
Fitzgerald, Edward, 290
Florovsky, Father Georges, 278, 280
Forgiveness, 75-76, 157-58, 172, 174-75, 185, 187, 191, 208, 210
Forsyth, P. T., 138, 208, 227-40, 265, 309, 310, 313, 327
Franks, R. S., 82, 142, 162, 164, 168-69, 181-86, 242
Fry, Elizabeth, 139

Gabriel, 299
Gibbon, Edward, 139
Gnosis, 39, 48
God
   the Father, 38, 40, 50, 76, 123, 141
   the Fatherhood of, 144
   Holiness of, 234-39
   Providence of, 190, 305
Goodwin, Thomas, 121-26
Gospels
   the Atonement in, 82, 172-75, 198, 199, 201, 261, 381
   Baptism in. See Baptism of John
   the Lord's Supper in, 43n., 361-64
Gray, G. Buchanan, 28
Gregory of Nazianzus, 57, 69, 278
Gregory of Nyssa, 54-56
Grotius, Hugo, 115, 116, 126, 247, 303; see also under Arminianism, Atonement, Rectoral Theory

Harnack, A., 182
Healing Ministry, 155
Hebrews, the views of the writer of, 53, 178, 198

Heidelberg Catechism, 111
Heilsgeschichte, 100, 225
Heim, Karl, 182
Herod, 95
Hicks, F. C. N., 145, 159, 257-63, 278-79, 302
Hobbes, Thomas, 257
Hodges, H. A., 275-78, 310
Hodgson, Leonard, 256, 275, 277, 280, 309
Holy Spirit, 148-49, 165, 167, 175, 180, 209-10, 337-38
Hopkins, Samuel, 247
Howard, John, 139

Ignatius, 41, 43, 44, 45
Immaculate Conception, 289
Incarnation, 39-40, 72-73, 98, 100, 101, 141, 144, 152, 153, 155, 159, 180, 208, 218, 227, 240, 270, 273, 282-86, 371-74; see also Atonement
Infant Baptism, 344-47
Infant "Dedication," 351
Inspiration of Scripture, 212
Irenaeus, 47-53, 71, 100
Israel, New, 328, 347, 354

James, the Apostle, 331, 333
James, the Just, the Epistle of, 200, 207
Jeremiah, 347, 375-76
Jesus Christ
  baptism of, 328
  circumcision of, 329-30
  the cross of, 39, 224, 230-31, 260, 301, 331-32
  the death of, 41, 43, 45, 58-59, 81, 103, 121, 176, 185, 196-97, 203, 208, 210, 224, 260
  the passion of, 40, 42, 85, 146, 265
  the person of, 71, 177, 199, 208, 264, 288, 291, 331-32
  "Second Adam," 48, 57
  the victory of. See Resurrection, Atonement, Ransom theory
  the work of, 36, 38, 40, 42, 57, 72, 100, 104, 105, 142, 163, 165, 167-68, 196, 200, 222, 237
Job, 96
Johannine literature, 178, 199, 361-64
John, the Apostle, 316, 331, 333
John the Baptist (and the Baptism of John), 330, 331, 332, 333, 334, 335, 337, 339, 351, 352, 353
Jonah, 56
Joseph, the husband of Mary, 299
Joshua, 300n., 368
Jowett, Benjamin, 169, 198, 204
Judicial Theory of Atonement. See Atonement, Penal theory
Justification, 115, 176-77
Justin Martyr, 39

INDEX

Kant, E., 184
Knox, John, 253
Knudson, A. C., 248

Lanfranc, 65, 66
Last Supper, 89, 174
"Latin Theory." See Atonement, Anselm
Laud, William, 135
Law, 101, 156-157, 189, 252
Laying on of Hands, 356-57
Letter to Diognetus, 40, 41
Lidgett, J. Scott, 148, 211n., 216, 217
Liturgy, 61
Lord's Supper, 32, 44-46, 51, 88-90, 165, 240, 257, 261, 262, 266-68, 281, 308-18, 359, 360, 378-86
Luther, Martin, 92-97, 151, 178, 200, 254-55
Luther's Shorter Catechism, 111

Magi, 299
Manning, B. L., 347
Marshman, Joshua, 138
Martineau, James, 205
Martyrdom of Polycarp, 45
Mary, the Mother of our Lord, 44, 49, 80n., 218, 226, 289, 299, 329
Mary, Magdalene, 315
Mascall, E. L., 298
Maurice, F. D., 204, 228
McIntyre, J., 68n.
Melanchton, Philip, 111
Micklem, Nathaniel, 280, 317, 377
Mill, John Stuart, 304
Moberly, Canon R. C., 148-49, 162-68, 172, 204
Montagu, Richard, 117
Moral Influence Theory of Atonement. See Atonement
Moses, 101, 170, 189, 364, 365
Mozley, J. K., 234, 279
"Mystical" Theory of Atonement, 63n., 219

Nebuchadnezzar, 288
Nicoll, Robertson, 228
Niebuhr, Reinhold, 253
Nominalists, 183

Obedience (of Christ), 99, 107, 113, 115, 144, 164-65, 167, 218, 266
Occam, William of, 91
Oman, John, 203
Origen, 54, 178
Orsborn, General Albert E., 385
Orthodox Liturgy, 374

Owen, John, 117, 126-27, 130
Oxford Movement, 246, 349

Paine, Thomas, 139
Patristic Theory of Atonement. See Atonement, Ransom theory
Paul, 154, 161
    the Atonement in the writings of, 51, 53, 74, 101, 106, 107, 109 175-178, 198, 199, 200, 214, 265
    the Sacraments in the writings of, 210, 266, 348, 384
    Baptism in the writings of, 322-25, 337, 339, 340, 341, 343, 348-49
    the Lord's Supper in the writings of, 364-68, 376
    the "Body of Christ" in the writings of, 282; see also Church
    the "Second Adam" in the writings of, 48, 57
Peel, Albert, 230
Pelagius, 62
Penal Theory of Atonement. See Atonement, Penal Substitutionary Theory
Penitence, 163
Pentecost, 148, 165, 175
Person of Christ. See Jesus Christ
Peter, 273, 314, 315, 316, 338, 351, 382
Peter, Epistles of, 178, 199, 339
Pfleiderer, 214
Pharaoh, 288
Pilate, 39, 44, 95, 112, 151
Polycarp, 45
Propitiation, 147, 203, 208; see also Atonement
Punishment, 163
Puritans, 117-31, 135, 138, 205; see also John Owen, Thomas Goodwin, and Jonathan Edwards

Quick, O. C., 71, 274, 276, 280, 360-361, 363, 370, 374

Ransom Theory of Atonement. See Atonement, Ransom Theory
Rashdall, Hastings, 46, 49, 54, 162, 168-81, 182, 202
Recapitulation, 44, 99, 107
Reconciliation. See Atonement
Rectoral Theory of Atonement. See Atonement, Rectoral Theory
Redemption, 38, 50, 51, 53, 71, 89, 129, 156, 161, 281, 282
Reformation, 48, 91, 142, 178, 188
Reformer's Theory of Atonement. See Atonement, Penal Substitutionary Theory, Ransom Theory, and Sacrificial Theory; also Calvin and Luther
Remensnyder, J. B., 248
Resurrection, 87, 209, 210, 226, 286, 298, 300, 371
Ritschl, A., 182
Robinson, H. Wheeler, 343, 349
Roman Catholic Church, 348
Roman Catholic Mass, 374
Rousseau, Jean-Jacques, 139
Rufinus, 55

INDEX

Sacrament of the Body and Blood of Our Lord. See Lord's Supper
Sacraments, 67n., 80n., 88-90, 149, 167, 185, 210-11, 216, 217, 240, 246, 257, 266, 268, 280-81, 319, 326, 327, 357, 361, 365, 366, 372, 377, 382, 386, Chapter IX passim
Sacrifice, 108-9, 144
Sacrificial Theory of Atonement. See Atonement, Sacrificial Theory
Salvation, doctrine of, 251
Satisfaction, 47-48, 86, 145
Sayers, Dorothy, 173, 290
Schleiermacher, 182, 185
Scholasticism, 178
Scottish Confession, 112
Scotus, Duns, 91
Second Adam. See Jesus Christ, Paul
Second Epistle of Clement, 38
Sermon on the Mount, 189, 292
Shaw, G. B., 42
Shorter Catechism, 109, 113
Simeon, 300, 352
Sin, 69, 70-72, 163, 172, 187, 232
Smith, George Adam, 53-56, 150
Smith, Robertson, 28
"Social Gospel," 224
Socinians (ism), 115-16, 126, 139, 211, 212
Socinus, Faustus, 114, 123
Spurgeon, Charles H., 169
Stewart, J. S., 177
Substitutionary Theory of Atonement. See Atonement, Penal Substitutionary Theory
Suffering Servant, 183, 265, 287
Synod of Dort, 116

Taylor, Vincent, 110, 256, 263-68, 309
Tertullian, 47, 178
Thirty-Nine Articles, 113
Thomas, 315
Tillich, Paul, 253
Toplady, Augustus, 136, 146
Torrance, T. F., 37, 46, 76
Transfiguration, 314
Transubstantiation, 314, 372
Trinity, 31, 78, 115, 123-26, 130, 150, 154, 161, 166, 180, 205, 235, 265, 273, 278, 288
Troeltsch, Ernst, 182
Turrettini, Francois, 126

Unitarianism. See Socinianism
Unity of Scripture, 207

Van Dyke, Henry, 248
Vicarious Confession, 166-67
Vicarious Penitence, 166-67
Vicarious Sacrifice, 153-54, 161, 167
Virgin Birth, 44, 72
Virgin Mary, 44, 49

Watts, Isaac, 135
Wedel, T. O., 189
Weiss, J., 214
Weisse, C. H., 182
Wesley, Charles, 135-37
Wesley, John, 136, 344
Westcott, B. F., Bishop of Durham, 166, 173, 218-27
Westminster Confession, 113
Westminster Confession's *Shorter Catechism*, 109
Whale, J. S., 276-77, 281
Whitefield, George, 135-37, 146, 167
Wilson, J. M., 219, 223-24
Wolf, William J., 253, 277
Worship, 61, 312

Xavier, Francis, 280

Zacharias, 299
Zwingli, 97, 313

www.ingramcontent.com/pod-product-compliance
Lightning Source LLC
Chambersburg PA
CBHW052139300426
44115CB00011B/1445